Yours truly

T. B. Searight

THE OLD PIKE.

A HISTORY OF

THE NATIONAL ROAD,

WITH

INCIDENTS, ACCIDENTS, AND ANECDOTES
THEREON.

ILLUSTRATED.

BY

THOMAS B. SEARIGHT.

UNIONTOWN, PA.:
PUBLISHED BY THE AUTHOR.
1894.

COPYRIGHT, 1894, BY T. B. SEARIGHT.

Facsimile Reprint

Published 1990 by

HERITAGE BOOKS, INC.
1540-E Pointer Ridge Place
Bowie, MD 20716
(301) 390-7709

ISBN 1-55613-407-X

PRESSES OF
M. CULLATON & CO.,
RICHMOND, IND.

LETTER FROM JAMES G. BLAINE.

Hon. T. B. Searight,
Uniontown, Pa.

Stanwood, Bar Harbor, Maine, }
September 8th, 1892.   }

My Dear Friend:—

I have received the sketches of the "Old Pike" regularly and have as regularly read them, some of them more than once, especially where you come near the Monongahela on either side of it, and thus strike the land of my birth and boyhood. I could trace you all the way to Washington, at Malden, at Centreville, at Billy Greenfield's in Beallsville, at Hillsboro (Billy Robinson was a familiar name), at Dutch Charley Miller's, at Ward's, at Pancake, and so on—familiar names, forever endeared to my memory. I cherish the desire of riding over the "Old Pike" with you, but I am afraid we shall contemplate it as a scheme never to be realized.

Very sincerely,
Your friend,
JAMES G. BLAINE.

CONTENTS.

CHAPTER XVIII.

8   CONTENTS.

CHAPTER XXIX.

CHAPTER XXX.

CHAPTER XXXI.

CHAPTER XXXII.

CHAPTER XXXIII.

CHAPTER XXXIV.

CHAPTER XXXV.

CHAPTER XXXVI.

CHAPTER XXXVII.

CHAPTER XXXVIII.

CHAPTER XXXIX.

CHAPTER XL.

ILLUSTRATIONS.

STAGE HOUSE AND STABLES AT MT. WASHINGTON.

THE OLD PIKE.

CHAPTER I.

Inception of the Road — Author's Motive in Writing its History — No History of the Appian Way — A Popular Error Corrected — Henry Clay, Andrew Stewart, T. M. T. McKennan, Gen. Beeson, Lewis Steenrod and Daniel Sturgeon — Their Services in Behalf of the Road — Braddock's Road — Business and Grandeur of the Road — Old and Odd Names — Taverns — No Beer on the Road — Definition of Turnpike — An Old Legal Battle.

The road which forms the subject of this volume, is the only highway of its kind ever wholly constructed by the government of the United States. When Congress first met after the achievement of Independence and the adoption of the Federal Constitution, the lack of good roads was much commented upon by our statesmen and citizens generally, and various schemes suggested to meet the manifest want. But, it was not until the year 1806, when Jefferson was President, that the proposition for a National Road took practical shape. The first step, as will hereinafter be seen, was the appointment of commissioners to lay out the road, with an appropriation of money to meet the consequent expense. The author of this work was born and reared on the line of the road, and has spent his whole life amid scenes connected with it. He saw it in the zenith of its glory, and with emotions of sadness witnessed its decline. It was a highway at once so grand and imposing, an artery so largely instrumental in promoting the early growth and development of our country's wonderful resources, so influential in strengthening the bonds of the American Union, and at the same time so replete with important events and interesting incidents, that the writer of these pages has long cherished a hope that some capable hand would write its history and collect and preserve its legends, and no one having come forward to perform the task, he has ventured upon it himself, with unaffected diffidence and a full knowledge of his inability to do justice to the subject.

It is not a little singular that no connected history of the renowned Appian Way can be found in our libraries. Glimpses of its existence and importance are seen in the New Testament and in some

2 (13)

old volumes of classic lore, but an accurate and complete history of
its inception, purpose, construction and development, with the incidents, accidents and anecdotes, which of necessity were connected
with it, seems never to have been written. This should not be said
of the great National Road of the United States of America. The
Appian Way has been called the Queen of Roads. We claim for our
National highway that it *was* the King of Roads.

Tradition, cheerfully acquiesced in by popular thought, attributes
to Henry Clay the conception of the National Road, but this seems to
be error. The Hon. Andrew Stewart, in a speech delivered in Congress, January 27th, 1829, asserted that "Mr. Gallatin was the very
first man that ever suggested the plan for making the Cumberland
Road." As this assertion was allowed to go unchallenged, it must be
accepted as true, however strongly and strangely it conflicts with the
popular belief before stated. The reader will bear in mind that the
National Road and the Cumberland Road are one and the same. The
road as constructed by authority of Congress, begins at the city of
Cumberland, in the State of Maryland, and this is the origin of the
name Cumberland Road. All the acts of Congress and of the legislatures of the States through which the road passes, and they are
numerous, refer to it as the Cumberland Road. The connecting link
between Cumberland and the city of Baltimore is a road much older
than the Cumberland Road, constructed and owned by associations
of individuals, and the two together constitute the National Road.

While it appears from the authority quoted that Henry Clay was
not the planner of the National Road, he was undoubtedly its ablest
and most conspicuous champion. In Mallory's Life of Clay it is
stated that "he advocated the policy of carrying forward the construction of the Cumberland Road as rapidly as possible," and with what
earnestness, continues his biographer, "we may learn from his own
language, declaring that he had to *beg, entreat* and *supplicate* Congress,
session after session, to grant the necessary appropriations to complete the road." Mr. Clay said, "I have myself toiled until my
powers have been exhausted and prostrated to prevail on you to make
the grant." No wonder Mr. Clay was a popular favorite along the
whole line of the road. At a public dinner tendered him by the mechanics of Wheeling, he spoke of "the great interest the road had
awakened in his breast, and expressed an ardent desire that it might
be prosecuted to a speedy completion." Among other things he said
that "a few years since he and his family had employed the whole or
greater part of a day in traveling the distance of about nine miles
from Uniontown to Freeman's,* on Laurel Hill, which now, since the
construction of the road over the mountains, could be accomplished,
together with seventy more in the same time," and that "the road

---

* Benjamin Freeman kept a tavern on the old Braddock Road, a short distance south of
Mt. Washington. Locating his house on Laurel Hill, was an error of Mr. Clay, but of little consequence, and readily made under the circumstances. A monument was erected, and is still
standing, on the roadside near Wheeling, commemorative of the services of Mr. Clay in behalf
of the road.

GEN. HENRY W. BEESON.

was so important to the maintenance of our Union that he would not consent to give it up to the keeping of the several States through which it passed."

Hon. Andrew Stewart, of Uniontown, who served many years in Congress, beginning with 1820, was, next to Mr. Clay, the most widely known and influential congressional friend of the road, and in earnestness and persistency in this behalf, not excelled even by Mr. Clay. Hon. T. M. T. McKennan, an old congressman of Washington, Pennsylvania, was likewise a staunch friend of the road, carefully guarding its interests and pressing its claims upon the favorable consideration of Congress. Gen. Henry W. Beeson, of Uniontown, who represented the Fayette and Greene district of Pennsylvania in Congress in the forties, was an indomitable friend of the road. He stoutly opposed the extension of the Baltimore and Ohio railroad west of Cumberland, through Pennsylvania, and was thoroughly sustained by his constituents. In one of his characteristic speeches on the subject, he furnished a careful estimate of the number of horse-shoes made by the blacksmiths along the road, the number of nails required to fasten them to the horses' feet, the number of bushels of grain and tons of hay furnished by the farmers to the tavern keepers, the vast quantity of chickens, turkeys, eggs and butter that found a ready market on the line, and other like statistical information going to show that the National Road would better subserve the public weal than a steam railroad. This view at the time, and in the locality affected, was regarded as correct, which serves as an illustration of the change that takes place in public sentiment, as the wheels of time revolve and the ingenuity of man expands. Lewis Steenrod, of the Wheeling district, was likewise an able and influential congressional friend of the road. He was the son of Daniel Steenrod, an old tavernkeeper on the road, near Wheeling; and the Cumberland, Maryland, district always sent men to Congress who favored the preservation and maintenance of the road. Hon. Daniel Sturgeon, who served as a senator of the United States for the State of Pennsylvania from 1840 to 1852, was also an undeviating and influential friend of the road. He gave unremitting attention and untiring support to every measure brought before the Senate during his long and honorable service in that body, designed to make for the road's prosperity, and preserve and maintain it as the nation's great highway. His home was in Uniontown, on the line of the road, and he was thoroughly identified with it alike in sentiment and interest. He was not a showy statesman, but the possessor of incorruptible integrity and wielded an influence not beneath that of any of his compeers, among whom were that renowned trio of Senators, Clay, Webster and Calhoun.

Frequent references will be made in these pages to the Old Braddock Road, but it is not the purpose of the writer to go into the history of that ancient highway. This volume is devoted exclusively to the National Road. We think it pertinent, however, to remark that Braddock's Road would have been more appropriately named Washington's Road. Washington passed over it in command of a detachment of Virginia troops more than a year before Braddock ever saw it. Mr. Veech, the eminent local historian. says that Braddock's Road and Nemicolon's Indian trail are identical, so that Nemicolon, the Indian, would seem to have a higher claim to the honor of giving name to this old road than General Braddock. However, time, usage and common consent unite in calling it Braddock's Road, and, as a rule, we hold it to be very unwise, not to say downright foolishness, to undertake to change old and familiar names. It is difficult to do, and ought not to be done.

From the time it was thrown open to the public, in the year 1818, until the coming of railroads west of the Allegheny mountains, in 1852, the National Road was the one great highway, over which passed the bulk of trade and travel, and the mails between the East and the West. Its numerous and stately stone bridges with handsomely turned arches, its iron mile posts and its old iron gates, attest the skill of the workmen engaged on its construction, and to this day remain enduring monuments of its grandeur and solidity, all save the imposing iron gates, which have disappeared by process of conversion prompted by some utilitarian idea, savoring in no little measure of sacrilege. Many of the most illustrious statesmen and heroes of the early period of our national existence passed over the National Road from their homes to the capital and back, at the opening and closing of the sessions of Congress. Jackson, Harrison, Clay, Sam Houston. Polk, Taylor, Crittenden, Shelby, Allen, Scott, Butler, the eccentric Davy Crockett, and many of their contemporaries in public service, were familiar figures in the eyes of the dwellers by the roadside. The writer of these pages frequently saw these distinguished men on their passage over the road, and remembers with no little pride the incident of shaking hands with General Jackson, as he sat in his carriage on the wagon-yard of an old tavern. A coach, in which Mr. Clay was proceeding to Washington, was upset on a pile of limestone, in the main street of Uniontown, a few moments after supper at the McClelland house. Sam Sibley was the driver of that coach, and had his nose broken by the accident. Mr. Clay was unhurt, and upon being extricated from the grounded coach, facetiously remarked that: "This is mixing the Clay of Kentucky with the limestone of Pennsylvania."

As many as twenty-four-horse coaches have been counted in line at one time on the road, and large, broad-wheeled wagons, covered with white canvass stretched over bows, laden with merchandise and drawn by six Conestoga horses, were visible all the day long at every point, and many times until late in the evening, besides innumerable caravans of horses, mules, cattle, hogs and sheep. It looked more like the leading avenue of a great city than a road through rural districts.

The road had a peculiar nomenclature, familiar to the tens of thousands who traveled over it in its palmy days. The names, for example, applied to particular localities on the line, are of striking

HON. DANIEL STURGEON.

import, and blend harmoniously with the unique history of the road. With these names omitted, the road would be robbed of much that adds interest to its history. Among the best remembered of these are, The Shades of Death, The Narrows, Piney Grove, Big Crossings, Negro Mountain, Keyser's Ridge, Woodcock Hill, Chalk Hill, Big Savage, Little Savage, Snake Hill, Laurel Hill, The Turkey's Nest, Egg Nog Hill, Coon Island and Wheeling Hill. Rich memories cluster around every one of these names, and old wagoners and stage drivers delight to linger over the scenes they bring to mind.

The road was justly renowned for the great number and excellence of its inns or taverns. On the mountain division, every mile had its tavern. Here one could be seen perched on some elevated site, near the roadside, and there another, sheltered behind a clump of trees, many of them with inviting seats for idlers, and all with cheerful fronts toward the weary traveler. The sign-boards were elevated upon high and heavy posts, and their golden letters winking in the sun, ogled the wayfarer from the hot road-bed and gave promise of good cheer, while the big trough, overflowing with clear, fresh water, and the ground below it sprinkled with droppings of fragrant peppermint, lent a charm to the scene that was well nigh enchanting.

The great majority of the taverns were called wagon stands, because their patrons were largely made up of wagoners, and each provided with grounds called the wagon-yard, whereon teams were driven to feed, and rest over night. The very best of entertainment was furnished at these wagon stands. The taverns whereat stage horses were kept and exchanged, and stage passengers took meals, were called "stage houses," located at intervals of about twelve miles, as nearly as practicable.

The beer of the present day was unknown, or if known, unused on the National Road during the era of its prosperity. Ale was used in limited quantities, but was not a favorite drink. Whisky was the leading beverage, and it was plentiful and cheap. The price of a drink of whisky was three cents, except at the stage houses, where by reason of an assumption of aristocracy the price was five cents. The whisky of that day is said to have been pure, and many persons of unquestioned respectability affirm with much earnestness that it never produced delirium tremens. The current coin of the road was the big copper cent of United States coinage, the "fippenny bit," Spanish, of the value of six and one-fourth cents, called for brevity a "fip," the "levy," Spanish, of the value of twelve and a half cents, the quarter, the half dollar, and the dollar. The Mexican and Spanish milled dollar were oftener seen than the United States dollar. The silver five-cent piece and the dime of the United States coinage were seen occasionally, but not so much used as the "fip" and the "levy." In times of stringency, the stage companies issued scrip in denominations ranging from five cents to a dollar, which passed readily as money. The scrip was similar to the postal currency of the war

period, lacking only in the artistic skill displayed in the engraving of
the latter. A hungry traveler could obtain a substantial meal at an
old wagon stand tavern for a "levy," and two drinks of whisky for a
"fippenny bit." The morning bill of a wagoner with a six-horse
team did not exceed one dollar and seventy-five cents, which included
grain and hay for the horses, meals for the driver, and all the drinks
he saw proper to take.

The National Road is not in a literal sense a turnpike. A turnpike, in the original meaning of the word, is a road upon which pikes
were placed to turn travelers thereon through gates, to prevent them
from evading the payment of toll. Pikes were not used, or needed
on the National Road. It was always kept in good condition, and
travelers thereon, as a rule, paid the required toll without complaining. At distances of fifteen miles, on the average, houses were erected
for toll collectors to dwell in, and strong iron gates, hung to massive
iron posts, were established to enforce the payment of toll in cases of
necessity. These toll houses were of uniform size, angular and
round, west of the mountains constructed of brick, and through the
mountains, of stone, except the one six miles west of Cumberland,
which is of brick. They are all standing on their old sites at this
date (1893), except the one that stood near Mt. Washington, and the
one that stood near the eastern base of Big Savage Mountain. At
the last mentioned point, the old iron gate posts are still standing,
firmly rooted in their original foundations, and plastered all over with
advertisements of Frostburg's business houses, but the old house and
the old gates have gone out of sight forever.

It is curious to note how the word turnpike has been perverted
from its literal meaning by popular usage. The common idea is that
a turnpike is a road made of stone, and that the use of stone is that
alone which makes it a turnpike. The common phrase, "piking a
road," conveys the idea of putting stones on it, whereas in fact, there
is no connection between a stone and a pike, and a road might be a
turnpike without a single stone upon it. It is the contrivance to turn
travelers through gates, before mentioned, that makes a turnpike.
We recall but one instance of a refusal to pay toll for passing over
the National Road, and that was a remarkable one. It grew out of a
misconception of the scope of the act of Congress, providing for the
exemption from toll of carriages conveying the United States mails.
The National Road Stage Company, commonly called the "Old
Line," of which Lucius W. Stockton was the controlling spirit, was a
contractor for carrying the mails, and conceived the idea that by
placing a mail pouch in every one of its passenger coaches it could
evade the payment of toll. Stage companies did not pay toll to the
collectors at the gates, like ordinary travelers, but at stated periods
to the Road Commissioner. At the time referred to, William Searight, father of the writer, was the commissioner in charge of the
entire line of the road through the state of Pennsylvania, and it was
fifty years ago. Upon presenting his account to Mr. Stockton, who

lived at Uniontown, for accumulated tolls, that gentleman refused payment on the ground that all his coaches carried the mail, and were therefore exempt from toll. The commissioner was of opinion that the act of Congress could not be justly construed to cover so broad a claim, and notified Mr. Stockton that if the toll was not paid the gates would be closed against his coaches. Mr. Stockton was a resolute as well as an enterprising man, and persisted in his position, whereupon an order was given to close the gates against the passage of his coaches until the legal toll was paid. The writer was present, though a boy, at an execution of this order at the gate five miles west of Uniontown. It was in the morning. The coaches came along at the usual time and the gates were securely closed against them. The commissioner superintended the act in person, and a large number of people from the neighborhood attended to witness the scene, anticipating tumult and violence, as to which they were happily disappointed. The drivers accepted the situation with good nature, but the passengers, impatient to proceed, after learning the cause of the halt, paid the toll, whereupon the gates were thrown open, and the coaches sped on. For a considerable time after this occurrence an agent was placed on the coaches to pay the toll at the gates. Mr. Stockton instituted prosecutions against the commissioner for obstructing the passage of the United States mails, which were not pressed to trial, but the main contention was carried to the Supreme Court of the United States for adjudication on a case stated, and Mr. Stockton's broad claim was denied, the court of last resort holding that "the exemption from tolls did not apply to any other property (than the mails) conveyed in the same vehicle, nor to any persons traveling in it, unless he was in the service of the United States and passing along the road in pursuance of orders from the proper authority; and further, that the exemption could not be claimed for more carriages than were necessary for the safe, speedy and convenient conveyance of the mail." This case is reported in full in 3d Howard U. S. Reports, page 151 *et seq.*, including the full text of Chief Justice Taney's opinion, and elaborate dissenting opinions by Justices McClean and Daniel. The attorneys for the road in this controversy were Hon. Robert P. Flenniken and Hon. James Veech of Uniontown, and Hon. Robert J. Walker of Mississippi, who was Secretary of the Treasury in the cabinet of President Polk. After this decision, and by reason of it, the Legislature of Pennsylvania enacted the law of April 14th, 1845, still in force, authorizing the collection of tolls from passengers traveling in coaches which at the same time carried the mail.

CHAPTER II.

Origin of the Fund for Making the Road.—*Acts for the Admission of Ohio, Indiana, Illinois and Missouri*—*Report of a Committee of Congress as to the Manner of Applying the Ohio Fund*—*Distances from Important Eastern Cities to the Ohio River*—*The Richmond Route Postponed*—*The Spirit and Perseverance of Pennsylvania*—*Maryland, "My Maryland," not behind Pennsylvania*—*Wheeling the Objective Point*—*Brownsville a Prominent Point*—*Rivers tend to Union, Mountains to Disunion.*

Act of April 30, 1802, for the admission of Ohio, provides that one-twentieth part of the net proceeds of the lands lying within the said State sold by Congress, from and after the 30th of June next, after deducting all expenses incident to the same, shall be applied to laying out and making public roads leading from navigable waters emptying into the Atlantic to the Ohio, to the said State and through the same, such roads to be laid out under the authority of Congress, with the consent of the several States through which the road shall pass.

Act of April 19, 1816, for the admission of Indiana, provides that five per cent. of the net proceeds of lands lying within the said territory, and which shall be sold by Congress from and after the first day of December next, after deducting all expenses incident to the same, shall be reserved for making public roads and canals, of which three-fifths shall be applied to those objects within the said State under the direction of the Legislature thereof, and two-fifths to the making of a road or roads leading to the said State under the direction of Congress.

Act of April 18, 1818, for the admission of Illinois, provides that five per cent. of the net proceeds of the lands lying within the said State, and which shall be sold by Congress from and after the first day of January, 1819, after deducting all expenses incident to the same, shall be reserved for the purposes following, viz: Two-fifths to be disbursed under the direction of Congress in making roads leading to the State, the residue to be appropriated by the Legislature of the State for the encouragement of learning, of which one-sixth part shall be exclusively bestowed on a college or university.

Act of March 6, 1820, admitting Missouri, provides that five per cent. of the net proceeds of the sale of lands lying within the said Territory or State, and which shall be sold by Congress from and after the first day of January next, after deducting all expenses incident to the same, shall be reserved for making public roads and canals, of which three-fifths shall be applied to those objects within the State under the direction of the Legislature thereof, and the other two-fifths in defraying, under the direction of Congress, the expenses to be incurred in making a road or roads, canal or canals, leading to the said State.

No. 195.

NINTH CONGRESS — FIRST SESSION.

CUMBERLAND ROAD.

Communicated to the Senate December 19, 1805.

Mr. Tracy, from the committee to whom was referred the examination of the act entitled, "An act to enable the people of the eastern division of the territory northwest of the river Ohio to form a Constitution and State Government, and for the admission of such State into the Union on an equal footing with the original States, and for other purposes;" and to report the manner in which, in their opinion, the money appropriated by said act ought to be applied, made the following report:

That, upon examination of the act aforesaid, they find "the one-twentieth part, or five per cent., of the net proceeds of the lands lying within the State of Ohio, and sold by Congress from and after the 30th day of June, 1802, is appropriated for the laying out and making public roads leading from the navigable waters emptying into the Atlantic to the river Ohio, to said State, and through the same; such roads to be laid out under the authority of Congress, with the consent of the several States through which the road shall pass."

They find that by a subsequent law, passed on the 3d day of March, 1803, Congress appropriated three per cent. of the said five per cent. to laying out and making roads *within* the State of Ohio, leaving two per cent. of the appropriation contained in the first mentioned law unexpended, which now remains for "*the laying out and making roads from the navigable waters emptying into the Atlantic to the river Ohio, to said State.*"

They find that the net proceeds of sales of land in the State of Ohio,

From 1st July, 1802, to June 30, 1803, both inclusive, were........$124,400 92
From 1st July, 1803, to June 30, 1804............................ 176,203 35
From 1st July, 1804, to June 30, 1805........................ ..... 266,000 00
From 1st July, 1805, to Sept. 30, 1805 .... 66,000 00

Amounting, in the whole, to..............................$632,604 27

Two per cent. on which sum amounts to $12,652. Twelve thousand six hundred and fifty-two dollars were, therefore, on the 1st day of October last, subject to the uses directed by law, as mentioned in this report; and it will be discerned that the fund is constantly accumulating, and will, probably, by the time regular preparations can be made for its expenditure, amount to eighteen or twenty thousand dollars. The committee have examined, as far as their limited time and

2a

the scanty sources of facts within their reach would permit, the various routes which have been contemplated for laying out roads pursuant to the provisions of the act first mentioned in this report. They find that the distance from Philadelphia to Pittsburg is 314 miles by the usual route, and on a straight line about 270.

From Philadelphia to the nearest point on the river Ohio, contiguous to the State of Ohio, which is probably between Steubenville and the mouth of Grave creek, the distance by the usual route is 360 miles, and on a straight line about 308.

From Baltimore to the river Ohio, between the same points, and by the usual route, is 275 miles, and on a straight line 224.

From this city (Washington) to the same points on the river Ohio, the distance is nearly the same as from Baltimore; probably the difference is not a plurality of miles.

From Richmond, in Virginia, to the nearest point on the river Ohio, the distance by the usual route is 377 miles; but new roads are opening which will shorten the distance fifty or sixty miles; 247 miles of the contemplated road, from Richmond northwesterly, will be as good as the roads usually are in that country, but the remaining seventy or eighty miles are bad, for the present, and probably will remain so for a length of time, as there seems to be no existing inducement for the State of Virginia to incur the expense of making that part of the road passable.

From Baltimore to the Monongahela river, where the route from Baltimore to the Ohio river will intersect it, the distance as usually traveled is 218 miles, and on a straight line about 184. From this point, which is at or near Brownsville, boats can pass down, with great facility, to the State of Ohio, during a number of months in every year.

The above distances are not all stated from actual mensuration, but it is believed they are sufficiently correct for the present purpose.

The committee have not examined any routes northward of that leading from Philadelphia to the river Ohio, nor southward of that leading from Richmond, because they suppose the roads to be laid out must strike the river Ohio on some point contiguous to the State of Ohio, in order to satisfy the words of the law making the appropriation; the words are: "Leading from the navigable waters emptying into the Atlantic, to the river Ohio, to the said State, and through the same."

The mercantile intercourse of the citizens of Ohio with those of the Atlantic States is chiefly in Philadelphia and Baltimore; not very extensive in the towns on the Potomac, within the District of Columbia, and still less with Richmond, in Virginia. At present, the greatest portion of their trade is with Philadelphia; but it is believed their trade is rapidly increasing with Baltimore, owing to the difference of distance in favor of Baltimore, and to the advantage of boating down the Monongahela river, from the point where the road strikes it, about 70 miles by water, and 50 by land, above Pittsburg.

The sum appropriated for laying out and making roads is so small that the committee have thought it most expedient to direct an expenditure to one route only. They have therefore endeavored to fix on that which, for the present, will be most accommodating to the citizens of the State of Ohio; leaving to the future benevolence and policy of congress, an extension of their operations on this or other routes, and an increase of the requisite fund, as the discoveries of experience may point out their expediency and necessity.

The committee being fully convinced that a wise government can never lose sight of an object so important as that of connecting a numerous and rapidly increasing population, spread upon a fertile and extensive territory, with the Atlantic States, now separated from them by mountains, which, by industry and an expense moderate in comparison with the advantages, can be rendered passable.

The route from Richmond must necessarily approach the State of Ohio in a part thinly inhabited, and which, from the nature of the soil and other circumstances, must remain so, at least for a considerable time; and, from the hilly and rough condition of the country, no roads are or can be conveniently made, leading to the principal population of the State of Ohio.

These considerations have induced the committee to postpone, for the present, any further consideration of that route.

The spirit and perseverance of Pennsylvania are such, in the matter of road making, that no doubt can remain but they will, in a little time, complete a road from Philadelphia to Pittsburg, as good as the nature of the ground will permit. They are so particularly interested to facilitate the intercourse between their trading capital, Philadelphia, not only to Pittsburg, but also to the extensive country within that State, on the western waters, that they will, of course, surmount the difficulties presented by the Allegheny mountain, Chesnut Ridge and Laurel Hill, the three great and almost exclusive impediments which now exist on that route.

The State of Maryland, with no less spirit and perseverance, are engaged in making roads from Baltimore and from the western boundary of the District of Columbia, through Fredericktown, to Williamsport. Were the Government of the United States to direct the expenditure of the fund in contemplation upon either of these routes, for the present, in Pennsylvania or Maryland, it would, probably, so far interfere with the operations of the respective States, as to produce mischief instead of benefit; especially as the sum to be laid out by the United States is too inconsiderable, alone, to effect objects of such magnitude. But as the State of Maryland have no particular interest to extend their road across the mountains (and if they had it would be impracticable, because the State does not extend so far), the committee have thought it expedient to recommend the laying out and making a road from Cumberland, on the northerly bank of the Potomac, and within the State of Maryland, to the river Ohio, at the most convenient place between a point on the easterly bank of said river,

opposite to Steubenville, and the mouth of Grave creek, which empties into said river Ohio a little below Wheeling, in Virginia. This
route will meet and accommodate the roads leading from Baltimore
and the District of Columbia; it will cross the Monongahela river, at
or near Brownsville, sometimes called Redstone, where the advantage
of boating can be taken; and from the point where it will probably
intersect the river Ohio, there are now roads, or they can easily be
made over feasible and proper ground, to and through the principal
population of the State of Ohio.

Cumberland is situated at the eastern foot of the Allegheny
mountains, about eighty miles from Williamsport, by the usual route,
which is circuitous, owing to a large bend in the river Potomac, on
the bank of which the road now runs, the distance on a straight line
is not more than fifty or fifty-five miles, and over tolerable ground for
a road, which will probably be opened by the State of Maryland,
should the route be established over the mountains, as contemplated
by this report.

From Cumberland to the western extremity of Laurel Hill, by
the route now travelled, the distance is sixty-six miles, and on a straight
line about fifty-five; on this part of the route, the committee suppose
the first and very considerable expenditures are specially necessary.
From Laurel Hill to the Ohio river, by the usual route, is about
seventy miles, and on a straight line fifty-four or five; the road is
tolerable, though capable of amelioration.

To carry into effect the principles arising from the foregoing
facts, the committee present herewith a bill for the consideration of
the Senate. They suppose that to take the proper measures for carrying into effect the section of the law respecting a road or roads to the
State of Ohio, is a duty imposed upon Congress by the law itself, and
that a sense of duty will always be sufficient to insure the passage of
the bill now offered to the Senate. To enlarge upon the highly important considerations of cementing the union of our citizens located
on the Western waters with those of the Atlantic States, would be an
indelicacy offered to the understandings of the body to whom this report is addressed, as it might seem to distrust them. But from the
interesting nature of the subject, the committee are induced to ask
the indulgence of a single observation : Politicians have generally
agreed that rivers unite the interests and promote the friendship of
those who inhabit their banks ; while mountains, on the contrary,
tend to the disunion and estrangement of those who are separated by
their intervention. In the present case, to make the crooked ways
straight, and the rough ways smooth will, in effect, remove the intervening mountains, and by facilitating the intercourse of our Western
brethren with those on the Atlantic, substantially unite them in interest, which, the committee believe, is the most effectual cement of
union applicable to the human race.

All which is most respectfully submitted .

CHAPTER III.

The Act of Congress Authorizing the Laying Out and Making of the Road.

An Act to Regulate the Laying Out and Making a Road from Cumberland, in the State of Maryland, to the State of Ohio.

Be it enacted by the Senate and House of Representatives of the United States of America in Congress assembled, That the President of the United States be, and he is hereby authorized to appoint, by and with the advice and consent of the Senate, three discreet and disinterested citizens of the United States, to lay out a road from Cumberland, or a point on the northern bank of the river Potomac, in the State of Maryland, between Cumberland and the place where the main road leading from Gwynn's to Winchester, in Virginia, crosses the river, to the State of Ohio; whose duty it shall be, as soon as may be, after their appointment, to repair to Cumberland aforesaid, and view the ground, from the points on the river Potomac hereinbefore designated, to the river Ohio; and to lay out in such direction as they shall judge, under all circumstances the most proper, a road from thence to the river Ohio, to strike the same at the most convenient place, between a point on its eastern bank, opposite the northern boundary of Steubenville, in said State of Ohio, and the mouth of Grave creek, which empties into the said river a little below Wheeling, in Virginia.

Sec. 2. *And be it further enacted,* That the aforesaid road shall be laid out four rods in width, and designated on each side by a plain and distinguishable mark on a tree, or by the erection of a stake or monument sufficiently conspicuous, in every quarter of a mile of the distance at least, where the road pursues a straight course so far or farther, and on each side, at every point where an angle occurs in its course.

Sec. 3. *And be it further enacted,* That the commissioners shall, as soon as may be, after they have laid out said road, as aforesaid, present to the President an accurate plan of the same, with its several courses and distances, accompanied by a written report of their proceedings, describing the marks and monuments by which the road is designated, and the face of the country over which it passes, and pointing out the particular parts which they shall judge require the most and immediate attention and amelioration, and the probable expense of making the same passable in the most difficult parts, and through the whole distance; designating the State or States through which said road has been laid out, and the length of the several parts which are laid out on new ground, as well as the length of those parts laid out on the road now traveled. Which report the President is hereby authorized to accept or reject, in the whole or in part. If he accepts, he is hereby further authorized and requested to pursue such measures, as in his opinion shall be proper, to obtain consent for making the road, of the State or States through which the same has been laid out. Which consent being obtained, he is further authorized to take prompt and effectual measures to cause said road to be made through the whole distance, or in any part or parts of the same as he shall judge most conducive to the public good, having reference to the sum appropriated for the purpose.

SEC. 4 *And be it further enacted*, That all parts of the road which the President shall direct to be made, in case the trees are standing, shall be cleared the whole width of four rods; and the road shall be raised in the middle of the carriageway with stone, earth, or gravel and sand, or a combination of some or all of them, leaving or making, as the case may be, a ditch or water course on each side and contiguous to said carriageway, and in no instance shall there be an elevation in said road, when finished, greater than an angle of five degrees with the horizon. But the manner of making said road, in every other particular, is left to the direction of the President.

SEC. 5. *And be it further enacted*, That said Commissioners shall each receive four dollars per day, while employed as aforesaid, in full for their compensation, including all expenses. And they are hereby authorized to employ one surveyor, two chainmen and one marker, for whose faithfulness and accuracy they, the said Commissioners, shall be responsible, to attend them in laying out said road, who shall receive in full satisfaction for their wages, including all expenses, the surveyor three dollars per day, and each chainman and the marker one dollar per day, while they shall be employed in said business, of which fact a certificate signed by said commissioners shall be deemed sufficient evidence.

SEC. 6. *And be it further enacted*, That the sum of thirty thousand dollars be, and the same is hereby appropriated, to defray the expense of laying out and making said road. And the President is hereby authorized to draw, from time to time, on the treasury for such parts, or at any one time, for the whole of said sum, as he shall judge the service requires. Which sum of thirty thousand dollars shall be paid, first, out of the fund of two per cent. reserved for laying out and making roads *to* the State of Ohio, by virtue of the seventh section of an act passed on the thirtieth day of April, one thousand eight hundred and two, entitled, "An act to enable the people of the eastern division of the territory northwest of the river Ohio to form a constitution and State government, and for the admission of such State into the Union on an equal footing with the original States, and for other purposes." Three per cent. of the appropriation contained in said seventh section being directed by a subsequent law to the laying out, opening and making roads *within* the said State of Ohio; and secondly, out of any money in the treasury not otherwise appropriated, chargeable upon, and reimbursable at the treasury by said fund of two per cent. as the same shall accrue.

SEC. 7. *And be it further enacted,* That the President be, and he is hereby requested, to cause to be laid before Congress, as soon as convenience will permit, after the commencement of each session, a statement of the proceedings under this act, that Congress may be enabled to adopt such further measures as may from time to time be proper under existing circumstances.

Approved, March 29, 1806.   TH. JEFFERSON.

UNITED STATES OF AMERICA,   )
DEPARTMENT OF STATE.)

To all to whom these presents shall come, Greeting:

I certify that hereto annexed is a true copy of an Act of Congress, approved March 29, 1806, the original of which is on file in this Department, entitled: "An Act to regulate the laying out and making a road from Cumberland, in the State of Maryland, to the State of Ohio."

In testimony whereof, I, James G. Blaine, Secretary of State of the United States, have hereunto subscribed my name and caused the seal of the Department of State to be affixed.

Done at the City of Washington, this seventh day of March, A. D. 1891, and of the Independence of the United States the one hundred and fifteenth.

JAMES G. BLAINE.

CHAPTER IV.

Special Message of President Jefferson—Communicating to Congress the First Report of the Commissioners—They View the Whole Ground—Solicitude of the Inhabitants—Points Considered—Cumberland the First Point Located—Uniontown Left Out—Improvement of the Youghiogheny—Distances— Connellsville a Promising Town — " A Well Formed, Stone Capped Road — Estimated Cost, $6,000 per Mile, exclusive of Bridges.

No. 220.

NINTH CONGRESS — SECOND SESSION.

January 31, 1807.

To the Senate and House of Representatives of the United States:

In execution of the act of the last session of Congress, entitled, " An act to regulate the laying out and making a road from Cumberland, in the State of Maryland, to the State of Ohio," I appointed Thomas Moore, of Maryland, Joseph Kerr, of Ohio, and Eli Williams, of Maryland, commissioners to lay out the said road, and to perform the other duties assigned to them by the act. The progress which they made in the execution of the work, during the last season, will appear in their report now communicated to Congress; on the receipt of it, I took measures to obtain consent for making the road of the States of Pennsylvania, Maryland and Virginia, through which the commissioners propose to lay it out. I have received acts of the Legislatures of Maryland and Virginia, giving the consent desired; that of Pennsylvania has the subject still under consideration, as is supposed. Until I receive full consent to a free choice of route through the whole distance, I have thought it safest neither to accept nor reject, finally, the partial report of the commissioners.

Some matters suggested in the report belong exclusively to the legislature.

TH. JEFFERSON.

The commissioners, acting by appointment under the law of Congress, entitled " An act to regulate the laying out and making a road from Cumberland, in the State of Maryland, to the State of Ohio, beg leave to report to the President of the United States, and to premise that the duties imposed by the law became a work of greater magnitude, and a task much more arduous, than was conceived before entering upon it; from which circumstance the commissioners did not allow themselves sufficient time for the performance of it before the severity of the weather obliged them to retire from it, which was the case in the first week of the present month (December). That, not having fully accomplished their work, they are unable fully to report a discharge of all the duties enjoined by the law; but as the most material and principal part has been performed, and as a communication of the progress already made may be useful and proper, during the present session of Congress, and of the Legislatures of those States through which the route passes, the commissioners respectfully state that at a very early period it was conceived that the maps of the country were not sufficiently accurate to afford a minute knowledge of the true courses between the extreme points on the rivers, by which the researches of the commissioners were to be governed; a survey for that purpose became indispensable, and considerations of public economy suggested the propriety of making this survey precede the personal attendance of the commissioners.

Josias Thompson, a surveyor of professional merit, was taken into service and authorized to employ two chain carriers and a marker, as well as one vaneman, and a packhorse man and horse, on public account; the latter being indispensable and really beneficial in excelerating the work. The surveyors' instructions are contained in document No. 1, accompanying this report.

Calculating on a reasonable time for the performance of the instructions to the surveyor, the commissioners, by correspondence, fixed on the first day of September last, for their meeting at Cumberland to proceed in the work; neither of them, however, reached that place until the third of that month, on which day they all met.

The surveyor having, under his instructions, laid down a plat of his work, showing the meanders of the Potomac and Ohio rivers, within the limits prescribed for the commissioners, as also the road between those rivers, which is commonly traveled from Cumberland to Charleston, in part called Braddock's road; and the same being produced to the commissioners, whereby straight lines and their true courses were shown between the extreme points on each river, and the boundaries which limit the powers of the commissioners being thereby ascertained, serving as a basis whereon to proceed in the examination of the grounds and face of the country; the commissioners thus prepared commenced the business of exploring; and in this it was considered that a faithful discharge of the discretionary powers vested by the law made it necessary to view the whole to be able to judge of a preference due to any part of the grounds, which imposed a task of examining a space comprehending upwards of two thousand square miles; a task rendered still more incumbent by the solicitude and importunities of the inhabitants of every part of the district, who severally conceived their grounds entitled to a preference. It becoming necessary, in the interim, to run various lines of experiment for ascertaining the geographical position of several points entitled to attention, and the service suffering great delay for want of another surveyor, it was thought consistent with the public interest to employ, in that capacity, Arthur Rider, the vaneman, who had been chosen with qualification to meet such an emergency ; and whose service as vaneman could then be dispensed with. He commenced, as surveyor, on the 22d day of September, and continued so at field work until the first day of December, when he was retained as a necessary assistant to the principal surveyor, in copying field notes and hastening the draught of the work to be reported.

The proceedings of the commissioners are specially detailed in their general journal, compiled from the daily journal of each commissioner, to which they beg leave to refer, under mark No. 2.

After a careful and critical examination of all the grounds within the limits prescribed, as well as the grounds and ways out from the Ohio westwardly, at several points, and examining the shoal parts of the Ohio river as detailed in the table of soundings, stated in their journal, and after gaining all the information, geographical, general and special, possible and necessary, toward a judicial discharge of the duties assigned them, the commissioners repaired to Cumberland to examine and compare their notes and journals, and determine upon the direction and location of their route.

In this consultation the governing objects were:

1st. Shortness of distance between navigable points on the eastern and western waters.

2d. A point on the Monongahela best calculated to equalize the advantages of this portage in the country within reach of it.

3d. A point on the Ohio river most capable of combining certainty of navigation with road accommodation; embracing, in this estimate, remote points westwardly, as well as present and probable population on the north and south.

4th. Best mode of diffusing benefits with least distance of road.

In contemplating these objects, due attention was paid as well to the comparative merits of towns, establishments, and settlements already made, as to the capacity of the country with the present and probable population.

In the course of arrangement, and in its order, the first point located for the route was determined and fixed at Cumberland, a decision founded on propriety, and in some measure on necessity, from the circumstance of a high and difficult mountain, called Nobley, laying and confining the east margin of the Potomac so as to render it impossible of access on that side without immense expense, at any point between Cumberland and where the road from Winchester to Gwynn's crosses, and even there the Nobley mountain is crossed with much difficulty and hazard. And this upper point was taxed with another formidable objection; it was found that a high range of mountains, called Dan's, stretching across from Gwynn's to the Potomac, above this point, precluded the opportunity of extending a route from this point in a proper direction, and left no alternative but passing by

Gwynn's; the distance from Cumberland to Gwynn's being upward of a mile less than from the upper point, which lies ten miles by water above Cumberland, the commissioners were not permitted to hesitate in preferring a point which shortens the portage, as well as the Potomac navigation.

The point on the Potomac being viewed as a great repository of produce, which a good road will bring from the west of Laurel Hill, and the advantages which Cumberland, as a town, has in that respect over an unimproved place, are additional considerations operating forcibly in favor of the place preferred.

In extending the route from Cumberland, a triple range of mountains, stretching across from Jenings' run in measure with Gwynn's, left only the alternative of laying the road up Will's creek for three miles, nearly at right angles with the true course, and then by way of Jenings' run, or extending it over a break in the smallest mountain, on a better course by Gwynn's, to the top of Savage mountain; the latter was adopted, being the shortest, and will be less expensive in hill-side digging over a sloped route than the former, requiring one bridge over Will's creek and several over Jenings' run, both very wide and considerable streams in high water; and a more weighty reason for preferring the route by Gwynn's is the great accommodation it will afford travelers from Winchester by the upper point, who could not reach the route by Jenings' run short of the top of Savage, which would withhold from them the benefit of an easy way up the mountain.

It is, however, supposed that those who travel from Winchester by way of the upper point to Gwynn's, are in that respect more the dupes of common prejudice than judges of their own ease, as it is believed the way will be as short, and on much better ground, to cross the Potomac below the confluence of the north and south branches (thereby crossing these two, as well as Patterson's creek, in one stream, equally fordable in the same season), than to pass through Cumberland to Gwynn's. Of these grounds, however, the commissioners do not speak from actual view, but consider it a subject well worthy of future investigation. Having gained the top of Allegany mountain, or rather the top of that part called Savage, by way of Gwynn's, the general route, as it respects the most important points, was determined as follows, viz.:

From a stone at the corner of lot No. 1, in Cumberland, near the confluence of Will's creek and the north branch of the Potomac river; thence extending along the street westwardly, to cross the hill lying between Cumberland and Gwynn's, at the gap where Braddock's road passes it; thence near Gwynn's and Jesse Tomlinson's, to cross the big Youghiogheny near the mouth of Roger's run, between the crossing of Braddock's road and the confluence of the streams which form the Turkey foot; thence to cross Laurel Hill near the forks of Dunbar's run, to the west foot of that hill, at a point near where Braddock's old road reached it, near Gist's old place, now Colonel Isaac Meason's, thence through Brownsville and Bridgeport, to cross the

Monongahela river below Josias Crawford's ferry; and thence on as straight a course as the country will admit to the Ohio, at a point between the mouth of Wheeling creek and the lower point of Wheeling island.

In this direction of the route it will lay about twenty-four and a half miles in Maryland, seventy-five miles and a half in Pennsylvania, and twelve miles in Virginia; distances which will be in a small degree increased by meanders, which the bed of the road must necessarily make between the points mentioned in the location; and this route, it is believed, comprehends more important advantages than could be afforded in any other, inasmuch as it has a capacity at least equal to any other in extending advantages of a highway, and at the same time establishes the shortest portage between the points already navigated, and on the way accommodates other and nearer points to which navigation may be extended, and still shorten the portage.

It intersects Big Youghiogheny at the nearest point from Cumberland, then lies nearly parallel with that river for the distance of twenty miles, and at the west foot of Laurel Hill lies within five miles of Connellsville, from which the Youghiogheny is navigated; and in the same direction the route intersects at Brownsville the nearest point on the Monongahela river within the district.

The improvement of the Youghiogheny navigation is a subject of too much importance to remain long neglected; and the capacity of that river, as high up as the falls (twelve miles above Connellsville), is said to be equal, at a small expense, with the parts already navigated below. The obstructions at the falls, and a rocky rapid near Turkey Foot, constitute the principal impediments in that river to the intersection of the route, and as much higher as the stream has a capacity for navigation; and these difficulties will doubtless be removed when the intercourse shall warrant the measure.

Under these circumstances the portage may be thus stated:

From Cumberland to Monongahela, 66½ miles. From Cumberland to a point in measure with Connellsville, on the Youghiogheny river, 51½ miles. From Cumberland to a point in measure with the lower end of the falls of Youghiogheny, which will lie two miles north of the public road, 43 miles. From Cumberland to the intersection of the route with the Youghiogheny river, 34 miles.

Nothing is here said of the Little Youghiogheny, which lies nearer Cumberland; the stream being unusually crooked, its navigation can only become the work of a redundant population.

The point which this route locates, at the west foot of Laurel Hill, having cleared the whole of the Allegheny mountain, is so situated as to extend the advantages of an easy way through the great barrier, with more equal justice to the best parts of the country between Laurel Hill and the Ohio. Lines from this point to Pittsburg and Morgantown, diverging nearly at the same angle, open upon equal terms to all parts of the Western country that can make use of this portage; and which may include the settlements from Pittsburg.

up Big Beaver to the Connecticut reserve, on Lake Erie, as well as those on the southern borders of the Ohio and all the intermediate country.

Brownsville is nearly equi-distant from Big Beaver and Fishing creek, and equally convenient to all the crossing places on the Ohio, between these extremes. As a port, it is at least equal to any on the Monongahela within the limits, and holds superior advantages in furnishing supplies to emigrants, traders, and other travelers by land or water.

Not unmindful of the claims of towns and their capacity of reciprocating advantages on public roads, the commissioners were not insensible of the disadvantage which Uniontown must feel from the want of that accommodation which a more southwardly direction of the route would have afforded; but as that could not take place without a relinquishment of the shortest passage, considerations of public benefit could not yield to feelings of minor import. Uniontown being the seat of justice for Fayette county, Pennsylvania, is not without a share of public benefits, and may partake of the advantages of this portage upon equal terms with Connellsville, a growing town, with the advantage of respectable water-works adjoining, in the manufactory of flour and iron.

After reaching the nearest navigation on the western waters, at a point best calculated to diffuse the benefits of a great highway in the greatest possible latitude east of the Ohio, it was considered that, to fulfill the objects of the law, it remained for the commissioners to give such a direction to the road as would best secure a certainty of navigation on the Ohio at all seasons, combining, as far as possible, the inland accommodation of remote points westwardly. It was found that the obstructions in the Ohio, within the limits between Steubenville and Grave creek, lay principally above the town and mouth of Wheeling; a circumstance ascertained by the commissioners in their examination of the channel, as well as by common usage, which has long given a decided preference to Wheeling as a place of embarcation and port of departure in dry seasons. It was also seen that Wheeling lay in a line from Brownsville to the centre of the State of Ohio and Post Vincennes. These circumstances favoring and corresponding with the chief objects in view in this last direction of the route, and the ground from Wheeling westwardly being known of equal fitness with any other way out from the river, it was thought most proper, under these several considerations, to locate the point mentioned below the mouth of Wheeling. In taking this point in preference to one higher up and in the town of Wheeling, the public benefit and convenience were consulted, inasmuch as the present crossing place over the Ohio from the town is so contrived and confined as to subject passengers to extraordinary ferriage and delay, by entering and clearing a ferry-boat on each side of Wheeling island, which lies before the town and precludes the opportunity of fording when the river is crossed in that way, above and below the island.

From the point located, a safe crossing is afforded at the lower point of the island by a ferry in high, and a good ford at low water.

The face of the country within the limits prescribed is generally very uneven, and in many places broken by a succession of high mountains and deep hollows, too formidable to be reduced within five degrees of the horizon, but by crossing them obliquely, a mode which, although it imposes a heavy task of hill-side digging, obviates generally the necessity of reducing hills and filling hollows, which, on these grounds, would be an attempt truly Quixotic. This inequality of the surface is not confined to the Allegheny mountain; the country between the Monongahela and Ohio rivers, although less elevated, is not better adapted for the bed of a road, being filled with impediments of hills and hollows, which present considerable difficulties, and wants that super-abundance and convenience of stone which is found in the mountain.

The indirect course of the road now traveled, and the frequent elevations and depressions which occur, that exceed the limits of the law, preclude the possibility of occupying it in any extent without great sacrifice of distance, and forbid the use of it, in any one part, for more than half a mile, or more than two or three miles in the whole.

The expense of rendering the road now in contemplation passable, may, therefore, amount to a larger sum than may have been supposed necessary, under an idea of embracing in it a considerable part of the old road; but it is believed that the contrary will be found most correct, and that a sum sufficient to open the new could not be expended on the same distance of the old road with equal benefit.

The sum required for the road in contemplation will depend on the style and manner of making it; as a common road cannot remove the difficulties which always exist on deep grounds, and particularly in wet seasons, and as nothing short of a firm, substantial, well-formed, stone-capped road can remove the causes which led to the measure of improvement, or render the institution as commodious as a great and growing intercourse appears to require, the expense of such a road next becomes the subject of inquiry.

In this inquiry the commissioners can only form an estimate by recurring to the experience of Pennsylvania and Maryland in the business of artificial roads. Upon this data, and a comparison of the grounds and proximity of the materials for covering, there are reasons for belief that, on the route reported, a complete road may be made at an expense not exceeding six thousand dollars per mile, exclusive of bridges over the principal streams on the way. The average expense of the Lancaster, as well as Baltimore and Frederick turnpike, is considerably higher; but it is believed that the convenient supply of stone which the mountain affords will, on those grounds, reduce the expense to the rate here stated.

As to the policy of incurring this expense, it is not the province of the commissioners to declare; but they cannot, however, withhold assurances of a firm belief that the purse of the nation cannot be more seasonably opened, or more happily applied, than in promoting the speedy and effectual establishment of a great and easy road on the way contemplated.

In the discharge of all these duties, the commissioners have been actuated by an ardent desire to render the institution as useful and commodious as possible; and, impressed with a strong sense of the necessity which urges the speedy establishment of the road, they have to regret the circumstance which delays the completion of the part assigned them. They, however, in some measure, content themselves with the reflection that it will not retard the progress of the work, as the opening of the road cannot commence before spring, and may then begin with marking the way.

The extra expense incident to the service from the necessity (and propriety, as it relates to public economy,) of employing men not provided for by law, will, it is hoped, be recognized, and provision made for the payment of that and similar expenses, when in future it may be indispensably incurred.

The commissioners having engaged in a service in which their zeal did not permit them to calculate the difference between their pay and the expense to which the service subjected them, cannot suppose it the wish or intention of the Government to accept of their services for a mere indemnification of their expense of subsistence, which will be very much the case under the present allowance; they, therefore, allow themselves to hope and expect that measures will be taken to provide such further compensation as may, under all circumstances, be thought neither profuse nor parsimonious.

The painful anxiety manifested by the inhabitants of the district explored, and their general desire to know the route determined on, suggested the measure of promulgation, which, after some deliberation, was agreed on by way of circular letter, which has been forwarded to those persons to whom precaution was useful, and afterward sent to one of the presses in that quarter for publication, in the form of the document No. 3, which accompanies this report.

All which is, with due deference, submitted.

ELI WILLIAMS,
THOMAS MOORE,
JOSEPH KERR.

DECEMBER 30, 1806.

CHAPTER V.

Pennsylvania Grants Permission to Make the Road Through Her Territory — Union-
town Restored, Gist Left Out, and Washington, Pennsylvania, Made a Point —
Simon Snyder, Speaker of the House — Pressly Carr Lane, a Fayette County Man,
Speaker of the Senate, and Thomas McKean, Governor — A Second Special Mes-
sage From President Jefferson, and a Second Report of the Commissioners —
Heights of Mountains and Hills — On to Brownsville and Wheeling — An Im-
perious Call Made on Commissioner Kerr.

An Act authorizing the President of the United States to open a road through
that part of this State lying between Cumberland, in the State of Maryland, and the Ohio river.

WHEREAS, by an Act of the Congress of the United States, passed
on the twenty-ninth day of March, one thousand eight hundred and
six, entitled "An act to regulate the laying out and making a road
from Cumberland, in the State of Maryland, to the State of Ohio,"
the President of the United States is empowered to lay out a road
from the Potomac river to the river Ohio, and to take measures for
making the same, so soon as the consent of the legislatures of the
several States through which the said road shall pass, could be obtained:
And whereas, application hath been made to this legislature, by the
President of the United States, for its consent to the measures aforesaid: Therefore,

SECTION 1. *Be it enacted by the Senate and House of Representa-*
tives of the Commonwealth of Pennsylvania, in General Assembly met,
and it is hereby enacted by the authority of the same, That the President
of the United States be, and he is hereby authorized to cause so much
of the said road as will be within this State, to be opened so far as it
may be necessary the same should pass through this State, and to
cause the said road to be made, regulated and completed, within the
limits, and according to the intent and meaning of the before recited
Act of Congress in relation thereto; *Provided, nevertheless,* That the
route laid down and reported by the commissioners to the President
of the United States, be so altered as to pass through Uniontown, in
the county of Fayette, and Washington, in the county of Washington,
if such alteration can, in the opinion of the President, be made, con-
sistently with the provisions of an act of Congress passed March 29th,
1806, but if not, then over any ground within the limit of this State,
which he may deem most advantageous.

SEC. 2. *And be it further enacted by the authority aforesaid,* That
such person or persons as are or shall be appointed for the pur-
(36)

pose of laying out and completing the said road, under the authority of the United States, shall have full power and authority to enter upon the lands through which the same may pass, and upon any land near or adjacent thereto, and therefrom to take, dig, cut and carry away such materials of earth, stone, gravel, timber and sand as may be necessary for the purpose of completing, and for ever keeping in repair, said road; *Provided*, That such materials shall be valued and appraised, in the same manner as materials taken for similar purposes, under the authority of this Commonwealth are by the laws thereof, directed to be valued and appraised, and a certificate of the amount thereof shall, by the person or persons appointed, or hereafter to be appointed under the authority of the United States for the purpose aforesaid, be delivered to each party entitled thereto, for any materials to be taken by virtue of this act, to entitle him, her or them to receive payment therefor from the United States.

SIMON SNYDER,
Speaker of the House of Representatives.
P. C. LANE,
Speaker of the Senate.

Approved, the ninth day of April, one thousand eight hundred and seven. THOMAS M'KEAN.

TENTH CONGRESS—FIRST SESSION.

Communicated to Congress February 19, 1808.

To the Senate and House of Representatives of the United States :

The States of Pennsylvania, Maryland and Virginia having, by their several acts consented that the road from Cumberland to the State of Ohio, authorized by the act of Congress of March 29, 1806, should pass through those States, and the report of the commissioners communicated to Congress with my message of January 31, 1807, having been duly considered, I have approved of the route therein proposed for the said road as far as Brownsville, with a single deviation since located, which carries it through Uniontown.

From thence the course to the Ohio, and the point within the legal limits at which it shall strike that river, is still to be decided.

In forming this decision, I shall pay material regard to the interests and wishes of the populous parts of the State of Ohio, and to a future and convenient connection with the road which is to lead from the *Indian* boundary near Cincinnati, by Vincennes, to the Mississippi, at St. Louis, under authority of the act of April 21, 1806. In this way we may accomplish a continuous and advantageous line of communication from the seat of the General Government to St. Louis, passing through several very interesting points, to the Western country.

I have thought it advisable, also, to secure from obliteration the trace of the road so far as it has been approved, which has been executed at such considerable expense, by opening one-half of its breadth through its whole length.

3

The report of the commissioners herewith transmitted will give particular information of their proceedings under the act of March 29, 1806, since the date of my message of January 31, 1807, and will enable Congress to adopt such further measures, relative thereto, as they may deem proper under existing circumstances.

TH. JEFFERSON.

FEBRUARY 19, 1808.

The undersigned, commissioners appointed under the law of the United States, entiled "An act to regulate the laying out and making a road from Cumberland, in the State of Maryland, to the State of Ohio," in addition to the communications heretofore made, beg leave further to report to the President of the United States that, by the delay of the answer of the Legislature of Pennsylvania to the application for permission to pass the road through that State, the commissioners could not proceed to the business of the road in the spring before vegetation had so far advanced as to render the work of exploring and surveying difficult and tedious; from which circumstance it was postponed till the last autumn, when the business was again resumed. That, in obedience to the special instructions given them, the route heretofore reported has been so changed as to pass through Uniontown, and that they have completed the location, gradation and marking of the route from Cumberland to Brownsville, Bridgeport, and the Monongahela river, agreeably to a plat of the courses, distances and grades in which is described the marks and monuments by which the route is designated, and which is herewith exhibited; that by this plat and measurement it will appear (when compared with the road now traveled) there is a saving of four miles of distance between Cumberland and Brownsville on the new route.

In the gradation of the surface of the route (which became necessary) is ascertained the comparative elevation and depression of different points on the route, and taking a point ten feet above the surface of low water in the Potomac river at Cumberland, as the horizon, the most prominent points are found to be elevated as follows, viz.:

	Feet.	10ths.
Summit of Wills mountain	581	3
Western foot of same	304	4
Summit of Savage mountain	2022	24
Savage river	1741	6
Summit Little Savage mountain	1900	4
Branch Pine Run, first Western water	1699	9
Summit of Red Hill (after called Shades of Death)	1914	3
Summit Little Meadow mountain	2026	16
Little Youghiogheny river	1322	6
East Fork of Shade Run	1558	92
Summit of Negro mountain, highest point	2328	12
Middle branch of White's creek, at the west foot of Negro mountain	1360	5
White's creek	1195	5
Big Youghiogheny river	645	5

	Feet.	10ths.
Summit of a ridge between Youghiogheny river and Beaver waters	1514	5
Beaver Run	1123	8
Summit of Laurel Hill	1550	16
Court House in Uniontown	274	65
A point ten feet above the surface of low water in the Monongahela river, at the mouth of Dunlap's creek	119	26

The law requiring the commissioners to report those parts of the route as are laid on the old road, as well as those on new grounds, and to state those parts which require the most immediate attention and amelioration, the probable expense of making the same passable in the most difficult parts, and through the whole distance, they have to state that, from the crooked and hilly course of the road now traveled, the new route could not be made to occupy any part of it (except an intersection on Wills mountain, another at Jesse Tomlinson's, and a third near Big Youghiogheny, embracing not a mile of distance in the whole) without unnecessary sacrifices of distances and expense.

That, therefore, an estimate must be made on the route as passing wholly through new grounds. In doing this the commissioners feel great difficulty, as they cannot, with any degree of precision, estimate the expense of making it merely passable; nor can they allow themselves to suppose that a less breadth than that mentioned in the law was to be taken into the calculation. The rugged deformity of the grounds rendered it impossible to lay a route within the grade limited by law otherwise than by ascending and descending the hills obliquely, by which circumstance a great proportion of the route occupies the sides of the hills, which cannot be safely passed on a road of common breadth, and where it will, in the opinion of the commissioners, be necessary, by digging, to give the proper form to thirty feet, at least in the breadth of the road, to afford suitable security in passing on a way to be frequently crowded with wagons moving in opposite directions, with transports of emigrant families, and droves of cattle, hogs, etc., on the way to market. Considering, therefore, that a road on those grounds must have sufficient breadth to afford ways and water courses, and satisfied that nothing short of well constructed and completely finished conduits can insure it against injuries, which must otherwise render it impassable at every change of the seasons, by heavy falls of rain or melting of the beds of snow, with which the country is frequently covered; the commissioners beg leave to say, that, in a former report, they estimated the expense of a road on these grounds, when properly shaped, made and finished in the style of a stone-covered turnpike, at $6,000 per mile, exclusive of bridges over the principal streams on the way; and that with all the information they have since been able to collect, they have no reason to make any alteration in that estimate.

The contracts authorized by, and which have been taken under the superintendence of the commissioner, Thomas Moore (duplicates of which accompany this report), will show what has been undertaken

relative to clearing the timber and brush from part of the breadth of
the road. The performance of these contracts was in such forwardness on the 1st instant as leaves no doubt of their being completely
fulfilled by the first of March.

The commissioners further state, that, to aid them in the extension of their route, they ran and marked a straight line from the
crossing place on the Monongahela, to Wheeling, and had progressed
twenty miles, with their usual and necessary lines of experiment, in
ascertaining the shortest and best connection of practical grounds,
when the approach of winter and the shortness of the days afforded
no expectation that they could complete the location without a needless expense in the most inclement season of the year. And, presum-
ing that the postponement of the remaining part till the ensuing
spring would produce no delay in the business of making the road,
they were induced to retire from it for the present.

The great length of time already employed in this business, makes
it proper for the commissioners to observe that, in order to connect
the best grounds with that circumspection which the importance of
the duties confided to them demanded, it became indispensably necessary to run lines of experiment and reference in various directions,
which exceed an average of four times the distance located for the
route, and that, through a country so irregularly broken, and crowded
with very thick underwood in many places, the work has been found
so incalculably tedious that, without an adequate idea of the difficulty,
it is not easy to reconcile the delay.

It is proper to mention that an imperious call from the private
concerns of Commissioner Joseph Kerr, compelled him to return home
on the 29th of November, which will account for the want of his sig-
nature to this report.

All of which is, with due deference, submitted, this 15th day of
January, 1808.   ELI WILLIAMS,
                                         THOMAS MOORE.

NOTE.—It will be observed that Keyser's Ridge, which is unques-
tionably the highest point on the road, is not mentioned by the commissioners. This is, no doubt, because, at the date of their report,
the locality did not bear the name Keyser's Ridge, and was known as
a peak of Negro mountain. Soon after the location of the road, one
Keyser acquired the property at the ridge, and it took its name from
him. It will also be observed that the measurement of heights by
the commissioners was made from "a point ten feet above the surface
of low water in the Potomac at Cumberland." A table of heights
given in a subsequent chapter, the authority for which is not ascertainable, differs from that in the commissioners' report, but their
report must be accepted as accurate from their point of measurement.
The other table referred to, gives the heights above the Atlantic and
above Cumberland, and embraces more hills than the commissioners'
report.

CHAPTER VI.

Albert Gallatin, Secretary of the Treasury, called upon for Information respecting the Fund Applicable to the Roads mentioned in the Ohio Admission Act — His Responses.

TENTH CONGRESS — FIRST SESSION.

Communicated to the House of Representatives March 8, 1808.

TREASURY DEPARTMENT, March 3, 1808.

Sir: In answer to your letter of the 1st instant, I have the honor to state:

1st. That the 5 per cent. reserved by the act of 30th April, 1802, on the net moneys received for public lands in the State of Ohio, sold since 1st July, 1802, has amounted to the following sums, viz:

From 1st July, 1802, to 30th June, 1803..........................$	6,220 00
From 1st July, 1803, to 30th June, 1804..........................	8,810 17
From 1st July, 1804, to 30th June, 1805..........................	13,994 30
From 1st July, 1805, to 30th June, 1806..........................	31,442 20
From 1st July, 1806, to 30th June, 1807..........................	28,827 92
From 1st July, 1807, to 31st December, 1807 (estimated)...........	15,000 00

$104,294 59

And that the said 5 per cent. will henceforth probably amount to $30,000 a year.

2d. That, of the $30,000 appropriated by act of 29th March, 1806, there has been expended, in laying out the Cumberland road from Cumberland to Brownsville, about....................$10,000
That there may be wanted to complete the location, about .. 5,000

$15,000

3d. That contracts have been made for opening one-half of the breadth of said road, which, as verbally informed by one of the commissioners, will require about $3,000, leaving, probably, about $12,000 of the appropriation for the further improvement of the road.

4th. That the portion of the road actually located and confirmed, no part of which exceeds an angle of five degrees, extends from the navigable waters of the Potomac, at Cumberland, to the navigable waters of the Monongahela, at Brownsville (Red Stone Old Fort), and it is stated, though no official report has been made to me, at about seventy miles.

5th. That that road can be considered as a national object only if completed as a turnpike, whereby all the flour and other produce of the western adjacent countries may be brought to a market on the Atlantic shores; and the transportation of all the salt and other commodities and merchandise whatever, imported from the Atlantic ports to the western country generally, may be reduced probably one dollar per cwt.

And, Lastly, that the expense of completing that part of the road in such manner, is estimated at $400,000.

I have the honor to be, respectfully, sir, your obedient servant,

ALBERT GALLATIN.

Hon. John Montgomery, of Maryland, Chairman, etc., in Congress.

COMMITTEE ROOM, Dec. 22, 1808.

Sir: The committee appointed on the message of the President, transmitting a report of the commissioners concerning a road from Cumberland to Ohio, have directed me to request that you would cause to be laid before them such information as may be in possession of the Treasury Department respecting the fund applicable by law to " the laying out and making public roads leading from the navigable waters emptying into the Atlantic, to the Ohio," etc. (1) The unexpended balance of the $30,000 appropriated by the act of the 29th of March, 1806; (2) The amount of moneys, exclusive of the above, now in the treasury, and in the hands of the receiver of public moneys, applicable to that object; and (3) an estimate of the probable amount of moneys that will accrue to the fund within the two succeeding years.

I have the honor to be, very respectfully, sir, your obedient servant, JEREMIAH MORROW.

To the Hon. Secretary of the Treasury.

TENTH CONGRESS — SECOND SESSION.

Cumberland Road.

Communicated to the House of Representatives, February 16, 1809.

TREASURY DEPARTMENT, Dec. 29, 1808.

Sir: In answer to your letter of the 22d instant, I have the honor to state, for the information of the committee:

1st. That the unexpended balance of the appropriation, made by the act of March 29, 1806, for opening a road from Cumberland, on the Potomac, to the river Ohio, amounts to $16,075.15; part of which sum will probably be wanted in order to complete the location and opening of the road. It is probable that about $13,000 will remain applicable to making the road.

2dly. That the total amount received, either at the treasury, or by the receivers of public moneys on account of roads, and calculated at the rate of 5 per cent. of the net proceeds of the sales of lands in the State of Ohio, subsequent to the 30th day of June, 1802, was, on

the 30th day of September last $104,692
leaving, if that mode of calculating be correct, and after deducting the sum appropriated by the above mentioned act..   30,000

a sum applicable to the road of ....$ 74,692
in addition to the above mentioned unexpended balance of..   16,075

and making together a sum of ....$ 90,767
But if the amount applicable to roads be calculated at the
rate of 2 per cent. only, on the net proceeds of the sales of
lands, this will, on the 30th of September last, have produced
only ....$ 41,876
from which, deducting the appropriation of..............   30,000

leaves an unappropriated balance of ....$ 11,876
which, added to the unexpended balance of the appropriation   16,075

makes an aggregate of only............................$ 27,951

3dly. That the probable receipts on account of that fund may, for
the two ensuing years, be estimated at $22,500 a year, if calculated at
the rate of 5 per cent., and at $9,000 a year, if calculated at the rate
of 2 per cent. on the sales of lands.

I have the honor to be, respectfully, sir, your obedient servant,

ALBERT GALLATIN.

Hon. Jeremiah Morrow, Chairman of the Land Committee.

P. S.—Amount of the 2 per cent. of the net proceeds of the lands
within the State of Ohio:

From 1st July, 1802, to 30th June, 1803, 2 per cent.................$ 2,400 00
From 1st July, 1803, to 30th June, 1804, 2 per cent................   3,524 06
From 1st July, 1804, to 30th June, 1805, 2 per cent.   5,597 72
From 1st July, 1805, to 30th June, 1806, 2 per cent................ 11,243 55
From 1st July, 1806, to 30th June, 1807, 2 per cent................   9,120 75
From 1st July, 1807, to 30th June, 1808, 2 per cent. 9,902 80
Estimated July, 1808, to 31st October, 1808, 2 per cent.............   2,815 60

Total $44,692 48

The sum of $30,000 appropriated per act of 29th of March to be
paid therefrom; of which $13,924.85 seems to have been paid.

A. G.

CHAPTER VII.

The Life of the Road Threatened by the Spectre of a Constitutional Cavil — President Monroe Vetoes a Bill for its Preservation and Repair — General Jackson has Misgivings — Hon. Andrew Stewart comes to the Rescue.

SPECIAL MESSAGE.

To the House of Representatives: MAY 4, 1822.

Having duly considered the bill, entitled "An act for the preservation and repair of the Cumberland Road," it is with deep regret (APPROVING, AS I DO, THE POLICY), that I am compelled to object to its passage, and to return the bill to the House of Representatives, in which it originated, under a conviction that Congress do not possess the power, under the Constitution, to pass such a law. A power to establish turnpikes, with gates and tolls, and to enforce the collection of the tolls by penalties, implies a power to adopt and execute a complete system of internal improvements. A right to impose duties to be paid by all persons passing a certain road, and on horses and carriages, as is done by this bill, involves the right to take the land from the proprietor on a valuation, and to pass laws for the protection of the road from injuries; and if it exist, as to one road, it exists as to any other, and to as many roads as Congress may think proper to establish. A right to legislate for one of these purposes, is a right to legislate for the others. It is a complete right of jurisdiction and sovereignty for all the purposes of internal improvement, and not merely the right of applying money under the power vested in Congress to make appropriations (under which power, with the consent of the States through which the road passes, the work was originally commenced, and has been so far executed). I am of opinion that Congress do not possess this power — that the States individually cannot grant it; for, although they may assent to the appropriation of money within their limits for such purposes, they can grant no power of jurisdiction of sovereignty, by special compacts with the United States. This power can be granted only by an amendment to the Constitution, and in the mode prescribed by it. If the power exist, it must be either because it has been specifically granted to the United States, or that it is incidental to some power, which has been specifically granted. If we examine the specific grants of power, we do not find it among them, nor is it incidental to any power which has been specifically granted. It has never been contended that the power was specifically granted. It is claimed only as being incidental

(44)

to some one or more of the powers which are specifically granted. The following are the powers from which it is said to be derived: (1) From the right to establish post offices and post roads; (2) From the right to declare war; (3) To regulate commerce; (4) To pay the debts and provide for the common defence and general welfare; (5) From the power to make all laws necessary and proper for carrying into execution all the powers vested by the Constitution in the government of the United States, or in any department or officer thereof; (6) And lastly, from the power to dispose of and make all needful rules and regulations respecting the territory and other property of the United States. According to my judgment, it cannot be derived from either of these powers, nor from all of them united, and in consequence it does not exist. Having stated my objections to the bill, I should now cheerfully communicate at large the reasons on which they are founded, if I had time to reduce them to such form as to include them in this paper. The advanced stage of the session renders that impossible. Having, at the commencement of my service in this high trust, considered it a duty to express the opinion that the United States do not possess the power in question, and to suggest for the consideration of Congress the propriety of recommending to the States an amendment to the Constitution, to vest the power in the United States, my attention has been often drawn to the subject since, in consequence whereof, I have occasionally committed my sentiments to paper respecting it. The form which this exposition has assumed is not such as I should have given it had it been intended for Congress, nor is it concluded. Nevertheless, as it contains my views on this subject, being one which I deem of very high importance, and which, in many of its bearings, has now become peculiarly urgent, I will communicate it to Congress, if in my power, in the course of the day, or certainly on Monday next.   JAMES MONROE.

General Jackson, in his famous veto of the Maysville Road bill (May 27, 1830), refers to the Cumberland Road, and to the above message of President Monroe, in the following terms:

"In the administration of Mr. Jefferson we have two examples of the exercise of the right of appropriation, which, in the consideration that led to their adoption, and in their effects upon the public mind, have had a greater agency in marking the character of the power than any subsequent events. I allude to the payment of fifteen millions of dollars for the purchase of Louisiana, and to the ORIGINAL APPROPRIATION FOR THE CONSTRUCTION OF THE CUMBERLAND ROAD; the latter act deriving much weight from the acquiescence and approbation of three of the most powerful of the original members of the confederacy, expressed through their respective legislatures. Although the circumstances of the LATTER CASE may be such as to deprive so much of it as relates to the actual construction of the road of the force of an obligatory exposition of the Constitution, it must nevertheless be admitted that so far as the mere appropriation of money is con-

3ᵃ

cerned, they present the principle in its most imposing aspect. No less than twenty-three different laws have been passed through all the forms of the Constitution, appropriating upwards of two millions and a half of dollars out of the national treasury in support of that improvement, with the approbation of every president of the United States, including my predecessor, since its commencement. The views of Mr. Monroe upon this subject were not left to inference. During his administration, a bill was passed through both houses of Congress, conferring the jurisdiction and prescribing the mode by which the federal government should exercise it in the case of THE CUMBERLAND ROAD. He returned it with objections to its passage, and in assigning them, took occasion to say that in the early stages of the government he had inclined to the construction that it had no right to expend money except in the performance of acts authorized by the other specific grants of power, according to a strict construction of them; but that on further reflection and observation his mind had undergone a change; that his opinion then was: 'that Congress had an unlimited power to raise money, and that in its appropriation they have a discretionary power, restricted only by the duty to appropriate it to purposes of common defence and of general, not local, National, not State benefit;' and this was avowed to be the governing principle through the residue of his administration."

On the 27th of January, 1829, the Hon. Andrew Stewart, of Pennsylvania, in a vigorous speech on the floor of Congress, repelled the proposition that the general government was lacking in power and authority to make and preserve the road, from which the following extracts are taken:

"Mr. Stewart expressed his regret that gentlemen had deemed this a fit occasion to draw into discussion all the topics connected with the general power over the subject of internal improvements. If repeated decisions, and the uniform practice of the government could settle any question, this, he thought, ought to be regarded as settled. The foundation of this road (the National or Cumberland) was laid by a report made by Mr. Giles, the present Governor of Virginia, in 1802, and was sanctioned the next session by a similar report, made by another distinguished Virginian (Mr. Randolph), now a member of this House—it was the offspring of Virginia, and he hoped she would not now abandon it as illegitimate. Commenced under the administration of Mr. Jefferson, it had been sanctioned and prosecuted by every president, and by almost every Congress, for more than a quarter of a century. *　*　*　*

"Without roads and canals, of what avail was it to the people of the West to possess a country, abounding with all the essential elements of wealth and prosperity—of what avail was it to have a country abounding with inexhaustible mines of coal and ore; to possess a fruitful soil and abundant harvests, without the means of transporting them to the places where they were required for consumption? Without a market, the people of the West were left without a motive

HON. ANDREW STEWART.

for industry. By denying to this portion of the Union the advantages of internal improvements, you not only deprive them of all the benefits of governmental expenditures, but you also deprive them of the advantages which nature's God intended for them. Possessing the power, how, he asked, could any representative of the interior or western portions of this Union vote against a policy so essential to the prosperity of the people who sent him here to guard their rights, and advance their interests? * * * *

"The right of this government to construct such roads and canals as were necessary to carry into effect its mail, military, and commercial powers, was as clear and undoubted as the right to build a post office, construct a fort, or erect a lighthouse. In every point of view the cases were precisely similar, and were sustained and justified by the same power." * * * *

The power, said Mr. S., "to establish post offices and post roads," involves the power and duty of transporting the mail, and of employing all the means necessary for this purpose. The simple question, then, was this: Are roads necessary to carry the mail? If they were, Congress had expressly the right to make them, and there was an end to the question. Roads were, he contended, not only necessary to carry into effect this power, but they were absolutely and indispensably necessary; you cannot get along without them, and yet we are gravely told that Congress have no right to make a mail road, or repair it when made! That to do so would ruin the States and produce consolidation — ruin the States by constructing good roads for their use and benefit; produce consolidation by connecting the distant parts of the Union by cheap and rapid modes of inter-communication. If consolidation meant to confirm and perpetuate the Union, he would admit its application, but not otherwise. But we are told that the *States* will make roads to carry the mails. This was begging the question. If the States would make all the roads required to carry into effect our powers, very well; but if they did not, then we may undoubtedly make them ourselves. But it was never designed by the framers of the Constitution that this government should be dependent on the States for the means of executing its powers: "its means were adequate to its ends." This principle was distinctly and unanimously laid down by the Supreme Court in the case already referred to: "No trace," says the Chief Justice, "is to be found in the Constitution of an intention to create a dependence of the government of the Union on the States for the execution of the powers assigned to it — its means are adequate to its ends. To impose on it the necessity of resorting to means it cannot control, which another government may furnish or withhold, would render its course precarious, the result of its measures uncertain, and create a dependence on other governments, which might disappoint the most important designs, and is incompatible with the language of the Constitution." And this was in perfect harmony with the constant and uniform practice of the government. * * *

Mr. S. begged gentlemen to turn their attention for a moment to the statute book, and see what the practice of the government had been; what had been already done by Congress in virtue of this power of "establishing post offices and post roads." In 1825 an act had been passed, without a word of objection, which went infinitely further than the bill under consideration. His colleague (Mr. Buchanan) was then a member of this House, and, no doubt, voted for it. His eloquence was then mute—we heard nothing about States rights, spectres, and sedition laws. This bill, regulating the post office establishment, not only created some thirty or forty highly penal offences, extending not only over the Cumberland Road, but over every other road in the United States, punishing with severest sanctions, even to the taking away the liberty and the lives of the citizens of the States, and requiring the State courts to take cognizance of these offences and inflict these punishments. This was not all: this act not only extended over all the mail roads, but all other roads running parallel with them, on which all persons are prohibited, under a penalty of fifty dollars, from carrying letters in stages or other vehicles performing regular trips; and authorizing, too, the seizure and sale of any property found in them for the payment of the fines. The same regulations applied to boats and vessels passing from one town to another. Compare that bill with the one under debate. This bill had two or three trifling penalties of ten dollars, and was confined to one road of about one hundred and fifty miles in extent, made by the United States, while the other act, with all its fines and forfeitures, pains and penalties, extended not only to all the mail roads in the United States, but also to all parallel roads; yet no complaint was then heard about the constitutionality of this law, or the dreadful consequences of carrying the citizens hundreds of miles to be tried. Under it no difficulties had ever been experienced, and no complaint had ever been heard. There had been no occasion for appointing United States Justices and creating federal courts to carry this law into effect, about which there was so much declamation on this occasion: this was truly choking at gnats and swallowing camels. To take away *life* by virtue of the post office power for robbing the mail, is nothing; but to impose a fine of ten dollars for wilfully destroying a road which has cost the government a million of dollars, is a dreadful violation of State rights! An unheard of usurpation, worse than the sedition law; and went further towards a dissolution of the Union than any other act of the government. Such were the declarations of his colleague; he hoped he would be able to give some reason for thus denouncing this bill, after voting for the act of 1825, which carried this same power a hundred times further than this bill, both as regards the theatre of its operations, and the extent of its punishments. * * * *

Having thus established, and, as he thought, conclusively, the right to construct roads and canals for mail and military purposes, he came next to say a few words on the subject of those which appertained to the express power of "regulating commerce with foreign nations and *among the several States.*" This power carried with it, as a necessary incident, the right to construct commercial roads and canals. From this grant Congress derived exactly the same power to make roads and canals that it did sea-walls, light-houses, buoys, beacons, etc., along the seaboard. If the power existed over the one it existed over the other in every point of view; the cases were precisely parallel; it was impossible to draw a distinction between them. This power was essential to every government—there was no government under the sun without it. All writers on national law and political economy considered the right to construct roads and canals as belonging to the commercial power of all governments.   *   *   *

There were great arteries of communication between distant divisions of this extensive empire, passing through many States or bordering upon them, which the States never could and never would make. These works were emphatically national, and ought to be accomplished by national means.

He instanced the road now under consideration—it passed through Maryland, Pennsylvania and Virginia, yet neither of these States would have given a dollar to make it. It passed mostly through mountainous and uninhabited regions. He adverted to the Potomac, Ohio, and Mississippi rivers. Important as these were to all the States, yet they were the internal concerns of none—they were mere boundaries to which the States would give nothing, while they had so many objects exclusively internal requiring all their means. For these reasons he was utterly opposed to the project of dividing the surplus revenue of the general government among the several States; this would be to surrender the national means which the people had confided to this purpose to mere local and sectional objects, while those truly national would remain forever unprovided for. He did not claim for this government the power to make roads and canals for all purposes. The powers of this government and of the States were distinct and well defined. To the national government belonged, under the Constitution, the power of making national roads and canals for national purposes. To the States belonged the power of providing for state and local objects. The roads and canals projected and executed by the States and private companies were often highly important in a national point of view; and to such, in his opinion, this government ought always to afford aid in a proportion corresponding with the interest the nation had in their accomplishment. When individuals were willing to go before and vest millions of their private funds in works strictly and truly national, connecting the remote sections of the Union together (of which we had two distinct examples, one in this district and the other in a neighboring city, Baltimore), could this government, charged with the care and guardianship of all the great interests of the nation, look on with cold indifference? Was it not our duty to lend a helping hand to encourage, to cheer, and to sustain them in their noble and patriotic efforts?   *   *   *   *

Mr. Stewart said he would now proceed to answer, as briefly as possible, some leading arguments urged by gentlemen in opposition to the bill under consideration. His colleague (Mr. Buchanan) had said that this bill proposed a greater stretch of power than the sedition law. This was an argument "ad captandum vulgus." He would not do his colleague the injustice to suppose that he was so ignorant of the Constitution of his country as seriously to address such an argument to the understanding of this House. The bill under consideration was necessary to carry into effect the express power of transporting the mail. What power of this government was the sedition law intended to carry into effect? None. It was therefore not only clearly unconstitutional on this ground, but it went directly to abridge the freedom of the press, and, of course, was a plain and palpable violation of that provision in the Constitution, which declares that "Congress shall make no law abridging the freedom of speech or of the press." Now, if his colleague could show any provision in the Constitution in the slightest degree impugning the right of Congress to pass this bill, then he might have some excuse for offering such an argument, otherwise he had none. The gentleman had, in a very labored effort, endeavored to prove that this government had no kind of jurisdiction or control whatever over this road. Yet his own amendment recognized the existence of the very power which he denies. By his amendment he proposes what? That this government shall cede the roads to the States, with the power to erect gates and collect as much toll as was necessary to keep it in repair. But his whole argument went to prove that Congress did not possess the very power which his amendment assumed and proposed to the States. The gentleman's amendment, and his speech therefore, were at open war with each other, and would perhaps both perish in the conflict. Certainly, both could not survive—one or the other must fall.

The gentleman, proceeding in his argument, had assumed premises which nobody would admit, and then, with an air of great triumph, he drew conclusions which even his own premises would not support. He takes for granted that this government, with all its mail, military, and commercial powers, has no more right to make a road to carry these powers into effect, through a State, than any individual possessing none of these powers would have. Thus, having assumed what was utterly inadmissible, he triumphantly inquires whether an individual, having obtained leave to make a road through another's land, could put up gates and exact toll? The gentleman says, surely not. But he said, surely yes, unless expressly prohibited by the contract. Suppose, by permission, I build a mill, said Mr. S., upon that gentleman's estate, and construct a bridge and turnpike road to get to it, have not I as much right to demand toll at the bridge as at the mill? Most undoubtedly; so that the gentleman's premises and his conclusions were alike fallacious and unsound. This position had been taken by both the gentlemen from Virginia (Mr. Barbour and Mr. Archer), to whom he would make the same reply.

A most extraordinary argument had been advanced against military roads: the public enemy may get possession of them in war!! Was it possible that an American statesman could, at this time of day, urge such an argument? It might be addressed to a set of timid savages, secure in the midst of the wilderness. The enemy get possession of our roads, and therefore not make them! Such cowardly arguments would deprive us of every possible means of defence. The enemy, it might be said with equal propriety, may get our ships, our forts, our cannon, our soldiers, and therefore we ought not to provide them. What would the brave freemen of this country say to the men who would deny them roads to travel on, lest the enemy might take them from us in war? They would reply, with Spartan magnanimity, "Let them come and take them." * * *

A great deal has been said on the subject of jurisdiction; that, if it existed at all, it must be exclusive; that it could not attach to soil, and much metaphysical refinement of this sort, which had little to do with the subject. On this point, the only sound and practical rule was, that this government had a right to assume such jurisdiction over their roads as was necessary for their preservation and repair by such means as should be deemed most expedient, leaving everything beyond that to the States. Thus far the Constitution declared the legislation of Congress to be "the supreme law of the land, anything in the constitution and laws of any State to the contrary nothwithstanding." This left to the laws of the States, the right to punish all offences and other acts committed upon the road, in the same manner as though they had occurred in any other part of their territory. Such had been the uniform practice of the government in executing all its powers up to the present time, and no complaint had ever been made or inconvenience experienced.

It has been universally conceded on all hands in this debate, that the consent of the States could not confer any jurisdiction or powers on this government beyond what it had derived from the Constitution. This was too clear a proposition to admit of doubt. Yet the names of Jefferson, Madison, Monroe, and Gallatin, were introduced and relied on. Did gentlemen forget that Mr. Gallatin was the very first man that ever suggested the plan for making the Cumberland road, and that it had been sanctioned and actually constructed under the administrations of Jefferson, Madison, and Monroe? Their opinions were thus reduced to practice, which was the best evidence in the world — "By their fruits shall ye know them."

CHAPTER VIII.

State Authority prevails — The Road surrendered by Congress — The erection of Toll Gates authorized — Commissioners appointed by the States to receive the Road — They wrangle over its bad condition, and demand that it be put in thorough repair by Congress, before the States will accept it — Old and familiar names of the Commissioners —The Road accepted by the States.

At the session of the year 1831, the Pennsylvania Legislature passed a bill, which was approved April 4th, of that year, by George Wolf, governor, the preamble to, and the first, and part of the second, and all of the tenth sections of which read as follows:

"Whereas, that part of the Cumberland Road lying within the State of Pennsylvania is in many parts in bad condition for want of repairs, and as doubts have been entertained whether the United States have authority to erect toll gates on said road, and collect toll; and as a large proportion of the people of this commonwealth are interested in said road, and its constant continuance and preservation; therefore,

SECTION 1. *Be it enacted by the Senate and House of Representatives of the commonwealth of Pennsylvania, in general assembly met, and it is hereby enacted by authority of the same;* That as soon as the consent of the government of the United States shall have been obtained, as hereinafter provided, WILLIAM F. COPLAN, DAVID DOWNER, of Fayette county, STEPHEN HILL, BENJAMIN ANDERSON, of Washington county, and THOMAS ENDSLEY, of Smithfield, Somerset county, shall be, and they are hereby appointed commissioners, a majority of whom shall be sufficient to transact business, who shall hold their offices for three years after the passage of this act, after which the right of appointing said commissioners shall vest in the governor of this commonwealth, to build toll houses, and erect toll gates at suitable distances on so much of the Cumberland Road as lies within the State of Pennsylvania; *Provided,* that if any one or more of the commissioners should die, resign, or refuse to serve, the Governor shall appoint one or more other commissioners to fill the vacancies so happening; *And provided, also,* that nothing herein contained shall be construed to prevent the Governor from re-appointing the commissioners named in this act, if he thinks proper.

SEC. 2. That for the purpose of keeping so much of the said road in repair as lies within the State of Pennsylvania, and paying the expense of collection and other incidental expenses, the commissioners

TOLL HOUSE.

shall cause to be erected on so much of the road as passes within this State at least six gates, and that as soon as said gates and toll-houses shall be erected, it shall be the duty of the toll collectors, and they are hereby required to demand and receive for passing the said gates, the tolls hereafter mentioned; and they may stop any person riding, leading or driving any horses, cattle, sulky, chair, phæton, cart, chaise, wagon, sleigh, sled or other carriage of burden or pleasure from passing through the said gates, until they shall respectively have paid for passing the same, that is to say: (Here follow the rates).

SEC. 10.   That this act shall not have any force or effect, until the Congress of the United States shall assent to the same, and until so much of the said road as passes through the State of Pennsylvania, be first put in a good state of repair, and an appropriation made by Congress for erecting toll-houses and toll-gates thereon, to be expended under the authority of the commissioners appointed by this act: *Provided*, The legislature of this State may at any future session thereof, change, alter or amend this act, provided that the same shall not be so altered or amended, as to reduce or increase the rates of toll hereby established, below or above a sum necessary to defray the expenses incident to the preservation and repair of said road, for the payment of the fees or salaries of the commissioners, the collectors of tolls, and other agents. *And provided further*, That no change, alteration, or amendment, shall ever be adopted, that will in any wise defeat or affect, the true intent and meaning of this act.

Ohio was a little in advance of Pennsylvania in accepting the road, and less exacting in her terms.   The legislature of that State, on the 4th of February, 1831, passed an act authorizing the acceptance, without requiring that the road should be put in repair as a condition precedent.   On the 23d of January, 1832, Maryland, by an act of her legislature, agreed to accept the road upon the same condition required by Pennsylvania, and on the 7th of February, 1832, Virginia accepted in an act similar to that of Ohio.   On the 3d of July, 1832, Congress declared its assent to the above mentioned laws of Pennsylvania and Maryland in these words: "To which acts the assent of the United States is hereby given, to remain in force during the pleasure of Congress," and on the 2d of March, 1833, assented to the act of Virginia with a similar limitation.

JANUARY 19, 1835.

REFERRED TO THE COMMITTEE OF THE WHOLE HOUSE, TO WHICH IS COMMITTED BILL No. 221.

To the Senate and House of Representatives of the United States in Congress assembled:

The undersigned beg leave to represent that they have been appointed commissioners, under the act of the Legislature of Pennsylvania, to accept from the general government so much of the Cumberland Road as lies within the limits of that State, and erect toll gates as soon as it is put in such a state of repair as is required by the provisions of that act. That they have every disposition to relieve the government from the burden of the road, so soon as they can feel themselves justified, under the law, in doing so; but they beg leave to respectfully represent that the road has not yet been put in that condition that would enable them to accept of it.

On some parts no more than six inches, and west of the Monongahela river, three inches only of metal have been put upon it, and it is apparent that this will be totally insufficient to preserve it under the heavy travel upon that road. Besides, the bridges throughout the whole road remain untouched. Under these circumstances, it is impossible for us, in the discharge of our duty, to accept of it; and we would most earnestly but respectfully urge upon Congress the propriety of making such an appropriation as will complete the repairs in a substantial manner, as required by the act of our own legislature. We will not undertake to prescribe the amount which may be necessary; but, to satisfy your honorable bodies that we are disposed to go as far as the faithful discharge of our duty will permit, we hereby pledge ourselves, so soon as Congress shall make an appropriation of so much money as may be estimated by the department as necessary for that purpose, to accept of the road, and have toll gates erected without delay. We, therefore, beg leave most respectfully to submit to the wisdom of your honorable bodies to determine whether it will be better to make the necessary appropriation to justify us in accepting the road, and relieving the government from all future charge, or to keep it in its present state, subject to annual appropriations for its preservation, as heretofore.

THO. ENDSLEY.
STEPHEN HILL.
DAVID DOWNER.
WILLIAM F. COPLAN.
January 7, 1835. BENJAMIN ANDERSON.

To the Honorable the Senate and House of Representatives of the United States in Congress assembled:

The undersigned beg leave to represent that they have been appointed commissioners, under the act of Assembly of the State of Maryland, to report to the Governor and Council of said State when that part of the Cumberland Road which lies within the limits of said State shall have been put in that state of repair contemplated by the act of Congress, and the act of Assembly of the State of Maryland, agreeing to receive the road and to keep it in repair; that they will with great pleasure report the road to the Governor and Council the moment they can with propriety do so. And they beg leave to represent that they feel authorized to say that the Governor and Council will, with great pleasure, authorize them to receive the road whenever it shall be put in that condition which would justify the State in accepting it. They further represent that the road has not yet been put in that condition that would justify them in advising the State to receive it. On some parts of the road no more than three and a half inches of metal has been put, and it is evident that this covering will be totally insufficient to preserve it in a fit state for use under the heavy travel which is constantly passing over it. The bridges also, throughout the whole distance, remain in a ruinous and dilapidated condition. They further respectfully represent that the new location from Cumberland, through the narrows of Wills creek and along Braddock's run, a distance of upwards of six miles, has had but three and a half inches of metal upon it; and the bridge over Wills creek and the bridges over Braddock's run were to be permanent stone structures, by the act of Assembly of Maryland, authorizing the President to change the location of the road. The undersigned are also advised that it is contemplated by the superintendent to put up wooden structures for bridges, in lieu of the stone bridges required by the act of Assembly of Maryland, authorizing the change in the location of the road, which would be in direct violation of that act. They further represent that the floors of wooden bridges must be removed every two or three years, and the whole structure of the bridges themselves must be built every twenty or twenty-five years.

Under these circumstances it would be impossible for the undersigned, in the discharge of their duty, to recommend to the State the acceptance of the road. And they would most earnestly but respectfully urge upon Congress the propriety of making such an appropriation as will be sufficient to complete the repairs on the old road, and to finish the new location in a substantial manner, as contemplated and required by the act of the Legislature of Maryland. The undersigned will not undertake to prescribe the sum which may be necessary for this purpose; but, to satisfy your honorable bodies that they are disposed to go as far as the faithful discharge of their duty will permit, they hereby pledge themselves that so soon as Congress shall make an appropriation of so much money as may be estimated by the department as necessary for the completion of the repairs of the old road, and the finishing of the road on the new location, together with the construction of permanent stone bridges, they will forthwith report to the Governor and Council the state of the road, and recommend that the State receive such part of the road as may be completed, and to collect tolls on it to keep it in repair, thereby relieving the United States from any further expense for repairs on such part. They further beg leave most respectfully to submit to the wisdom of your honorable bodies to determine whether it will be better to make the necessary appropriation to enable them to recommend the road as in a fit condition to be received by the State, and thus relieve the government from any further burden, or to let it remain in its present state, subject to appropriations for its preservation, as heretofore.

JOHN HOYE,
MESHECK FROST,
Commissioners of the State of Maryland.

On April 1, 1835, Pennsylvania accepted the road in the following brief terms, embodied in the third section of an act of her legislature of that date : " The surrender by the United States of so much of the Cumberland Road as lies within the State of Pennsylvania is hereby accepted by this State, and the commissioners to be appointed under this act are authorized to erect toll gates on the whole or any part of said road, at such time as they may deem it expedient to do so."

Maryland, Virginia, and Ohio also accepted the road, and thenceforth it was, and remains under the control of the several States through which it passes.

CHAPTER IX.

ENGINEER DEPARTMENT,
WASHINGTON, July 23, 1832.

Lt. J. K. F. Mansfield, Corps of Engineers:

SIR: By direction of the Secretary of War, you have been assigned, temporarily, to the superintendence of the repairs of the Cumberland Road east of the Ohio river; and in the discharge of your duties in this capacity, you will be governed by the following instructions:

1st. Respecting the parts to be repaired. The extreme limits within which your operations will be confined are, the point of intersection of the road with the western boundary line of the State of Pennsylvania, and Cumberland, in the State of Maryland; the dividing line between these States will be considered as dividing the line of the road to be repaired into two divisions, and the division within the State of Pennsylvania will be subdivided into six equal sections, and that within the State of Maryland, into two; then, having made a thorough examination of each of these sections, with a view to make yourself acquainted with their exact condition, you will classify them in the order of their condition, placing the worst first, the next worst second, and so on, making the best the last. You will then make an estimate for the repairs of each of these sections, to ascertain how far the appropriation, which is one hundred and fifty thousand dollars, will go toward repairing the whole road. Separate contracts will then be made for executing the repairs, commencing with No. 1, and passing regularly through the sections, as classified, to the best section; and these repairs will be prosecuted with as much despatch as the nature of the case will allow. Should you deem it advisable, in letting out these sections, to retain any portion of them which may seem to require but slight repairs, and which repairs could be executed with greater economy by having overseers and laborers to act under your immediate direction, you are at liberty to do so, bearing in mind, however, that whenever the repairs of the road can be made

·with equal economy, it is the wish of the department that they should be made by contract. As soon as one or more of these sections are finished, you will notify the commissioners appointed to receive this road by the laws of Pennsylvania and Maryland, approved, that of the former on the 4th day of April, 1831, and that of the latter on the 4th day of January, 1832, that these sections are ready to be turned over to the State, and you will accordingly turn them over.

2d. Respecting the mode of repairs. In order to insure efficient and permanent repairs, they are to be made on that which is called the Macadam system; that is to say, the pavement of the old road must be entirely broken up, and the stones removed from the road; the bed of which must then be raked smooth, and made nearly flat, having a rise of not more than three inches from the side to the center, in a road thirty feet wide; the ditches on each side of the road, and the drains leading from them, are to be so constructed that the water cannot stand at a higher level than that which is eighteen inches below the lowest part of the surface of the road; and, in all cases, when it is practicable, the drains should be adjusted in such a manner as to lead the water entirely from the side ditches. The culverts are to be cleared out, and so adjusted as to allow the free passage of all water that may tend to cross the road.

Having thus formed the bed of the road, cleaned out the ditches and culverts, and adjusted the side drains, the stone, reduced to a size not exceeding four ounces in weight, must be spread on with shovels, and raked smooth. The old material should be used only when it is of sufficient hardness, and no clay or sand must be mixed with the stone.

In replacing the covering of stone, it will be found best to lay it on in strata of about three inches thick, admitting the travel for a short interval on each layer, and interposing such obstructions from time to time as will insure an equal travel over every portion of the road; taking care to keep persons in constant attendance to rake the surface when it becomes uneven by the action of the wheels of carriages. In those parts of the road, if any, where materials of good quality cannot be obtained from the road in sufficient quantity to afford a course of six inches, new stone must be procured to make up the deficiency to that thickness; but it is unnecessary, in any part, to put on a covering of more than nine inches. None but limestone, flint or granite, should be used for the covering, if practicable; and no covering should be placed upon the bed of the road till it has become well compacted and thoroughly dried. At proper intervals, on the slopes of hills, drains or paved catch-waters must be made across the road, when the cost of constructing culverts would render their use inexpedient. These catch-waters must be made with a gradual curvature, so as to give no jolts to the wheels of carriages passing over them; but whenever the expense will justify the introduction of culverts, they will be used in preference; and in all cases where the water crosses the road, either in catch-waters or under culverts, sufficient pavements and overfalls must be constructed to provide against the possibility of the road or banks being washed away by it.

The masonry of the bridges, culverts, and side walls, must be repaired, when it may be required, in a substantial manner, and care must be taken that the mortar used be of good quality, without admixture of raw clay. All the masonry to be well pointed with hydraulic mortar, and in no case must the pointing be put on after the middle of October; all masonry finished after this time will be well covered, and pointed early in the following spring. Care must be taken, also, to provide means for carrying off the water from the bases of walls, to prevent the action of frost on their foundations; and it is highly important that all foundations in masonry should be well pointed with hydraulic mortar to a depth of eighteen inches below the surface of the ground.

As the laws on the subject of this road do not seem to justify a deviation from the original location, you will be careful to confine your operations to the road as you find it located; but, as it is believed that its axis may be dropped without adding much to the expense in those places where its inclination with the horizon exceeds four degrees, you are authorized, under the exercise of a sound discretion, to make this change.

In making your contracts, it must be understood that you are to have the general supervision of their execution, and that it will be your duty to see that all labor and materials (provided for by them) be applied in the most faithful and substantial manner. These contracts must provide in their specifications for all the work that can be anticipated, and should it happen that additional stipulations are afterwards found to be necessary for either workmanship or supplies not originally provided for, the facts must be reported to this department, and, with its approbation, if obtained, new contracts will be made for the additional services and supplies required; and it must be distinctly understood by the contractors that no payment will be made for work not provided for by their contracts.

Mr. L. W. Stockton, of Uniontown, has been engaged on this road and is intimately acquainted with every part of it, as well as with the adjacent country; and, as he has offered his services, you would do well to call upon him and avail yourself of them in any capacity that may seem to you best.

As soon as it can be done, a drawing of the whole road, with details of construction, will be forwarded, to be filed in this office.

You will take up your headquarters at any point on the road where your services may appear to you to be most needed; and, as soon as you shall have completed such an examination of the road as will place you in possession of the information necessary to draw up the specifications to your contracts, you will invite proposals for those contracts through the public prints. These contracts will be closed with as little delay as the interest of the road will allow, when the work will be commenced, and the contracts, together with the proper estimates, forwarded to this office. For the mode of making these estimates, keeping your accounts, and conducting your correspondence with this office, you are referred to the regulations of the Engineer Department.

Captain Delafield has been assigned to the permanent superintendence of the repairs of this road, and has been directed to join you on or before the 1st of October next. You will, therefore, immediately on his arrival, turn over to him these instructions, together with all the papers and public property that may be in your possession relating to the road. As soon as you shall have completed the necessary examinations on the road, you will commence and continue the repairs simultaneously in both States.

You will make application for such instruments and funds as may appear necessary to enable you to execute the foregoing instructions.   I am, &c.,

C. GRATIOT,
Brigadier General.

CUMBERLAND, MD., August 1, 1832.

Sir: I have this evening returned from a general reconnoissance of the road in this State. I find the road in a shocking condition, and every rod of it will require great repair; some of it is now almost impassable. I purpose leaving here to-morrow, on a particular measurement and survey of the road as it is, and the requisites to put it in complete repair.

The object of this communication is to request to be permitted to deviate, according to circumstances, from so much of my instructions as requires the old bed in all cases to be lifted, and the rise in the middle three inches; for there are parts of the road where the top of the old bed is full low, and where it will be more expensive, and less firm, to remove the old bed and fill in with earth, than to bring stone and Macadamize on the top of the old bed to the thickness of nine inches; and there are cases on the sides of the mountains where a greater rise than three inches, such, for instance, as some parts of it now have, which is more advantageous than a less one to confine the water to the gutters in cases of torrents, and thereby preventing a general sweep over the whole road, which would carry off the smallest stuff of a Macadamized road.

The repairs made by Mr. Giesey, about two years since, have the radical fault resulting from having lifted the old road indiscriminately, and not giving sufficient rise to the center for a mountainous country.

I have the honor to be, sir,

Very respectfully, your most obedient,
J. K. F. MANSFIELD,
Lieut. of Engineers.

Gen. Chas. Gratiot, Chief Engineer.

ENGINEER DEPARTMENT,

WASHINGTON, August 9, 1832.

Sir: Your letter of the 1st instant, requesting permission to deviate, according to circumstances, from so much of the instructions of the department to you, on the subject of the repairs of the Cumberland Road, as requires the old road in all cases to be lifted, and the rise in the middle to be made three inches, has been under consideration, and I have to inform you that this permission cannot be granted.

In withholding the sanction of the department to any deviation from the prominent features of your instructions on the subject of these repairs, it may, perhaps, be proper to state, for your information, the views of the department on this subject.

By referring to the report of Mr. Weaver, a printed copy of which you have in your possession, who made an examination of the Cumberland Road in 1827, you will perceive that the mode of constructing it was that of digging a trench, or of sinking the bed of the road below the natural surface of the ground; that this trench was filled with large stones, and that these were covered with stones a size smaller, and so on. By this construction, it was intended that the weight of the carriages passing over the road should be supported by the large stones, and that the smaller stones were only intended to present an even surface for the easy passage of vehicles over it. The great objections to this construction are, that the bed being lower than the surface of the ground on each side, the ditches can hardly ever be sunk sufficiently deep to intercept the passage of water from the ground adjacent to the road to the ditch or trench in which the road is made; this water, by keeping the bed constantly wet, would cause the heavy stones of the first layer to sink into the ground, and thus break up the surface of the road, and allow the free passage of water through the covering itself. In the winter, the frost acting upon the bed, rendered wet by the free passage of water to it in every direction, would heave the stones to such a degree that the road in a little time would be perfectly impassable; and if any evidence, in addition to that presented by the testimony of the most experienced and approved road builders, were necessary to convince the department that the present dilapidated state of the road under your charge is owing entirely to the operation of the causes above alluded to, it is believed that that evidence is found in the report made by Capt. Delafield, who inspected the repairs of this road made by Mr. Giesey. By pursuing the course suggested in your letter, it is believed that these objections and difficulties would still obtain, and that in a little time, however faithfully the repairs might be made on the top of the large stones, the road would be in as bad order as it is at present, since the great cause of these evils would remain, viz.: that of having the bed which supports the stones, and which in fact should

4

be the real support of the traffic on the road, lower than the neighboring ground.

It is the intention of the department that the defects of the first construction of the road shall be remedied in its repair, and as it is believed that the adoption, as nearly as practicable, of the Macadam system, in all its important features, presents the only means of effecting this remedy, and as this system forms the basis of your instructions, it is recommended that they be departed from as little as possible.

It is by no means the intention of the department to take from you all discretion in the discharge of your duties; such a course would defeat the object had in view in sending an officer of engineers on the road; but it is believed to be highly important that the exercise of this discretion should be limited to an extent that will insure the adoption of such principles and rules as cannot fail to render these repairs permanent. For these principles and rules, you are referred to Mr. Macadam's work on the construction and repairs of roads, a copy of which is in your possession. In removing the metal from the old road, whenever hollows present themselves in the old bed, it is recommended that they be filled with earth; indeed, the whole bed of the road should be elevated, and its form given to it, before any of the covering of stone be replaced. The earth necessary for this may be taken from the ditches, or even from the sides of the road, where it can be done without encroaching upon the privileges of persons residing on the road.   I am, &c., &c.,

                                        C. GRATIOT.
Lt. J. K. F. Mansfield,
       Corps of Engineers, Uniontown, Pa.

EXTRACTS FROM NOTICES FOR CONTRACTS.

PLAN OF REPAIRS.

The plan for repair is to lift the pavement of the old road in all cases, and deposit the stone off the bed; then to repair the culverts, clear the drains, ditches, and culverts, so as to admit the free passage of water, and graduate the bed of the road, so that, when well packed by travel or other means, it will be three inches higher in the middle than at either side, for a bed of thirty feet. Having thus formed the bed of the road, the hard stone (if there be any) of the old road, broken to a size not exceeding four ounces, is to be placed on the bed of the road to a breadth of twenty feet, and a thickness not exceeding nine inches, and in cases where there is a deficiency of the old material, limestone or whinstone is to be procured to supply the deficiency to the required thickness of nine inches. Catch-waters and hollow-ways to be permanently constructed on the sides of hills, and at other places where it will be thought necessary by the superintending engineer, but in no case to exceed one in every twelve rods.

In those sections where pieces of hitherto Macadamized road are included, the sand is to be taken off, and, before new metal is added, the surface loosened with a pick.   The metal added to be three inches thick in the cases heretofore Macadamized.

JOS. K. F. MANSFIELD,
Lieutenant Corps of Engineers.

ENGINEER DEPARTMENT,

WASHINGTON, August 27, 1832.

Sir: I have to acknowledge the receipt of your letter of the 24th inst., inclosing two printed advertisements for proposals to contract for the repairs of the Cumberland Road under your charge.

In answer, the department would call your attention to your remarks under the head " Plan of Repairs," and would suggest that, instead of removing the stones from the bed of the road before the drains, ditches, and culverts are put in repair, to allow the free passage of water from the road, this latter operation should be first attended to, to the end that the removal of the stone from the road might be effected without the fear of being annoyed by the accumulation of water from heavy rains.   Besides, thus preparing the drains, ditches, &c., in the first place, would enable the bed to become perfectly dry by the time the stones are prepared to be replaced.

I am, &c.,
C. GRATIOT.

Lt. J. K. F. Mansfield,
Corps of Engineers, Uniontown, Pa.

CHAPTER X.

Lieut. Mansfield superseded by Capt. Delafield—The Turning of Wills Mountain— Contractors not Properly Instructed—Capt. Delafield suggests a Change of Plan, and enforces his Views by Copious Quotations from Macadam—He is Permitted to exercise his own Discretion—Too much sand between Uniontown and Cumberland — Operations at Wills Creek suspended —A Collision with the Chesapeake and Ohio Canal Company—The difficulty adjusted, and operations resumed.

ENGINEER DEPARTMENT,

WASHINGTON, October 5, 1832.

Sir: On the arrival of Captain Delafield, of the engineers, on the Cumberland Road in Pennsylvania and Maryland, you will hand to him the enclosed communication, which assigns to him the superintendence of the repairs of that road which have heretofore been conducted under your supervision. You will, also, turn over to him all the funds, books, papers, and public property in your possession appertaining to this road, and close your account with it.

Very respectfully, &c.,

By order: WM. H. C. BARTLETT,

Lieut. and Assistant to Chief Engineer.

Lieut. J. K. F. Mansfield,
     Corps of Engineers, Uniontown, Pa.

———

UNIONTOWN, December 13, 1832.

Sir: The surveys of a route for turning Wills mountain by the valley of Braddock's run and Wills creek are progressing, being retarded only by the weather. I have examined the whole route, and can confirm the most satisfactory account you may have heard of it. The ground over which the road will pass is a uniform inclined plane, requiring very few culverts, two small bridges over Braddock's run of about fifteen feet span each, with side hill in no other part than about 300 yards in the "Narrows" of Wills creek, where a most simple and expedient plan will be to use the level and smooth bottom of the creek for the road, by building a wall not to exceed ten feet in height, thus throwing the stream on the opposite bank, peculiarly well formed for this construction, being a low bottom of alluvion. The idea of cutting into the mountain would be expensive, and no better than throwing the creek from its present bed.

On the arrival of Mr. Pettit, I shall divide the road into four sections, giving him one. The present condition of the road is most unpromising. Nearly every contractor has formed his bed in the valley made by the removal of the old pavement, the consequence of which is, that, with the mild season and rainy weather, the bed is not drained, nor can it be, until the side roads are cut down to the bottom of the stone strata—a measure I directed as the only means of correcting the evil. Time, and the headstrong obstinacy of some of the contractors, have prevented much of the work being so attended to. All the contracts made by Lieut. Mansfield distinctly specify that the road for 30 feet in width shall be graded in such manner as to avoid this difficulty; yet in carrying the contracts into effect, the superintendents have, in no instance, instructed the contractors in the proper course. They have, in most instances too, permitted the stone to be broken on the road; the consequences of this are, much sand and dirt in the metal, and a bed graded without proper attention. This is the more remarkable, as in my report on the work executed two years since by one of the present superintendents, these errors were pointed out as serious evils, yet they are not corrected. It must be expected, therefore, that all that part of the road now under construction will be very indifferently made, and by no means such as the Macadam system calls for. By the time the superintendents acquire a knowledge of their business, the present contracts will be completed. Instead of giving out any more of the work under the present system, as I had contemplated and advertised, I shall postpone doing so until I am better assured that the work can be properly executed. I look anxiously for Mr. Pettit, trusting his intelligence may correct some of the defects in the section he will be called upon to superintend.

To instruct the superintendents in their duties, I shall be compelled to have printed a manual or primer, with a few lithographic sections, that the sight may aid the mind in a proper understanding of the business. To persevere in the present plan, where neither contractors, superintendents, nor laborers, understand their business, is highly inexpedient, and I shall forthwith commence maturing a system that must be productive of more good with less money, or it were better to leave the work undone, for I am satisfied that durability can not be looked for under the present system.

My first business will be to draw the operations to a close, and then endeavor to bring about the correction. You will be apprised of my views before carrying any of them into effect, observing that, in anticipation of a change, I have suspended making the contracts alluded to in my communication of the 27th ultimo.

Respectfully, your obedient servant,
RICH'D DELAFIELD,
Captain of Engineers.

Brig. Gen. Charles Gratiot,
Chief Engineer.

BALTIMORE, May 6, 1833.

Sir: The instructions of the department of the 23d July last, relating to the method of repairing the Cumberland Road east of the Ohio, are founded upon principles upon which I differ in opinion, and beg leave to request your reconsideration, involving, as they do, an expenditure of not less than $250,000, when compared with what I judge to be the most judicious method of making the repairs.

It is in relation to the propriety of breaking up the old bed of the road in all cases. I apprehend the department was not aware that the bed is a substantial, yet rough pavement, and not formed of loose, detached masses of quarry stone thrown together, without order. It is important to consider this particular when examining the authorities on road making.

My own views are that it is decidedly preferable to retain the old pavement in all cases where its continuity is unbroken, even mending small parts that may be deranged, and Macadamizing over it. In this, I think, I am borne out by Macadam, Dean, Telford, and Farey, whose ideas on the subject are annexed, as extracted from "Macadam on Roads."

The only two arguments against the method I propose are, first, that the metal will grind to dust by being placed over large stone. In answer to which, I say, that the road passing through a rocky country, even after removing the pavement, there still remains a rocky foundation; and where the pavement is well bedded in sand or clay, we have all the elasticity necessary from the clay or sand bed through the pavement. In support of which, see the sample of metal taken from the road through Uniontown, where the under strata have not worn or crushed an iota, presenting angles as sharp as the day they were first placed there. Were the metal placed upon an unyielding rock, it would doubtless soon grind to dust; but placing it upon a pavement laid in sand or gravel, preserves the elasticity so necessary for this kind of road. Second: That large stone, placed under Macadam metal, will work to the surface. This is doubtless true when detached pieces are surrounded by the metal, but with a pavement the case is very different. I find pieces of this Cumberland Road, repaired as far back as 1827, by Mr. Ewing, over the old pavement, in perfect order to this day; as, also, some parts done in this way by Giesey in 1829, that are much better than any of the repairs he made at the same time; and a piece through Uniontown, by the authorities of the place, in 1830, remains in perfect order.

I have been led to reflect upon this subject from learning that the Ohio road had cut through and was impassable at certain places during the months of February and March, and seeing the state of the road under my supervision between Cumberland and Wheeling, comparing the parts repaired last season, those under Giesey, Ewing, and the town authorities, with the old pavement that has stood sixteen years without a cent of money in repair, and to this day is a very good wagon road, rough, it is true, yet never cutting through during the fall, winter, or spring, where the pavement is continuous. To throw away so firm a foundation I cannot think advisable, and beg you to reflect upon the subject and favor me with your views. The road in Ohio has worn six years (nearly) without repairs, and was impassable this spring. The old Cumberland Road has worn sixteen years, and mile after mile has never been known to cut through at any season. Parts of it covered with Macadamized metal, and worn for five years, are in fine order, and present a very smooth surface, never having cut through. Other parts, where the old pavement has been removed and Macadamized, were impassable during the spring after three years' wear. We have to bear in mind the impossibility of keeping the ditches and drains open in the mountains during the winter. Ice forming in the drains will, of course, throw the melting snows on the surface of the road, which is destructive to a Macadamized road on clay or sand, whereas, if on the old pavement, it has strength enough to resist the travel until either dried by frost, or sun. This is a consideration that the English road-makers had not to consider with the same weight. As to keeping the drains open, and the road surface free from water in the winter, I conceive it impracticable in the mountains; hence the further propriety of preserving a foundation that will secure a firm road at all seasons, even if the wear should prove some five or ten per cent. more rapid, which I do not even think will be the case on the plan suggested of Macadamizing upon a pavement, and not on an unyielding, rocky bottom.   Respectfully, your obedient servant,

RICHARD DELAFIELD,

Brig. Gen. C. Gratiot,   Captain of Engineers.
      Chief Engineer.

EXTRACTS FROM "MACADAM ON ROADS," MADE BY CAPTAIN DELAFIELD IN SUPPORT OF HIS VIEWS RELATING TO THE PAVEMENT FORMING THE BED OF THE "CUMBERLAND ROAD EAST OF THE OHIO."

Page 39. — "It would be highly unprofitable to lift and relay a road, even if the materials should have been originally too large. The road between Cirencester and Bath is made of stone too large in size. In this case I recommend cutting down the high places," &c.

Page 40. — "A part of the road in the Bath district is made of freestone, which it would be unprofitable to lift. Other cases of several kinds have occurred where a different method must be adopted, but which it is impossible to specify, and must be met by the practical skill of the officer, and who must constantly recur to general principles."

Page 42. — "The price of lifting a road, &c., leaving the road in a finished state, has been found in practice to be from 1d. to 2d. per superficial yard, lifted four inches deep."

Page 47.—"It is well known to every skillful and observant road-maker, that if strata of stone of various sizes be placed on a road, the largest stones will constantly work up." (This is in no manner applicable to a pavement, and a road made even in the manner he alludes to was lifted only four inches deep.—R. D.)

Page 105.—"How deep do you go in lifting the roads? That depends upon circumstances, but I have generally gone four inches deep. I take up the materials four inches, and, having broken the large pieces, I put them back again."

"Does the plan which you have mentioned, of breaking up the roads, apply to gravel roads, or only to those roads composed of hard stones? In gravel roads, and in some other roads, it would be impossible to break them up to advantage; and, in several places, I should think it unprofitable to lift a road at all. I did not order the road near Reading to be lifted, but I directed, whenever a large piece of flint was seen, it should be taken up, broken, and put down again. I am speaking of a gravel road now."

Page 107.—" There are other cases besides that of gravel, in which I should think it unprofitable to lift a road. The road between ———— and ———— is made of very soft stone, and is of so brittle a nature, that if it were lifted it would rise in sand, and there would be nothing to lay down again that would be useful. I should not recommend lifting of freestone roads, for the same reason, because it would go so much to sand that there would be very little to lay down again. I will explain what I have done to the road between Cirencester and Bath. I was obliged to lift a little of the sides of the road, in order to give it shape, but in the center of the road we 'shoved it.' It was before in the state which the country people call gridirons: that is, it was in large ridges, with long hollows between, and we cut down the high part to a level with the bottom of the furrows, and took the materials and sifted them at the side of the road, and returned what was useful to the center."

(So far we have the views of Mr. Macadam. From the same work I continue to quote.—R. D.)

Page 153.—"Considering the very great traffic upon White-chapel road, is it your opinion (addressed to Mr. Farey) that it would be advantageous to pave any part of that road? I think it would be desirable to pave it within some feet of the footpath," &c.

Page 158.—"In the neighborhood of London the materials that are to be procured are of too tender and brittle a nature to endure the wear of the heavy carriages. I, therefore, am of the opinion that it would be proper to pave the sides of all the principal entrances into London."

Page 166.—"James Walker says, 'The traffic upon the Commercial rail road, both up and down, is very great. I am quite sure that the expense of this road would have been very much greater, probably much more than doubled, if it had not been paved. The road has been paved for about sixteen years, and the expense of supporting it has been small. During the thirteen years that the East India dock branch has been paved, the paving has not cost £20.' "

Page 167. — " But as the paving is always preferred for heavy carriages," &c.

Page 172. — " The thickness ought to be such, that the greatest weight will not effect more than the surface of the shell, in order to spread the weight which comes upon a small part only of the road over a large portion of the foundation."

Page 173. — " If the foundation is bad, breaking the bottom stone into small pieces is expensive and injurious, upon the principle I have above described, for the same reason that an arch formed of whole bricks, or deep stones, is preferred to one of the same materials broken into smaller pieces, for, in some countries, the materials will admit of the foundation of the road being considered as of the nature of a flat arch, as well as being supported by the strata directly under it. But the error of laying stones in large pieces upon the surface is more common and more injurious."

Page 183. — " James Dean says, ' Near to great towns it would be highly advantageous if the center of the road, for about twelve feet in width, were to be paved with hard, well-squared stones, nine inches deep.' "

Page 188. — " Thomas Telford, Esq., says, ' The improvements made in North Wales I beg leave to submit as models for the roads through hilly countries. Great pains have been taken in constructing firm and substantial foundations for the metallic part of the roadway.' "

Page 189. — " There has been no attention paid to constructing a good and solid foundation for the roadway."

Page 192. — " Are you of the opinion that it would be advisable or practicable to procure, from any particular part of the country. better materials, so as to form perfect roads without the necessity of paving them? That these materials could be procured, is evident; but I am satisfied that the most economical and preferable mode would be by the means of paving."

ENGINEER DEPARTMENT.

WASHINGTON, May 8, 1833.

Sir: Your communication of the 6th instant, submitting your views in regard to lifting the old bed in prosecuting the repairs of the Cumberland road east of the Ohio, and requesting a reconsideration of so much of the instructions of the department of the 23d July last as relates to this matter, has just been received. That part of the instructions alluded to, which requires that the old bed shall, in all cases, be taken up, will be considered as suspended, and you are hereby authorized to exercise your discretion in this particular.

Very respectfully, &c..

Capt. R. Delafield.   C. GRATIOT. Brig. General.
Corps of Engineers. Uniontown, Pa.
4*

UNIONTOWN, PA., June 11, 1833.

Sir: I find upon an examination of the National Road, under your superintendence, from Cumberland to this place, that too great a portion of sand and other perishable stone has been allowed to be put on it. In almost the whole distance, little or no regard has been paid to the keeping the side drains open, at least sufficiently so to carry the water freely from the road. The culverts are too few and small, particularly on the long slopes; and the manner of constructing the hollow-ways and catch-waters is defective. These errors of construction cause the water, in many places, to pass over the road, to its rapid destruction. I am aware of the difficulties you have to contend with under the contract system, and that to this cause most of the evils complained of may be traced. As it is all important that they should be remedied, as soon as practicable, you will enforce the early completion of the several contracts, according to their conditions, after making due allowance for the stoppage arising from your order for suspending operations during last winter. On the completion of the road, should it be found not to possess the requisite properties to secure its permanency, you will make such additions under your own agency as will place it in the condition contemplated by the government, before turning it over to the States. Not less than six inches of lime or sandstone should be put upon the surface, and where lime is exclusively used, the thickness should not be less than nine inches. The side ditches should, when practicable, be at least eighteen inches below the bed of the road; and when this cannot be done, culverts, 2′ x 3′, should be constructed at convenient distances to carry off the water, which, in no instance, should be allowed to rise above the level of the bed of the road. The catch-waters should be constructed in such a manner, that while they subserve the purposes for which they are intended, they should admit the passage of vehicles without jolting; and, in every case, with a view to prevent their being washed into deep gullies. As this frequently happens when they are constructed with broken stone, it will be proper to pave them with shingle stones, if to be had; or, when this cannot be obtained, with limestone firmly imbedded in the road. It should especially be observed that, before breaking up the road for the reception of the metal, the ditches should be first prepared, and then the culverts. This will keep the roadway dry for travel, and better prepare it for the reception of its covering. As it is found impracticable to keep the travel from the center of the road, and the deep ruts that are formed, then, as a consequence, I would recommend, instead of the present system of blocking, that rakers should be constantly employed to preserve the transverse profile. If it does not come within the spirit of the contract, that this labor should be performed by the contractors, you will hire men to do it yourself. This operation, in addition to the draining system before recommended, will, it is presumed, preserve the road from further ruin, and place it in a condition to receive its last coat of limestone. Finally.

while studying due economy in your administration of the affairs of the road, you should constantly bear in mind that the wishes of the government are to have a superior road, both as regards workmanship, and the quality of the materials used in its construction. With this understanding, it is expected that you will avail yourself of all the facilities within your reach to effect, in a satisfactory manner to yourself and the public at large, the great end proposed—the construction of a road unrivaled in the country. These are the views and special instructions of the Secretary of War.

I am, respectfully, &c.,

C. GRATIOT, Brig. General.

Capt. R. Delafield,
Corps of Engineers, Uniontown, Pa.

ENGINEER DEPARTMENT,

WASHINGTON, July 16, 1833.

Sir: You will forthwith cause all operations to cease on that part of the new location of the Cumberland Road on the east of Wills creek. You shall in a few days receive further instructions on this subject. Very respectfully, &c.,

WM. H. C. BARTLETT,
Lieut. and Assistant to Chief Engineer.

Capt. R. Delafield,
Corps of Engineers, Uniontown, Pa.

ENGINEER DEPARTMENT,

WASHINGTON, July 20, 1833.

Sir: On the 16th you were advised to delay any further action as to the location of the Cumberland Road until you were again written to.

Mr. Purcell reports to the Board of the Chesapeake and Ohio Canal Company that the road being at the site now chosen will occasion an increased cost to the Canal Company of upwards of $16,000. It is very desirable to avoid this state of things, for, as their charter claims precedence, it would necessarily create a demand upon the government commensurate with the injury sustained.

Major Eaton, president of the Canal Company, will direct Mr. Purcell, the engineer, to proceed forthwith to Cumberland, with you, to ascertain the best mode of making the location by which to avoid any injury or increased expense to the Canal Company. You are instructed to confer freely with Mr. Purcell, holding the object suggested steadily in view, and give such direction to the location of the road as may best attain this object. This done, you will forward a plan of the route agreed on, and a minute detail of everything, particularly what increased expense to the Canal Company will probably be occasioned. On receiving your report, the case will be considered here, and you be advised immediately of the course to be pursued.

Very respectfully, &c., &c.,

By order :   WM. H. C. BARTLETT,
                              Lieut. and Assistant to Chief Engineer.
Capt. R. Delafield,
      Corps of Engineers, Uniontown, Pa.

PHILADELPHIA, July 26, 1833.

Sir: The order of your department of the 16th instant was received by me at Cumberland, and its injunctions forthwith carried into effect. The communication of the 20th has since been received, explanatory of that order. In relation to locating that part of the National Road that might probably interfere with the Canal Company, measures were taken to procure from the Company such information as would enable me to locate the road without coming in contact with any part of the Canal route; and, so far as the information was furnished, I have endeavored so to do. I enclose copies of the letter and information received from the president of the company, in reply to a request for such information as would enable me to "ascertain at what point the Chesapeake and Ohio Company contemplate erecting their dam across Wills creek, and to what height it will be raised above low water. The information desired is for enabling me to locate the bridge for the road at a point, and elevate its arches to such a height that the interest of the Canal Company will not be effected; and that I may at the same time, fulfill the objects contemplated by the law authorizing the new location."

In reply to which you will perceive "the location of the canal is that recommended by General Bernard, and the Board of Internal Improvement, over which he presided," and that it was proposed to feed the canal at Cumberland, and below by a dam to be erected across the Potomac about a mile above Cumberland. The water of the Potomac was to be carried over Wills creek twenty-one or two feet above ordinary water in the creek.

Such is the information furnished me by the president of the Canal Company, and by which I have been governed in the location of the road. On the eastern side of Wills creek the grading is finished to the site of the bridge; on the western side I have directed no work to be executed that can have any bearing upon this point.

You perceive it has been my study to avoid conflicting with the interests of the Canal Company; but, from the want of knowing the exact location of their works, will occasion to them an increased expense, as reported by Mr. Purcell, of 16,000 dollars if the bridge is constructed at the point now chosen. If, then, the Company will cause the Canal to be located through the gap of Wills mountain, and give me bench marks from which to ascertain the cuttings and embankments they propose making, I will then locate the road on such ground as not to interfere in any manner with their operations, and such as shall be most advantageous for the public interest. I judge the communication of the department was written under the impression that an interference with the works of the Canal Company was unavoidable, and that some compromise of advantages and disadvantages would necessarily have to be made. Such, however, I do not conceive to be the case.

I have located as high up the creek as would give room for a six horse team to turn off and on a bridge at right angles with the stream with facility. If the Canal Company make choice of this ground, I have but to make a bridge oblique with the current, and thus avoid the work of the Canal Company. To ascertain this, it is essential that the Canal Company should make choice of the ground and locate their works; after having so done, if they will favor me with plans and sections, with bench marks of reference of the part in the valley of the creek, the road shall be made not to interfere with their interest, which has always been looked upon by me as claiming precedence.

I have here pointed out a course for the consideration of the department, differing materially from the one ordered by the letter of the 20th instant. First, in consideration of its not being acquainted with the nature of the case, and, next, with its requiring me to perform a service in no way necessary to a proper understanding of the interests of the Government connected with the road; to do which, surveys, levels, calculations of excavation and embankment must be made, that the time of neither myself nor the officers associated with me could accomplish.

What I ask is, information from the Company as to their own works solely. It will suffice for all purposes connected with the location of the road.

Be pleased to address me at New Castle, and on any matter relating to the section of the road near Cumberland requiring immediate attention, a copy of the communication forwarded to Lieutenant Pickell, at that place, would prevent any delay; Lieutenant P. being the officer to whom I have assigned this particular section of the road.

Respectfully, your obedient servant,

RICH'D DELAFIELD.

Brig. Gen. Charles Gratiot,   Captain of Engineers.
Chief Engineer.

WASHINGTON, D. C., May 10, 1832.

Sir: Your letter to Mr. Ingle, the clerk of the Chesapeake and Ohio Canal Company, has been handed over to me, and I am authorized, on the part of the president and directors, to express to you our thanks for the considerate regard you have paid to the location adopted by the Chesapeake and Ohio Canal Company, for the part of their work which will pass through Cumberland. The location adopted is that recommended by General Bernard, and the Board of Internal Improvement, over which he presided.

When the proposed change of the Cumberland Road immediately above the town was under consideration of the Committee on Roads and Canals, I suggested the very precaution you now practice, which was to see that no conflict would arise in hereafter conducting the canal over its long established route, by a conflict with the location of the improved road, the value of which I know well how to appreciate. The hill above Cumberland, which it is proposed to avoid, was the worst between that place and Wheeling, if reference be had to the inclination of its surface. General Bernard proposed to feed the canal at Cumberland, and for some distance below it, as far, at least, as the mouth of the South branch, by means of a dam to be erected at a ledge of rocks crossing the Potomac about a mile above Cumberland. The dam was to be elevated so high as to conduct the canal over Wills creek at Cumberland, with an elevation of twenty-one or twenty-two feet above ordinary water in the creek. This was to be effected by an aqueduct across the creek. I presume at this season of the year the ledge of rocks is visible above Cumberland. Enclosed I send you extracts from General Bernard's report, which accompanied the President's message to Congress of December 9, 1826, and is now a congressional record. From that you may perhaps infer all that is essential to your purpose of avoiding a collision with the rights of the Chesapeake and Ohio Canal Company, who have adopted for the location of the canal General Bernard's report.

C. F. MERCER,
President of the Chesapeake and Ohio Canal Company.

EXTRACTED—PAGE 55, DOC. No. 10, 19TH CONGRESS, 2D SESSION.—
EXECUTIVE PAPERS.

"The difficulties of this passage (down Wills creek) are great, and continue for more than a mile. The ground then becomes favorable (*i. e.*, in descending Wills creek from the west), permitting the canal to pass at the outskirts of Cumberland, to join with the eastern section. Adjoining Cumberland, the canal will receive a feeder from the Potomac for a supply below, and more especially to complete what is necessary in relation to the first subdivision of the eastern section.

"This feeder is proposed to be made navigable, in order to accommodate the trade of the Potomac above Cumberland. Its length is one mile, its width at the water line thirty feet, its depth four feet. At its point of departure from the Potomac, a basin is formed in the bed of the river, by means of a dam erected at the first ledge above Cumberland.

" This basin, comprehending an extent of about eight miles, will afford a constant supply of water, and also accommodate the canal trade of the Potomac. The levees around the basin, the dam, the guard lock of the feeder, and its aqueduct over Wills creek, are included in the estimate of this subdivision.

" In the table of quantities and cost, this feeder is made to cost a very large sum (two or three words illegible in the MS.) if the dam above Cumberland is supposed to be ever changed from the above location. The aqueduct over Wills creek is computed to cost $41,601; the length of the aqueduct, seventy yards; the number of arches, three; the span of the arch, thirty feet; the height of the piers, sixteen feet."

The above is a true copy.   C. F. MERCER.
May 10, 1833.

ENGINEER DEPARTMENT.

WASHINGTON, August 10, 1833.

Sir: The Secretary of War has just returned to this place, having passed over the Cumberland Road east of the Ohio. He feels great interest in this road, and is anxious that the operations on it shall be so directed as to obtain the best possible results. His confidence in your ability induced him to select you as its superintendent, knowing that under your management his wishes would be realized; and deeming it a work of much greater importance than that with which you are occupied on the Delaware, he has expressed a wish that by far the greater portion of your time should be passed upon the road. You will, therefore, repair to Cumberland without loss of time, ascertain the exact location of the Chesapeake and Ohio canal along the valley of Wills creek, and so adjust that of the road as shall remove the present difficulties, and avoid any interference with the interests of the Canal Company. This being done, you will communicate to the department the result.

Very respectfully, &c.,

WM. H. C. BARTLETT,
Capt. R. Delafield.   Lt. and Ass't to Ch. Eng'r.
Corps of Engineers, New Castle, Del.

ENGINEER DEPARTMENT.

WASHINGTON, September 12, 1833.

Sir: Your letter of the 9th instant, enclosing a plan and sections of part of Wills' creek, exhibiting the location of the National Road "as now constructed;" the ground selected by the engineer of the Chesapeake and Ohio Canal Company for its canal, and the new location of the National Road, in consequence of the Canal Company having made choice of the route upon which the road was constructed, has been received. The plan has been submitted, with the approval of this department, to the Secretary of War, and by him adopted; and the construction of the road on the new location will, therefore, be proceeded with.   I am, sir, &c.,

C. GRATIOT,

Capt. R. Delafield,   Brig. General.
Corps of Engineers, Cumberland, Md.

CUMBERLAND ROAD, AT STODDARD'S, MD.,
September 17, 1833.

Sir : I enclose herewith plan and sections of part of the Cumberland Road between Cumberland and Frostburg, where an alteration has just been made in the location, by which a very steep hill is avoided, and the distance decreased.

By the new route there is a slope of $18\frac{2}{10}$ feet in a distance of 1,600; by the old road the slope was 53.9' in 700 feet on one side of the hill, and 35.7' in 900 feet on the other side.

This is now undergoing construction. The foundation of the center pier of the bridge over Wills creek is raised above water.

Respectfully, your obedient servant,

RICH'D DELAFIELD,

Brig. Gen. Charles Gratiot,   Captain of Engineers.
Chief Engineer.

ENGINEER DEPARTMENT,
WASHINGTON, September 25, 1833.

Sir : Your letter of the 17th inst., enclosing a plan and sections of part of the Cumberland Road between Cumberland and Frostburg, where you had made an alteration in the location, thereby avoiding a steep hill, and decreasing the distance, was duly received; and I have to inform you that the alteration referred to has been approved.   I am, &c.,

C. GRATIOT,

Capt. R. Delafield,   Brig. General.
Corps of Engineers, Cumberland, Md.

CHAPTER XI.

ENGINEER DEPARTMENT,

WASHINGTON, June 25, 1834.

Sir: In addition to the views of the department, communicated to you this morning, I now have to request that you will proceed to apply the funds available for the Cumberland Road east of the Ohio, with the utmost despatch consistent with the public interest. It is greatly to be desired that the repairs of this road may be completed before the termination of the coming fall.

I am, &c..   C. GRATIOT,

Capt. R. Delafield.   Brigadier General.

Corps of Engineers. New Castle, Del.

CUMBERLAND, Md., July 23, 1834.

Sir: I beg leave to call your attention to the act of the Legislature of Maryland, giving its consent to change the location of the National Road near this place, to turn Wills mountain by the route of Wills creek and Braddock's run, in which it is provided that certain bridges shall be constructed of stone, and to compare this act with that of the last session of Congress, and inform me whether or not I will be justified in constructing the bridges with stone abutments and wing-walls, and *wooden* superstructures. There is a necessity growing out of the cost, the law requiring the road to be finished with $300,000.

From the most advantageous offers received, the bridge over Wills creek will not cost less than $15,000, constructed of stone, and if built of wood, planed, and painted with three coats of white lead.

(77)

roofed with shingles, will cost not to exceed $7,000. There are two other bridges on the same new route to be constructed, the ratio of expense of which will not materially vary.   *   *   *
                    Respectfully, your obedient servant,
                                    RICH'D DELAFIELD,
Brig. Gen. Charles Gratiot,   Captain of Engineers.
            Chief Engineer.

                                    CUMBERLAND, July 24, 1834.
    Sir: I have just finished comparing the numerous offers for work to be done on the 16 miles of road immediately west of this place. There is great competition among very excellent and responsible men of the country, as well as from the railroad and canal below us.
    The offers for the bridge render its construction with stone next to impracticable, under the law, to finish the road with $300,000. They are as follows: $22,000, $21,930, $23,323, $22,680, $24,000.
    To construct the abutments I have offers at $3.80 cents per perch; that would, with the superstructure of wood, make the whole cost not to exceed $6,500 to $7,000. We cannot with propriety expend so large a sum for a stone bridge, with such limited means. I strongly recommend a wooden superstructure if compatible with existing laws under which we act, and beg to be advised as requested in my letter of yesterday.
                    Respectfully, your obedient servant,
                                    RICH'D DELAFIELD,
Brig. Gen. Charles Gratiot,   Captain of Engineers.
            Chief Engineer.

                    ENGINEER DEPARTMENT,

                    WASHINGTON, July 29, 1834.
    Sir: It has just been determined by the War Department that the substitution of wood for stone, in the superstructures of the bridges on the new piece of road around Wills hill would be deemed by the State of Maryland a substantial compliance with the requirements of her law giving assent to the change from the old to the present location of that part of the road. You will, therefore, build the abutments of those bridges in a good and durable manner, of the best stone to be had in your immediate neighborhood, and make the superstructure of wood. These last, when completed, must be well covered, and painted in the best manner. This is communicated in answer to your two letters of the 23d and 24th instant, on the subject, which are at hand.   I am, &c.,
                                    C. GRATIOT.
Capt. R. Delafield,
        Corps of Engineers. Cumberland. Md.

COPY OF INSTRUCTIONS SENT BY THE SUPERINTENDENT OF THE CUMBERLAND ROAD, EAST OF THE OHIO, TO EACH OF HIS ASSISTANTS ON THE LINE OF THE ROAD.

WHEELING, May 29, 1834.

Sir: In conducting the operations for repairing the section of the road under your supervision, during the present season, two very important alterations will be made in the system of last year.

The first is to retain, in all cases, the old bed or pavement, breaking down with sledges the prominent or projecting pieces into the ruts and holes, and smoothing the grade with quarry chips, or stone broken on the face of the road with sledge-hammers, slightly covering the bed so prepared with the earth from the ditches, observing to put no more earth than is barely sufficient to prevent the metal coming in contact with the large stone of the bed.

Where there is no stone in the old bed, restore the grade with the best and hardest material to be found in the vicinity, making it a point to have stone to fill the large holes. This formation of the bed for the metal on top of the old bed will enable large and sufficient ditches to be formed for carrying off the water. The most particular attention must be given to these ditches, as upon them depends the preservation of the road.

All the earth taken from the ditches, side roads, and slopes, not required to make good the grade and side roads, must be thrown down the hill side, and on no account whatever upon the slope of a side hill cutting, from whence it soon washes back into the ditches. The minimum size of the ditches should not be less than three feet wide on top, one foot deep, and one foot wide in the bottom; the whole depth to be below the bed of the road. Rock and peculiar side slopes can alone prevent this being practiced.

The side slopes must be cut to a slope of 45, with berms, as a minimum; and as low as 60 wherever it is practicable.

Wherever earth is required for a filling to make good the side roads, require that it be taken from some near side slope or other point that will improve such part of the road. The minimum side road is to be five feet; wherever the natural ground will permit, cause it to be increased to admit of summer roads, placing the ditches outside of such increased side road.

The second alteration is, to have the whole work done by contract, instead of job work and day labor, as was practiced last year.

To effect this, the greatest precaution is necessary to specify what work has to be done on each chain of four rods of the road, the particular grade for such portion, the depth and size of the ditches, the side roads and slopes, and from whence the required earth is to be taken to restore the grade, and where the surplus earth is to be taken from the ditches, drains, side slopes, &c.

In the delivery of stone for the metal, the contract must provide that the stone be delivered and broken on the side roads in rectangular piles or strings of such dimensions as you require on the several parts of the road, and the measurement made of the cubic contents of the stone thus prepared ; from which measurement you will ascertain the number of perches, by previously having a mass, containing five perches of stone, as it comes from the quarry, as compactly piled as can be without the use of a hammer, taking large and small indiscriminately. Have this mass broken to the size of four ounces ; ascertain the cubic contents of the bulk it shall produce, the fifth part of which you will take as a perch, and the unit of measurement for paying for the number of perches to be delivered.

The metal is to be thrown on the road at such favorable periods as you shall designate, after it has been measured, and not until the contractor has prepared the required quantity for half a mile at a time.

You will require the contractor to commence the grade at one end of the piece he is to repair, and continue regularly through, not permitting him to seek the parts requiring least work to execute first ; and when delivering stone, to commence the delivery at a point giving a mean distance for hauling from the quarry ; a mean rate of payment is then equitable, otherwise it would not be.

The work on your section may be divided into two distinct classes : the one, where nothing has as yet been done ; and the other, the part graded and stone prepared for the metal during the past season.

On the first class, you will make contracts to grade, deliver, and put on three perches of limestone where the old bed remains firm, and four perches where the old bed has disappeared, requiring the grade to be finished by the 15th of October ; and if the metal is all prepared by that date, to be put on by the 1st of November, the contractor continuing to rake the road, change the travel, and preserve the whole work in order, until the succeeding 1st of April. Should the contractor, however, not be able to prepare the metal to put it on the road by the 1st of November, then he is to preserve the grade of the road in order until the first favorable state of the weather after the 15th of March ensuing, when he is to put on the metal, raking and smoothing the surface for twenty days after the whole metal shall have been put on the road.

You will observe that the contract is to call for preserving the road in either case during the winter ; in one case, by adding metal, raking, &c., and in the other, by breaking with a sledge stone to fill the ruts, covering such stone in the spring lightly before putting on the metal.

The second class of work is the unfinished part of last year's operations, upon which there will be time to put three and a half additional perches per rod on such parts as were covered last year, and four perches per rod on such as had none, requiring that it be put on by the 1st of November, and be preserved, raked, &c., until the succeeding 1st of April, during the winter filling ruts made by travel with additional metal, to be prepared and ready at convenient points on the road.

For the culverts you will make a contract with one person for all that may be necessary on half your section, and with a second person for the other half, the work to be paid by the perch of twenty-five cubic feet, measured by the plan and dimensions you shall designate for each locality, and according to which plan the work must be constructed. For this work you will require the stone to be of good proportions, with parallel beds and faces, and not smaller than two cubic feet in each piece, in no case ever permitting a stone to be placed " on edge," a very common practice, destructive of good masonry. The covering stone to be of such additional dimensions as you shall judge necessary for each locality. The bottoms of the culverts to be paved or flagged with stone, and such an apron constructed at each end as to guard against the ends being undermined by the passage of the water.

The repairs of the masonry of the bridges and walls on Wheeling Hill it is very desirable to effect by contract, if practicable. On Wheeling Hill the object may be effected by requiring the masonry to conform with that already executed, particularly in regard to the size and quality of the stone, paying for it by the perch measured in the wall when finished, reserving the one-fifth of the value from monthly payments as security for the faithful execution of the whole work. The repairs of the bridge may be executed in like manner, specifying the masonry of the bridge now building over Wheeling Creek as the standard, excepting stones placed on edge.

It is desirable to postpone the repair of all masonry to the latest date, excepting only such parts as are necessary to perfect the grade ; you will make your contracts accordingly. The masonry of the culverts and some of the bridges must be finished in time, including the filling to make good the roadway, to permit the contractor for grading to comply with his agreement. The usual one-fifth of the value of work done being retained until the expiration of the time for completing the whole work, when this sum is to be applied either to carry into effect the remaining provisions of the agreement, as stipulated to be executed, or paid to the contractor, if the work has been faithfully executed according to the tenor of the agreement.

You will make all your payments by checks drawn on the bank through which I shall make your remittances, taking duplicate receipts for moneys thus paid, attached to a bill giving the quantity rate, cost, and date of the receipt of the article clearly and distinctly expressed.

Your check book must be added up, and the balance in bank ascertained every Saturday evening, which balance must be reported in the weekly reports to be forwarded to me, as required last season.

The balance of your account, as appears by your ledger account with me, must also form an item in the weekly report. The assistant engineer will make an inspection of these books, and report to me, whenever he comes on your section of the road.

The receipted vouchers you will forward to the office at Browns- ville, of all payments made during the week at the end of such week, reserving the duplicate until called for by myself or the assistant engineer.

So soon as you are apprised by me of funds being available you will immediately advertise by hand bills, and through the public prints, that contracts will be made for repairing the section of road under your supervision, and that proposals for executing the work will be received for twenty days from the date of your advertisement, for repairing each mile of the road according to stipulations and particular information, to be had on enquiring of you on or after such date as you are enabled to collect it.   Let the advertisements express that the repairs consist principally in grading the road over the old bed, cleaning out the ditches and drains, restoring the side roads to their width of five feet and covering the road thus prepared with limestone broken to four ounce pieces, in such quantities as shall be specified for each rod, varying from two to four perches per rod, and keeping the whole in order until the first of April next, by which date the contracts are to be completed.

To ascertain the work to be done on the different mile sections, and on the particular parts of each mile, you will, the instant funds are available, make a measurement of the road, noting the work to be done on each chain (as specified in the previous parts of this communication) in the most minute detail.

This statement, reduced as much as practicible to a tabular form, you will cause to be printed, as the information to be given to persons upon which to make their proposals, and it will be embodied in or at- tached to the articles of agreement as a specification of the work to be done.

As you will find it convenient to have the prepared metal piled in uniform masses, admitting of the application of a gauge to ascer- tain whether or not the required quantity is in the pile, you will cause such gauges to be made with slopes of 45 degrees and in no in- stance permit a measurement of stone to be made without having previously verified the dimensions of the gauge.   The necessity for this you will perceive by reflecting that the end of the gauge may be cut off and the angles altered to make a material difference in the quantity, without being perceptible to the eye.

The following are some of the frauds heretofore practiced, and now enumerated that you may look cautiously to their not being practiced upon your section of the road :

1st.   Diminishing the size and altering the angle of the gauge.

2d.   Loosening the pile of metal just before the measurement, to increase its bulk.

3d.   Concealing or covering up in the piles of metal large masses of stone or other matter.

4th. Breaking stone of a softer or otherwise inferior quality than the sample agreed upon.

5th. Breaking the metal to a larger size than that agreed upon.

6th. Removing the prepared metal from one point to another after it has been measured.

7th. Taking metal from the face of the road, of the first or second stratum, to make it appear the desired quantity has been broken to fill the gauge.

8th. On parts of the road where limestone has already been delivered, wagoners, with a partial load, passing from the quarries to the point of delivery, have been detected in stealing a piece from several piles, thus making a full load from what has already been paid for.

Very many other frauds have been detected upon receiving and paying for stone perches before breaking. No corrective offers for the many that may be practiced under this system. It is, therefore, in no case, to be adopted. Always measuring the stone after it is broken, and reserving one-fifth of its value until the whole agreement has been fully and faithfully complied with, are the best securities against fraudulent practices.

Immediately after concluding the contracts on your section for the season, you will forward me a statement of the funds required to carry them into effect, and the times such funds will probably be required. Respectfully, your obedient servant,

RICH'D DELAFIELD,
Captain of Engineers.

PHILADELPHIA, December 28, 1834.

Sir: The enclosed letter of the 29th May was prepared as the instructions for Lieutenant Vance, conducting the operations on the seventh division of the road, and a copy thereof was forwarded to the officer of each division, with directions to conform thereto on their respective sections, suiting the phraseology to their divisions.

On the 27th June, on being made acquainted with the particulars of the act of Congress making the appropriation for the year's service, the following instructions were communicated to the officers of the several divisions, slightly changed to suit each particular division:

"*Sir:* Funds having been made available for continuing the repairs of the Cumberland Road, east of the Ohio, you will cause the preparatory measures to be taken immediately, and notice given as required by my letter of the 29th of May, a copy of which has been forwarded to you from Brownsville.

" The act of Congress grants a specific sum for finishing the repairs of the road; you will, therefore, in your arrangements, provide for the stone bridges on the new road, and three and a half perches of stone to the rod on the surface of the road as metal; the latter to be furnished by the 31st of December, and kept raked and additional metal put on until the 15th day of February ensuing; the masonry of the bridges to be finished by the 15th of October, with proposals of the terms for finishing the same work by the 30th day of June, 1835.

"The form of a contract has also been forwarded to you from Brownsville, which, with the letter of instructions accompanying it, connected with the tenor of this communication, you will make your guide in the management of the section of road confided to your supervision.

"You will observe the form of the contract provides for work that may not occur in your division. You will, in preparing the form to be printed, be cautious to suit the same to your particular division, as to distance, &c., &c. Mile sections are desirable for subdividing the road, and as the portion to be given under contract to an individual: on your division other subdivisions will be found more convenient, and your attention must, in consequence, be given to make the phraseology of the instrument conform with the facts of the case.

"Hereafter, you will commence and continue your weekly reports to me. Apprise me of the date you limit the reception of proposals, that I may be with you at the time.

"RICH'D DELAFIELD, Captain of Engineers."

The instructions to the officer of the third division required him to provide for the work to be done on his division not exceeding three and a half perches of stone to a rod on the surface of the road as metal, reducing the quantity to two or one perch, as might be requisite to keep the whole in repair until finally completed.

For a copy of the form of contract forwarded to the officers of the several divisions, see the contracts on file in your office, for the *fourth* division of the road.

I enclose the statement called for by the letter of your department of the 9th instant.

Respectfully, your obedient servant,
RICH'D DELAFIELD,
Brig. Gen. Charles Gratiot,   Captain of Engineers.
                Chief Engineer.

REPORT AND ESTIMATE FOR THE CUMBERLAND ROAD EAST OF THE OHIO, UNDER A RESOLUTION OF THE SENATE OF THE UNITED STATES, CALLING FOR THE CONDITION OF THE MASONRY, THE THICKNESS OF METAL ON VARIOUS PARTS, &c., &c., DECEMBER, 1834.

The plan of repair adopted and continued for this road to July, 1834, was that of Macadam, with nine inches of metal in three strata.

The provisions of the act of Congress of the last session made a change in the plan of operation necessary. The sum of $300,000 was appropriated to finish the repairs of the road from Cumberland to Wheeling, a distance of one hundred and thirty-two miles, of which fifty-four miles had not been commenced.

To conform with the provisions of the law, it became necessary to confine the expenditure of this sum to the most indispensable parts of the system, and adopt a less expensive and less permanent repair; abandoning the plan of finishing the mountain division with limestone throughout, and to a width of twenty feet; confining the metal on the more expensive parts of these divisions to a width of from twelve to fifteen feet, instead of twenty; abandoning further repairs to the masonry of the parapets of the bridges; depositing the stone that had been prepared for this purpose on the side roads, and leaving the side walls on Wheeling Hill in their unfinished state; limiting the stratum of metal to be put on this season to three perches and a half, on an average, per rod, on the whole line of the road; transporting the stone that had previously been collected for an additional thickness of metal to parts that had not been supplied with any; substituting wooden bridges for stone over Wills creek and Braddock's run, and abandoning altogether the construction of any bridge over Dunlap's creek. The repairs thus modified are fast drawing to a close, when the road will present parts covered with thicknesses of metal varying from three to nine inches, as follows:

First division, in Maryland, sixteen miles, one hundred and sixty rods, including new location, is covered with three inches of metal.

Second division, in Maryland, sixteen miles, one hundred and ninety-four rods, is covered with six inches of metal.

Third division, in Pennsylvania, two hundred rods, is covered with four inches and a half of metal.

Third division, in Pennsylvania, twenty-five miles, one hundred rods, to a width of from twelve to fifteen feet, is covered with nine inches of metal.

Fourth division, in Pennsylvania, one mile, seven rods, is covered with three inches of metal.

Fourth division, in Pennsylvania, fourteen miles, one hundred and twenty-three rods, to a width of from twelve to fifteen feet, is covered with six inches of metal.

Fifth division, in Pennsylvania, eighteen miles, nine rods, is covered with three inches of metal.

Sixth division, in Pennsylvania, twenty-one miles, two hundred and seventy-three rods, is covered with three inches of metal.

Seventh division, in Virginia, five miles, is covered with three inches of metal.

Seventh division, in Virginia, nine miles, two hundred and sixteen rods, is covered with six inches of metal.

The number of inches of metal put on that part which has been located anew, the first six miles of the first division, being three inches, and the number of inches of metal put upon that part of the road which lies between the Monongahela and the Ohio, the fifth, sixth, and seventh divisions, being three inches of metal on forty-four miles and two hundred and eighty-two rods, and six inches of metal on nine miles and two hundred and sixteen rods.

5

To make this a permanent and substantial road, such that the heavy transportation wagons shall not force their wheels through the metal into the bed, not less than the original contemplated thickness of three strata of three inches each, or the same number of strata of three perches and a half of stone each, appears sufficient. That three inches of metal will not suffice to bear up the travel passing over this road, is proved by the experience of the last two years. Nor will six inches answer the purpose on all parts of the road, during a long or continued wet spell of weather, when, from absorption alone, the solidity and contiguity of the metal has become weakened and lessened. On the crests of the hills it will be solid, with a thickness of six inches, when, in the valley and grades under one degree, the evidence of its insufficiency are apparent. Nothing less than the three strata of three inches each has been found sufficient; the last stratum being unequally applied according to the firmness and dryness, and the slope or grade of the bed. Such was judged necessary for a Macadam road from Cumberland to Wheeling, and the results tend to confirm the necessity of a thickness of nine inches on an average, to secure the object contemplated by the instructions of the Chief Engineer.

The condition of the masonry on the whole line of the road is in an unfinished state, so far as regards many of the parts upon which repairs have been commenced; and where nothing had been done toward repairing the bridges, many of their side-walls or parapets are in a dilapidated state, or torn down to the level of the roadway. In repairing the road under the last act of Congress, no more masonry was undertaken than the construction of culverts to drain the road, and repairing such parts as were necessary to perfect the roadway twenty feet in width; all other parts were left in the unfinished and decayed state in which they were when the appropriation of the year caused an abandonment of further repairs to this part of the work.

To carry into effect the repairs originally contemplated, and to secure the uniform strength throughout the whole line of the road equivalent to nine inches of metal, the following sums will be necessary, after applying the means now on hand, and which are pledged for the work commenced and contracted for in July last.

By reference to the annexed statement, it will be perceived the price per perch for delivered stone prepared as metal on the road varies from ninety-three cents to $2.50, and is stated for each section throughout the whole line of the road. Three quarries supply upward of twenty miles of the road, there being none nearer or accessible. Quarries of the best limestone are numerous and not remote from the road between Wheeling and the eastern base of Laurel hill; from thence to Frostburg they are few in number, situated in deep ravines, and remote from the road; from Frostburg to Cumberland they are comparatively numerous and of easy access. It will be seen that the price agrees with the difficulty of procuring the stone, and in the ratio above stated, from ninety-three cents to $2.50 per perch.

CHAPTER XII.

Gen. Lewis Cass, Secretary of War, transmits a Report — More about the Wooden Bridges for the New Location near Cumberland — The War Department thinks they will do — John Hoye stoutly Objects — The Governor of Maryland takes a hand against Wooden Bridges — John Hoye to the Front Again — The Pennsylvania Commissioners make another demand that the Road be put in Repair.

WAR DEPARTMENT, January 3, 1835.

Sir: Herewith I have the honor to transmit a report from the Chief Engineer, which furnishes the information called for by the resolution of the House of Representatives of the 12th ultimo, respecting the Cumberland Road east of the Ohio.

Very respectfully, your most obedient servant,

LEW. CASS.

Hon. John Bell,
 Speaker of the House of Representatives.

ENGINEER DEPARTMENT,

WASHINGTON, January 3, 1835.

Sir: I have the honor to hand you the information called for by the House of Representatives on the 12th ultimo, relating to the Cumberland Road east of the Ohio,

And remain, sir, very respectfully, your obedient servant,

C. GRATIOT,
Chief Engineer.

The Hon. Lewis Cass,
 Secretary of War.

ENGINEER DEPARTMENT,

WASHINGTON, July 28, 1834.

Sir: In making the repairs of the Cumberland Road east of the Ohio river, it was deemed expedient, in the fall of 1832, to change that part of the old location which is immediately west of Cumberland, in the State of Maryland, for the purpose of turning Wills hill. By this an abrupt rise of several hundred feet would be avoided. A survey, preparatory to this change, was made, and the result submitted to Congress, in the session of 1832–'33; the proposed change was authorized, and the location, as exhibited on the drawing of the survey, adopted. This change of location involved the construction of a bridge over the mill-race in the town of Cumberland, and another over Wills creek, as well as other bridges of minor importance, with several culverts. The Legislature of the State of Maryland passed an act giving assent to the change in question, with the proviso, however, "that the part of the road embraced in this change should be made of the best material, upon the Macadam plan, and that a good, substantial stone bridge should be made over the mill-race, in the town of Cumberland, and over Wills creek at the place of crossing, and that substantial stone bridges and culverts should be made wherever the same may respectively be necessary along the line of said road."

In the estimates which were prepared, and submitted at the commencement of the last session of Congress for its action, the sum proposed for the completion of the repairs of the entire road from Cumberland to the Ohio river, contemplated the erection of the bridges on the new location, in conformity to the requirements of the law of Maryland just referred to. But, as is known to you, more than one-half of this sum was stricken from the bill, which embodied the whole amount of the estimate. The act appropriating the remainder requires that the whole of the repairs shall be completed for this diminished sum. Under these circumstances, it becomes necessary to change the plan upon which it was proposed to execute the work, and the object of this communication is to ascertain the extent to which the department may be allowed to carry this change on the new part of the road embraced by the law of Maryland. If the bridges alluded to be built of stone, the expense will be much greater than the sum allotted to that section would bear: whereas, if the abutments be built of stone, and the superstructure of wood, the same ends would be attained as would result from bridges built entirely of stone, but the letter of the Maryland law would be departed from. Good wooden superstructures, well covered and painted, would last, with a little care, at least forty years, and perhaps longer. To abandon this new location, and return to the old road, would be to sacrifice a large amount of money already expended on the former, which is now in a state of forwardness, and would soon be finished. Besides, a bridge must, in any event, be constructed over Wills creek, and every consideration of convenient and easy traveling conspires to render its location on the new line of the road desirable.

The officer charged with the repairs of the road is now engaged in giving out the work to contract, and making other arrangements necessary to a speedy application of the funds. It is, therefore, very desirable that an early decision may be had of this question, and it is accordingly respectfully requested.

I have the honor to be, &c.,

C. GRATIOT, Brig. Gen.

Hon. Secretary of War.

I approve of the course recommended by General Gratiot with regard to the bridges — the abutments to be of stone, and the super-structure of wood — believing that such a course would be deemed by Maryland a substantial compliance with the law, under the circum-stances of the case.

JOHN FORSYTH,

July 28, 1834.   Act. Sec'y of War.

CUMBERLAND, August 5, 1834.

Sir: I was this day informed that the bridge across Wills creek, on the new location of the Cumberland road up Braddock's run, is to be built of wood. By the act of the Legislature of Maryland, author-izing the President to change the location of the road, it is enacted that the road may be located up Wills creek through the narrows, pro-vided the bridges were all built of stone. I am decidedly of the opin-ion that, by the provisions of that law, the President had no right to change the location of the road unless he strictly complied with every provision and requisition of said law. You will, on examination of the act of Maryland, passed at December session, 1832, chapter 55, see that the bridges are to be all built of stone. I sincerely hope you will, on examining the law, and reflecting on the subject, direct the bridges to be built in strict compliance with the law authorizing the change in location; it would, in all probability, save money and time.

I am sure the State will not receive the road without the stone bridges. I shall be gratified to hear from you on this subject by return mail.

Your most obedient,

General C. Gratiot.   JOHN HOYE.

ENGINEER DEPARTMENT,

WASHINGTON, August 14, 1834.

Sir: Your communication in behalf of the citizens of Cumber-land, remonstrating against the erection of bridges of wooden super-structures over Wills creek, &c., addressed to me under date of 6th instant, is received. The measure to which the citizens of Cumber-land object, grows, of necessity, out of existing circumstances; and the bridges will have to be built in the manner and of the materials named in the instruction of the department to the superintendent of the road, or the new location to turn Wills hill must be abandoned. The people of Cumberland are doubtless aware that estimates were submitted to Congress last fall for funds sufficient to put up the structures in conformity with the law of Maryland, to which you refer; and it is hoped that they are also aware that these funds were reduced more than one-half in amount, and that the act appropriating the residue imposes the task of completing all the repairs on the whole road east of the Ohio, with the sum rendered available by it.

You will perceive, sir, that there was no other course left to the department than to change the plan and system of repairs.

The bridges which it is proposed to construct will, with care, last at least forty years.

Very respectfully, &c.,

C. GRATIOT,

Brig. Gen. and Chief Engineer.

B. S. Pigman, Esq., Cumberland, Md.

EXECUTIVE DEPARTMENT,

ANNAPOLIS, September 10, 1834.

Sir: By an act of the General Assembly, passed at December session, 1832, (of which, at your request, an authenticated copy was transmitted to you on the 29th day of March, 1833), the consent of this State was given to a change of the location of a part of the Cumberland or National Road within our limits, upon certain conditions; among which, "that a good and substantial stone bridge shall be made over the mill-race in the town of Cumberland, and over Wills creek at the place of crossing, and that substantial stone bridges or culverts shall be made wherever the same may respectively be necessary along the line of said road."

By the same act, John Hoye and Meshach Frost, Esqrs., and the superintendent for the time being of the said road, appointed by the President of the United States, were appointed commissioners "to report the said National Road, when finished and repaired within the limits of this State, to the Governor and Council."

A communication has been received from John Hoye, Esq., in which he states that "the War Department has now directed and contracted to have all the bridges on said new location built of wood."

I beg leave to call your attention to this subject, in the fullest confidence that there has been some mistake or misapprehension on the part of some of the agents or persons employed upon the work in question, and that you will cause the terms and conditions upon which the consent of the State was given to the proposed improvements to be respected and carried into effect.

With great respect, I have the honor to be,

Your obedient servant,

Hon. Lewis Cass,   JAMES THOMAS.

Secretary of War.

WAR DEPARTMENT,

WASHINGTON, September 12, 1834.

Sir: I have had the honor to receive your letter of the 10th instant, respecting the construction of the bridge on the National Road near Cumberland, and for your information I beg leave to enclose the accompanying report from the Engineer Department, which explains the course which has been taken, and the necessity of it. I trust that you will find that the act of the State of Maryland has been substantially complied with, and certainly so far as the means within this department permitted.

Very respectfully, &c.

His Excellency James Thomas,   LEW. CASS.
  Governor of Maryland, Annapolis.

ENGINEER DEPARTMENT,

WASHINGTON, September 12, 1834.

Sir: In answer to your inquiries of this morning respecting certain bridges on the Cumberland Road, in the State of Maryland, I have the honor to submit the following statement :

In applying the money appropriated by Congress at the session of 1831 and '32, for the repairs of the Cumberland Road east of the Ohio river, it was deemed highly important to change the location of that part of the road immediately west of Cumberland to turn Wills mountain, as, by that means, a rise of several hundred feet, within a few miles, would be avoided. A survey was accordingly made, and submitted to Congress, and the change was approved. The State of Maryland assented, provided the part of the road embraced in the change should be "made of the best materials, upon the Macadam plan, and that a good and substantial stone bridge should be made on the mill-race, in the town of Cumberland, and over Wills creek at the place of crossing, and that substantial stone bridges and culverts should be made wherever the same may respectively be necessary along the line of said road."

Estimates were prepared last fall for the entire completion of the repairs of the road from Cumberland to the Ohio. These estimates, which contemplated the construction and erection of bridges, in strict conformity with the law of Maryland giving her consent to the change of location, were submitted to Congress at the commencement of its recent session, and amounted to six hundred and fifty-two thousand one hundred dollars. Full and ample explanations accompanied these estimates, so there could have been no misunderstanding respecting them. A bill of appropriation was introduced, embracing their entire amount. This amount, after much discussion, was reduced to less than one-half, to-wit: $300,000, and the bill became a law, containing a section which requires that as soon as the sum of $300,000, or as much thereof as is necessary, shall be expended on the road agreeably to the provisions of this act, the same shall be surrendered to the States, respectively, through which the road passes; "and the United States shall not thereafter be subject to any expense for repairing said road." Under these circumstances, it was plain that the system of repairs upon which the estimates were predicated could not be executed, and a change became necessary. The stone bridges referred to in the law of Maryland constituted a heavy item in the estimates, and it was entirely out of the question to build them without absorbing more of the appropriation than the absolute requirements of other sections of the road would admit. There being no obligation to finish the new location further than that imposed by the very great advantage resulting from its adoption, the question arose whether it would be best to abandon it, and return to the old road or not. After adopting every expedient, consistent with a faithful execution of the law, to diminish the expenses on other portions of the road, it was found that a sufficient sum would be left to construct this new portion of the best material, on the Macadam plan, and to build the abutments and piers of all the bridges on it of good stone, and in the best manner, provided the superstructures were made of wood. This was the best that could be done; and when it was considered that these superstructures, being made of the best materials, would, when covered and well painted, last, with a little care, from thirty to forty years, it was recommended to the acting Secretary of War, during your absence, to adopt them in preference to surrendering all the benefits that will result from the new road. The acting Secretary, considering that the approval of the measure would, under this state of things, be a substantial compliance with the law of Maryland, directed instructions to that effect to be issued to the superintendent of the road, which was accordingly done.

With great respect, &c.,

By order :

WM. H. C. BARTLETT,
Lieut. and Assist. to Chief Engineer.

The Hon. Secretary of War.

CUMBERLAND, December 12, 1834.

Sir: As one of the commissioners appointed by the Legislature of Maryland to report to the Governor and Council of said State when that part of the National Road within the limits of this State shall have been repaired agreeably to the provisions of the law of the State agreeing to receive that part of the road lying within the limits of this State; and a further act of the Legislature of Maryland, authorizing the President of the United States to change the location of a part of said road within the limits of Maryland, the change of location was authorized to be made on certain and positive conditions that the bridges over Wills creek and Braddock's run should all be permanent stone bridges; and the road to be constructed with the best materials, on the Macadam plan (see the law of Maryland, passed December session, 1832, chapter 55). The plan of the bridges has been changed by the superintendent to wooden bridges, in direct violation of the engagements with this State. The President had no right to change the location of the road, unless the law of this State authorizing the change was fully complied with.

The metal on the new location is not more than three and a half inches, and every wagon that passes over it, when the road is wet, cuts entirely through the stone, and turns up the clay. I am advised that there is a part of the road, fourteen miles west of Cumberland, which has had but three and a half inches of metal put on it over the original pavement. I am gratified to have it in my power to state that, from observation, and the best information I have been able to collect, the last appropriation for the road has been most judiciously expended. I believe that it is the first that has been well laid out.

I must say that we cannot report in favor of this State receiving the road until the permanent stone bridges are erected, and the road in that state of repair contemplated by the law.

I beg leave to refer you to my letter to General C. Gratiot, dated in August last, which, with my communication to his excellency James Thomas, Governor of Maryland, a copy of which, I presume, he communicated to your department during the last summer, you will please to consider a part of this communication. I should have addressed you at an earlier period, but was prevented by severe indisposition.

I remain, with respect, your most obedient,

JOHN HOYE.

Hon. Lewis Cass,
Secretary of War, Washington City.

NOVEMBER 17, 1834.

Sir: The undersigned commissioners, appointed by the Governor of Pennsylvania to erect gates and superintend the collection of tolls on the Cumberland Road "after it shall be put in a good state of repair by the United States," respectfully represent:

That, from a full and careful examination of the subject, they are satisfied that they are not authorized, by the terms of the law under which they are appointed, to accept the road from the United States, or erect gates for the collection of tolls, until provision is made by Congress for completing the repairs on the plan already adopted by the agents of the United States, and sanctioned by several appropriations to carry it into effect. Without this it is evident that a considerable portion of the road, which has received but a single stratum of stone, will be left in a condition so weak and imperfect as soon to become again totally impassable for a considerable portion of the year.

The law of Pennsylvania expressly requires that, before the road is accepted by the Commissioners, it must be put in good and complete repair by the United States. To this act and all its provisions, Congress, on the 3d of July, 1832, gave its assent; an appropriation was made, and a plan of repair was accordingly adopted by the agents of the government, and two subsequent appropriations made by Congress to carry this plan and compact into effect. The complete repair of the road is made by the compact a condition precedent to be performed

5a

by the United States. It is not performed, as appears by the report of the agents of the United States, and, until it is, the Commissioners appointed by the State cannot be justified in accepting the road or exacting tolls. Besides, it is evident that the tolls established, even if raised to the maximum, will be totally inadequate to the preservation and repair of the road, unless first put in a state of complete and substantial repair. This, a statement of a single fact will fully demonstrate. It appears by a report lately received from the superintendent of that part of the road which lies between Hagerstown and Cumberland, that the tolls there collected amount to $312 per mile per annum; of this $45 is required to pay gate keepers and superintendents, leaving $267 for repairs. The tolls on that part of the road are more than three times as high as those proposed on this, so that the amount of tolls applicable to the repair of this road will not exceed $89 per mile per annum, a sum barely sufficient to preserve the road after it is put in the best possible state of repair. The undersigned do not presume to prescribe a plan of repair; they are satisfied with that adopted and partly executed by the agents of the United States; and they now distinctly declare and pledge themselves, that so soon as Congress shall appropriate the sum required by the Secretary of War to complete the repair of the road on the plan adopted in his report at the last session, we will, with all possible despatch, proceed to erect the gates, and relieve the United States from all further charge or expense on account of said road, after the appropriation so made shall be expended.

Very respectfully, your most obedient servants,

THOMAS ENDSLEY.
DANIEL DOWNER.
WILLIAM F. COPLAN.
STEPHEN HILL.
BENJAMIN ANDERSON.

Hon. Lewis Cass,
　　Secretary of War.

NOTE.—The bridges near Wills creek were in the end built of stone.

IRON BRIDGE.

CHAPTER XIII.

The Iron Bridge over Dunlap's Creek at Brownsville — Interesting facts relating to its projection and construction — The first step — Several respectable Gentlemen of Brownsville call the attention of the Government's Agent to the subject.

NATIONAL ROAD, 85⅝ MILES FROM CUMBERLAND,

August 15, 1832.

Sir: Yesterday, as I passed through Brownsville, I was waited on by several of the most respectable gentlemen of that place, who were anxious to have me examine the bridge over Dunlap's creek, between Brownsville and Bridgeport, to see its condition, and to give my opinion as to its renewal. Accordingly, I observed that I thought the bridge would not stand a twelve-month, and that I did not feel myself authorized to renew it, as the bridge had never been made by the government, but recommended that they write to the department for a decision ; and, agreeably to their request, observed that I would likewise report the actual condition of the bridge. Consequently, I enclose to the department a leaf from my note book, giving a rough sketch of the bridge, and pointing out its defects. The reason why this bridge was not originally constructed by the government, as well as a bridge over the Monongahela river, are better known to the department than I am able to conjecture.

I have to observe that a company is now constructing a substantial bridge over the Monongahela river, across from Bridgeport, thereby making the bridge over Dunlap's creek an important link in the road ; and that a bridge, to ensure the purpose of a common highway, would not be suitable for the only connecting point between two important and increasing towns.

I have the honor to be, sir,

Very respectfully, your most obedient servant,

J. K. F. MANSFIELD,

Gen. C. Gratiot, Lieutenant Corps of Engineers.
Chief Engineer.

THE SUBJECT TO BE EXAMINED.

ENGINEER DEPARTMENT,

WASHINGTON, August 20, 1832.

Sir: Your letter of the 15th inst., informing the department that you had, at the request of the citizens of Brownsville, made an examination of the bridge over Dunlap's creek, with a view to an opinion on the question of its removal, and transmitting a rough sketch of the bridge as it at present exists, is received.

In consequence of the views presented in your letter, it will be necessary to make a thorough examination of this bridge to ascertain whether it is sufficiently substantial to answer all the purposes of the road, by putting proper repairs upon it, or whether it will be necessary to remove it entirely, and to build a new one.

You will accordingly make this examination, and with your report on the subject you will transmit such drawings and explanatory notes as may be necessary to present a full and clear view of the repairs, or new bridge, as the case may be, accompanied by the proper estimates for their execution.

You will also ascertain, by the best oral testimony that can be obtained in the vicinity of the bridge, whether it is on the line of the road as originally located, and make known the fact in your report.

The Secretary of War has been written to on the subject, and, as soon as his decision is known at the department, you will be instructed accordingly. I am, &c., &c.,

C. GRATIOT.

Lieut. J. K. F. Mansfield,
    Corps of Engineers, Uniontown, Pa.

AN EXAMINATION MADE, AND AN ADVERSE DECISION RENDERED.

UNIONTOWN, PA., August 24, 1832.

Sir: I have the honor to acknowledge the receipt of the letter of the department on the subject of the bridge over Dunlap's creek, at Brownsville, and to state that I have completed the examination of the road to the Virginia line, and have already given out notices for contracts, two of which are enclosed for the perusal of the department. I am, &c.,

J. K. F. MANSFIELD,
Lieutenant Corps of Engineers.

Gen. Charles Gratiot,
    Chief Engineer.

ENGINEER DEPARTMENT,

WASHINGTON, October 11, 1832.

Sir: You were informed by letter from the department, under date of 20th August last, that the Secretary of War had been written to on the subject of building a new bridge over Dunlap's creek in the place of that which is at present in the line of the Cumberland Road, between Brownsville and Bridgeport, and which was referred to in your communication to the Chief Engineer of the 15th of August last. I now have to inform you that the Secretary of War has decided that the bridge in question cannot be built at the expense of the government, under the law making appropriation for the repairs of the Cumberland Road east of the Ohio river.

Very respectfully, &c.,

By order: WM. H. C. BARTLETT,

Lieut. of Engineers, and Assistant to Chief Engineer.

Lieut. J. K. F. Mansfield,

Corps of Engineers, Uniontown, Pa., or Capt. Delafield.

THE DECISION REVERSED, AND THE BRIDGE TO BE BUILT.

ENGINEER DEPARTMENT,

WASHINGTON, May 13, 1833.

Sir: The Secretary of War has determined that a new bridge shall be built across the mouth of Dunlap's creek, in the line of the Cumberland Road; you will, therefore, be pleased to submit a plan, and estimate, with as little delay as practicable, with the view to the erection of this bridge during the present year.

I am, sir, &c.,

Capt. R. Delafield,   C. GRATIOT,

Corps of Engineers, Uniontown, Pa.   Brig. General.

A SERIOUS QUESTION AS TO LOCATION ARISES — A REQUEST THAT BARRIERS BE USED ON THE ROAD.

Extract from a letter dated   BROWNSVILLE, May 14, 1834.

Sir: To establish the location of Dunlap's creek bridge, I desire the field notes of the commissioners, if on file in your office, and Mr. Shriver's notes of location. From these, I am inclined to believe it will appear that the most favorable route for the bridge was pointed out by the commissioners, and the route over the bridge now used, no part of the National Road, but a county bridge, that we have no right to interfere with. May I request such information as is within your reach on this subject?

The road may be called a very excellent turnpike between this and Frostburg, at the present time; so smooth that already the stage proprietors have commenced the use of a "rough lock," that materially injures the surface. Some defects are clearly observable, growing out of the constant travel and wear of the center of the road from the prohibition to use barriers to change the travel.

Without being permitted to use barriers of logs, stumps and stones, it is out of our power ever to make a perfect Macadamized road, and far from being as good as the expenditure should produce. Such a system has been resorted to on every road I have seen made, and every officer associated with me concurs in the opinion that we cannot succeed without using them. Permit me to ask a reconsideration of the order prohibiting their use.

Respectfully, your obedient servant,

Brig. Gen. Charles Gratiot,   RICH'D DELALFIELD,

Chief Engineer.   Captain of Engineers.

THE USE OF BARRIERS PERMITTED—A ROAD BEGINNING AT UNIONTOWN, AND
ENDING AT WASHINGTON.

ENGINEER DEPARTMENT,

WASHINGTON, May 20, 1834.

Sir: Your communication, dated the 14th instant, was duly
received. In conformity with your request, a detail of two officers,
as your assistants on the Cumberland Road, has been applied for.
Herewith is transmitted a book containing, as stated, "the notes of a
location of the United States western road, beginning at Uniontown,
and ending at the turnpike near Washington," which is the only
document among the papers transferred from the Treasury Department to this office, relating to the Cumberland Road, embraced in the
notes, required to be forwarded to you.

(On the subject of regulating the travel so as to preserve the
surface of the road from injury mentioned in your letter, you will
again resort to the use of barriers, wood only, to be used for the purpose, and placed only on one side of the road at the same time, provided the object can thus be accomplished, and so elevated as to be
very conspicuous, that the travel by night may not be endangered
by the barriers).   I am, &c.,

C. GRATIOT,

Capt. R. Delafield,   Brig. General.

Corps of Engineers, Brownsville, Pa.

A BIG APPROPRIATION, BUT THE BRIDGE ABANDONED.

ENGINEER DEPARTMENT,

WASHINGTON, June 25, 1834.

Sir: Three hundred thousand dollars have just been appropriated for the repairs of the Cumberland Road east of the Ohio. You
will perceive by the law, a printed copy of which is herewith enclosed, that the intention is that this sum shall complete the repairs.
You will, therefore, take your measures accordingly, and put the road
in as good condition as this sum will admit of. The new section to
turn Wills hill will be completed on the plan already commenced,
but the plan of operations on the other sections must be modified to
suit the requirements of the law. The iron bridge over Dunlap's
creek will be abandoned. Your project, when matured, will be transmitted for the approval of the department.

Very respectfully, &c.,

By order: WM. H. C. BARTLETT,

Lieut. and Assistant to Chief Engineer.

Capt. R. Delafield,

Corps of Engineers, New Castle, Del.

ANOTHER AND FINAL CHANGE—THE BRIDGE TO BE BUILT ON THE SITE OF THE OLD ONE.

ENGINEER DEPARTMENT,

WASHINGTON, August, 14, 1834.

Sir: I have to acknowledge the receipt of your communication, dated 31st ultimo, in reference to the bridge over Dunlap's creek, on the Cumberland Road, east of the Ohio. The subject of rebuilding this bridge was brought to the notice of the Secretary of War during the summer of 1832, when he refused to take any action in the matter, on the ground that it was a county bridge, which should be repaired or rebuilt by the county authorities, as the United States, in adopting a system of repairs, had undertaken to repair only that which they had originally constructed. It was thought on the other side, that notwithstanding the United States had not built this bridge, yet, as they had enjoyed the free benefit of it, and as it lay on the tacitly acknowledged line of the road, they were bound, under the act of Congress authorizing the repairs of the road to work on every part of it without reference to original constructors or proprietors. In this state of the case, it was submitted to Mr. Taney, then Attorney General, who decided verbally in favor of the latter view, and instructions in conformity thereto were issued to the superintendent of the road, requiring him to cause the bridge to be either repaired or rebuilt. This question having been settled, the next is, whether Dunlap's creek can be crossed at any other point than where the county bridge now stands. It is the opinion of the department that it cannot. It would seem there is no evidence on record that any location was ever finally fixed upon by the commissioners, and reported by them to the President, for the part of the road in the immediate vicinity of this creek; but the fact that the road was actually made in its present location, and used ever since its original construction, without any opposition, is strong proof that this route was adopted by the Government; at all events, in the absence of all other evidence, the department feels constrained to act upon this. Now, the appropriations having been made for the repairs of the road, and not for constructing any part of it, except the new section to turn Wills hill, it is not perceived how any part of the funds can be applied to the new location proposed by you. These views having been submitted to the acting Secretary of War, he concurs in them. Your operations will, therefore, be confined to the old road on which the bridge must be located.   Very, &c.,

C. GRATIOT,

Capt. Richard Delafield,

Corps of Engineers, Brownsville, Pa.

CHAPTER XIV.

Appropriations by Congress at various times for Making, Repairing, and Continuing the Road — Aggregate of Appropriations, $6,824,919.33.

1. Act of March 29, 1806, authorizes the President to appoint a commission of three citizens to lay out a road four rods in width "from Cumberland or a point on the northern bank of the river Potomac in the State of Maryland, between Cumberland and the place where the main road leading from Gwinn's to Winchester, in Virginia, crosses the river, * * * to strike the river Ohio at the most convenient place between a point on its eastern bank, opposite to the northern boundary of Steubenville and the mouth of Grave creek, which empties into the said river a little below Wheeling, in Virginia." Provides for obtaining the consent of the States through which the road passes, and appropriates for the expenses, to be paid from the reserve fund under the act of April 30, 1802.....................................$ 30,000 00

2. Act of February 14, 1810, appropriates to be expended under the direction of the President, in making the road between Cumberland and Brownsville, to be paid from fund act of April 30, 1802 60,000 00

3. Act of March 3, 1811, appropriates to be expended under the direction of the President, in making the road between Cumberland and Brownsville, and authorizes the President to permit deviations from a line established by the Commissioners under the original act as may be expedient; *Provided*, that no deviation shall be made from the principal points established on said road between Cumberland and Brownsville, to be paid from fund act of April 30, 1802......................... 50,000 00

4. Act of February 26, 1812, appropriates balance of a former appropriation not used, but carried to surplus fund................................ 3,786 60

Carried forward ....$ 143,786 60

Brought forward...........................$ 143,786 60

5. Act of May 6, 1812, appropriates to be expended under direction of the President, for making the road from Cumberland to Brownsville, to be paid from fund act of April 30, 1802................ 30,000 00

6. Act of March 3, 1813 (General Appropriation Bill), appropriates for making the road from Cumberland to the State of Ohio, to be paid from fund act of April 30, 1802........................ 140,000 00

7. Act of February 14, 1815, appropriates to be expended under the direction of the President, for making the road between Cumberland and Brownsville, to be paid from fund act of April 30, 1802.. 100,000 00

8. Act of April 16, 1816 (General Appropriation Bill), appropriates for making the road from Cumberland to the State of Ohio, to be paid from the fund act, April 30, 1802......................... 300,000 00

9. Act of April 14, 1818, appropriates to meet claims due and unpaid........................... 52,984 60
    Demands under existing contracts............. 260,000 00
    from money in the treasury not otherwise appropriated.

10. Act of March 3, 1819, appropriates for existing claims and contracts....................... 250,000 00
    Completing road............................. 285,000 00
    To be paid from reserved funds, acts admitting Ohio, Indiana, and Illinois.

11. Act of May 15, 1820, appropriates for laying out the road between Wheeling, Va., and a point on the left bank of the Mississippi river, between St. Louis and the mouth of the Illinois river, road to be eighty feet wide and on a straight line, and authorizes the President to appoint Commissioners. To be paid out of any money in the treasury not otherwise appropriated.............. 10,000 00

12. Act of April 11, 1820, appropriates for completing contract for road from Washington, Pa., to Wheeling, out of any money in the treasury not otherwise appropriated.......................... 141,000 00

13. Act of February 28, 1823, appropriates for repairs between Cumberland and Wheeling, and authorizes the President to appoint a superintendent at a compensation of $3.00 per day. To be paid out of money not otherwise appropriated............. 25,000 00

Carried forward $1,737,771 20

Brought forward.............................$1,737,771 20

14. Act of March 3, 1825, appropriates for opening
and making a road from the town of Canton, in
the State of Ohio, opposite Wheeling, to Zanesville, and for the completion of the surveys of the
road, directed to be made by the act of May 15,
1820, and orders its extension to the permanent
seat of government of Missouri, and to pass by the
seats of government of Ohio, Indiana, and Illinois,
said road to commence at Zanesville, Ohio; also
authorizes the appointment of a superintendent
by the President, at a salary of $1,500 per annum,
who shall make all contracts, receive and disburse
all moneys, &c.; also authorizes the appointment
of one commissioner, who shall have power according to provisions of the act of May 15, 1820;
$10,000 of the money appropriated by this act is to
be expended in completing the survey mentioned.
The whole sum appropriated to be advanced from
moneys not otherwise appropriated, and replaced
from reserve fund, acts admitting Ohio, Indiana,
Illinois, and Missouri.........................   150,000 00

15. Act of March 14, 1826 (General Appropriation
Bill), appropriates for balance due superintendent,
$3,000; assistant superintendent, $158.90; contractor, $252.13.............................   3,411 03
from moneys not otherwise appropriated.

16. Act of March 25, 1826 (Military Service), appro-
propriates for continuation of the Cumberland
Road during the year 1825...................   110,749 00

17. Act of March 2, 1827 (Military Service), appropriates for construction of road from Canton to Zanesville, and continuing and completing the survey
from Zanesville to the seat of government of Missouri, to be paid from reserve fund, acts admitting
Ohio, Indiana, Illinois, and Missouri...........   170,000 00
For balance due superintendent, from moneys not
otherwise appropriated 510 00

18. Act of March 2, 1827, appropriates for repairs between Cumberland and Wheeling, and authorizes
the appointment of a superintendent of repairs, at
a compensation to be fixed by the President. To
be paid from moneys not otherwise appropriated.
The language of this act is, "For repairing the
public road from Cumberland to Wheeling".....   30,000 00

Carried forward $2,202,441 23

	Brought forward	$2,202,441 23
19.	Act of May 19, 1828, appropriates for the completion of the road to Zanesville, Ohio, to be paid from fund, acts admitting Ohio, Indiana, Illinois, and Missouri	175,000 00
20.	Act of March 2, 1829, appropriates for opening road westwardly, from Zanesville, Ohio, to be paid from fund, acts admitting Ohio, Indiana, Illinois, and Missouri	100,000 00
21.	Act of March 2, 1829, appropriates for opening road eighty feet wide in Indiana, east and west from Indianapolis, and to appoint two superintendents, at $800 each per annum, to be paid from fund, acts admitting Ohio, Indiana, Illinois, and Missouri	51,600 00
22.	Act of March 3, 1829, appropriates for repairing bridges, &c., on road east of Wheeling	100,000 00
23.	Act of May 31, 1830 (Internal Improvements), appropriates for opening and grading road west of Zanesville, Ohio, $100,000; for opening and grading road in Indiana, $60,000, commencing at Indianapolis, and progressing with the work to the eastern and western boundaries of said State; for opening, grading, &c., in Illinois, $40,000, to be paid from reserve fund, acts admitting Ohio, Indiana, Illinois, and Missouri; for claims due and remaining unpaid on account of road east of Wheeling, $15,000; to be paid from moneys in the treasury not otherwise appropriated	215,000 00

To this act is appended the following note:

"I approve this bill, and ask a reference to my communication to Congress of this date in relation thereto.

"ANDREW JACKSON."*

	Carried forward	$2,844,041 23

*The following is the communication referred to by President Jackson:

SPECIAL MESSAGE.

MAY 30, 1830.

To the Senate of the United States :

Gentlemen : I have approved and signed the bill entitled "An act making appropriations for examinations and surveys, and also for certain works of internal improvement," but as the phraseology of the section, which appropriates the sum of eight thousand dollars for the road from Detroit to Chicago, may be construed to authorize the application of the appropriation for the continuance of the road beyond the limits of the territory of Michigan, I desire to be understood as having approved this bill with the understanding that the road, authorized by this section, is not to be extended beyond the limits of the said territory. ANDREW JACKSON.

Brought forward...........................$2,844,041 23

24. Act of March 2, 1831, appropriates $100,000 for
     opening, grading, &c., west of Zanesville, Ohio;
     $950 for repairs during the year 1830; $2,700 for
     work heretofore done east of Zanesville; $265.85
     for arrearages for the survey from Zanesville to
     the capital of Missouri; and $75,000 for opening,
     grading, &c., in the State of Indiana, including
     bridge over White river, near Indianapolis, and
     progressing to eastern and western boundaries;
     $66,000 for opening, grading, and bridging in Illi-
     nois; to be paid from the fund, acts admitting Ohio,
     Indiana, Illinois, and Missouri..................   244,915 85

25. Act of July 3, 1832, appropriates $150,000 for re-
     pairs east of the Ohio river; $100,000 for contin-
     uing the road west of Zanesville; $100,000 for
     continuing the road in Indiana, including bridge
     over east and west branch of White river: $70,000
     for continuing road in Illinois; to be paid from the
     fund acts admitting Ohio, Indiana and Illinois,.... 420,000 00

26. Act of March 2, 1833, appropriates to carry on
     certain improvements east of the Ohio river, $125,-
     000; in Ohio, west of Zanesville, $130,000; in
     Indiana, $100,000; in Illinois, $70,000; in Vir-
     ginia, $34,440................................   459,440 00

27. Act of June 24, 1834, appropriates $200,000 for
     continuing the road in Ohio; $150,000 for continu-
     ing the road in Indiana; $100,000 for continuing
     the road in Illinois, and $300,000 for the entire
     completion of repairs east of Ohio, to meet provi-
     sions of the Acts of Pennsylvania (April 4, 1831).
     Maryland (Jan. 23, 1832), and Virginia (Feb.
     7, 1832), accepting the road surrendered to the
     States, the United States not thereafter to be sub-
     ject for any expense for repairs. Places engineer
     officer of army in control of road through Indi-
     ana and Illinois, and in charge of all appropria-
     tions. $300,000 to be paid out of any money in
     the Treasury not otherwise appropriated, balance
     from acts admitting Ohio, Indiana and Illinois...   750,000 00

28. Act of June 27, 1837, (General Appropriation) for
     arrearages due contractors...................   1,609 36

29. Act of March 3, 1835, appropriates $200,000 for
     continuing the road in the State of Ohio; $100,000
     for continuing road in the State of Indiana; to be

Carried forward $4,720,006 44

Brought forward $4,720,006 44

out of fund acts admitting Ohio, Indiana and Illinois, and $346,186.58 for the entire completion of repairs in Maryland, Pennsylvania and Virginia; but before any part of this sum can be expended east of the Ohio river, the road shall be surrendered to and accepted by the States through which it passes, and the United States shall not thereafter be subject to any expense in relation to said road. Out of any money in the Treasury not otherwise appropriated 646,186 58

30. Act of March 3, 1835, (Repair of Roads) appropriates to pay for work heretofore done by Isaiah Frost on the Cumberland Road, $320; to pay late Superintendent of road a salary, $862.87 .... 1,182 87

31. Act of July 2, 1836, appropriates for continuing the road in Ohio, $200,000; for continuing road in Indiana, $250,000, including materials for a bridge over the Wabash river; $150,000 for continuing the road in Illinois, provided that the appropriation for Illinois shall be limited to grading and bridging, and shall not be construed as pledging Congress to future appropriations for the purpose of macadamizing the road, and the moneys herein appropriated for said road in Ohio and Indiana must be expended in completing the greatest possible continuous portion of said road in said States so that said finished part thereof may be surrendered to the States respectively; to be paid from acts admitting Ohio, Indiana, Illinois and Missouri 600,000 00

32. Act of March 3, 1837, appropriates $190,000 for continuing the road in Ohio; $100,000 for continuing the road in Indiana; $100,000 for continuing road in Illinois, provided the road in Illinois shall not be stoned or graveled, unless it can be done at a cost not greater than the average cost of stoning and graveling the road in Ohio and Indiana, and provided that in all cases where it can be done the work to be laid off in sections and let to the lowest substantial bidder. Sec. 2 of the act provides that Sec. 2 of act of July 2, 1836, shall not be applicable to expenditures hereafter made on the road, and $7,183.63 is appropriated by this act for repairs east of the Ohio river; to be paid from the acts admitting Ohio, Indiana and Illinois 397,183 63

Carried forward $6,364,559 52

Brought forward..........................$6,364,559 52

33. Act of May 25, 1838, appropriates for continuing
the road in Ohio, $150,000; for continuing it in
Indiana, including bridges, $150,000; for continu-
ing it in Illinois, $9,000; for the completion of a
bridge over Dunlap's creek at Brownsville; to be
paid from moneys in the Treasury not otherwise
appropriated and subject to provisions and conditions of act of March 3, 1837................. 459,000 00

34. Act of June 17, 1844, (Civil and Diplomatic) appropriates for arrearages on account of survey to
Jefferson, Mo............................... 1.359 81

Total................................$6,824,919 33

Note—The appropriation of $3,786 60, made by act of Feb. 26, 1812, is
not included in the above total for the reason that it was a balance from a
former appropriation.

The act of March 3, 1843, appropriates so much as is necessary to settle
certain claims on contract for building bridges over Kaskaskia river and constructing part of Cumberland Road.

HON. T. M. T. McKENNAN.

CHAPTER XV.

*Speech of Hon. **T. M. T.** McKennan, delivered in Congress, June 6, 1832 — The Road a Monument of National Wealth and Greatness —A Bond of Union — Business of the Road — Five Thousand Wagons unload in Wheeling in a single year — Facilities afforded by the Road for transporting the Mails and Munitions of War.*

This road, Mr. Speaker (the National Road), is a *magnificent one* — magnificent in extent; it traverses seven different States of this Union, and its whole distance will cover an extent of near eight hundred miles. Magnificent in the difficulties overcome by the wealth of a nation, and in the benefits and advantages and blessings which it diffuses, east and west, far and wide, through the whole country. It is, sir, *a splendid monument of national wealth and national greatness, and of the deep interest felt by the government in the wealth and prosperity and happiness of the people.*

It is not, sir, like the stupendous monuments of other countries and of other times, which have been erected merely for the purpose of show and of gratifying the pride of some despotic monarch; but this and all similar national improvements are *works of utility; they tend to cement the bond of union; they bring together the distant parts of this exalted republic; they diffuse wealth and happiness among a free people, and will be a source of never failing prosperity to millions yet unborn.*

It is, sir, *a great commercial, military, mail, national work.* To give the House, or those of its members who are unacquainted with the fact, some idea of the immense commercial advantages which the eastern as well as the western country has derived from the construction of this road, let me call their attention to the amount of merchandise transported to the Ohio river in a single year after its completion; and here, sir, I avail myself of an estimate made by an honorable member of the other House on another occasion, when he strongly urged the propriety and importance of the extension of the road through the State of Ohio.

In the year 1822, shortly after the completion of the road, a single house in the town of Wheeling unloaded 1,081 wagons, averaging about 3,500 pounds each, and paid for the carriage of the goods $90,000. At that time there were five other commission houses in the same place, and estimating that each of them received two-thirds the amount of goods consigned to the other, there must have been nearly 5,000 wagons unloaded, and nearly $400,000 paid as the cost of transportation. But, further, it is estimated that at least every tenth wagon passed through that place into the interior of Ohio, Indiana, &c., which would considerably swell the amount. These wagons take their return loads and carry to the eastern markets all the various articles of production and manufacture of the West—their flour, whisky, hemp, tobacco, bacon, and wool. Since this estimate was made, the town of Wheeling is greatly enlarged; its population has nearly doubled; the number of its commercial establishments has greatly increased; and the demand for merchandise in the West has increased with the wealth and improvement and prosperity of the country.

But, further, sir,-before the completion of this road, from four to six weeks were usually occupied in the transportation of goods from Baltimore to the Ohio river, and the price varied from six to ten dollars per hundred. Now they can be carried in less than half the time and at one-half the cost, and arrangements are making by some enterprising gentlemen of the West to have the speed of transportation still increased, and the price of carriage diminished.

Equally important are the benefits derived by the government and the people from the rapid, regular, and safe transportation of the mail on this road. Before its completion, eight or more days were occupied in transporting the mail from Baltimore to Wheeling; it was then carried on horseback, and did not reach the western country by this route more than once a week. Now it is carried in comfortable stages, protected from the inclemency of the weather, in forty-eight hours; and no less than twenty-eight mails weekly and regularly pass and repass each other on this road. To show this fact, and the absolute necessity and importance of keeping the road in a good state of repair, in order to enable the postoffice department to fulfill the expectations of the public, I will ask the favor of the clerk to read to the House a communication received from the Postmaster General on the subject. [Here the clerk read an extract from a letter of the Postmaster General]. The facilities afforded by such a road in time of war for the transportation of the munitions of war, and the means of defence from one point of the country to another, need scarcely be noticed; they must be palpable and plain to every reflecting mind, and I will not take up the time of the House in detailing them.

As I said before, the road traverses seven different States of this Union, and in its whole extent will cover a distance of near 800 miles. Who, then, can doubt its nationality? Who can question the allegation that it is an immensely important national work? *Who can reconcile it to his conscience and his constituents to permit it to go to destruction?*

CHAPTER XVI.

Life on the Road — Origin of the Phrase Pike Boys — Slaves Driven Like Horses — Race Distinction at the Old Taverns — Old Wagoners — Regulars and Sharpshooters — Line Teams — John Snider, John Thompson, Daniel Barcus, Robert Bell, Henry Clay Rush, and other Familiar Names.

As the phrase "Pike Boys" is frequently used in this volume, it is considered pertinent to give its origin. When first used, it was confined in its application to boys — sons of wagoners, stage drivers, tavern keepers, farmers, and in fact the sons of persons of every occupation who lived on or adjacent to the road, in the same sense that the boys of a town are called "town boys." Its meaning and import, however, expanded in course of time, until it embraced, as it now does, all persons in any manner and at any time identified with the road, whether by residence or occupation, and without "regard to age, race, color or previous condition of servitude," as the statute puts it, for be it remembered that negro slaves were frequently seen on the National Road. The writer has seen them driven over the road arranged in couples and fastened to a long, thick rope or cable, like horses. This may seem incredible to a majority of persons now living along the road, but it is true, and was a very common sight in the early history of the road and evoked no expression of surprise, or words of censure. Such was the temper of the times. There were negro wagoners on the road, but negro stage drivers were unknown. Stage driving was quite a lofty calling, and the acme of many a young man's ambition. The work was light and the whirl exciting and exhilarating. Wagoners, white and black, stopped over night at the same taverns, but never sat down together at the same table. A separate table was invariably provided for the colored wagoners, a custom in thorough accord with the public sentiment of the time, and seemingly agreeable to the colored wagoners themselves. Country life in the olden time was enlivened by numerous corn huskings, balls, spelling matches, school exhibitions and frolics of all kinds. Young men and boys along the road, were in the habit of attending these gatherings, going as far as three miles and more in the back country, to reach them, some on foot and others on horseback. A young man would think nothing of getting a girl up behind him on a horse, and hieing away after nightfall, four and five miles to a country dance, and many of the girls of the period considered it but pleasant recreation to walk two or three miles with their lovers, to a

6 (109)

spelling match or a revival meeting. A feeling of jealousy always existed between the young men and boys, living along and near the road, and those in the back country, and the occasions before mentioned furnished opportunities from time to time for this feeling to break out, as it often did, in quarrels and fights. The country boys would get together in anticipation of an approaching gathering at some school house, and organize for offense or defense, as the exigencies might require, always calling their rivals and imaginary enemies, "Pike Boys," and this was the origin of that familiar phrase.

The men who hauled merchandise over the road were invariably called wagoners, not teamsters, as is the modern word, and they were both, since Webster defines wagoner as one who conducts a wagon, and teamster as one who drives a team. The teams of the old wagoners consisting, as a rule, of six horses, were very rarely stabled, but rested over night on the wagon yards of the old taverns, no matter how inclement the weather. Blankets were used to protect them in the winter season. Feed troughs were suspended at the rear end of the wagon bed, and carried along in this manner, day after day all the year round. In the evening, when the day's journey was ended, the troughs were taken down and fastened on the tongues of the wagon to which the horses were tied, three on a side, with their heads to the trough. Wagoners carried their beds, rolled up, in the forepart of the wagon, and spread them out in a semi-circle on the bar room floor in front of the big bar room fire upon going to rest. Some of the old bar room grates would hold as much as six bushels of coal, and iron pokers from four to six feet in length, weighing eight and ten pounds, were used for stirring the fires. To get down an icy hill with safety, it was necessary to use an ice cutter, a rough lock, or a clevis, and sometimes all combined, contingent upon the thickness and smoothness of the ice, and the length and steepness of the hill. The ice cutter was of steel or iron, in appearance like a small sled, fitted on the hind wheels, which were first securely locked. The rough lock was a short chain with large, rough links, and the clevis was like that used on an ordinary plow, except that it was larger and stronger. These instruments were essential parts of the wagoners' "outfit." There were two classes of wagoners, the "regular" and the "sharpshooter." The regular was on the road constantly with his team and wagon, and had no other pursuit than hauling goods and merchandise on the road. The sharpshooters were for the most part farmers, who put their farm teams on the road in seasons when freights were high, and took them off when prices of hauling declined; and there was jealousy between the two classes. The regular drove his team about fifteen miles a day on the average, while the sharpshooter could cover twenty miles and more. Line teams were those controlled by an association or company. Many of the regular wagoners became members of these companies and put in their teams. The main object of the combination was to transport goods more rapidly than by the ordinary method. Line teams were sta-

JOHN THOMPSON.

tioned along the road, at distances of about fifteen miles, and horses were exchanged after the manner of the stage lines. Many of the old wagoners had bull-dogs tied at the rear of their wagons, and these dogs were often seen pressing with all their strength against the collar about their necks, as if to aid the horses in moving their load; and this is probably the origin of the common form of boast about a man being equal in strength to "a six-horse team with a cross dog under the wagon."

The whip used by old wagoners was apparently five feet long, thick and hard at the butt, and tapering rapidly to the end in a silken cracker. Battley White, of Centerville, Washington county, Pa., made more of these whips than any other man on the road. The interior of his whip was a raw hide. John Morrow, of Petersburg, Somerset county, Pa., also made many whips for the old wagoners. There was another whip, much used by old wagoners, known as the "Loudon Whip." The inner portion of this whip was an elastic wooden stock, much approved by the wagoners. It was manufactured in the village of Loudon, Franklin county, Pa., and hence its name. It was used almost exclusively on what was called the "Glade Road," from Philadelphia to Pittsburg, via Chambersburg and Bedford.

Some of the old wagoners of the National Road became rich. John Snider was one of these. He drove a six-horse team on the road for twenty years, and died on his farm near Uniontown in December, 1889, much lamented. Few men possessed more of the higher attributes of true manhood than John Snider. The author of this volume gratefully and cheerfully acknowledges his indebtedness to John Snider for many of the facts and incidents it contains. He was a clear-headed, intelligent, sober, discreet, and observing man, whose statements could be relied on as accurate.

It would be an impossible task to collect the names of all the old wagoners of the National Road. They number thousands, and many of them left the road long since to seek fortunes in new and distant sections of our widely extended country. The most of them have gone to scenes beyond the boundaries of time. It is the author's aim to collect as many of their names as is practicable and write them down in history. The names of John Thompson, James Noble, and John Flack are recalled. These worthy old wagoners are still living in the vicinity of Taylorstown, Washington county, Pa., and highly respected by all their neighbors. The point at which they first entered upon the road was the famous "S" bridge. Thompson drove his father's team when quite young, in fact, a mere boy. The first trip he made over the road was in the spring of 1843, in company with the veteran wagoner, George Hallam, of Washington, Pa. Thompson's father was a pork packer, and the youthful wagoner's "down loads," as those moving eastwardly were called, consisted for the most part of bacon. His recollections of the road are vivid, and warmly cherished. He can sit down in a room, at his comfortable home, and "in his mind's eye" see every mile post along the road and recall the distances to points inscribed thereon. In the year 1852, he went to California, engaged in mining, and was successful. With the instinct planted in every human breast, he returned to his native land, and with his accumulations bought his father's homestead farm. The old farm enhanced in value by reason of the oil developments, and landed the old wagoner in the ranks of the rich.

The name Noble is a familiar one on the National Road, and suggestive of rank. "Watty" and William Noble were stage drivers. James Noble, the old wagoner, drove a team for the late Hon. Isaac Hodgens, who was at one time a pork salter. He remained on the road as a wagoner until its tide of business ceased, and retired to Taylorstown to take his chances in the on-moving and uncertain affairs of life. He seemed possessed of the idea that there was undeveloped wealth in the vicinity of Taylorstown, and made up his mind to gain a foothold there and wait the coming of events. He managed by the exercise of industry and economy to become the owner of a farm, and the discovery of oil did the rest for him. He is rich.

John Flack's career is similar to those of Thompson and Noble, culminating in like good fortune. "He struck oil, too."

We have in the story of these old wagoners, examples of the possibilities for achievement, under the inspiring genius of American institutions. Poor boys, starting out in life as wagoners, with wages barely sufficient for their subsistence, pushing on and up with ceaseless vigilance, attaining the dignity of farmers, in all ages the highest type of industrial life, and now each bearing, though meekly, the proud title of "freeholder," which Mr. Blaine said in his celebrated eulogium of Garfield, "has been the patent and passport of self-respect with the Anglo-Saxon race ever since Horsa and Hengist landed on the shores of England."

Otho and Daniel Barcus, brothers, were among the prominent wagoners of the road. They lived near Frostburg, Md. Otho died at Barton, Md., in 1883. Daniel is now living in retirement at Salisbury, Somerset county, Pa. In 1838 he engaged with John Hopkins, merchant at the foot of Light and Pratt streets, Baltimore, to haul a load of general merchandise, weighing 8,300 pounds, to Mt. Vernon, Ohio. "He delivered the goods in good condition" at the end of thirty days from the date of his departure from Baltimore. His route was over the National Road to Wheeling, thence by Zanesville and Jacktown, Ohio, thence thirty-two miles from the latter place to the point of destination, the whole distance being 397 miles. He received $4.25 per hundred for hauling the goods. At Mt. Vernon he loaded back with Ohio tobacco, 7,200 pounds in hogsheads, for which he received $2.75 per hundred. On the return trip he upset, between Mt. Vernon and Jacktown, without sustaining any damage, beyond the breaking of a bow of his wagon bed, and the loss caused by detention. The expense of getting in shape for pursuing his journey, was the price of a gallon of whisky. Mt. Vernon is not on the line of the road, and Mr. Barcus writes that "when he reached

DANIEL BARCUS.

the National Road at Jacktown, he felt at home again." Mr. Barcus also states in a letter to the writer of these pages, that the first lot of goods shipped over the Baltimore and Ohio railway, after its completion to Cumberland, destined for Wheeling, was consigned to Shriver and Dixon, commission merchants of Cumberland, and by that firm consigned to Forsythe and Son, of Wheeling. This lot of goods aggregated 6,143 pounds, an average load for a six-horse team, and Mr. Barcus contracted with Shriver and Dixon to haul it through to Wheeling in six days for fifty cents a hundred, which he accomplished. He further states that a delegation of wholesale and retail merchants of Wheeling met him at Steenrod's tavern, east of Wheeling Hill, and escorted him to town, then a place of 4,000 or 5,000 inhabitants, and in the evening there was public rejoicing over the unprecedented event of goods reaching Wheeling from Baltimore in the short space of seven days. Mr. Barcus concludes his letter as follows: " I stayed many nights at Hopwood with Wilse Clement, and many with Natty Brownfield, in Uniontown. I often stayed with Arthur Wallace, five miles east of Brownsville. I remember one night at Wallace's, after caring for my team, I accompanied his two fine and handsome daughters to a party about a mile distant in the country, where I danced all night, till broad daylight, and then walked home with the girls in the morning."

John Grace was another old wagoner, who became wealthy. The old pike boys will remember him as the driver of a black team. He was a Maryland man. When the old road yielded its grasp on trade, to the iron railway, Grace settled in or near Zanesville, Ohio, where he still lives, or was living a few years ago, worth a hundred thousand dollars. He transported his family to Ohio in his big road wagon.

Jesse Franks, and his son Conrad, of High House, Fayette county, Pa., were old wagoners. Conrad's team ran off near Cumberland, on one of his trips, overthrowing the wagon, and causing an ugly dislocation of Conrad's thigh, from which he suffered great pain for many weeks.

John Manaway, late owner of the Spottsylvania House, Uniontown, drove a team on the road for many years, and no man enjoyed the business more than he.

There was an Ohio man of the name of Lucas, called Gov. Lucas, because a man of like name was an early Governor of Ohio, who was an old wagoner, and his team consisted of but five horses, yet he hauled the biggest loads on the road. He was the owner of the team he drove. In the year 1844, one of his loads weighed twelve thousand pounds—"one hundred and twenty hundred," as the old wagoners termed it, and the biggest load ever hauled over the road up to that date.

William King, of Washington county, Pa., an old wagoner, was noted for his steady habits. On one of his trips over the road, and going down the eastern slope of Laurel Hill, when it was covered with ice, his wagon slipped from the road and fell over the bank near the old Price residence, dragging the team after it. Strange to say, the horses were uninjured and but little damage done to the wagon. The contents of the load were Ohio tobacco and bacon. After getting things restored, King drove to Jimmy Snyder's, stayed all night, and the next morning proceeded on his journey to Baltimore. He was the owner of a farm in Washington county.

Joseph Thompson, an old wagoner on the road, is now and has been for many years in charge of the large and valuable coal farm belonging to the estate of the Hon. James G. Blaine, on the Monongahela river, near Pittsburg. A trusty old wagoner, he has approved himself the trusty agent of the great statesman.

Jacob Probasco was an old wagoner, and also kept a tavern at Jockey Hollow. He went west and founded a fortune.

Joseph Lawson, an old wagoner, kept tavern for many years in West Alexander, Washington county, Pa., and died the possessor of a valuable estate. The author of this book took dinner, in 1848, at Lawson's tavern, in company with James G. Blaine, the late distinguished Secretary of State.

Matthias Fry, an old wagoner, kept the Searight House in 1840, and subsequently presided as landlord over several houses at different times in Hopwood. He was one of the best men on the road. His large and well proportioned form will be readily recalled by the old pike boys. He was a native of Old Virginia, and died in Hopwood.

David Hill was one of the most noted wagoners of the road. He was an active, bustling man, and given to witty sayings. He belonged to Washington county, Pa., and was the father of Dr. Hill, of Vanderbilt, and the father-in-law of the Rev. J. K. Melhorn, who preached for many years in the vicinity of McClellandtown, Fayette county, Pa.

Andrew Prentice, who died recently in Uniontown, the possessor of considerable money, drove a team on the old road in his early days.

Henry Clay Rush, a prominent citizen of Uniontown, and ex-jury commissioner, was once the proud driver of a big six-horse team. He drove through from Baltimore to Wheeling, and can recount incidents of every mile of the road to this day. None of the old pike boys enjoys with keener relish a recital of the stories of the old pike than Rush.

William Worthington, who died not long since in Dunbar township, Fayette county, Pa., aged upwards of ninety years, was one of the earliest wagoners on the road. When he made his first trip he was only thirteen years old, and the road was then recently opened for travel. He continued as a wagoner on the road for many years, and located in Dunbar township, where he purchased property, which subsequently became very valuable by reason of the coal development.

William Chenriewith, who recently, and probably at the present time, keeps a hotel near Bedford Springs, was an old wagoner of the National Road.

HENRY CLAY RUSH.

John Thomas, who kept a hotel and livery stable in Baltimore, was an old wagoner, and is well remembered along the road.

George Buttermore, father of Dr. Smith Buttermore, of Connellsville, was at one time a wagoner on the National Road.

John Orr, now a prosperous and well-known farmer of the vicinity of West Newton, Westmoreland county, Pa., was an old wagoner of the road.

James Murray, an old wagoner, is remembered for his extravagance of speech. One of his sayings was, that "he saw the wind blow so hard on Keyser's Ridge, that it took six men to hold the hair on one man's head."

E. W. Clement, of Hopwood, was an old wagoner, and invariably used bells on his horses. He subsequently kept a tavern in Hopwood, and built the house there known as the "Shipley House."

Robert Bell was an old wagoner with quaint ways. He was rich, and owned his team, which was the poorest equipped of any on the road. Horses in his team were not infrequently seen without bridles. He was a trader, and often bought the goods he hauled and sold them out to people along the road. His reputation for honesty was good, but he was called "Stingy Robert."

George Widdle, an old wagoner of the age of eighty and upwards, still living in Wheeling, drew the single line and handled the Loudon whip over a six-horse team for many years, between Wheeling and Baltimore, and accounts the days of those years the happiest of his existence. He was also a stage driver for a time. Nothing affords him so much pleasure as a recital of the incidents of the road. He says there never were such taverns and tavern keepers as those of the National Road in the days of its glory, and of his vigorous manhood.

James Butler, like Bell, was a trader. Butler drove a "bell team," as teams with bells were called. He was a Virginian, from the vicinity of Winchester. It was the tradition of the road that he had a slight infusion of negro blood in his veins, and this assigned him to the side table of the dining room. When he quit the road he returned to Winchester, started a store, and got rich.

Neither tradition or kindred evidence was necessary to prove the race status of Westley Strother. He showed up for himself. He was as black as black could be, and a stalwart in size and shape. He was well liked by all the old wagoners, and by every one who knew him. He was mild in manner, and honest in purpose. He had the strongest affection for the road, delighted in its stirring scenes, and when he saw the wagons and the wagoners, one after another, departing from the old highway, he repined and prematurely died at Uniontown.

CHAPTER XVII.

Old Wagoners continued —Harrison Wiggins, Morris Mauler, James Mauler, John Marker, John Bradley, Robert Carter, R. D. Kerfoot, Jacob F. Longanecker, Ellis B. Woodward — Broad and Narrow Wheels — A peculiar Wagon — An experiment and a failure — Wagon Beds — Bell Teams.

Harrison Wiggins, widely known as a lover of fox hunting, and highly respected as a citizen, was one of the early wagoners. His career as a wagoner ceased long before the railroad reached Cumberland. He hauled goods from Baltimore to points west. His outfit, team and wagon, were owned by himself and his father, Cuthbert Wiggins. Harrison Wiggins was born in the old Gribble house, two miles east of Brownsville, on the 30th of April, 1812. About the year 1817 his father moved to Uniontown, and kept a tavern in a frame building which stood on the lot adjoining the residence of P. S. Morrow, Esq. He remained here until 1821, when he went to the stone house at the eastern base of Chalk Hill, and was its first occupant. His house at Uniontown numbered among its patrons, Hon. Nathaniel Ewing, Samuel Cleavenger, Mr. Bouvier, John A. Sangston, John Kennedy, John Lyon, and other eminent men of that period. In 1832 or '33, Harrison Wiggins married a daughter of John Risler, a noted tavern keeper of the road, one of the very best, a talent which descended to his children. At the date of the marriage Mr. Risler was keeping the stone house at Braddock's run, and the wedding occurred in that house. In 1839 Harrison Wiggins went to Iowa, with a view of locating in that State, but returned the next year and leased the property on which he now lives from Charles Griffith. In ten years thereafter he bought this property, and it has been his home for more than half a century. Under the careful and sagacious management of Mr. Wiggins, it has become one of the prettiest and most valuable properties in the mountains. It has been a long time since he was a wagoner, but he enjoys a recital of the stirring scenes he witnessed on the old road in the days of its glory.

There is not a more familiar name among the old pike boys than that of Morris Mauler. He was an old wagoner, stage driver and tavern keeper. He was born in Uniontown in the year 1806. The house in which he first beheld the light of day, was a log building on the Skiles corner, kept as a tavern by his father. Before he reached the age of twenty-one he was on the road with a six-horse team and

HARRISON WIGGINS.

a big wagon, hauling goods from the city of Baltimore to points west. He continued a wagoner for many years, and afterward became a stage driver. He drove on Stockton's line. From stage driving he went to tavern keeping. His first venture as a tavern keeper was at Mt. Washington, when the old tavern stand at that point was owned by the late Hon. Nathaniel Ewing. He subsequently and successively kept the old Probasco house at Jockey Hollow, the old Gaither house, the Yeast house, and a house in Hopwood. He always furnished good entertainment for strangers and travelers, as well as for friends and acquaintances, and as a consequence, was well patronized. He died about seven years ago at Fairchance, and when his light went out a shadow of sorrow passed over the hearts of all the old pike boys.

James Mauler, a son of Morris, above mentioned, is also an old wagoner. He went on the road with a team in the year 1830, and remained on it as long as he could obtain a load of goods to haul over it. He is still living and in robust health, at Brownfield station, four miles south of Uniontown.

John Marker, now residing in the east end of Uniontown, is an old wagoner. He was born at the Little Crossings in the State of Maryland, in the year 1816, and while yet a lad began to drive a team on the road for Joseph Plucker. In 1839 he quit the service of Plucker and came to Wharton township, Fayette county, Pa., and soon thereafter began driving again, first for Sebastian Rush and next for Nicholas McCartney. He is a near relative of the Shipley, McCollough and McCartney families, all of the old pike. Marker says he never suffered an "upset" himself, but saw a great many "upsets" on the road. He also states that he saw a stage driver killed near Little Crossings in 1835 by the "running off" of his team and the "upsetting" of the coach. The name of this unfortunate stage driver was James Rhodes, and he drove on Stockton's line. John Marker, in his prime, was one of the stoutest men on the road, upwards of six feet in height, and rounded out in proportion, but, being of an amiable temperament, he never engaged in broils, realizing, no doubt, and acting upon the poetic sentiment that:

> "It is excellent to have a giant's strength,
> But tyrannous to use it as a giant."

He still clings to the old road, breaking stone to repair it, when his health will permit. He is in the 76th year of his age.

John Bradley, brother of Daniel, of Jockey Hollow, is an old wagoner. He drove a team for Benjamin Brownfield, Jr., now residing near Newark, Ohio., son of Col. Ben., the centennarian of South Union township, and grand marshal of Democratic processions of the olden time. John Bradley also worked on the construction of the Baltimore and Ohio railroad in 1839, near Oldtown, Md., fifteen miles east of Cumberland. His employer on this work was the late Zalmon Ludington, of Uniontown, who had a contract at the point mentioned. John Bradley is now living in the city of Pittsburg.

6ª

Robert Carter was a well known old wagoner, a native of Washington county, Pa., a "regular," and a very energetic, persevering and keen sighted man. He took a prominent part in many of the festivities of the old road, but never lost his head. He was a money maker, and unlike most of that class, kind hearted and generous. He married the eldest daughter of Thomas Moxley, the old tavern keeper, whose house was three miles west of Uniontown. After his marriage he bought a small farm, known as the Solomon Colley farm, near Hatfield's, in Redstone township, Fayette county, Pa., subsequently merged in the Hatfield estate. He operated this farm for a short time, but while engaged as a farmer, kept his team on the road in charge of a hired driver. He sold his farm and leased the Bar house in Bridgeport, and kept tavern there for some time. When business ceased on the road, he gave up his team and his tavern, and moved with his family to Iowa, where he engaged extensively in farming and stock raising.

R. D. Kerfoot, the well known miner and labor leader of Everson, was at one time a wagoner on the National Road. He was born in Lancaster county, Pa., and before reaching the full stature of manhood in point of age, went to Washington county, Md., where he engaged as a driver for one J. B. Bear, a farmer of that county and State, and was put in charge of a fine six-horse team, and a broad wheeled wagon, with which he hauled goods, wares and merchandise to and from Baltimore and Wheeling. He enjoyed the stirring scenes of the old road, and recalls with a keen relish the bounteous tables of the old taverns.

Jacob F. Longanecker, who served as county commissioner of Fayette county, Pa., from 1854 to 1857, was an old wagoner. He owned a farm in German township, and was a good practical farmer, but spent much of his time, for many years, on the road with his team. He enjoyed life on the road, and seemed loath to relinquish the occupation of a wagoner.

Ellis B. Woodward, of Menallen township, Fayette county, Pa., is an old wagoner with experience hardly sufficient to entitle him to be classed as a "regular," and yet almost enough to take him from the list of "sharp-shooters." He kept his big road wagon on his farm for many years after the road ceased to be a profitable avenue of transportation, and felt a pride in exhibiting it as a reminder of his identification with the great highway, in the days of its prosperity. He still lives and warmly cherishes the memories of the old road.

The first wagons used on the National Road were made with narrow rimmed wheels, like those in use at the present day on farms and country roads. It was not long, however, after the opening of the road, until the broad wheeled, or "broad tread wagon," as it was called, was introduced, and came into general use by the "regulars." The "sharpshooters," as a rule, retained the narrow tread, as their wagons were designed mainly for farm service. The width of the broad tread was about four inches, and lighter tolls were exacted at

JOHN MARKER.

the gates from broad than from narrow tread wagons for the obvious reason that narrow wheels cut deeper into the road than broad wheels.

A gentleman of Wheeling interested in the transportation business at one time, conceived the idea of constructing a wagon that would make so wide a track as to be allowed to pass over the road for a very low rate of toll, if not entirely exempt. His model was a wagon with the rear axle four inches shorter than the front one, so that a track was made of eight inches in width. To this wagon nine horses were attached — three abreast. It passed over the road several times, with Joseph Sopher as driver, attracting much attention, but turning out a failure as well in the matter of saving toll as in being an impracticable vehicle of transportation.

The bed of the regular road wagon was long and deep, bending upward at the bottom in front and rear. The lower broad side was painted blue, with a movable board inserted above, painted red. The covering was of white canvas stretched over broad wooden bows, so that the old road wagon, probably more as a matter of taste than design, disclosed the tri-colors of the American escutcheon, red, white and blue.

An average load was 6,000 pounds, but loads weighing 10,000 pounds, "a hundred hundred," as all old wagoners boastfully put it, were frequently hauled over the road.

The reader who never saw the endless procession on the old pike, in the days of its glory, may have the impression that the bells used by some of the old wagoners on their teams were like sleigh bells, or those of the milk wagon of the present day, and in like manner strapped around the horses. But that was not the way of it. The bells of the old wagoners were cone shaped, with an open end, not unlike a small dinner bell, and were attached to a thin iron arch, sprung over the tops of the hames. The motion of the horses caused a quiver in the arch, and the bell teams moved majestically along the road attracting attention and eliciting admiration. The great majority of wagoners did not use bells.

CHAPTER XVIII.

Old Wagoners continued — John Deets — His story told by himself — David Church —
John Snider loads up with Butter — Billy Ashton, John Bradfield, Frank
Bradfield — An Escapade — William Hall, Henry Puffenberger and Jacob
Breakeron — Collision between a "regular" and a "sharpshooter" — Joseph
Lawson, Jeff. Manypenny, Joseph Arnold, The Sophers, Robert Beggs, Thomas
Gore, and John Whetsel.

John Deets was a wagoner on the road as early as 1826, before
the invention of the rubber, or at least before its application to
wagons on the National Road. He had a brother, Michael, who preceded him as a wagoner on the road. John Deets located in Guernsey county, Ohio, in 1835, whence he went from Menallen township,
Fayette county, Pa. He is still living. The following from his own
pen furnishes a graphic account of life on the road in his day:

MR. SEARIGHT: I will try to give you as much information as I
can at this time. My brother, Michael Deets, about four years older
than myself, was among the first that wagoned on the pike. That
was about the year 1822. He first drove his father's team, and the
first load of goods he hauled from Baltimore was to Uniontown for
Isaac Beeson or Isaac Skiles, I am not certain which. After that he
drove for Abram Beagle, who lived in the west end of Uniontown.
After that he bought a team, and a few years after bought two more,
so that he owned three teams at one time. He drove one of the teams
himself and hired drivers for the other two. The team he drove
himself was a bell team. One of his drivers was George Richards,
and the other, Jesse Barnet, a colored man, who lived in the east end
of Uniontown. When they took up the old bed of the road, and
macadamized it, my brother took a contract and put his teams to
hauling stones. After finishing his contract, he resumed the hauling
of merchandise on the road and continued until about 1837, when he
moved to Ohio, thence to Illinois, and thence to Missouri, where he
died.

The pike boys had some hard times and they had some good
times. They were generally very fond of sport, and mostly tried to
put up where the landlord was a fiddler, so that they could take a
hoe-down. Every one carried his own bed, and after they had all
the sport they wanted they put their beds down on the floor in a circle, with their feet to the fire, and slept like a mouse in a mill. They
were generally very sociable and friendly with each other, but I must

JOHN DEETS.

note one thing just here: Two of the boys met at David Barnett's, some three miles east of Hancock, and got into a dispute, which was not often the case. Elias Meek and Abner Benley were the two. Meek was for fight, Benley was for peace. But Meek pushed on Benley and Benley run, but Meek caught him. Then Benley knew he had to fight, and turned on Meek and gave him a wonderful thrashing, so that he was not able to drive his team for some time. And now with regard to getting up and down the hills. They had no trouble to get up, but the trouble was in getting down, for they had no rubbers then, and to tight lock would soon wear out their tires. They would cut a small pole about 10 or 11 feet long and tie it to the bed with the lock chain and then bend it against the hind wheel and tie it to the feed trough, or the hind part of the wagon bed, just tight enough to let the wheel turn slow. Sometimes one driver would wear out from 15 to 20 poles between Baltimore and Wheeling. Sometimes others would cut down a big tree and tie it to the hind end of the wagon and drop it at the foot of the hill. When there was ice, and there was much of it in winter, they had to use rough locks and cutters, and the wagon would sometimes be straight across the road, if not the hind end foremost. The snow was sometimes so deep that they had to go through fields, and shovel the drifts from the fences, and often had to get sleds to take their loads across Nigger Mountain, and on as far as Hopwood. Those of us who had to go through the fields were three days going nine miles. This was in the neighborhood of Frostburg, Md. There were no bridges then across the Monongahela or the Ohio rivers. Wagoners had to ferry across in small flat-boats, and sometimes to lay at the rivers for some days, until the ice would run out or the river freeze over. A small bridge across Dunlap's creek, at Brownsville, broke down with one of the pike boys and did a great deal of damage. Sometimes a barrel of coffee would spring a leak and the coffee would be scattered along the road, and women would gather it up and be glad for such a prize. The writer has scattered some in his time. Some of the old citizens of Uniontown, no doubt, well remember the time, when scores of poor slaves were driven through that place, handcuffed and tied two and two to a rope that was extended some 40 or 50 feet, one on each side. And thousands of droves of hogs were driven through to Baltimore, some from Ohio. Sometimes they would have to lay by two or three days on account of the frozen road, which cut their feet and lamed them. While the writer was wagoning on the old pike, the canal was made from Cumberland to Harper's Ferry. The pike boys were bitterly opposed to railroads and so were the tavern keepers. The writer heard an old tavern keeper say "he wished the railroad would sink to the lower regions." That great phenomenon that occurred the 13th of November, 1833, or, as it is often called, the Shooting stars. That circumstance caused a great deal of excitement. Some became very much alarmed, and it was reported that some went crazy, and thought the world was coming to an end. The writer was at Hopwood that night with his team and wagon. The phenomenon was also seen in Ohio. It was reported in Ohio that there was a box of money hid on the old Gaddis farm, near the pike, about two miles west of Uniontown, supposed to have been hid there by Gen. Braddock. It was sought for but never found. The taverns we mostly put up at in Baltimore were the Maypole, on Paca street, south of Gen. Wayne, and at Thomas Elliott's, near the Hill market; and where we mostly loaded our goods was at J. Taylor & Sons and at Chauncey Brook's, on Baltimore and Howard streets. Our first day's drive out of Baltimore was 19 miles, to Enoch Randall's, or 20, to John Whalon's. The second day to Frank Wathers—who could almost outswear the world. And one thing more: Before this writer became a pike boy he plowed many a day with a wooden mold-board plow, and after being engaged on the road for about ten years, he left the road and went to Ohio, and then made a public profession of religion and united with the Baptist church. In conclusion, will say to make as good a history as you possibly can, and I hope you shall be well rewarded for your labor, and above all never forget your Creator, as in Him we live, move and have our being.

Yours respectfully,

JOHN DEETS.

David Church was an old wagoner, a native of Wheeling, and when the old pike ceased to ring with the clatter of travel and trade, he purchased a farm in Wharton township, near Farmington, Fayette county, Pa., took up his residence thereon, and died a mountain farmer. He was a large, fat man, of ruddy complexion and reddish hair. The leader in his team was of a dun color, and as it approached the old taverns and the big water-troughs, was recognized as the team of David Church by the color of the leader. Charley Rush often invited Church to take a chair and be seated when he visited the store at Farmington, but he invariably declined, remarking that he could rest as well standing as sitting. He felt like nearly all the old wagoners, that his occupation was gone when transportation ceased on the old road, and could never fully adapt himself to the new order of things.

In the year 1842 John Snider hauled a load of butter from Wheeling to Washington, D. C. The owner of this butter was a man by the name of Oyster, a butter dealer of Wheeling. He could have shipped his butter from Cumberland to its destination by rail, as the Baltimore & Ohio road had just then been finished to Cumberland; but his animosity against railroads was so deep-seated that he engaged Snider to haul it all the way through with his big team. On his way to Washington with this load he struck off from the National Road at Frederick City, Maryland. He reached that city on Christmas night and "put up" at Miller's tavern. The guests of that old tavern danced all of that night, and early in the morning of the day after Christmas, Snider "pulled out" on a strange road for

JOHN SNIDER.

the city of Washington with his load of butter. He was three days on a mud road between Frederick and Washington, but, nevertheless, delivered his butter in "good condition" to the consignee. This butter was bought up in small quantities in the vicinity of Wheeling for ten cents per pound, and Snider got two dollars and fifty cents per hundred pounds for hauling it to Washington.

William Ashton, a well-known old wagoner, was an Englishman by birth. He was also an old tavern keeper. He was noted for his mental vivacity, and for his achievements as an athlete. At Petersburg he once bounded over the top of one of the big road wagons with the aid of a long pole. He kept a tavern at Funkstown, seventy miles west of Baltimore, and was largely patronized by wagoners. While keeping tavern he had two teams on the road in charge of hired drivers. This was as early as 1835. His drivers were Samuel Kelly and William Jones, and they hauled goods from Hagerstown, Maryland (then the terminus of the railroad), to Terre Haute, Indiana, and to Springfield, Illinois, involving a trip of four months duration, and the compensation was six dollars per hundred pounds.

John Bradfield was one of the most prominent old wagoners on the road. He was the general agent of the first transportation company on the road. He was also a tavern keeper. He kept the brick house west of, and a short distance from, Petersburg, and owned it. He was a native of Virginia.

Frank Bradfield, son of John, before mentioned, was also a wagoner. Fifty years ago, when but a boy, he drove one of his father's teams to Baltimore, "pulled up" on the wagon yard of the old Maypole tavern, in that city, attended to his team, remained over night, and the next day mysteriously disappeared. Search was instituted, but he could not be found. He had enlisted as a soldier in the regular army. His friends thought he was dead. He served through the Mexican war, and yet his relatives knew not of his existence. When that war was over he stepped one morning from a steamboat to the wharf at Brownsville. Nobody recognized him. He took a seat in a coach at Brownsville, and in a few hours thereafter entered his father's house, near Petersburg. He called for supper and lodging, and the person he addressed was his father, who did not recognize him, and to whom he did not make himself known. Supper was announced, and his father showed him to the dining room and withdrew. His mother, who was attending at the table, immediately after he was seated, recognized him, and fell fainting in his arms, and there was joy in that household, although inaugurated by a great shock. Frank Bradfield subsequently became a clerk in the Adams Express Company, and entered the Pittsburg office when it was first established in that city, and remained in its service until his death, a few years ago. He has a brother at this time in the office of the Adams Express Company at Pittsburg, where he has been employed for many years, and esteemed as a faithful and efficient clerk.

William Hall was a fine specimen of the old wagoner in the

palmy days of the road — a regular of regulars, zealous in his calling, and jealous of his rights. Robert Bell, the quaint old wagoner before referred to, was his uncle and his friend, who, it is said, rendered him substantial aid in securing a foothold on the great National highway. There was a certain kind of *esprit de corps* among the old regular wagoners, and William Hall possessed it in a high degree. He was well attired, and clean in person and conversation. He was born in Adams county, Pennsylvania, and his first appearance on the road was in the year 1838. He was a great admirer of Thomas Corwin, and was in Ohio with his team on the day that old-time statesman and orator was chosen Governor, a circumstance he frequently referred to in after years with feelings of pride and pleasure. He married a daughter of Aaron Wyatt, and granddaughter of Major Paul, old tavern keepers, and this formed a silken cord that bound him to the destinies of the old pike. In the declining years of the road he became a stage proprietor, and in conjunction with Redding Bunting (not a stranger to these pages), operated a line of coaches between Cumberland and Washington, Pennsylvania. This line had nothing of the whirl and dash of the older lines of coaches. When wagons and stages ceased to enliven the road, William Hall located in Cumberland, and is living there at this time, one of the leading citizens of that place. Soon after he cast his lot in Cumberland he was appointed Superintendent of the Maryland Division of the road by Governor Hicks, and served in that office for a number of years previous to the late war. He had a brother, Robert, who was also an old wagoner, and subsequently, and for several years, a postal clerk on the Baltimore & Ohio railroad between Cumberland and Pittsburg.

Henry Puffenberger, a "regular," given to blustering, but not a vicious man, and Jacob Breakiron, a "sharpshooter" and a fat man, met one day on the road and indulged in a wrangle about the right of way. Strings of fresh broken stone on either side of the road, as was often the case, left but a narrow passage where the meeting occurred, and this led to the difficulty. "Old Puff," as he was called, demanded of Breakiron, with an air of authority, that he should "turn out." Breakiron declined to obey, and showed a determined spirit of resistance. After an exchange of angry words Puffenberger inquired of Breakiron his name, and he answered, "my name is Breakiron." "That," said Puffenberger, "is a hard name, but you look harder than your name." "I am as hard as my name," said Breakiron, "and what is your name?" "Puffenberger," was the reply. "That," said Breakiron, "is a windy name." "Yes," rejoined Puffenberger, "but there is thunder with it." After this explosion of wit the contestants compromised, shook hands, and passed without colliding. Puffenberger was a Maryland man, became a Confederate soldier, and was killed in battle. Breakiron was a farmer of Georges township, Fayette county, Pennsylvania, and died on his farm a number of years ago.

WILLIAM HALL.

Turner Brown, brother of Henry, famous for the big loads he hauled, was an old wagoner. After a number of years' experience as a wagoner he moved to Ohio and settled in Guernsey county, where he became wealthy and was elevated to the office of Probate Judge. Persons who remember him say he was "pompous" in manner, but honest in his dealings. He was a native of Fayette county, Pa., born and reared in the vicinity of Brownsville, and of the family of Browns prominently identified with the National Road in its early days. He had a number of sons, three of whom—Samuel, Turner and Levi—were Union soldiers in the late war. Another, Thomas, published for a time *The Ohio Farmer*, at Cleveland; and another, William, took to theology, and is engaged in missionary work in some remote quarter of the globe.

Joseph Lawson was, like his fellow teamster, John Galwix, considered a fancy wagoner. He took pride in his calling, and his team consisted of six stallions, well mated and of gigantic size. The gears he used were the very best of the John Morrow pattern, and his "outfit" attracted attention and evoked words of praise from the throngs that lined the road in that day. There was a regulation tread and an air about the old wagoner, especially of the regular line, that rose almost, if not altogether, to the standard of dignity.

Jeff. Manypenny was an old wagoner, and a son of the old tavern keeper of Uniontown, referred to in a subsequent chapter.

Joseph Arnold is said to have hauled the first "eighty hundred load" ever hauled on the road, and it gave him great fame. It was in 1837.

Joseph Sopher tried the experiment of using nine horses in his team, driven three abreast. It did not prove practicable or profitable, and he soon abandoned it and returned to the ordinary six-horse team. There were four Sophers on the road and they were brothers, viz: Joseph, Nimrod, Jack and William, and they were stage drivers as well as wagoners.

Robert Beggs, an old wagoner, prosecuted Jacob Probasco for perjury. The prosecution grew out of an affidavit made by Probasco alleging that Beggs, who was indebted to him, was about to remove his goods from the State with intent to defraud his creditors. This prosecution gave Probasco much trouble and involved him in considerable expense, and is said to have been the cause of his removal from Fayette county, Pennsylvania.

Thomas Gore was one of the first wagoners on the road, and a regular. He lived in Hopwood when that village was known as Woodstock. He drove a "bell team," and owned it. He was well known all along the road, but it is so long ago that but few of the pike boys of this day remember him. He gave up wagoning long before business ceased on the road, and settled in Franklin township, Fayette county, Pennsylvania, where he died thirty years ago. Robinson Addis, a well known and much esteemed citizen of Dunbar township, Fayette county, Pennsylvania, married a daughter of

Thomas Gore; and a grandson of the old wagoner, bearing the name Thomas Gore Addis, is one of the trusted and trustworthy superintendents of the H. Clay Frick Coke Company, with headquarters at Brownfield Station, on the Southwest Railway.

John Whetzel, called "Johnny," a regular old wagoner, was small in stature, quiet in disposition, and of swarthy complexion. He talked but little, rarely using a word beyond the size of a monosyllable, and was well known and highly esteemed all along the road. When the career of the road as a great National highway ended, "Johnny" Whetzel retired to a farm in Saltlick township, Fayette county, Pennsylvania, where he still lives, bending under the weight of many years, but enjoying the confidence and respect of all his neighbors.

JOHN WALLACE.

CHAPTER XIX.

Old Wagoners continued — The Harness they Used — John Morrow a maker of Harness — Capt. Elias Gilmore encounters a Man Eater — Perry Gaddis, William G. Patterson, Alfred Bailes, the Scarboroughs and McLaughlins — Hill, who respected Sunday — James Riley and Oliver Pratt, Robert Carr, Robert Allison, David Herr, William Keefer, Abram Beagle, Samuel Youman, Robert Cosgrove, James Brownlee, John Collier, Darius Grimes, Fielding Montague, James Smith, Elisha Maxon, Jacob Marks, Thomas Starr, Thomas Hastings, Henry Foster, John Smasher, Maj. Jesse B. Gardner, McWilliams, Pixler, Riley and Hankins.

John Morrow, of Petersburg, mentioned hereinbefore as a manufacturer of the wagoner's whip, was likewise a saddle and harness maker, and had the reputation of making the best harness on the road. He was a man of thin visage and energetic habit.

Gears was the name old wagoners applied to harness. The gears used on the team of the regular wagoner were of immense proportions. The back bands were fifteen and the hip straps ten inches wide, and heavy black housing covered the horses' shoulders down to the bottom of the hames. The traces used were iron chains with short and thick links. It required a strong man to throw these heavy gears on the back of a big horse. Heavy and broad as they were, these gears were not out of proportion to the large fat horses of the old teams, and looked well on their broad and shining backs. The wagoner's saddle was unique. It was made over an ordinary wooden model, covered with thick, black leather, and had long and wide skirts or aprons, cut straight on the edges and ends. Daniel P. Gibson, the well known capitalist of Uniontown, learned the trade of saddle and harness making with John Morrow in Petersburg, and worked many a day on the big gears and odd saddle, above described.

Capt. Elias Gilmore was not strictly an old wagoner, but a pike boy to all intents and purposes, yet his home was not immediately on the road. He had a team which he employed for the most part in hauling stones for repairs on the road. He was a contractor, and an energetic one. He was an amiable man, in a general way, but given at times to pugilistic encounters, and it is said that no man along the road could outdo him in a fight. A stage driver once came upon the road who was called "the man eater." He drove from Uniontown to Mt. Washington on the Good Intent line. Gilmore, hearing of this famous "man eater," was desirous of meeting him, and calling one day at Mt. Washington, inquired where he was. Upon being introduced, Gilmore said to him : "You are a pretty stout looking man, but I can lick you," and at it they went, without further ceremony, and Gilmore did lick him. At another time Gilmore was in Uniontown with a load of lumber, and stood his team across the street, which caused John P. Sturgis, who was constable then, to take him to task for obstructing the street, whereupon Gilmore fell upon Sturgis and gave him a tremendous beating, for which he was fined by the burgess. Gilmore was born in Wharton township, Fayette county, Pa., and owned and lived on a farm near "Sugar Loaf," in the vicinity of Ohiopyle. His wife was a sister of Boss Rush, "the prince of landlords." Captain Gilmore moved, with his family, to Illinois thirty years ago, and subsequently to York county, Nebraska, where he is still living in comfortable circumstances, a farmer and stock dealer. He long since abandoned the profitless pastime of sowing wild oats, and is esteemed as one of the most respectable and influential citizens of Nebraska. John Rush, a brother of Boss, and brother-in-law of Gilmore, an old wagoner and tavern keeper, went west with Gilmore, and lives near him now, in Nebraska.

Perry Gaddis, who died a few years ago at Dunbar, Pennsylvania, was an old wagoner. His first service on the road as driver was for Isaac Bailey, who kept a tavern near the old red house east of Brownsville, subsequently postmaster at Brownsville, and a member of the Fayette county, Pennsylvania, bar. Gaddis married a daughter of Robert Shaw, an old tavern keeper, and many years ago steward of the county home near Uniontown. She was a schoolmate of the author of these pages, as was also her sister, who became the wife of Robert S. McDowell, another well known pike boy. William D. Beggs, father-in-law of the late Dr. Smith Fuller, blessed be his memory, was our faithful old teacher. Mrs. Gaddis, Perry's widow, is still living at Dunbar.

*William G. Patterson, of Jefferson township, Fayette county, Pennsylvania, an old wagoner, has a record worthy of special mention. When on the road he was called "Devil Bill," and this name followed him to his farm, and adhered to him for many years. To see him now at his ancestral home, bending beneath his four score years and more, gentle in manner and intelligent and entertaining in conversation, surrounded by all the needful comforts of this life, one wonders how he ever got the name of "Devil Bill." His first appearance on the National Road as a driver was in the year 1820, when he assisted in driving a lot of hogs for his father to Baltimore. It required almost a month to drive a lot of hogs from the vicinity of Brownsville to the city of Baltimore. He made his first trip over the road as a wagoner in 1823, going clear through to Baltimore. The first team he drove was his father's, but it was not long until he became the owner of a team himself. He was on the road many years as a wagoner. The farm on which he now resides descended from his grandfather to his father, and then to himself. His father died on this farm on Christ-

*Died in Iowa in 1892.

ALFRED BAILES.

mas day of the year 1827. His grandfather came out from Dauphin county, Pennsylvania, at an early day.

Alfred Bailes, of Dunbar, Pennsylvania, is probably the oldest man living who drove a team on the National Road. He was first a wagoner, and subsequently and for many years a stage driver. He was born in Loudon county, Virginia, and came upon the road about the year 1830, at the solicitation of John Bradfield, who was also a native of Virginia, and agent of the first line of wagons on the road. Alfred Bailes was born in 1804, and although closely approaching his ninetieth year, his eye is undimmed and his natural vigor unabated. Samuel Luman, of Cumberland, is two years younger than Bailes, but two years his senior as a stage driver. Bailes was one of the most commanding figures on the road, upwards of six feet in height, with broad chest and shoulders, and long arms. Noted for great strength, he was never quarrelsome. As a driver he performed his functions faithfully and carefully. He is a most interesting relic of the road, and his memory is well stored with interesting reminiscences of its faded glory.

Samuel and William Scarborough were old wagoners. They lived on the old William Elliott farm, in Jefferson township, Fayette county, Pa., and were brothers. William Hogg, the pioneer merchant of Brownsville, was the owner of the William Elliott farm at the time referred to, and the Scarboroughs paid their rent by hauling a load of merchandise for Mr. Hogg once a year, from Baltimore to his store in Brownsville.

George McLaughlin, still living near Uniontown, but now, and for a long time, a sufferer from rheumatism, is an old wagoner. It may be that exposure, when a wagoner, to the snow storms of the mountains, is the source of the rheumatism which now afflicts him. His brother, Abraham, who lives at Mt. Braddock, is also an old wagoner, and, when a boy, broke stone on the pike at a "levy" a perch.

There was an old wagoner whose name was Hill, and he lived at Triadelphia, now West Virginia, then "Old Virginia never tire," who never drove his team on Sunday. He seems not to have lost anything by resting his team and himself on Sunday, for he made as good time on his trips as any other wagoner, and in the end became rich.

Michael Teeters, a spluttering old wagoner, was noted for his profanity. He was possessed with the fatal delusion that hard swearing was evidence of superior intelligence. He, of course, had some good traits, as the worst of men have; but when age and infirmity came upon him, he exchanged the tramp over the hills of the old pike for a " walk over the hills to the poor house," and died in the county home of Washington county, Pennsylvania. Had he followed the example of Hill, who rested on Sunday, it may not be said that he would have grown rich, but it is pretty certain that the surroundidgs of his dying hours would have been different from what they were.

James Riley and Oliver Pratt were among the oldest of the old wagoners—veterans in every sense. Riley was a large man, with florid face and very white hair, and was called "Old Whitey." He lived and died in Hopwood. Pratt was also a large man, and stout, a steady drinker, with red-rimmed eyes. He was a good driver, and devoted to his calling. He married a Miss Bird, of the old family of that name, in Henry Clay township, Fayette county, Pennsylvania, and when flush times ended on the road, went west and died, far from the scenes of the grand old highway.

Robert Carr, who died in Uniontown about two years ago, was an old wagoner. He was on the road as early as 1825. He drove first for Benjamin Miller, grandfather of Ben, Sam and Jeff Miller, of Uniontown. He subsequently married a daughter of Abner Springer, of North Union township, Fayette county, who owned a road team which was placed in charge of Carr, and he drove it several years. He was also a stage driver.

Robert Q. Fleming, now residing in Uniontown, is an old wagoner. He hauled whiskey from the old Overholt distillery, near Mt. Pleasant, to Baltimore for many years, and loaded back with merchandise to various points in the west. One of his earliest back loads consisted of oysters for Pittsburg, *via* Brownsville. The oyster boxes were piled up to the canvass covering, and upon reaching Brownsville he was required to drive down the wharf to the steamboat landing, which was "sidling," and at the time icy. Some of the top boxes fell out and were broken, whereupon the bystanders helped themselves to fresh shell oysters. They were not carried away, but the eager oyster lovers picked them up, cracked open the shells on the wagon wheels and gulped down the juicy bivalves on the ground. Fleming was "docked," as they termed the abating of loss, from the freight charges.

Robert Allison, one of the best known of the old wagoners, was a fighting man. He did not seem to be quarrelsome, yet was often, as by some sort of untoward destiny, involved in pugilistic encounters along the road. In one of these at Fear's tavern, on Keyser's Ridge, he bit off the nose of a stage driver.

David Harr was a good fiddler, and William Keefer was a good dancer, and these two old wagoners warmed the bar room of many an old tavern between Baltimore and Wheeling, in the good old days when every mile of the National Road bristled with excitement.

Abram Beagle was a widely known old wagoner. He lived with David Moreland in Uniontown as early as 1820, and probably before that time, and subsequently became a tavern keeper. The house he kept was twelve miles east of Wheeling, and he married it. That is to say: The Widow Rhodes owned the tavern stand, and he married *her*. He kept a good house, and was largely patronized. Old citizens of Uniontown who remember Abram Beagle, and there are not many of them living, speak of him as a good and worthy citizen of the olden time.

Samuel Youman, of Washington county, Pa., was an old wagoner, stage driver and tavern keeper. He drove stage from Hillsboro to Washington, and subsequently kept tavern in Hillsboro. He had the

GERMAN D. HAIR.

distinction of being next to the largest man on the road, "Old Mount" being admittedly the largest. Youman was a man full of zeal, as to all pursuits and interests relating to the National Road. He understood the art of driving horses to perfection, was kindly in disposition, and attracted attention by reason of his immense size. He had a son, Israel, who was also a stage driver and a lively fellow. Father and son are presumably both dead, but the marks they made on the memories of the old pike are indelible.

Poor old Robert Cosgrove, who once traversed the road with all the pride and pomp of a "regular," finally succumbed to the adverse tides of life and time, and to avoid "the slings and arrows of outrageous fortune," took refuge in the "county home," where he remains, indulging the memories of better days and awaiting the summons to rejoin the companionship of old wagoners who have passed over the dark river.

James Brownlee was one of the old wagoners who suffered the experience of a genuine "upset." It occurred near Hagen's tavern, east of Cumberland. He had a high load, and encountered a big snow drift which he thought he could overcome by pulling out and around, but he failed, and his wagon capsized. His main loss was in time, which was "made up" by the good cheer at Hagen's old tavern.

John Collier, father of Daniel Collier, was a wagoner on the road when it was first opened up for travel. He had been a wagoner on the Braddock road for years before the National Road was made. He lived in Addison, Somerset county, Pa., as early as 1795, and was one of the foremost wagoners of his day. He was the grandfather of Mrs. Amos S. Bowlby, of Fayette street, Uniontown.

Darius Grimes was among the first crop of wagoners, and gave up the whip and line long before the termination of the road's prosperous era. When the writer first knew him he was living a retired life on the roadside at the foot of Graham's lane, three miles west of Uniontown. He was one of the earliest tavern keepers on the road, beside being a wagoner. He kept the old Abel Colley house, west of and near Searight's, before Abel Colley owned that property, and that was a long time ago. William Johnson, farmer and dealer in fruits and vegetables, well known to the people of Uniontown, married a daughter of Darius Grimes.

Fielding Montague, an old wagoner and stage driver, is still living on the road. His residence is in Henry Clay township, Fayette county, Pennsylvania, where his sleep is undisturbed by the clatter which in other years was heard at all hours of the night as well as day. Montague was not a driver on the old stage lines, but after they were withdrawn from the road, drove the mail hack for a considerable length of time between Uniontown and Somerfield. He was, however, a regular wagoner in the palmy days of the road.

*James Smith, now living in Wharton township, Fayette county, Pennsylvania, well and favorably known, is an old wagoner. He en-

*Deceased.

joyed the grand march along the old road, and was deeply grieved when stillness took the place of the bustling activity that marked its palmy days. The old veteran is bending to the storms of time, but glows with enthusiasm when recounting the scenes he witnessed on the old highway "in the days of yore."

Elijah Maxon was an old wagoner. His home was near the Charlestown school house, in Luzerne township, Fayette county, Pennsylvania. He owned the team he drove, and made money on the road. He moved west many years ago, and in all probability has gone to that bourne whence no traveler returns.

Jacob Marks was an old wagoner, and subsequently, like so many of his fellows, became a tavern keeper. He first kept the stone house at Malden, between Brownsville and Centreville, and afterward the old Workman House at Brownsville. The glory of the old road had departed before he took charge of the Workman House, and business was dull; but the road was flush when he entertained the public at Malden, and he did a thriving business there.

Thomas Starr was an old wagoner, and drove for John Riley, an old tavern keeper of Bridgeport, Fayette county, Pa. The old citizens of Bridgeport and Brownsville will remember Starr and Riley, as they were conspicuous pike boys in their day.

Thomas Hastings was an old wagoner and tavern keeper. He kept the house well known and well patronized in his day about four miles east of Washington.

Henry Foster, late of North Union township, Fayette county, Pa., a well known farmer in his day, was an old wagoner. He drove a six-horse team to Baltimore in 1837, when but nineteen years old. His first load was bacon, consigned to a Baltimore house by Edward Gavin, of Uniontown. His return load was merchandise, consigned to William Bryson, a merchant of that day at Uniontown.

David Blakely was an old wagoner and became a tavern keeper. He kept a tavern in Washington in 1838, and subsequently in Wheeling. He was a prominent man, well known all along the road. He was also an agent of one of the transportation lines, and a very competent man for that business.

John Smasher, an old wagoner, was noted as a nimble and expert dancer, and had many opportunities to display his talent in this line on the old road. It frequently happens that a good dancer makes a ready "smasher."

Major Jesse B. Gardner, of Uniontown, ex-jury commissioner and ex-soldier of two wars, drove a team several trips on the old road for Archibald Skiles, who kept a tavern at Monroe, and was a thorough pike boy.

Huston McWilliams, Joseph Pixler and John Riley were old wagoners who retired to farms in German township when the steam railway usurped the functions of the old pike.

William Hankins, a well known farmer of North Union township, still living, is an old wagoner, and made many a dollar on the

ELLIS B. WOODWARD.

road. He is a son of James Hankins, who owned the farm at Frost's Station, and was reputed to have a barrel of money. One Hook, P. U., merchant and auctioneer of Uniontown, and member of the Legislature, was accustomed to speak of ready cash as "Hankins' Castings," in allusion to the Hankins barrel. He had a small store in an old frame house near the store room and residence of the late Col. Ewing Brownfield, on which he nailed a rough board for a sign, bearing the legend: "Hook and Hankins versus Boyle and Rankin." Boyle and Rankin kept a rival store further up town. Hook also frequently advertised his business under the firm name of "Hook and Wife." He was well known and is well remembered by the old citizens of Uniontown.

James Ambrose was a regular. He drove from Baltimore to Wheeling. He was a strong driver, and well known on the road. He married the youngest daughter of Robert Shaw, the old tavern keeper near Braddock's Grave. After business ceased on the road, he engaged in mining coal in the Connellsville coke district, and died near Vanderbilt, in January, 1892. His wife survives him.

Isaac Hurst was a sharpshooter, and appeared on the road near the close of its prosperous era. He hauled flour from his father's mill on George's Creek, Fayette county, Pennsylvania, to Cumberland, and "loaded back" with merchandise to Brownsville. His experience on the road as a wagoner was confined between the points named. He subsequently became first, Treasurer, and afterward, Commissioner of Fayette county, Pennsylvania. He is still living in Uniontown, pursuing the calling of a contractor, and taking an active interest in public affairs.

7

CHAPTER XX.

The political campaign of 1840, as is well known, was one of the most spirited and exciting contests ever witnessed in the United States. It was a campaign made memorable by log cabins, hard cider, coon skins and glee clubs. William Henry Harrison, the hero of Tippecanoe, and grandfather of the late chief executive, Benjamin Harrison, was the Whig candidate for President, and John Tyler, of Virginia, was his running mate, and the whole country resounded with shouts for "Tippecanoe and Tyler too." Martin Van Buren was the Democratic candidate for President, and his associate on the ticket was Col. Richard M. Johnston, of Kentucky. Harrison and Tyler were triumphantly elected. One day during this exciting campaign Neri Smith, an old wagoner, drove his big six-horse team through Uniontown, exhibiting from the front of his wagon a petticoat, in allusion to a partisan and groundless charge of cowardice made against General Harrison, the Whig candidate. The coming of the wagon with the petticoat was made known to the Whigs of Uniontown before it reached the place, and a delegation met Smith a short distance east of town and requested him to take down the offensive symbol, but he stubbornly refused. Upon reaching Uniontown an attempt was made by some of the muscular Whigs, led by John Harvey, to "tear down the dirty rag," but an equal number of muscular Democrats rallied to the support of the old wagoner, and the attempt failed. The affair caused great excitement in Uniontown, leading to violence and almost to the shedding of blood.

Isaac Stuck, now residing in Perryopolis, Fayette county, Pennsylvania, in service on the extensive Fuller estate, near that place, was an old wagoner, and is not forgotten and never will be forgotten by the old pike boys. He drove a fine " bell team," which was notice to all the world that he was on the road in earnest and to stay. The team belonged to William Stone, the well remembered old farmer of Menallen, and tanner of Uniontown.

ASHAEL WILLISON.

John Short, an old wagoner, retired from the road at an early day and took up his abode in Franklin township, Fayette county, Pennsylvania. Before going on the road he learned the trade of a cooper, and upon leaving it resumed work at his trade. He was a good mechanic, and made most of the barrels used at Cook's and Sharples' mills, on Redstone creek, for many years. His team on the road was a good one, and he owned it. He met with an accident while working at his trade by cutting his knee with an adze, which crippled him for life. He died in Franklin township about eight years ago, aged nearly eighty. The old citizens of Franklin township all knew and respected him.

William Orr, a well known old wagoner, died of cholera at Keyser's Ridge in 1853. He left three sons. One of them died a soldier of the Northern army in the late war, leaving a widow surviving him, now residing in Cumberland and drawing a pension. Another son of the old wagoner is a watchman at the rolling mill in Cumberland, and the third is on the police force of that city.

Ashael Willison, another of the old wagoners, is still living in Cumberland, and one of the most prominent citizens of that place. He was postmaster at Cumberland during the first administration of President Cleveland. From the saddle horse of a six-horse team on the old pike to the control of a city postffice is distinctively an American idea, and a good one. The old wagoner made a capital postmaster. Mr. Willison is now deputy collector of Internal Revenue for the State of Maryland.

Robert Douglas, father of the well known real estate dealer of Uniontown, was an old wagoner. He owned his team and wagon, and hauled between Baltimore and Wheeling at an early day. He resided near West Newton, Westmoreland county, Pennsylvania, and died there in 1861. He was esteemed as an honest man, and was one of the few pike boys who never took a drink of liquor.

In the year 1839 John Snider, Isaac Browning and Black Westley, made a trip with their teams from Baltimore to Jonesboro, Tennessee, a distance of six hundred miles. They were loaded with goods for Jonesboro merchants, and were paid six dollars a hundred for hauling them. On their return they drove with empty wagons to Lynchburg, Virginia, a distance of two hundred miles, where they loaded up with pig lead, and got two dollars a hundred for hauling it to Baltimore.

Abram Brown, the wealthy land owner of the vicinity of Uniontown, was an old wagoner, a "sharpshooter," and always lucky in avoiding losses while pushing over the mountains. While on the road as a wagoner he formed the acquaintance of the girl who subsequently became his wife. She was Hannah, now deceased, the eldest daughter of Abel Colley, who kept the old tavern a short distance west of Searights. His wife was a good woman, and her seemingly premature death was much lamented by a wide circle of friends.

William Long, an old wagoner, after quitting the road, went to

Beaver county, Pennsylvania, and died there; and Samuel Weaver, a well remembered old wagoner, died about seven years ago in New Cumberland, West Virginia.

John Galwix, Black Wesley, Wilse Clement and James Pelter used bells on their teams. Galwix was called a "crack" wagoner, "swell," as it would be termed at this day.

Stephen Golden, an old wagoner, drove a team for John Gribble, who for many years kept the red tavern two miles east of Brownsville.

John Strong, one of the earliest regular wagoners, is still living in Cumberland, and has been Coroner at that place for many years.

John Kelso, a steady old regular, well remembered and well liked, died at Cumberland about two years ago.

Robert Nelson was run over by his wagon many years ago, and died from injuries inflicted by the accident.

Col. James Gardner was an old wagoner and an old soldier. He was a native of Winchester, Virginia, but spent the greater portion of his life in Uniontown.

John Phillips, of Washington county, Pennsylvania, an old wagoner, was noted for using the heaviest gears on the road. When in need of new ones he ordered them an inch wider than the widest in use. The gear pole boys at the old taverns groaned under the weight of Phillips' gears.

William C. McKean, nine years a deputy Sheriff of Fayette county, Pennsylvania, was in early life a regular wagoner of the road. He was a native of German township, Fayette county, Pennsylvania, and died in the Sheriff's house, at Uniontown, in 1859. He was noted for his energy and habit of pushing things. The prominent young attorney of Uniontown of the same name is a nephew of the old wagoner.

Peter Skiles, an old wagoner of the vicinity of Uniontown, died in Cumberland of typhoid fever, while at that place with his team and wagon.

Christian Herr, an old wagoner, was a very profane man, going to show that there is nothing in a name. He, Wilse Clement and Michael Teeters were the hardest swearers on the road.

Wyney Hunter, still living, an octogenarian, and rich, was an old wagoner. His residence is on the roadside five miles east of Hagerstown, Maryland.

Charles Allum and James Brownlee drove for Leonard Vail, an old pork-packer of the vicinity of Prosperity, Washington county, Pennsylvania. Lott Lantz, of Willow Tree, Greene county, Pennsylvania, had a pork-packing establishment in the olden time, and sent his produce over the road to Baltimore by the regular broad wheeled wagons in charge of hired drivers.

Isaac Browning, an old wagoner, at one time owned the "Browning farm," near Uniontown, whence its name is derived. This farm now belongs to Robert Hogsett.

John Wright, an old wagoner, is still living in Salisbury, Somer-

JACOB NEWCOMER.

set county, Pennsylvania, and has passed the ninetieth mile-post of his age.

Capt. James Gilmore was a sharpshooter. He owned a little farm in Menallen township, Fayette county, Pennsylvania, which he sold long ago and went West.

Noble McCormick, a regular old wagoner, was, while on the road, the owner of the Semans farm, near Uniontown. He sold his farm to Thomas Semans and went West. He is remembered as an habitual wearer of the broad-rimmed, yellow, long-napped regulation hat.

John Christy, an old wagoner, was eccentric as to his apparel, and careful of his money. He wore a full suit of buckskin, and improvised a savings bank by boring holes in blocks in which he placed his money, and secured it by plugging up the holes.

Charles Guttery, who recently died at an advanced age in Beallsville, Washington county, Pennsylvania, was one of the best known and most esteemed old wagoners of the road. After many years experience as a wagoner, he devoted the remainder of his life to tavern keeping.

John Yardley, as the saying goes, was a natural born wagoner. He loved the occupation, and was faithful in it, for many years. He was born in Maryland, but lived a long time at Searights, where he died. He was the father of William and Gus Yardley, of Uniontown.

David Newcomer, a farmer of German township, Fayette county, Pennsylvania, who served a term as County Commissioner, belongs to the long list of wagoners. His father, Jacob Newcomer, and Jacob F. Longanecker went to Loudon, Franklin county, Pennsylvania, in the year 1849, and each bought a new wagon and a new whip at that place. Jacob Newcomer soon thereafter became afflicted with rheumatism, and turned over his team and wagon to his son David, who traversed the road until the close of its busy era. Jacob Newcomer died in 1866, on the farm now owned and occupied by his son David.

John Ferren drove a six-horse team on the road many years for William Searight, and is remembered as a careful and discreet driver and an honest and industrious man. At the close of active business on the road, and while yet under the influence of its ancient grandeur, he married a daughter of "Wagoner Billy Shaw," and with his newly-wedded wife went to Iowa to work out his destiny, where he has achieved success as a farmer.

James E. Kline, a driver for Jacob A. Hoover, was a soldier in the late war between the States, and died in German township, Fayette county, Pennsylvania, after the conflict ended.

Robert Hogsett, the millionaire farmer, stock dealer, manufacturer, and coke operator of Fayette county, Pennsylvania, was a sharpshooter, and hauled many a load of goods from Cumberland to Brownsville at remunerative rates per hundred. His "down loads" consisted for the most part of corn of his own raising, which he sold out through the mountains at good prices.

Hiram Hackney, for many years a prosperous farmer of Menallen township, Fayette county, Pennsylvania, now a retired resident of Uniontown, and a director in the First National Bank of that place, was a sharpshooter and a drover.

Samuel Flowers was one of the earliest wagoners on the road, and of the regular order. He was a tall man, of quiet demeanor. His home was on Egg Nog Hill, where he lived until called away by the last summons.

John Means, an old wagoner, was killed by an accident on the road near Wheeling.

John Munce, of Washington, Pennsylvania, who became rich through the oil development in the vicinity of that place, is an old wagoner. He is still living.

John Olwine was an old wagoner, and by his union with the Widow Metzgar became a tavern keeper. He died at Chalk Hill a few years ago.

John Neff, an old wagoner, subsequently became a member of the Maryland Legislature, and played the role of statesmanship as gracefully as he drove a six-horse team on the old pike.

Abner and David Peirt, brothers, were natives of Lancaster county, Pennsylvania—steady-going, straightforward, honest "Pennsylvania Dutch," and wagoners on the road with teams of the genuine Conestoga strain.

John McIlree, called "Broadhead," was an old wagoner and a native of Adams county, Pennsylvania; and James Bell, William and Robert Hall were natives also of Adams county.

Arthur Wallace, an old wagoner devoted to the road, and esteemed for many good qualities of head and heart, subsequently became a tavern keeper. He was the father-in-law of Peter Frasher, the adamantine Democrat of 1844, and up to the date of his death, in 1893. Charles Wallace, a brother of Arthur, and an old wagoner, was killed by an accident on Laurel Hill many years ago.

William Reynolds, mentioned under the head of old tavern keepers, was likewise an old wagoner. He was on the road with a team as early as 1832. His son, John, present postmaster at Confluence, Somerset county, Pennsylvania, was also a wagoner.

Samuel Trauger, an old wagoner, fell from his lazy board while descending Laurel Hill, and was killed, the hind wheel of his wagon running over him.

John Curtis, who drove for William King, was accounted one of the best drivers on the road. His companions called him a "strong driver," meaning that he was skillful and careful. He followed the tide of emigration, and became a stage driver west of the Ohio river.

James and Benjamin Paul, sons of Major William Paul, were old wagoners.

Joseph Doak, of Washington county, Pennsylvania, was an old wagoner, subsequently a tavern keeper, and later a superintendent of the road.

JOHN FERREN.

Martin Horn, a native of Washington county, Pennsylvania, was known as the "swift wagoner." He made the trip from Cumberland to Wheeling with his six-horse team and a big load, in five days.

The following old wagoners were residents, when at home, and citizens of Fayette county, Pennsylvania: Harvey Grove, Adam Yeast, Solomon Bird, Louis Langley, James Paul, Joseph Wells, Isaiah Fouch, Ellis Campbell, William Sullivan, George Miller, William Bird, Barney Neiman, Jesse Hardin, John Hardin, James Marshall, Samuel Sidebottom, John Rutledge, Robert Hogsett, Samuel Milligan, Thomas Cook, Benjamin Paul, Jeff Nixon, George Miller, Moses Richer, John Rankin, Peter Fowler, William Ball, James Henshaw, William McShane, Henry Frasher, Peter Frasher, Jacob Wolf, West Jones, Daniel Turney, Eli Marlow, William Turney, William Cooper, Dawson Marlow, Robert Henderson, John Ferren, Robinson Murphy, Parker McDonald, William Betts, Rezin Lynch, Joseph Bixler, Moses Husted, William Pastoris, John McClure, Thomas Cochran, William Peirsol, Robert Lynch, Morgan Campbell, Martin Leighty, John Stentz, Philip D. Stentz, William Bosley, Charles McLaughlin, J. Monroe Bute, John Canon, Levi Springer, George Dearth, John McCurdy, Calvin Springer, Zachariah Ball, Michael Cochran, Caleb Hibbs, Jacob Newcomer, John Rinehart, Benjamin Goodwin, Harvey Sutton, Clark Hutchinson, James Ebbert, Mifflin Jeffries, Jacob Vance, William Ullery, Abram Hall, George Tedrick, Alexander Osborn, James Abel, Harper Walker, Jerry Fouch, Elias Freeman, George Wilhelm, father of Sheriff Wilhelm, of Uniontown, Caleb Langly, Jacob Wagoner, Oliver Tate, Jacob Strickler, George Shaffer, John Newcomer, Jesse J. Peirsol, James Shaffer, Samuel Harris, Caleb Antrim, William Cooper, Andrew Prentice, Ira Strong, William Gray, William Kennedy, Samuel Hatfield, Bernard Dannels, Stewart Henderson, David Dunbar, George Grace, Dicky Richardson, Reuben Woodward, John King, John Williams, George McLaughlin, Darlington Jeffries, John Nelson, John Moore, Bazil Sheets, Isaac Young, Jerry Strawn, Samuel Renshaw, Reuben Parshall, Hiram Hackney, James Martin.

The following were of Washington county, Pennsylvania, and there were many others from that county, as well as from Fayette and the other counties mentioned, whose names, very much to the writer's regret, are unascertainable: Eberon Hurton, James Bradley, Jerome Heck, James Dennison, James Bard, Thomas Bailes, Charles Thurston, William Kirkman, Otho Hartzell, Seldon King, William King, Zeph Riggle, John Guttery, Samuel Charlton, George Hallam, Lewis Hallam, David Hill, Charles Reddick, John Reddick, Joseph Arnold, Moses Kline, James Brownlee, Elisha Brownlee, Charles Allen, Philip Slipe, John Valentine, Daniel Valentine, John Quinter, Robert Magee, William Robinson, Arthur Robinson, John Cook, William Darlington, Griffith Darlington, Joseph Whisson, David Blakely, Samuel Boyd, Joseph King, Joseph Sopher, Nimrod Sopher, Jack Sopher, Peter Shires, John Smith, James Smith, Thomas Flack, James Blakely, William Darr, Robert Beggs, Josiah Brown, called "Squire" Brown.

James Arthur, George Munce, Joseph Lawson, Robert Judson, John A. Smith, Elisha Ely, Charles Bower, William Dennison, John Phillips, Joseph Doak, Moses Little, Samuel Guttery, William Shouse, William Jones, Robert Sprowl, William Hastings, James Thompson, Robert Doak, James Doak, Charles Allen, John Hastings (called Doc.).

The following were of Allegheny county, Maryland: Isaac Browning, James Browning, Michael Humbert, George McGruder, Peter Hager, Nathan Tracy, Thomas Plumer, Richard Gray (colored), Ben Carter, James McCartney, Joseph Brooks, John Carlisle, Joseph Turner, William Yeast, John Curtis, Louis Smith, John Smith, Fred Shipley, Alex. Greer, John Keener, David Swaggart, George Lehman, Andrew Lehman, William McClintock, Jacob Albright, Thomas Ashbel, Charles McAleer, Caleb Madden, William Lowry, Augustus Butler, John Sheeres, Edward Finch, James Clary, Daniel Barcus, Ashael Willison, Hanson Willison, Joseph Strong, Thomas Plumer, Josiah Porter, John Kelso, John Magraw, Ira Ryan, John Ryan, Moses McKenzie, Moses Porter, Henry Porter, John Porter, George Huff, Lewis Lachbaus, Neil Connor, John Long, George Long, Upton Long, William Dixon, Hanson Clary, James Porter, Josiah McKenzie.

The following were of Washington county, Maryland: Abram Herr, Fred Herr, David Herr, John Coffman, Samuel Kelly, William Jones, Joseph Watt, John Brentlinger, James Ambrose, James Dowler, William Ford, Robert Fowler, Peter Hawes, Samuel Emert, Michael Welty, John Duvall, Andrew Arnett, John Reinhart, Hiram Sutton, John Thomas, William Thomas, Barney Hitchin, Emanuel McGruder, William Orr, Emanuel Griffith, Michael Miller, John Makel, John Neibert, Samuel Brewer, Henry Stickle, Ezra Young, Joshua Johnson, Samuel Boyd, Joseph Myers, William Keefer, Peter Urtz, Jonas Speelman, Thomas Flack, David Connor, Eli Smith, John Galwix, Henry Urtz, Henry Puffenberger. John Snider, was born in Washington county, Maryland.

The following were of Somerset county, Pennsylvania: Michael Deets, Samuel Wable, Clem Engle, Samuel Thompson, John Livengood, Isaac Light, John Sloan, Joseph Light, Abram Hileman, Joseph Hileman, William Lenhart, Daniel Augustine, Andrew Hebner, James Klink, Andrew Bates, Robert Duncan, Robert Allison, John Dunbar, Alex. Dunbar, Joseph Skelly, James Irvin, John Fleck, William Moonshire, Thomas Collier, Frank Bradfield, Samuel Shoaf, John Bradfield, Eli Marble, Henry Renger, Michael Longstaff, John Mitchell, William McClintock, still living at Salisbury, nearly ninety years old.

The following were from the State of Ohio: James Gregory, William Hoover, David Hoover, Christian Hoover, Gov. Lucas, William Morely, Philip Slife, Samuel Breakbill, John Carroll, William Lefevre, John Lefevre, Alby Hall, Solomon Mercer, Jacob Breakbill, Joseph McNutt, John Scroggins, William Archie, Elias Petticord, Harvey Hamilton, Pryn Taylor, Alex. McGregor, Westley McBride, William George, Michael Neal, Tim Taylor, Joseph Vaughn, William

MORRIS MAULER.

Whittle, Daniel Kildo, Marion Gordon, Martin Kildo, George Clum, Oliver Mahon, William Chaney, Abner Bailey, Matthias Meek, John A. Smith, George Zane, Samuel Paxon, Benjamin McNutt, Knox Keyser, B. F. Dillon, Valentine Mann, Jacob Mann, Benjamin Corts, John Whittle, John Johnson (Old Sandy), William McDonald, John Moss, William Tracy, Joseph Watson, George Schaffer, William Reynolds, not the old tavern keeper.

Ohio county, Virginia, contributed the following names to the list of old wagoners: Wash. and Hiram Bennett, John Frasher, John Moss, John Weyman, Joseph Watson, Michael Detuck, James Johnson, David Church, William Brooks, Robert Boyce, Allen Davis, Thomas McDonald, James Jones, Charles Prettyman, John Christy, John Curtis, William, Adam, and David Barnhart, George Weddel, and William Tracy.

Greene county, Pennsylvania, contributed the following well remembered veterans: Christian and Washington Adams, John Snyder (not the old regular), Philip Snyder, George Miller, Samuel Milligan, Caldwell Holsworth, Joseph Milligan, Joseph Craft, Jack Dunaway, Otho W. Core, Thomas Chambers, Samuel Minor, Jacob Hart.

Frederic county, Maryland, contributed the following: John Crampton, Joseph Crampton, Samuel Brewer, Ross Fink, Grafton Shawn, Henry Smith, Jacob Wagoner, John Fink, John Miller, William Miller, and Henry McGruder.

Jacob and James Tamon were of Baltimore.

James Walker, Daniel Keiser, John Keiser, and Sharp Walker were of Franklin county, Pennsylvania.

The home of the regular wagoner was on the road, and a good home it was, in so far as mere subsistence and stimulus to the senses were concerned, and it is his nativity, that the author has endeavored to note. Regulars and sharpshooters are listed herein indiscriminately, but a majority of the names given as of Fayette county, Pennsylvania, are those of sharpshooters. The residences and homes of the following old wagoners could not be accurately ascertained, but they are familiar names, all well remembered by old inhabitants of the roadside, viz: William Kieger (a lively fellow, and a "regular"), James Dunbar, William Keefer, Rafe Rutlege, Samuel Jackson, Benjamin Hunter, David Greenland, John Strauser, Jacob Cox, Jonathan Whitton, Gus Mitchell, Samuel Dowly, James Patton, Joseph Freeman, James Hall, William Purcell, Samuel Rogers, John Nye, Israel Young, James Davis, Jacob Beem, Isaac Young, Martin Irwin, James Parsons, James Kennedy, Isaac Shaffer, John Lynch, Michael Longstaff, George Nouse, Peter Penner, James Shaffer, John McClure, John Cox, William Cox, Joseph Cheney, Frank Mowdy, Caldwell Shobworth, James Jolly, Andrew Sheverner, Jacob and James Layman, John Crampton, Henry Smith, William Miller, John Miller, Henry McGruder, Elias McGruder, Michael Miller, John Seibert, Henry Stickle, Ezra Young, Jonas Speelman, David Con-

7a

nor, Eli Smith, Jacob Everson, Nathaniel Everson, Joseph Shaw, James Irvin, John Chain, William Wiglington, Doug. Shearl, Marion Ritchie, John Vandyke, John Alphen, Daniel Carlisle, George Burke, Thomas Ogden, Michael Abbott, Charles Genewine, Herman Rolf, Isaac Manning.

The following letters from Jesse J. Peirsol, now a prosperous farmer of Franklin township, Fayette county, Pennsylvania, of vigorous health and unimpaired memory, furnish a graphic description of life on the road in its palmy days:

Mr. T. B. Searight: December 3, 1892.

Dear Sir: I have stayed over night with William Sheets, on Nigger mountain, when there would be thirty six-horse teams on the wagon yard, one hundred Kentucky mules in an adjacent lot, one thousand hogs in other enclosures, and as many fat cattle from Illinois in adjoining fields. The music made by this large number of hogs, in eating corn on a frosty night, I will never forget. After supper and attention to the teams, the wagoners would gather in the bar room and listen to music on the violin, furnished by one of their fellows, have a "Virginia hoe-down," sing songs, tell anecdotes, and hear the experience of drivers and drovers from all points on the road, and when it was all over, unroll their beds, lay them down on the floor before the bar room fire, side by side, and sleep, with their feet near the fire, as soundly as under the paternal roof. Coming out from Cumberland in the winter of 1851 or 1852, we stopped one night with Hiram Sutton, at Sand Springs, near Frostburg. The night was hazy, but not cold. We sat on our buckets, turned bottom up, and listened to a hundred horses grinding corn. One of our number got up in the night and complained that snow was falling on his face. This aroused us all, and we got up, went to the door and witnessed the most blinding snow storm I ever saw. Some of the horses broke loose from the tongue, and we had difficulty in finding them. We stayed up till morning, when the snow had risen to the hubs of the front wheels. We hitched eight or ten horses to a wagon, pulled out to Coonrod's tavern, one mile west, and returned to Sutton's for another wagon, and in this way all reached Coonrod's. The next morning we pulled out again, and on little Savage mountain found the snow deeper than ever, and a gang of men engaged in shoveling it from the road. I got stuck and had to be shoveled out. We reached Tom Johnson's that night, making three miles in two days. The next day John Ullery, one of our number upset at Peter Yeast's, and a barrel of Venetian Red rolled out from his wagon, which painted the snow red for many miles, east and west. We stayed with Yeast the third night after the storm. In the winter of 1848 a gang of us went down, loaded with tobacco, bacon, lard, cheese, flour, corn, oats and other products. One of our number was an Ohio man, named McBride. His team consisted of seven horses, the seventh being the leader. His load consisted of nine hogsheads of tobacco, five standing upright in the bed of his wagon, and four resting crosswise on top of the five. The hogsheads were each about four feet high and three and a half feet in diameter at the bulge, and weighing from nine to eleven hundred pounds each. This made a "top-heavy load," and on the hill west of Somerfield, and near Tom Brown's tavern, the road icy, McBride's load tumbled over, the tobacco in the ditches, and the horses piled up in all shapes. The work of restoring the wreck was tedious, and before we got through with it we had the aid of thirty or forty wagoners not of our company. Of course the occasion brought to the ground a supply of the pure old whisky of that day, which was used in moderation and produced no bad effects. After we had righted up our unfortunate fellow wagoner, we pushed on and rested over night at Dan Augustine's, east of Petersburg.

Yours truly,   JESSE J. PEIRSOL.

ANOTHER LETTER FROM THE SAME PERSON ON THE SAME SUBJECT.

February 2, 1893.

In September, 1844 or 5, my father came home from Uniontown late at night, and woke me up to tell me that there had been a big break in the Pennsylvania Canal, and that all western freights were coming out over the National Road in wagons. The stage coaches brought out posters soliciting teams. By sunrise next morning, I was in Brownsville with my team, and loaded up at Cass's warehouse with tobacco, bacon, and wool, and whipped off for Cumberland. I drove to Hopwood the first day and stayed over night with John Wallace. That night Thomas Snyder, a Virginia wagoner, came into Hopwood with a load of flour from a back country mill. When we got beyond Laurel Hill, Snyder retailed his flour by the barrel to the tavern keepers, and was all sold out when we reached Coonrod's tavern, on Big Savage. I was a mere boy, and Snyder was especially kind and attentive to me. After we pulled on to Coonrod's yard Snyder told me to unhitch and feed, but leave the harness on. At midnight we rose, hitched up, Snyder lending me two horses, making me a team of eight, pulled out, and reached Cumberland that night. On leaving Coonrod's the night was dark, and I shall never forget the sounds of crunching stones under the wheels of my wagon, and the streaks of fire rolling out from the horses' feet. In Cumberland, we found the commission houses, and the cars on sidings filled with goods, and men cursing loudly because the latter were not unloaded. Large boxes of valuable goods were likewise on the platform of the station, protected by armed guards. After unloading my down load I re-loaded at McKaig & Maguire's commission house for Brownsville. at one dollar and twenty-five cents a hundred. We reached Brownsville without incident or accident, made a little money, and loaded back again for Cumberland. On my return I found plenty of goods for shipment, and loaded up at Tuttle's house for Wheeling, at two dollars and twenty-five cents a hundred. In coming back, it looked as if the whole earth was on the road; wagons, stages, horses, cattle, hogs, sheep, and turkeys without number. Teams of every description appeared in view, from the massive outfit of Governor Lucas down to the old bates hitched to a chicken coop. The commission merchants, seeing the multitude of wagons, sought to reduce prices, whereupon the old wagoners called a meeting and made a vigorous kick against the proposed reduction. It was the first strike I ever heard of. Nothing worried a sharpshooter more than lying at expense in Cumberland waiting for a load. Two of the "sharps," unwilling to endure the delay caused by the strike, drove their four-horse rigs to a warehouse to load at the reduction. This excited the "regulars," and they massed with horns, tin buckets, oyster-cans and the like, and made a descent upon the "sharps," pelting and guying them unmercifully. An old wagoner named Butler commanded the striking regulars with a pine sword, and marched them back and forth through the streets. Finally the police quelled the disturbance, and the "sharps" loaded up and drove out sixteen miles, to find their harness cut and their axles sawed off in the morning. In this dilemma an old regular, going down empty for a load, took the contract of the "sharps," and made them promise to never return on the road, a promise they faithfully kept.

Yours truly,   JESSE J. PEIRSOL.

Many old wagoners wore a curious garment called a hunting shirt. It was of woolen stuff, after the style of "blue jeans," with a large cape trimmed with red. It was called a hunting shirt because first used by hunters in the mountains.

The origin of Pennsylvania tobies is worth recording, and pertinent to the history of the old wagoners. The author is indebted to J. V. Thompson, esq., president of the First National bank of Uniontown, for the following clipping from a Philadelphia paper concerning the "toby:" "It appears that in the old days the drivers of the Conestoga wagons, so common years ago on our National Road, used to buy very cheap cigars. To meet this demand a small cigar manufacturer in Washington, Pennsylvania, whose name is lost to fame, started in to make a cheap 'roll-up' for them at four for a cent. They became very popular with the drivers, and were at first called Conestoga cigars; since, by usage, corrupted into 'stogies' and 'tobies.' It is now estimated that Pennsylvania and West Virginia produce about 200,000,000 tobies yearly, probably all for home consumption."

It is probable that the manufacturer referred to in the above was George Black, as that gentleman made "tobies" in Washington at an early day, and continued in the business for many years, and until he became quite wealthy. In his later days his trade was very large and profitable. Old wagoners hauled his "tobies" over the road in large quantities, as they did subsequently the Wheeling "tobies," which were, and continued to be, a favorite brand. Many habitual smokers prefer a Washington or a Wheeling "toby" to an alleged fine, high

JAMES SMITH,
OF HENRY.

priced cigar, and the writer of these lines is one of them. As has been noted, the "rubber," called brake at this day, was not in use when the National Road was first thrown open for trade and travel. Instead, as related by John Deets, sapplings, cut at the summit of the hills, were shaped and fashioned to answer the ends of the "rubber," and at the foot of the hills taken off and left on the roadside. E. B. Dawson, esq., the well known, well posted and accurate antiquarian of Uniontown, and, by the way, deeply interested in the history of the National Road, is authority for the statement that one Jones, of Bridgeport, Fayette county, Pennsylvania, claimed to be the inventor of the "rubber." He, however, never succeeded in obtaining letters patent, if, indeed, he ever applied. There were other claimants, among them the Slifers, of Maryland, mentioned elsewhere in these pages. The real and true inventor seems to be unknown, and yet it is an invention of vast importance, and with legal protection would have yielded the inventor an immense fortune.

Old wagoners, as a class, were robust, hardy, honest and jovial. But one of the long list is remembered as a criminal. His name was Ben Pratt, and he belonged to Philadelphia. He turned out to be a counterfeiter of coin and currency, and suffered the punishment that all counterfeiters deserve. Many old wagoners were fond of fun and frolic, but very few of them were intemperate, although they had the readiest opportunities for unrestrained drinking. Every old tavern had its odd shaped little bar, ornamented in many instances with fancy lattice work, and well stocked with whiskey of the purest distillation, almost as cheap as water. In fact all kinds of liquors were kept at the old taverns of the National Road, except the impure stuff of the present day. The bottles used were of plain glass, each marked in large letters with the name of the liquor it contained, and the old landlord would place these bottles on the narrow counter of the little bar, in the presence of a room filled with wagoners, so that all could have free access to them. None of the old tavern keepers made profit from the sales of liquor. They kept it more for the accommodation of their guests, than for money making purposes. There was probably a tavern on every mile of the road, between Cumberland and Wheeling, and all combined did not realize as much profit from the sales of liquor in a year as is realized in that time by one licensed hotel keeper of Uniontown, at the present day.

When, at last, the Conestoga horse yielded up the palm to the Iron horse, and it became manifest that the glory of the old road was departing, never to return, the old wagoners, many of whom had spent their best days on the road, sang in chorus the following lament:

"Now all ye jolly wagoners, who have got good wives,
Go home to your farms, and there spend your lives.
When your corn is all cribbed, and your small grain is good,
You'll have nothing to do but curse the railroad."

CHAPTER XXI.

"My uncle rested his head upon his hands and thought of the busy bustling people who had rattled about, years before, in the old coaches, and were now as silent and changed; he thought of the numbers of people to whom once, those crazy, mouldering vehicles had borne, night after night, for many years, and through all weathers, the anxiously expected intelligence, the eagerly looked for remittance, the promised assurances of health and safety, the sudden announcement of sickness and death. The merchant, the lover, the wife, the widow, the mother, the school boy, the very child who tottered to the door at the postman's knock — how had they all looked forward to the arrival of the old coach! And where were they all now?"— *Charles Dickens.*

Stage drivers as a class did not rank as high morally as wagoners, but despite this there were among them men of good sense, honest intentions and steady habits. As typical of the better class, the reader who is familiar with the old road will readily recall Redding Bunting, Samuel Luman, Elliott Seaburn, Watty Noble, James Carroll, Aquila and Nat Smith, William Scott, David Gordon, James Burr, William Robinson, John Huhn, David Bell, John Guttery, John Ritter, Joseph Henderson and Peter Null. Others will be instantly recognized as their names shall appear on these pages. It is the sincere belief of all old pike boys that the stage lines of the National Road were never equalled in spirit and dash on any road, in any age or country. The chariots of the Appian Way; drawn by the fastest horses of ancient Italy, formed a dismal cortege in comparison with the sprightly procession of stage coaches on the old American highway. The grandeur of the old mail coach is riveted forever in the memory of the pike boy. To see it ascending a long hill, increasing speed, when nearing the summit, then moving rapidly over the intervening level to the top of the next hill, and dashing down it, a driver like the stately Redding Bunting wielding the whip and handling the reins, revealed a scene that will never be forgotten. And there was another

(146)

feature of the old stage lines that left a lasting mark on memory's tablet. It was the "Postilion." A groom with two horses was stationed at the foot of many of the long hills, and added to the ordinary team of four horses to aid in making the ascent. The summit gained, the extra horses were quickly detached and returned to await and aid the next coming coach, and this was the "Postilion. Nathan Hutton is a well remembered old postilion. He was a tall, spare man, and lived in a small log house on the roadside, a short distance west of the old Johnson tavern, and four and a half miles east of Brownsville. At the foot of the hill below his house, he re-enforced the coaches with his postilion both ways, east and west, up Colley's hill, going west, and the equally long hill, coming east from that point. When he wanted a man or horse to be faithful to duty he exhorted him to "stand by his 'tarnal integrity." The old postilion bade adieu to the scenes of earth long ago, and nothing is left to indicate the spot where his lowly dwelling stood except a few perishing quince bushes.

Hanson Willison, of Cumberland, when a boy rode postilion for Samuel Luman, and for Alfred Bailes. John Evans and Jacob Hoblitzell rode postilion through the mountains, east of Keyser's Ridge. Martin Massey rode out from Brownsville, and Thomas M. Fee, now crier of the courts of Fayette county, Pennsylvania, rode out from Uniontown, over Laurel Hill.

Excitement followed in the wake of the coaches all along the road. Their arrival in the towns was the leading event of each day, and they were so regular in transit that farmers along the road knew the exact hour by their coming, without the aid of watch or clock. They ran night and day alike. Relays of fresh horses were placed at intervals of twelve miles, as nearly as practicable. Ordinarily a driver had charge of one team only, which he drove and cared for. Mail drivers, however, in many instances, drove three or four teams and more, which were cared for by grooms at the stations. Teams were changed almost in the twinkling of an eye. The coach was driven rapidly to the station, where a fresh team stood ready harnessed and waiting on the roadside. The moment the team came to a halt the driver threw down the reins, and almost instantly the incoming team was detached, the fresh one attached, the reins thrown back to the driver, who did not leave his seat, and away again went the coach at full speed, the usual group of loafers, meanwhile, looking on and enjoying the exciting scene. The horses used were showy and superb, the admiration of all who beheld them. Mr. Stockton had a strain called the "Murat," and another known as the "Winflower," which have become extinct, but many expert horsemen contend that they have not, in later days, been surpassed for nerve, beauty or speed. A peculiar affliction came upon many of the "wheel horses," expressed by the phrase "sprung in the knees." It is said to have been produced by the efforts of the horses in "holding back," while descending the long and steep hills.

There was one mail coach that was especially imposing. On its gilded sides appeared the picture of a post boy, with flying horse and horn, and beneath it in gilt letters this awe inspiring inscription:

" He comes, the herald of a noisy world,
  News from all nations lumbering at his back."

No boy who beheld that old coach will ever forget it. The coaches were all handsomely and artistically painted and ornamented, lined inside with soft silk plush. There were three seats furnished with luxurious cushions, and three persons could sit comfortably on each, so that nine passengers made a full load as far as the interior was concerned. A seat by the side of the driver was more coveted in fair weather than a seat within. During the prosperous era of the road it was not uncommon to see as many as fifteen coaches in continuous procession, and both ways, east and west, there would be thirty each day.

James Kinkead, Jacob Sides and Abraham Russell put on the first line of passenger coaches west of Cumberland, and as early as 1818 John and Andrew Shaffer, Garrett Clark, Aaron Wyatt, Morris Mauler, John Farrell, Quill and Nathan Smith, and Peter Null, were drivers on this line. The Smiths and Null drove in and out from Uniontown. One of the Smiths subsequently became the agent of a stage line in Ohio. James Kinkead, above mentioned, was the senior member of the firm of Kinkead, Beck and Evans, who built most of the large stone bridges on the line of the road. This early line of stages was owned and operated in sections. Kinkead owned the line from Brownsville to Somerfield; Sides, from Somerfield to the Little Crossings, and thence to Cumberland Russell was the proprietor. Kinkead sold his section to George Dawson, of Brownsville, and Alpheus Beall, of Cumberland, bought out Russell's interest. This line was subsequently purchased by, and merged in, the National Road Stage Company, the principal and most active member of which was Lucius W. Stockton. The other members of this company were Daniel Moore, of Washington, Pennsylvania, Richard Stokes and Moore N. Falls, of Baltimore, and Dr. Howard Kennedy, of Hagerstown, Maryland. After the death of Mr. Stockton, in 1844, Dr. Kennedy and Mr. Acheson were the active members of the firm. John W. Weaver put a line of stages on the road at an early day, known as the People's Line. After a short run it was withdrawn from the road east of Wheeling, and transferred to the Ohio division. Previous to 1840, James Reeside put on a line which Mr. Stockton nick-named the "June Bug," for the reason, as he alleged, it would not survive the coming of the June bugs. Mr. Stockton subsequently bought out this line and consolidated it with his own. There was a line of stages on the road called the "Good Intent," which came to stay, and did stay until driven off by the irresistible force of the Steam King. This line was owned by Shriver, Steele & Company, and was equal in vim, vigor and general equipment to the Stockton line. The headquarters of the Good Intent line at Uniontown was the McClelland house. There passengers took their meals, and the horses were kept in the stables appurtenant. The "old line" (Stockton's) had its headquarters at the National house, on Morgantown street, now the private residence of that worthy and well known citizen, Thomas Batton. This little *bon mot* is one among a thousand, illustrative of the spirit of the competition between these rival lines. There was one Peter Burdine, a driver on the Good Intent line, noted for his dashing qualities, who was accustomed to give vent to his fidelity to his employers, and his confidence in himself in these words:

> "If you take a seat in Stockton's line,
> You are sure to be passed by Pete Burdine."

And this became a popular ditty all along the road.

On authority of Hanson Willison, the old stage driver of Cumberland, the first line of stages put on the road east of Cumberland, in opposition to the Stockton line, was owned, from Frederic to Hagerstown, by Hutchinson and Wirt; from Hagerstown to Piney Plains, by William F. Steele; from Piney Plains to Cumberland, by Thomas Shriver.

Thomas Corwin, the famous Ohio statesman and popular orator of the olden time, was not a stage driver, but he was a wagoner, and one of the rallying cries of his friends, in the campaign that resulted in his election as governor, was: "Hurrah for Tom Corwin, the wagoner boy." The introduction of his name, in connection with stages and stage drivers, becomes pertinent in view of the following anecdote: Corwin was of very dark complexion, and among strangers, and in his time, when race distinction was more pronounced than now, often taken for a negro. On one occasion, while he was a member of Congress, he passed over the road in a "chartered coach," in company with Henry Clay, a popular favorite all along the road, and other distinguished gentlemen, en route for the capital. A chartered coach was one belonging to the regular line, but hired for a trip, and controlled by the parties engaging it. The party stopped one day for dinner at an old "stage tavern," kept by Samuel Cessna, at the foot of "Town Hill," also known as "Snib Hollow," twenty-five miles east of Cumberland. Cessna was fond of entertaining guests, and particularly ardent in catering to distinguished travelers. He was, therefore, delighted when this party entered his house. He had seen Mr. Clay before, and knew him. The tall form of Mr. Corwin attracted his attention, and he noted specially his swarthy complexion, heard his traveling companions call him "Tom," and supposed he was the servant of the party. The first thing after the order for dinner was a suggestion of something to relieve the tedium of travel, and excite the appetite for the anticipated dinner, and it was brandy, genuine old cogniac, which was promptly brought to view by the zealous old landlord. Brandy was the "tony" drink of the old pike—brandy and loaf sugar, and it was often lighted by a taper and burnt, under the influence of a popular tradition that "if burnt brandy couldn't save a man" in need of physical tension, his case was hopeless. When the brandy was produced, the party, with the exception of Corwin, stepped up to the bar and each took a glass. Corwin, to encourage the illusion of the old landlord, stood back. In a patronizing way the landlord proffered a glass to Corwin, saying: "Tom, you take a drink." Corwin drank off the glass, and in an humble manner returned it to the landlord with modest thanks. Dinner was next announced, and when the party entered the dining room, a side table was observed for use of the servant, as was the custom at all old taverns on the road at that time. Corwin, at once recognizing the situation, sat down alone at the side table, while the other gentlemen occupied the main table. The dinner was excellent, as all were at the old taverns on the National Road, and while undergoing discussion, Mr. Clay occasionally called out to the lone occupant of the side table: "How are you getting on, Tom?" to which the modest response was, "Very well." After dinner the old landlord produced a box of fine cigars, and first serving the distinguished guests, took one from the box and in his hand proffered it to Mr. Corwin, with the remark: "Take a cigar, Tom?" When it was announced that the coach was in readiness to proceed on the journey, Mr. Clay took Corwin's arm, and, approaching the old landlord, said: "Mr. Cessna, permit me to introduce the Hon. Thomas Corwin, of Ohio." Cessna was thunder-struck. His mortification knew no bounds. Observing his mental agony, Mr. Corwin restored him to equanimity by saying: "It was all a joke, Mr. Cessna; do not, I beg you, indulge in the slightest feeling of mortification. I expect to be back this way before long, and will call again to renew acquaintance, and take another good dinner with you."

John Ritter, affectionately and invariably, by his acquaintances, called "Johnny," was noted for his honesty and steady habits. For many years after staging ceased on the road, he was a familiar figure about Washington, Pennsylvania. He assisted Major Hammond for thirty years in conducting the Valentine house, and acted as agent for Brimmer's line of mail hacks, and other similar lines, after the great mail and passenger lines were withdrawn. He was a bachelor, and a soldier of 1812, and drew a small pension. He died at the Valentine house, in Washington, on January 28th, 1879, in the eightieth year of his age, leaving behind him a good name and many friends.

The first line of passenger coaches put on the road between Brownsville and Wheeling was owned, organized and operated by Stephen Hill and Simms and Pemberton. This was in 1818, and a continuation of the early line before mentioned from Cumberland to Brownsville. Stephen Hill, while a stage proprietor, was also a tavern keeper in Hillsboro, Washington county, a small town, but an old town, which probably derived its name from his family. Under the inspiration of modern reformation, so called, the name of this old town has been changed and languishes now under the romantic appellation of Scenery Hill. When it was Hillsboro, and a stage station

WILLIAM WHALEY.

of the old pike, it was a lively little town. Under its present picturesque name it remains a little town, but not a lively one. The change of name, however, has not yet penetrated the thinned ranks of the old pike boys, and they still refer to it as Hillsboro.

The next station west of Hillsboro, where stage horses were changed, twelve miles distant, was Washington, where passengers also took meals. The Good Intent line stopped at the Mansion house, situate at the upper end of the town, and the "Old Line" stopped at the National, in the lower end. The next changing place west of Washington was Claysville, the next Roneys Point, and thence to Wheeling. About the year 1846 the Good Intent line stopped its coaches, or a portion of them, at the Greene house in Washington, kept by Daniel Brown, who, previous to that date, had, for a time, been a road agent of that line. Of all the good taverns on the road there were none better than Brown's. He had his pecularities, as most men have, but he knew how to keep a hotel. He enjoyed the occupation of entertaining guests, and glowed with good feeling while listening to the praises bestowed upon his savory spreads. This popular old landlord came to a sad and untimely end by being cut to pieces in a mill by a buzz saw, on what was once called the plank road, leading from Washington through Monongahela City, West Newton, Mt. Pleasant, Somerset and Bedford to Cumberland. Stages ran on that road, and at the time of the accident, Mr. Brown was in the service of a stage company and at the saw mill to urge forward the work of getting out plank for the road.

David Sibley, an old driver on Stockton's line, went with the Fayette county "boys in blue" to Mexico in 1847, a member of Co. H, 2d regiment of Pennsylvania volunteers. He participated in the engagement at Cerro Gordo, emerged from that conflict unscathed, but died soon after at Pueblo from ailments incident to an inhospitable climate.

William Whaley, a soldier of the war between the States, and a son of Capt. James Whaley, a soldier of 1812, was an old stage driver. He was born in Connellsville, but spent the prime of his life in Uniontown, and on the road. He used to tell the boys that one of the horses of his team died coming down Laurel Hill, but that he held him up until he reached the McClelland house in Uniontown. Whaley drove for a time on the Morgantown route from Uniontown, and died in the latter place twenty years and more ago.

James Turner, a Somerset county man, an old stage driver, also volunteered as a soldier in the Mexican war, and started out a member of Co. H, above mentioned. In crossing the Gulf he fell down a hatchway of the vessel and was killed, and the mortal remains of the old driver were buried in the deep sea.

James Gordon, a well remembered old stage driver, went with Co. H to Mexico, and died in the capital city of that Republic. He was the father-in-law of Peter Heck, a former postmaster of Uniontown.

Samuel Sibley, probably a brother of David, before mentioned, was a well-known driver. He was small in stature, but alert in movement. It was he who drove the coach that upset on a stone pile in the main street of Uniontown with Henry Clay as a passenger, the details of which have elsewhere been given.

Ben Showalter is remembered as an old driver, who sang little songs and performed little tricks of legerdemain for the amusement of the boys. He went to the war between the States as a private in Major West's cavalry of Uniontown, and died in the service.

Redding Bunting, mentioned before, was probably more widely known and had more friends than any other old stage driver on the road. His entire service on the road, covering many years, was in connection with the "old Line." He was a great favorite of Mr. Stockton, the leading proprietor of that line. His commanding appearance is impressed upon the memories of all who knew him. He stood six feet six inches high in his stockings, and straight as an arrow, without any redundant flesh. His complexion was of a reddish hue and his features pronounced and striking. His voice was of the baritone order, deep and sonorous, but he was not loquacious and had a habit of munching. He was endowed with strong common sense, which the pike boys called "horse sense," to emphasize its excellence. He was affable, companionable and convivial. He was a native of Fayette county, Pa., and born in Menallen township. He was not only a stage driver, but a trusted stage agent, stage proprietor, and also a tavern keeper. He once owned the property now known as the "Central Hotel," in Uniontown, and if he had retained it would have died a rich man. Despondency and depression of spirits seemed to have encompassed him, when business ceased on the road, and he appeared as one longing for the return of other and better days. During the presidency of Mr. Van Buren, it was deemed desirable by the authorities that one of his special messages should be speedily spread before the people. Accordingly arrangements were made by the Stockton line, which had the contract for carrying the mails, to transmit the message of the President with more than ordinary celerity. The Baltimore and Ohio railroad at the time was not in operation west of Frederic City, Maryland. Mr. Bunting, as agent of the company, repaired to that point to receive the coming document and convey it to Wheeling. He sat by the side of the driver the entire distance from Frederic to Wheeling to superintend the mission and urge up the speed. The distance between the points named is two hundred and twenty-two miles, and was covered in twenty-three hours and thirty minutes. Changes of teams and drivers were made at the usual relays, and the driver who brought the flying coach from Farmington to Uniontown was Joseph Woolley, who made the sparks fly at every step, as he dashed down the long western slope of Laurel Hill. Homer Westover drove the coach from Uniontown to Brownsville, covering the intervening distance of twelve miles in the almost incredible compass of forty-four minutes.

REDDING BUNTING.

The coach used on this occasion was called the "Industry," one of the early mail coaches with "monkey box" attachment, and it literally woke up the echoes in its rapid transit over the road. The Pittsburg *Gazette* had arranged for an early copy of the important message and agreed to pay Robert L. Barry and Joseph P. McClelland, of Uniontown, connected in various subordinate capacities with the stage lines, the sum of fifty dollars for a speedy delivery of the document at the office of that journal in Pittsburg. Brownsville was then the distributing point for all mail matter sent west over the National Road, consigned to Pittsburg, and Barry and McClelland went down to Brownsville on the "Industry" to obtain the message there and transmit it thence to Pittsburg by special convoy overland to the *Gazette;* but when the mail was opened it was discovered that it did not contain a package for the *Gazette*, and Barry and McClelland returned home disappointed, while the *Gazette* suffered still greater disappointment in not being able to lay an early copy of the message before its readers. The reader will bear in mind that at the time referred to the telegraph was unknown as an agency for transmitting news, and the railroad, as has been seen, had not advanced west of Frederic City, Maryland.

In the year 1846, after the railroad was completed to Cumberland, Redding Bunting rivaled, if he did not surpass, the feat of rapid transit above described. He drove the great mail coach from Cumberland to Wheeling. which carried the message of President Polk, officially proclaiming that war existed between the United States and Mexico. Leaving Cumberland at two o'clock in the morning, he reached Uniontown at eight o'clock of the same morning, breakfasted there with his passengers, at his own house (for he was then the proprietor of the National), and after breakfast, which was soon disposed of, proceeded with his charge, reaching Washington at eleven A. M. and Wheeling at two P. M., covering a distance of one hundred and thirty-one miles in twelve hours. He was not at that time an ordinary driver, but an agent of the line, and took the reins in person for the avowed purpose of making the highest speed attainable. Redding Bunting has been dead about ten years. His wife, who was a daughter of Capt. Endsley, the old tavern keeper at the Big Crossings, survived him about three years. He left two sons and two daughters. One of his sons, Henry Clay, is at present postmaster of Dunbar, Pa., and the other, William, is a printer, and at this writing foreman of the composing force of the Pittsburg *Times*. One of the daughters is the wife of Milton K. Frankenberry, a prominent citizen of Fayette county, Pa., and the other is the wife of Armor Craig, a leading merchant of Uniontown. The old driver has gone to his last home, but his memory remains fresh and fragrant all along the road.

Joseph Woolley, above mentioned, had a brother, William, who was also a well known stage driver. When the staging days on the road were ended, and the exciting incidents thereof relegated to the domain of history, Joseph and William Woolley sought and obtained employment in the service of the Baltimore and Ohio railroad company, and both ultimately became competent and trustworthy locomotive engineers.

Andrew J. Wable commenced driving stage in 1840, and continued uninterruptedly until 1851. He went to Illinois in 1867, and is still living, in good health and spirits. He frequently visits his old home in the mountains of Fayette county, where he was reared, and is there now, or was very recently. He drove first on the "Shake Gut," which was not a passenger line, but a line put on the road to carry light freights with rapidity. He drove next on the "Good Intent" line, and subsequently on the old, or Stockton line. He was a driver on the Good Intent line when William Scott was its agent, and on the old line during the agencies of Granger and Bunting. He drove on the Good Intent line from Somerfield to Keyser's Ridge, and on the old line from Keyser's Ridge to Piney Grove. He also drove between Washington and Wheeling, and from Uniontown to Farmington. His recollections of the old road are vivid, and he is fond of recounting incidents of its palmy days.

James Burr drove out westward from Washington. He was reputed to be a man of great muscular power, but with it all, a man of quiet demeanor. A Cincinnati man, name not given, had achieved the reputation of "licking" everybody in and around Cincinnati, and like Alexander of old, sighed for more victories. Hearing of Jim Burr, he resolved to encounter him, and struck out for Claysville, where he had been informed Burr could be found. He traveled by steamboat to Wheeling, thence by stage coach to Claysville. The Cincinnati man "put up" at the tavern of William Kelley, the stopping place of Burr's line at Claysville. Upon entering, the stranger inquired for Jim Burr, and was politely informed by Mr. Kelley, the old landlord, that Mr. Burr was at the stable looking after his team, and would soon be in. In a little while Burr came in, and Mr. Kelley remarked to the stranger, "this is Mr. Burr." The stranger, who was a somewhat larger man than Burr, saluted him thus: "Burr, I have been told that you are the best man in all this country, and I have come all the way from Cincinnati to fight you, and lick you, if I can." "Well," said Burr, "you have come a long distance for a job like that, and besides I don't know you, and there is no reason why we should fight." "But," rejoined the stranger, "you must fight me, I insist on it, and will not leave here until you do." Burr persisted in declining the proffered combat, and finally went upstairs to bed, and after a nap of half an hour's duration, came down without a thought of again meeting his aggressive visitor. To his utter surprise the Cincinnati bluffer met him at the foot of the stairs, and again demanded a trial of strength. This was more than Burr's good nature could withstand, and stepping back, he drew up in the attitude of a striker, warning his assailant at the same time to "look out." when with one blow of his fist, he felled him stone dead on the floor.

Burr then went to the water stand in a rear room of the tavern, washed his face and hands, and upon returning saw the victim of his deadly blow still lying prostrate upon the floor, and exclaimed: "My God, has that man not got up yet?" But the vanquished bully did, after a while, get up, and in rising discovered that he was a wiser, if not a better man. News of this singular encounter spread rapidly through the town of Claysville, and nearly every inhabitant thereof rushed to the scene to learn how it happened, and all about it. The facts were minutely and carefully made known to all inquirers by William Kelley, the old landlord, and cheers went up and out for Jim Burr, the hero of Claysville. At the time of this occurrence David Gordon was also driving out westwardly from Washington. Tradition has it that these two men had a reciprocal fear of each other, but they never collided, and it is a mooted question as to which of them was the better man in a physical sense. It is a long time since Burr and Gordon were seen on the front boot of a handsome Concord coach, wielding the reins and flourishing the whip over the backs of four dashing steeds with a grace and dignity befitting a more pretentious calling; and presumably they have answered the last summons, but living or dead, their names are indelibly stamped on the history of the National Road.

David Gordon was sent out from the east by James Reeside, and drove first on the "June Bug Line." Going out west from Claysville soon after he commenced driving his team ran off, with a full load of passengers. Discerning in a moment that the flying team could not be checked by ordinary methods, he pulled it off the road and turned the coach over against a high bank. The passengers were badly frightened, but none were hurt, and attributed their escape from injury to the skillfulness of the driver. After "righting up," the coach but little damaged, proceeded to Roney's Point without further casualty. This incident, or rather accident, gave Gordon a wide reputation as a cool and skillful driver, and he rapidly advanced to the front rank of his calling. The "June Bug Line" did not remain long on the road, and when it was withdrawn Gordon took service in the Good Intent line, and continued with it until all through lines of coaches were taken from the road. Gordon was a very stout man, six feet in height, and weighing about two hundred pounds, without any surplus flesh. It was said that he could fight, but was not quarrelsome. His motto seemed to be "*non tangere mihi*." On one occasion, as tradition has it, he was compelled to engage in a knock-down, in self defense. It was at Triadelphia, Virginia. Three "toughs" fell upon him at that place, with the intention, as they stated it, of "doing him up," but they failed ignominously. Gordon repulsed and routed them completely and decisively, and they never thereafter coveted a rencounter with Gordon, and the example of their fate rendered others with pugilistic proclivities a little shy about encountering him.

CHAPTER XXII.

Mr. A. J. Endsley, of Somerset, an intelligent, educated and observing gentleman, who was born and reared on the National Road, gives it as his judgment that old stage drivers, as a class, were better, morally, than old wagoners. He says that while some of the stage drivers were given to blaspheming and drinking, there were wagoners who would "discount them, especially in the matter of profanity." He names, as types of orderly, well behaved stage drivers, Thomas Grace, William and Alexander Thompson, John Mills, Charley Howell, John High, William Robinson, Isaac Frazee (still living in Markleysburg), Isaac Denny, Samuel Halsted, William White, Samuel Jaco, Thomas Moore, James A. Carroll, William Bishop and John Bunting. William Robinson and Pate Sides were expert penmen.

John E. Reeside, a son of Commodore James Reeside, the old stage proprietor, now residing in Baltimore, who had a general supervision of his father's lines on the National Road, gives three styles of stage driving, as follows, viz: (1) The Flat Rein (English); (2) the Top and Bottom (Pennsylvania); (3) the Side Rein (Eastern). In the first style Mr. Reeside says that John Bennett and Watty Noble excelled, and in the second, Jack Bailiss, Frank Lawson and Joe Bowers carried off the palm. He adds that the third mode was the one adopted by a majority of the best drivers, and in this, Isaac Page, Luda Adams, Peyton R. Sides, David Gordon, John Lanning, Abram Dedrick and David Johnson excelled all other drivers.

Mr. Endsley, before mentioned, divides the old stage drivers in four classes, as follows: "(1) Awkward, slovenly, careless drivers, such as handled the whip and 'ribbons' so clumsily, and kept their teams so unseemly together, up hill, down grades and on the level, that it was painful to see them on the box. Typical of this class were Tom Frantz, Dan Boyer, Pete Null and Abe Halderman. (2) Cruel men — their cruelty amounting almost to brutality. This class seemed to take a fiendish delight in whipping, lashing and gashing horses. Wash Alridge and a big, burly driver by the name of Robinson, were types of the cruel class. (3) Careful, easy-going, common, every day

JOHN BUNTING.

kind of drivers—men who never made pretensions to fancy styles. They were such as John Bunting (Old Judy), Jim Reynolds, James Carroll (Flaxey), Blanchard (Hatchet Face), Billy Armor and Josh. Boyce. (4) Well dressed drivers, clean and neat in person, and men who regarded sitting down to a meal in shirt sleeves as *contra, bonos mores.* This class manipulated the whip and 'ribbons' scientifically, and sat on the box in a way that showed they were masters of the situation. Prominent in this class were John High, Pate Sides, Peter Halderman, 'Yankee' Thompson, Sam Jerome, Jim Moore," &c. In this latter class might be ranked David Gordon, James Burr, and others of the western end of the road.

Samuel Luman, still living in Cumberland, and in good health, was one of the best equipped stage drivers on the road. His experience covers many of the most exciting and interesting events in the road's history. He commenced his career as a stage driver in 1832, the same year that Alfred Bailes began as a wagoner. He tells of a collision with highwaymen in the mountains, which was attended by thrilling details. On the 12th of August, 1834, he was on the road between Piney Grove and Frostburg, with a mail and passenger coach going east. After nightfall, and at a point studded by a thick growth of pine trees, he was confronted by a party of foot-pads, five in number, and strange to relate, one a woman, bent on felony. The outlook was alarming. Luman carried no fire-arms, and there was but one weapon among his passengers, a small, brass pistol, not brought into requisition, as the sequel shows. The assailants had thrown across the road an obstruction like a rude fence, made of logs, stumps and brush. As Luman's trusty leaders approached the obstruction, one of the highwaymen stepped out from his cover and seized a bridle, and the coach was stopped. The assailant ordered Luman to descend from his seat and surrender his charge. This he very politely, but very decidedly declined to do. "What do you want?" queried Luman, with seeming innocency. "We are traders," was the response. "Well," rejoined Luman, coolly, "I have nothing to trade; I am satisfied with my trappings, and not desirous of exchanging them." During this little parley the wood-be robber, who held a leader by the bridle, cried out to a partner in crime, who was near at hand, though under cover of darkness, to shoot the driver, and denounced him as a coward for not firing. The party thus addressed then leveled a pistol at Luman and pulled the trigger, but the result was nothing more than a "snap," the night air being damp and the powder failing to explode. These favorable surroundings, no doubt, saved Luman's life. The foot-pads at the heads of the leaders had, in the confusion and excitement of the moment, turned the horses squarely around, so that the leaders faced west, while the wheel horses stood to the east. In this conjuncture the party in charge of the leaders undertook to unhitch them, and to guard against the movements of Luman, wrapped a driving rein tightly around one of his arms. This was Luman's opportunity, and summoning all his resources, he poured a volley of stinging lashes upon

8

his antagonist, smiting him on the face and arm, alternately, and most vigorously. The bandit winced, and soon relinquished his grasp, when, almost in the twinkling of an eye, the team under Luman's skillful hands started up on a full run, leaping the improvised fence, and speeding on, leaving the foot-pads behind to lament their discomfiture. Mr. Luman relates that in crossing the improvised fence, he fairly trembled for the fate of himself and passengers, as the coach was within an ace of capsizing. He also states that the ruffian who seized his leader wore a gown that covered his whole person, tied around the middle of his body with a belt, and that another of his assailants wore a white vest, dark pantaloons, and covered his face with a black mask. The other three kept in the back ground during the attack, so that he is unable to recall their appearance. Mr. Luman further relates that when the first assault was made on him, he apprized his passengers of the impending danger and besought their assistance, but they crouched in their seats and made no effort to aid him or defend themselves. They were western merchants going east to buy goods, and had among them as much as sixty thousand dollars in cash. When the coach arrived safely at the Highland house, Frostburg, George Evans at that time proprietor thereof, the grateful passengers "took up" a collection for the benefit of their courageous and faithful driver and deliverer, but Luman says the sum proffered was so ludicrously small that he declined to receive it, and ever thereafter regarded that lot of passengers as a "mean set." Samuel Luman drove four teams between Cumberland and the Big Crossings. In 1839 he concluded to give up stage driving and try tavern keeping. His first venture in this line was at Piney Plains, east of Cumberland and near Cessna's old stand. He approved himself a popular landlord, and was well patronized. From Piney Plains he went to Frostburg, and took charge of the Franklin House. His next and last experience in tavern keeping was at the National House, in Cumberland. Luman interested himself in the detection and punishment of mail robbers, which drew upon him the animosity of suspected persons, and Mr. Stockton, fearing that the suspected ones might waylay and murder him, advised him to take service east of Cumberland, which he did. He is altogether one of the most interesting characters of the road.

George Fisher was a stage driver, who left his footprints very plainly on the limestone dust of the road. He was noted for his daring in the manipulation of fiery steeds. A fractious team was stationed at Claysville, which was the terror of all the drivers on that section of the road. It "ran off" several times, once killing a passenger outright, and seriously injuring others. This occurred on Caldwell's Hill, seven miles west of Washington, Pennsylvania. George Fisher was sent down from Washington to take charge of this team, and soon had it under complete control. He drove it many years without an accident. Fisher was a large, well proportioned, and fine looking man. He was driving the team mentioned in 1844, the year in which the celebrated political contest occurred, wherein James K.

SAMUEL LUMAN.

Polk and Henry Clay were opposing candidates for the presidency. Fisher was an ardent supporter of Polk, and quite bitter in his enmity against the Whigs. On the day of a large Whig meeting in Washington, an extra coach, not on regular time, but filled with passengers, passed over the road, going west. It fell to Fisher's lot to haul this coach from Claysville to Roney's Point, a relay beyond the State line, in Virginia. A delegation of Whigs, with banners and music, from West Alexander and vicinity, went up to Washington to attend the meeting, and on their return homeward in the evening, were overhauled by Fisher, who ran his team and coach into the Whig procession at several points, doing damage to buggies, carriages, and light wagons, and inflicting some quite serious personal injuries. Colin Wilson, a prominent citizen of Washington county at that date, was one of the persons injured by Fisher's inroad, and was seriously hurt. Fisher, in extenuation of his apparently criminal conduct, pleaded the irritability of his team, that it became frightened by the banners and music, was unmanageable, and the injuries inflicted were not intentional on his part, but purely accidental. The reputation of the team for pettishness was well known in the neighborhood of the occurrence, and served as a plausible excuse, and really saved Fisher from prosecution, and probably consequent punishment, but all the Whigs of that neighborhood went to their graves under the solemn belief that Fisher "did it a purpose." The following account of an accident, furnished by John Thompson, the old wagoner, no doubt relates to Fisher's team previous to the date at which he took charge of it: In the month of October, 1843, a stage team started to run from the locust tree near Caldwell's tavern. The driver lost control, and the team dashed down the long hill at a terrific gait. They kept in the road until Wickert's bridge was reached, at which point the coach, team, passengers, driver and all were violently thrown over the bridge. A Mr. Moses, a Kentucky merchant, and his nephew, were sitting by the side of the driver, and all remained firmly in their seats until the collapse occurred. The Kentucky merchant had a leg badly crushed, and in two days after the accident died, and was buried in the old graveyard at Washington. Doctors Stevens and Lane, of Washington, were promptly summoned and did all that medical and surgical skill could devise to aid the unfortunate sufferer, but gangrene ensued and baffled it all. The driver was severely hurt, and nursed at the Caldwell House until the spring of 1844, when he recovered. The nephew of Mr. Moses and all the other passengers escaped without injury. The remains of Mr. Moses were subsequently removed from Washington by his relatives, and interred near his home in Kentucky. Wickert's bridge is so called because a man of that name was murdered many years ago near it, and for a long time thereafter, according to neighborhood superstition, returned to haunt the bridge.

Daniel Leggett was an old stage driver, well known, and will be long remembered. He once had the distinction of hauling the celebrated Indian chief, Black Hawk, and his *suite*. The party ascended the Ohio river by steamboat, and took stage at Wheeling. Upon entering the coach at that point, Black Hawk showed shyness, fancying it might be a trap set for him by his pale faced enemies, and it required some persuasion by an interpreter, who accompanied his party, to induce him to enter and take a seat. The coach passed over the road without unusual incident until it reached Washington, Pennsylvania. Going down the main street of Washington, from the post-office, which was in the neighborhood of the court house, the breast strap of one of the wheel horses broke, causing a precipitation of the coach upon the leaders, and the team becoming frightened, dashed down the street at fearful speed. One of the party of Indians was seated by the driver, and thrown off, carrying down with him the driver. The team, thus left without a driver, rushed headlong for the stable of the National House, and at the corner of Main and Maiden streets, the coach upset. It contained nine passengers, eight Indians and one half-breed. The first one to show up from the wreck was Black Hawk, who stood upright in the middle of the street, disclosing a single drop of blood on his forehead, and manifesting much excitement and indignation, as he uttered "Ugh! Ugh! Ugh!" The interpreter had an arm broken, which was the only serious casualty attending the accident. Black Hawk now became almost wholly irreconcilable. The interpreter tried to explain to him the true situation, and to assure him that no harm was aimed at him, but the dusky warrior repelled the approaches of the friendly mediator, and refused to be reconciled. He was now certain that the white men intended to kill him. After a little while the excitement abated, and with it the temper of the unfortunate Indian chieftain. He was persuaded to enter the tavern, and observing that the surroundings were not hostile, threw off his sullenness, and became somewhat sensible of the situation, and apparently reconciled to it. Another coach of the line was provided, and the party proceeded on their journey to parley with the Great Father of the White House. The occasion marked an era in the life and career of the old driver, Daniel Leggett, which he referred to with intense interest on frequent occasions throughout the remainder of his life. The Black Hawk incident occurred in 1837, when Van Buren was president.

Tobias Banner, as if to do justice to his name, was an imposing driver. He was a chum of Jerry McMullin, another old driver, and the two together enjoyed many a game of bluff, while their teams were quietly resting in the well furnished old stables. They were both mail drivers in and out from Washington. McMullin at one time to vary the monotony of stage life, made a trip to Stockton's lane, in Greene county, to see the races, which occurred at regular periods at that place in that day. He engaged in a game of seven up, with a stalwart native of Greene county, for five dollars a side, and while he really won the game, his overgrown adversary claimed the stakes on an allegation of foul play. A quarrel and a fight ensued, and Jerry

McMullin returned to Washington with a blackened eye and diminished purse, vowing that he would never venture upon mud roads again.

George McKenna drove first on the Oyster line and afterwards a stage team. He was a Greene county man, and brother-in-law of Morgan R. Wise. After he quit driving he set up an oyster saloon in Waynesburg, and finally engaged with a travelling menagerie and lost his life in a railroad accident between New York and Philadelphia.

Paris Eaches, a strangely sounding name now, but once familiar to the ear of every pike boy, was a well known and well liked driver. He radiated from Washington, Pennsylvania, but left his mark all along the line. He was a jolly fellow and enjoyed the excitement of the road. He was always a favorite at social parties of young folks, and entertained them with songs. He had a good voice and sang well. "I have left Alabama," was one of his best songs, and he always sang it to the delight of his hearers.

Jack Bailiss was a widely known and popular driver, a married man, and a resident of Washington, Pennsylvania. He was accounted a reckless driver, and delighted in exciting the apprehension of his passengers, often filling them with terror by specimens of what they considered reckless driving. He knew the danger line however, and always kept within it. He drove the coach from Claysville to Washington, Pennsylvania, in which Gen. Taylor traveled on his way to the Capital to assume the Presidency.

Henry A. Wise, an old driver, is well remembered by the old people of the road on account of the quaintness of his character. He was not a driver on the National Road, but drove the mail coach from Uniontown to Morgantown, Virginia. Mr. Stockton had the contract for carrying the mail between these points, and Wise was his chief driver, and pursued this calling for many years. His headquarters in Uniontown were at the Old Hart tavern, Jackson's favorite stopping place, now the Hotel Brunswick. He was driving on this route as early as 1836. He was an odd genius, as Mr. John E. Reeside says of him, a "typical tide water Virginian." He claimed to be descended from blue blood, and simply drove stage for amusement. He always had plenty of slack in his reins, and as a consequence rarely kept his team straight in the road. It is said that on one occasion, while half a sleep on the box, his team turned from the road through an open gap into a field, and commenced eagerly to graze on the growing clover. Wise was tall and spare, and habitually wore a high silk hat.

John Huhn was a driver west of Washington, Pennsylvania. He married a daughter of John McCrackin, a well known and prosperous farmer of the vicinity of Claysville. When stage lines dissolved and stage coaches no longer rattled over the old pike, John Huhn engaged in the tanning business at Claysville, and was successful.

Peter Payne, an old driver east and west from Keyser's Ridge, was noted as an expert hand at a game of poker. He was usually a winner, and being a man of economic habits, saved his small accumulations from time to time and ultimately became rich. He often sat down to a game with Joseph Dilly, an old blacksmith of the mountain division of the road, a skillfull player, who, like Payne, also grew rich.

Frank Lawson, who subsequently kept tavern in Triadelphia, was a stage driver. He first drove on Weaver's Ohio line, next on a line in Kentucky, where he upset a coach causing the death of one or more of his passengers, and afterward came to the National Road and drove between Wheeling and Washington. He is mentioned by Mr. Reeside as an expert driver of the "Top and Bottom," or Pennsylvania mode of driving.

John Stotler was among the drivers on the first line of stages. He was stoutly built, a good reinsman and a popular driver. He drove out east and west from Cumberland. John Whitney, an Englishman, was an early driver, and noted for his caution in handling his team and caring for the comfort and safety of passengers.

Joseph Whisson drove from Washington to Claysville, and is well remembered and highly spoken of by all old citizens living on that section of the road. He is still living at Triadelphia, West Virginia.

Jason Eddy was one of the many drivers sent out on the road in an early day from New Jersey by "Commodore" Reeside, as James, the old stage proprietor, was frequently called. Eddy was an expert driver, and it was said of him that "he could turn his team and coach on a silver dollar." He was likewise a good musician, and played well on the bugle. He often entertained his passengers with stirring bugle blasts.

William Walker was a careful old driver, and so economical that he acquired property from the savings of his scanty wages.

William Craver, Edward Hays and the two Welches were old stage drivers, whose names were familiar along the road in its early history.

Isaac Page, first named by Mr. Reeside as a good driver in the Eastern style, was a Uniontown man, and died in that place before the glories of the old road had waned. He left a widow and a son, Charles, who went to New York, where the son engaged in business, prospered and became rich. His mother was highly esteemed by all who knew her, and to her example is attributed the success of the son.

Dr. Thayer, who subsequently became a circus proprietor, commenced driving stage on the National Road when eighteen years of age. He drove from Uniontown to Farmington on the "old line" previous to 1840. He was a skillful driver, and subsequently achieved success as a circus owner.

Gideon Bolton (nicknamed "Hoop-pole," from the circumstance of his coming from a hoop-pole region in Preston county, West Virginia), drove many years on the mountain division of the road, and is well remembered.

JOSEPH WHISSON.

James McCauley, an old driver, before reaching the dignity of the box, was a "postilion" for Redding Bunting on the mail coaches from Somerfield to Woodcock Hill, and to Winding ridge.

Jack Lee was a spirited driver, and would have been called a "dude" if he had not died before that term was applied to persons of fanciful and fashionable apparel. He drove in and out from Cumberland and was contemporaneous with Whitney.

David Bell, an old stage driver, subsequently kept a tavern in Claysville. His daughter became the wife of Calvin King, an officer of one of the Claysville banks.

William Corman, an old stage driver, is remembered as a *pal* of Dr. John F. Braddee in the celebrated mail robberies of 1840, at Uniontown. Braddee's office adjoined Stockton's stage yard. Corman drove the mail coach, and handed over the mail bags to Braddee, who rifled them. A full account of these mail robberies is given elsewhere in this volume.

John Bennett and James and John Bailiss drove out west from Washington, Pennsylvania, for many years, and were among the most careful and skillful drivers. Bennett died in Hillsboro.

Joshua Johnson, a Canadian, and an old stage driver, married a Miss Slicer, of Flintstone, Maryland, and subsequently kept a tavern in Cumberland.

CHAPTER XXIII.

The first mail coaches were arranged to carry but three passengers, in addition to the mail pouches, upon a model furnished by the postoffice department. Drivers and residents along the road called the passenger compartment of the early mail coach a "monkey box." This was at the front end of the vehicle, and rested on springs, and the mail pouches were placed behind it, on a lower plane, and in a long, tight, wooden box or bed, resting on the axles of the wagon, without springs. It made a loud noise when passing over the road, was altogether a curious contrivance, and after a short term of usage was abandoned, and the ordinary passenger coach substituted in its stead. Mr. Stockton established a coach factory in Uniontown, where many of the coaches of his line were made, and as necessity from time to time existed, repaired. Blacksmith shops were also set up in connection with this factory, where the stage horses of the Stockton line were shod. It was called the "stage yard," and located on Morgantown street, on the lot now covered by the residence and grounds of the Hon. Nathaniel Ewing. Many mechanics in different lines of work were employed in the "stage yard," and some of them still linger on the shores of time, and in Uniontown. *Philip Bogardus is probably the oldest of the surviving employees of the old stage yard, and is a well known and respected citizen of Uniontown. He was born in Dutchess county, New York, September 25, 1811, and came to Uniontown in 1838. On his journey to that place he halted for a season and worked at his trade, that of a coach trimmer, at Bloody Run, Bedford county, Pennsylvania, and there first met and formed the acquaintance of Henry Nycum, the well remembered and respected old blacksmith, who lived many years in Uniontown, and died there about a year ago. Soon after his arrival in Uniontown, Bogardus obtained employment in the stage yard. The foreman of the yard at the time was William Gaddis.

* Died recently.

MAJ. WILLIAM A. DONALDSON.

Next in seniority, among the surviving employees of the stage yard, is *Maj. William A. Donaldson, one of the best known citizens of Uniontown. He is a painter. He was born in Emmettsburg, Frederic county, Maryland, a village situate ten miles south of Gettysburg, on February 14, 1818, and came to Uniontown February 15, 1839. He located first at Brownsville, and remained there a year and upwards before going to Uniontown. His first engagement in Uniontown was with Col. William B. Roberts, in whose service he continued about a year, after which he entered the stage yard as a painter and ornamenter of coaches. He is not only a skillful artisan, but a gentleman well read in history, philosophy, theology, and politics, in short a good and useful citizen. When Dr. Braddee was first lodged in the Uniontown jail for robbing the mails, Maj. Donaldson called in the evening to see him. The accused was placed in charge of a special police force, which consisted of Zadoc Cracraft, George Martin, and Stewart Speers, who "stood guard" over the noted prisoner. Soon after Maj. Donaldson entered the jail the guardsmen informed him that they were very hungry, and desired to go down town to get some oysters, and requested him to remain in charge of the prisoner until they returned. To this Maj. Donaldson assented, provided the hungry guardsmen would speedily return. They went out for oysters and did not get back until one o'clock in the morning. The Major and the Doctor, being old acquaintances, spent the intervening time as pleasantly as circumstances would admit of, but it was not exactly the thing the Major had bargained for. Mr. Stockton had one of his coaches named John Tyler, in honor of the vice-president of the first Harrison administration. When Tyler, by the death of Harrison, succeeded to the presidency, and vetoed the United States bank bill, Mr. Stockton was very much angered thereat, and going into the stage yard, soon after the veto was announced, accosted Maj. Donaldson thus: "Donaldson, can't you erase that name (pointing to the Tyler coach) and substitute another? I won't have one of my coaches named for a traitor." "Certainly I can," replied Donaldson, "what shall the new name be?" "Call it Gen. Harrison," said Stockton. "All right," said Donaldson, and the change was made. Maj. Donaldson was a Democrat, and much amused by the incident.

Robert L. Barry, the well remembered old merchant of Uniontown, was, in his younger days, a painter in the old stage yard. Other painters in the stage yard were William McQuilken, William McMullin, William Crisfield, —— Mathiot, Ebenezer Matthews, George Starr, Alex. Fowler and Harrison Wiggins. Lewis Mobley was also a painter in the stage yard. He subsequently moved to Luzerne township, Fayette county, Pennsylvania, became a farmer and local politician. He had many good points of character and many warm friends. He died in Luzerne township a number of years ago. The Belfords, father and three sons, were of the stage yard force, workers in wood. They came from New Jersey, and were near relatives of the old and distinguished

* Died July 27th, 1893.

8a

Presbyterian preacher, Rev. A. G. Fairchild, D.D. The Belfords went west, and in all probability have passed from earth to scenes beyond.

Armstrong Hadden, the old postmaster and banker, of Uniontown worked a number of years in the stage yard on harness and "thorough braces." He learned his trade with Westley Frost, of Brownsville. Thorough braces were the leather springs, thick and wide, upon which the coach body was placed. Alex. McLean, the old clerk of the county commissioners, also worked on harness and braces.

Charles Brower was a trimmer. He came from Baltimore, and went from the stage yard in Uniontown to the State of Louisiana, since which time he has made no sign so far as known.

Abram Rogers was a worker on "thorough braces." Other workers in wood were Isaac and Simon Sampsell, Israel Hogue, and Frank Wilkinson. Among the blacksmiths of the old stage yard were James Rush, who subsequently went to Washington, Pennsylvania, where he lived many years, and until his death, which occurred recently, Thomas Haymaker, and his son, Leroy, Thomas Stewart, Michael Claybaugh, Jesse King, Thomas King, James Keenan, Fred Reamer, Abram Haldeman, Seth White, Hugh Rogers. and Jacob, Isaac and Robert Prettyman.

The inevitable company store was connected with the stage yard, but it was not so odious then as now. It was located on Morgantown street, in the building now occupied by the Ellis music store, and managed by John Keffer, who is well remembered by all the old citizens of Uniontown. George Martin was a clerk in the company store. Coaches were all named after the manner of steamboats, and more recently, sleeping cars on the leading railroads. The name of every State of the Union was utilized for this purpose, and the realms of fancy were likewise explored. The coach named for Pennsylvania bore the legend Keystone State; Ohio was honored under the name Buckeye State, New Hampshire, the Granite State, Massachusetts, the Bay State, and so on. Among the fancy names employed, the old pike boy will readily recall the following: Fashion, Palmetto, Central Route, Jewess, Beauty, Pathfinder, Samaratan, Highlander, Ivanhoe, Herald, Industry, National, Republic, Protection, Brilliant, Atlas, Sultana, Clarendon, Chancellor, Moravian, Miantonoma, Loch Lomond. Warriors, statesmen and old stagers were remembered and honored in the names following: Washington, Lafayette, General Wayne, General St. Clair, General Jackson, General Harrison, Rough and Ready, meaning General Taylor, General Worth, General Cass, Colonel Benton, Madison, Monroe, Henry Clay, The President, James K. Polk, Purviance, Daniel Moore, L. W. Stockton, General Moorehead, David Shriver, William H. Stelle, James C. Acheson, Columbus, Pocahontas, Santa Anna. Countries and cities were honored in the names that follow: Yucatan, Green Bay, Oronoco, Tampico, Bangor, Mexico, Buena Vista, New Orleans, Erie, Lexington, Vicksburg, Natchez, Trenton, San Francisco, Mobile, Troy, Wyandott,

Idaho, Ashland, Westmoreland, Allegany, Raritan, Youghiogheny, Gautemala, Panama, Hungarian, Montgomery, Paoli, Tuscaloosa. One coach took in a hemisphere, and was called America. Another was named Queen Victoria in the old stage days, as now, the reigning sovereign of England, while another rendered homage to dear old Ireland, by bearing the legend, Erin Go Bragh. When Harrison, the first, Polk and Taylor passed over the road to the capital, to be installed in the presidential office, a splendid new coach was provided for each occasion, called the President, in which the President-elect and his immediate family were conveyed. The presidential parties did not travel in the night time, but rested at stations along the road until morning. At Uniontown, President Harrison and party stopped over night at the Walker house, now called the Central. Polk lodged at the National and Taylor at the Clinton. The Walker and Clinton were not stage houses, but the distinguished passengers were quartered therein, respectively, for the purpose, probably, of conciliating some local political influences.

Henry Clay knew many of the old stage drivers personally, and would call them by name when he met them at different points along the road. He not only made acquaintances and friends of the drivers, but of the tavern keepers and persons in other employments on the road. David Mahaney, now living in Dunbar, kept tavern at various points on the mountain division of the road, and often entertained Mr. Clay, and became well acquainted with him. One Humes, of Claysville, was wont to boast of the familiarity with which he was recognized by Mr. Clay. While the teams were being changed at stations, Mr. Clay was in the habit of getting out of the coach and going in to the taverns. On occasion of one of these short stops, Humes was introduced to Mr. Clay. On the return trip, less than a year afterward, Humes heard of his coming, and hastened to the station to greet him. The coach was driven up and Mr. Clay got out, but before entering the tavern espied Humes approaching, and when near enough to be heard, said: "There comes my friend Humes," and gave him a cordial hand-shaking. Humes was delighted, and never wearied in telling the story of his acquaintance with Clay.

When Jennie Lind, the world renowned songstress, made her first professional visit to the United States, she returned east from her western tour by way of the National Road, in company with her troupe, and in "chartered" coaches of the Stockton line. This was at least forty years ago, probably a little more than that. P. T. Barnum, the celebrated showman, was the great singer's manager, and was with her on the occasion referred to. The party remained over night at Boss Rush's tavern, twelve miles east of Uniontown. The people along the road heard of the coming of the distinguished travelers, and a number assembled at the tavern in the evening to get a glimpse of them. William Shaffer drove the coach in which Barnum was seated, and when he halted in front of the tavern one of the curious called up to the driver on the box and inquired: "Which is Barnum?" Shaffer answered gruffly: "I don't know Barnum from the devil." Barnum, meanwhile, had emerged from the coach, and standing by its side overheard the inquiry and the driver's reply, and stepping up to the inquisitor said to him: "I am Barnum; the driver is right, it is hard to distinguish me from the devil." The party entered the good old tavern and were entertained and lodged in the handsome style for which Boss Rush was greatly and justly distinguished. Fresh trout were served for breakfast, which had been taken the day before in a near by mountain stream by F. B. Titlow and young Boss Rush, then a lad of sixteen. Titlow, now one of the best known citizens of the vicinity of Uniontown, and still a lover of fishing and hunting, was then an apprentice to the tailoring trade at Farmington, under tne guidance of John Hair. Young Boss, grown gray, still lingers about the portals of his father's old tavern, musing over the memories of the old pike.

William G. Beck, an old stage driver, still living in Fairfield, Iowa, has vivid recollections of the road. In a letter he states that, "if there is anything in the world that makes him, at the age of seventy-four, jump up and crack his heels together and wish he was a boy again, it is reading about the men and things of the National Road." He is a son of James Beck, of the old bridge building firm, and commenced to drive stage on the Old line when in his minority. He was born in Uniontown in 1819, went to Iowa in 1847, and was on the National Road as a stage driver as late as 1846. In his letter he states that in 1846 the Old line and the Good Intent both carried the mails. There was a "Lock mail" in leather pouches, and a "Canvass mail," the latter very frequently called "the second mail," carried in alternate months by the respective lines. In December, 1846, he says the Old line carried the "Lock mail." The details of an exciting race on the road he furnishes as follows: "A Good Intent coach was driven by Jacob Cronch to the railway station, immediately upon the arrival of the train at Cumberland, loaded up with the 'Canvass mail,' and started off under full speed for the West. The 'Lock mail,' which fell to me, was taken to the postoffice and overhauled, causing a considerable detention. While waiting in front of the post-office for the mail bags, Jacob Shuck and other Good Intent drivers chided me with the fact that the 'Canvass' had such a start that I could not get near it. I made up my mind that if it was in the hides of my two teams I would catch him, and pass him. It was after nightfall, and in crossing a water way in Cumberland my lamps went out, and what I deemed a calamity turned out in the end to be an advantage. As soon as I crossed the Wills creek bridge, I put my team in a full run and never pulled them up until I reached Rock Hill, seven miles out of Cumberland. At that point, in the winding of the road, I espied the lights on the coach of my rival, while he, by reason of the going out of my lights, was unable to see me, although, on the long stretches, he was constantly watching for a glimpse of me. Much to his surprise I drew up along side of him,

WILLIAM G. BECK.

and side by side we drove into Frostburg, lashing our tired teams at every jump. The grooms at the Frostburg station had my second team hitched to the coach by the time I was fairly stopped. A friendly driver ran with the way mail to the Frostburg postoffice, while another re-lit my lamps. I did not leave my seat. The reins over the fresh team were thrown up to me, and I was off again in a full run. The way mail bag was thrown into the front boot as I dashed past the postoffice. At Sand Spring (foot of Big Savage) I passed the 'Canvass' and held the lead, trotting my team every inch of the road to Piney Grove, the end of my route, which I reached twenty-two minutes in advance of my competitor. Lem Cross kept the tavern where our line stopped at Piney Grove. I made my route of twenty-two miles with two teams in two hours and ten minutes, fourteen miles of the distance, to the top of Big Savage, being ascending grade. James Reynolds relieved me at Piney Grove, and my competitor was relieved at that point by Joshua Boyd."

Among old stage drivers there was one conspicuous above all others, on account of his immense size. It was Montgomery Demmings, known as "Old Mount." He was six feet and upward in height, and his average weight was four hundred and sixty-five. It was a common remark, in the days of staging on the National Road, that " Old Mount on the front boot of a coach balanced all the trunks that could be put in the rear boot." As he grew old his weight increased, and at his death, upon authority of his widow, who is still living, was six hundred and fifty pounds. He was born and reared in Allentown, New Jersey, and was sent out on the road in 1836 by James Reeside. His first service was on the "June Bug Line," a line of brief existence, but full of dash and spirit. "Old Mount" married the widow of Joseph Magee, on May 3, 1839. The clergyman who performed the marriage ceremony was the Rev. John W. Phillips, of Uniontown. Joseph Magee was a blacksmith. His residence and shop were on the roadside, at the west end of Uniontown, near the present toll house. He owned sixteen acres of land on the northeast side of the road, which now forms a part of the Gilmore tract, and his widow, who is also the widow of "Old Mount," is still living with a third husband, one Thomas, of Wales. Her present home is in Allegheny City, Pa., and she continues to draw a dower interest from the land owned by her first husband, above mentioned. "Old Mount" has a son, Amos Frisbie Demmings, living near his mother, named after Amos Frisbie, who lived in Uniontown many years ago, and carried on the business of stove making. After driving a stage for a number of years, "Old Mount" relinquished his connection with the passenger coaches, and became a driver on the express line. This line carried small packages of light goods, and oysters, known as fast freight. and the people along the road, by way of derision, called it " The Shake Gut Line." The vehicles of this line were long and strong box-shaped wagons, something like the wagons used for transporting a menagerie. They were drawn by four horses, with relays at established points, driven by check reins or lines, as stage teams were driven. The speed of the express wagons was almost equal to that of the coaches of the stage lines. They made a great noise in their rapid passage over the road, and coming down some of the long hills, could be heard for miles. By the side of the drivers frequently sat one or more way-goers whose necessities impelled them to seek cheap transportation. What proportion of their meagre fares went to the driver, and what to the owners of the line, has never been definitely ascertained. "Old Mount" stuck to the road until its glory began to fade, and in April, 1851, left Uniontown and removed with his family to Brownsville, where he remained about eighteen months. While residing at Brownsville, he was engaged in hauling goods from the steamboat landing at that place to points in western Virginia, along the line of the Baltimore and Ohio railroad, then undergoing construction. He owned the team he drove in this employment. From Brownsville he went to South Side Pittsburg, then a separate municipality, called Birmingham. From that point he continued the hauling of goods to western Virginia, and also kept a boarding house. He did not remain in Birmingham longer than two years, probably not that long, and moved from there to McKeesport, where he engaged in the hotel business, having previously leased the Eagle House at that place. He died at McKeesport on March 4, 1855, and was buried there. His death occurred in less than a year after he went to McKeesport, and thus terminated the career of one whose name, half a century ago, was familiarly spoken in every town, tavern and wayside cabin, from Baltimore to Wheeling.

Simeon Houser was a stage driver. When stages left the road Simeon went to tavern keeping. He kept the old house which stood on the lot now occupied by the residence of Dr. Ewing, in Uniontown. It was called the "Buzzard's Roost," not by reason of any bad fame of Simeon Houser, for it had that name before he got there. Simeon was a very tall man, and raw boned, with strongly marked face and features. He served a number of years as constable of Uniontown. In 1851 William Bigler and William F. Johnson, rival candidates for governor, visited Uniontown. Bigler took in Greene county on his tour, and coming over to Fayette, struck the National Road at Searight's, where he met a popular ovation. His friends in that vicinity made a large raft of logs, which they placed on a strong wagon, and with a team of six white horses hauled to Uniontown, the Brownsville brass band seated on the raft and discoursing music, as the procession moved along the road. Bigler, in his early days, had been employed in constructing and running rafts on the Susquehanna river, and his supporters stirred up enthusiasm for him by calling him "The Raftsman of the Susquehanna." He was elected, not because he was a raftsman, but because the Democrats of that day outnumbered the Whigs. Johnston, his competitor, was a Whig. The present Republican party was not then in existence. Simeon Houser, aforesaid, drove the big white team that hauled the raft, and this is why allusion is made to the incident. It was a grand

HENRY FARWELL.

day for Simeon. Mr. Bigler spoke from the raft in Bierer's woods, west of Uniontown, to a great multitude, and Dr. Smith Fuller, standing on the same raft, made the speech of welcome. Simeon Houser, like hundreds of old pike boys, yielded up his life in defense of the Stars and Stripes.

Henry Farwell, father of the Broadway printer, was an old stage driver. He came to Uniontown in 1839, "the winter of the deep snow." He came on the Oyster Line from Little Crossings, working his way through the snow, which averaged a depth of four feet on the level, and was three days on the way. The oyster boxes were placed on a sled, drawn by six horses, and the Oyster Line made as good time as the stage lines while the deep snow lasted, and passenger coaches, like oyster boxes, were moved on sleds. Farwell came to Uniontown in obedience to an order of one of the stage lines, to take charge of a team at that place. He drove stage for ten years, one-half of the time in Ohio. When the staging days were over on the old road, Farwell located in Uniontown, and carried on the trade of shoemaking, which he learned before he took to stage driving. He owned the lot on which the National Bank of Fayette county now stands. He has been dead several years, and is well remembered by the older citizens of Uniontown.

Archie McNeil was of the class of merry stage drivers, and enlivened the road with his quaint tricks and humorous jokes. His service as a driver was confined for the most part to the western end of the road, between Brownsville and Wheeling. An unsophisticated youth from the back country, of ungainly form and manners, near the close of the forties, sauntered into Washington, Pennsylvania, to seek employment, with an ambition not uncommon among young men of that period, to become a stage driver. In his wanderings about the town he halted at the National House, then kept by Edward Lane, where he fell in with Archie McNeil, and to him made known the object of his visit. Archie, ever ready to perpetrate a joke, encouraged the aspirations of the young "greenhorn," and questioned him concerning his experience in driving horses and divers other matters and things pertaining to the work he proposed to engage in. Opposite the National House, on the Maiden street front, there was a long wooden shed, into which empty coaches were run for shelter, the tongues thereof protruding toward the street. McNeil proposed to the supplicating youth that he furnish a practical illustration of his talent as a driver, to which he readily assented, and crossing the street to the shed where the coaches were, he was commanded to climb up on the driver's seat, which he promptly did. McNeil then fastened a full set of reins used for driving, to the end of the coach tongue, and handed them up to the young man. He next placed in his hands a driver's whip, and told him to show what he could do. The coach bodies, it will be remembered, were placed on long, wide, and stout leather springs, which caused a gentle rocking when in motion. The young weakling, fully equipped as a driver, swayed himself back and forth, cracked the whip first on one side, and then on the other of the tongue, rocked the coach vehemently, manipulated the reins in various forms and with great pomp, and continued exercising himself in this manner for a considerable time, without evincing the slightest consciousness that he was the victim of a joke. A number of persons, the writer included, witnessed this ludicrous scene, and heartily enjoyed the fun. Among the spectators was James G. Blaine, then a student at Washington college. McNeil was a son-in-law of Jack Bailiss, the old driver before mentioned, and when stage lines were withdrawn from the road he moved with his family to Iowa, and settled in Oskaloosa.

Watty Noble might well be esteemed the Nestor of stage drivers. He commenced his career as a driver on the Bedford and Chambersburg pike. His route on that road was between Reamer's and the Juniata Crossings, *via* Lilly's and Ray's Hills, a distance of ten miles, and his average time between the points named, was one hour and thirty minutes. He drove one team on this route for a period of ten years without losing or exchanging a horse. He subsequently drove for five consecutive years on the National Road, between Brownsville and Hillsboro, and, as the old pike boys were accustomed to say, "leveled the road." When he "got the start," no other driver could pass him, unless in case of accident. He was not a showy reinsman, but noted for keeping his team well and long together. In personal habits he was quiet and steady, and no man ever impeached his honesty or fidelity. Jim Burr, the famous old driver elsewhere mentioned, was a son-in-law of Watty Noble.

Charley Bostick, a stage driver who lived in Uniontown, gained a somewhat unsavory reputation as one of the principals in a social scandal, involving the name of a prominent old Uniontown merchant. The incident produced great agitation in Uniontown society at the time, and its disagreeable details are stored away in the memories of all the older citizens of that place, but it is doubtful if three-fourths of its present inhabitants ever heard of it. On the night of the occurrence it fell to Bostick's lot in the rounds of his regular service as a driver, to take a coach from Uniontown to Farmington, but he was so prominently and closely identified with the event referred to that he deemed it expedient to employ a substitute, which he procured in the person of "Dumb Ike," competent for the service and the occasion, and ever ready for such exigencies.

Alfred Wolf, an old stage driver, is remembered as a large, fine looking and blustering sort of a man. His wife was a sister of Watson and Robinson Murphy, two well known, thrifty and highly esteemed farmers of Fayette county, Pennsylvania. The marriage ceremony that made Miss Martha Murphy the lawful wife of Alfred Wolf was performed by the late Hon. William Hatfield, when that gentleman was an acting Justice of the Peace for Redstone township, and the writer hereof was present at the wedding. When stage drivers were no longer required on the National Road, Alfred Wolf engaged in the business of tavern keeping, and for a number of years kept a public house in McClellandtown; and when the strife between the States culminated in actual hostilities, he enlisted as a Union soldier and perished in the cause. His widow went to Ohio, re-married, and is still living in that State.

Henry G. Marcy, called Governor, because of his near kinship to the old time, distinguished New York statesman of that name, who was at the head of the War Department during the conflict with Mexico, was a stage driver and lived in Uniontown. He was a small man in stature, but had a bright and clear intellect. He died in Uniontown a number of years ago at an advanced age, leaving a widow, still surving, but quite feeble by reason of her great age. George E. Marcy, also called Governor, a well known and active Democratic politician of Uniontown, is a son of the old driver.

Joseph Hughes, an old stage driver, is still living in Washington, Pennsylvania, vivacious and sprightly despite the weight of years piled upon his back. He was an expert and trusty driver, well known along the road, and cherishes the memory of the stirring times, when the road was the great highway of the Nation and he and his fellow drivers rode on the top wave of the excitement incident thereto.

James Bradley, an old stage driver, worked sometimes at repairs on the road. He made a breaker of unusual height on the hill east of Washington, Pennsylvania, and upon being questioned as to his motive for making it so high, replied that "he wanted to give some of the boys a lofty toss." A few days thereafter, he was in service as a driver himself, and going down the hill mentioned at a rapid rate, to "scoot the hollow," as he termed it, his coach struck the high breaker and he got the "lofty toss" himself, having been thrown from the box, a distance of nearly two rods, causing him a broken arm and other less serious injuries. He said, after this accident, that he would never again make high breakers on the road, or advise others to do so.

John Teed, husband of Mrs. Teed, who keeps the popular and prosperous boarding house on Morgantown street, Uniontown, was an old stage driver. His first engagement as a driver on the road was with the Express line, called derisively "The Shake Gut." After driving a short time on the Express, he was given a team on one of the regular coach lines. He was an approved driver and promoted to the office of guardsman. The guardsman was a person sent with the coach to superintend its progress, and aid in protecting it from the incursions of robbers, which were not uncommon in the night time on the mountainous sections of the road.

Thomas Poland was in every essential a stage driver, and zealously devoted to his calling. He drove out from Uniontown, east and west, as occasion required. He was a man rather below the average stature, but stoutly built and of swarthy complexion. Many old drivers were moved to grief when business ceased on the road, but no one felt the change more keenly than Thomas Poland.

John Guttery, of Washington, Pennsylvania, was one of the early stage drivers of the road, and a good and trusty one. He was a tall man, rounded out proportionately to his height, and closely resembled the renowned old driver, Redding Bunting. He was a brother of Charles Guttery, the old wagoner and tavern keeper mentioned in another chapter of this volume. John Guttery, after driving stage a number of years, gave up that exciting occupation and established a livery stable in Washington, which he conducted successfully until his death in that place a number of years ago.

CHAPTER XXIV.

Scharts' history of Western Maryland gives the following account of President Taylor's ride over the mountain division of the road, when on his way to Washington to be inaugurated:

"President Taylor and his party were, in 1849, conveyed over the road under the marshalship of that most indefatigable Whig, Thomas Shriver, who, with some other Cumberlanders, proceeded to the Ohio river and met the presidential party. Among the party were statesmen, politicians, and office-hunters, notably Col. Bullet, a brilliant editor from New Orleans, who was to occupy a relation to President Taylor something like that of Henry J. Raymond to Lincoln. The road was a perfect glare of ice, and everything above ground was literally plated with sleeted frost. The scenery was beautiful; to native mountaineers too common to be of much interest, but to a Southerner like Gen. Taylor, who had never seen the like, it was a phenomenon. In going down a spur of Meadow Mountain, the presidential coach, with the others, danced and waltzed on the polished road, first on one side and then on the other, with every sign of an immediate capsize, but the coaches were manned with the most expert of the whole corps of drivers. Shriver was in the rear, and in the greatest trepidation for the safety of the President. He seemed to feel himself responsible for the security of the head of the Nation. Down each hill and mountain his bare head could be seen protruding through the window of his coach to discover if the President's coach was still upon wheels. The iron gray head of the General could almost with the same frequency be seen outside of his window, not to see after anybody's safety, but to look upon what seemed to him an arctic panorama. After a ride of many miles the last long slope was passed and everything was safe. At twilight the Narrows were reached, two miles west of Cumberland, one of the boldest and most sublime views on the Atlantic slope. Gen. Taylor assumed authority and ordered a halt, and out he got in the storm and snow and looked at the giddy heights on either side of Wills creek, until he had taken in the grandeur of the scenery. He had beheld nothing like it before, even in his campaigns in Northern Mexico. The President-elect was tendered a reception on his arrival at Cumberland, and the next morning he and his party left on the cars for Washington."

At an early day there was a coach factory at or near the Little Crossings, where many of the first passenger coaches used on the road were made. They were without thorough braces, or springs of any kind. Their bodies were long, and the inside seats for passengers placed crosswise. They had but one door, and that was in the front, so that passengers on entering were compelled to climb over the front seats to reach those in the rear.

The first coach of the Troy pattern was placed on the road in the year 1829 by James Reeside, and tradition has it that he won this coach with a bet on Gen. Jackson's election to the presidency. Mr. Reeside was desirous that Gen. Jackson should be the first person to ride in this coach, and accordingly tendered it to the President-elect when on his way to Washington, who true to his habit of refusing gifts, declined the proffered compliment as to himself, but consented that his family might occupy the coach. Charley Howell was the driver, and his team was one of the finest on the road. Many coaches were brought out on the road afterward from the Troy and Concord factories. These coaches cost between five and six hundred dollars each.

John Buck was one of the oldest and best stage drivers on the road. He lived in Washington, Pennsylvania, and drove on the old line in the life-time of Daniel Moore, and was a great favorite of that ancient stage proprietor. When Lafayette visited Washington in 1825, Mr. Moore was active and prominent in arranging for his reception at that place, and assigned John Buck to drive the coach in which the illustrious visitor entered the town. It was a proud day for the old driver, who shared with the hero of the occasion, the plaudits of the people. Buck subsequently became the senior member of the firm of Buck, Lyon & Wolf, contractors, who built most of the locks and dams on the Muskingum river, in the State of Ohio. This old firm was called the "Menagerie Company," on account of the names of its members.

William Robinson (not "Billy") suffered an "upset" at Somerfield, in 1832, with a full load of passengers going west. The stage coach had but one door, and to bring up the door side to the Endsley tavern, in Somerfield, it was necessary to wheel around. Robinson turned his team with such rapidity as to overturn the coach, and the passengers were all tumbled out in a pile, but none of them were seriously hurt. Wash. Alridge threw a coach over on the Conway hill, near Somerfield, inflicting a severe spinal injury upon a passenger who lived in Cincinnati. The sufferer was cared for at the tavern in

THE NARROWS.

Jockey Hollow, kept at the time by Aaron Wyatt. The stage company (old line) paid the injured passenger a considerable sum in damages, without suit. A passenger by the name of Merrill, of Indianapolis, had a leg broken by the upsetting of a coach at the turn of the road, above Somerfield; Samuel Jaco was the driver. William Roach, a well known driver, was killed in an "upset" at the Little Crossings bridge, about the year 1837. This seems to have been a different accident from that which occurred near the same place in 1835, related in the sketch of John Marker. Marker witnessed the accident of 1835, and states that the driver who was killed at that time was James Rhodes. David Stinson, an old driver, was killed by an "upset" on Woodcock Hill. Woodcock Hill is a short distance west of Thomas Brownfield's old Mt. Augusta tavern, and is the highest peak on the road in Fayette county, Pennsylvania. Charley Howell upset in 1835, coming down the Winding Ridge Hill, and was badly hurt. He had a leg and arm broken, and was nursed at Connelly's tavern, in Petersburg, for many months before he recovered.

In 1834 or 1835, Mr. Stockton transferred a number of stage teams and drivers, from the Baltimore and Washington City road, to the National Road. Two of these teams ran in and out from Somerfield. One called "the Kangaroo team" was driven by John Mills. They were large, dark bays, and much admired by lovers of fine horses. Mills knew how to handle them. He was a superb driver. Another of these "transferred" teams was driven by William Bishop. The horses in this team were light bays, all "bob-tails," and notwithstanding there was but one good eye in the whole team, and all were "sprung in the knees," it is asserted by many old pike boys that this unique and "blemished" team was the fastest on the road. It was brought out from the Baltimore and Washington road by Charles Howell, who drove it a short time before it was turned over to William Bishop. Bishop was a capital reinsman.

The preservation of the National Road was considered so vital to the general welfare by everybody living upon its line and adjacent to it, that the deepest interest was manifested in the success of every measure proposed for its benefit. There was no powerful and paid "lobby" around the halls of Congress when the Cumberland Road was the highway of the Republic, as there is at this day, but all measures planned and presented for its preservation and repair, were carefully watched and guarded by such statesmen as Henry Clay, Daniel Sturgeon, Andrew Stewart, T. M. T. McKennan, Lewis Steenrod, W. T. Hamilton, and Henry W. Beeson. The following from a Cumberland paper published in that place sixty years ago shows the popular feeling in behalf of the road at that date:

"The citizens of the town on the 21st of May, 1832, in demonstration of their great joy growing out of the appropriation made by the National Government for the repair of the Cumberland Road, made arrangements for the celebration of that event. In pursuance of that arrangement, Samuel Slicer illuminated his large and splendid hotel, which patriotic example was followed by James Black. In addition to the illumination, Mr. Bunting (our famous 'old Red'), agent of L. W. Stockton, ordered out a coach, drawn by four large gray stallions, driven by George Shuck. The stage was beautifully illuminated, which presented to the generous citizens of this place a novelty calculated to impress upon the minds of all who witnessed it the great benefits they anticipated by having the road repaired. There were also seated upon the top of the vehicle several gentlemen who played on various instruments, which contributed very much to the amusement of the citizens and gave a zest to everything that inspired delight or created feelings of patriotism. They started from the front of Mr. Slicer's hotel, and as they moved on slowly the band played 'Hail Columbia,' 'Freemasons' March,' 'Bonaparte Crossing the Rhine,' 'Washington's March,' together with a new tune composed by Mr. Mobley, of this place, and named by the gentlemen on the stage, 'The Lady We Love Best,' and many others, as they passed through the principal streets of the town. On their return they played 'Home, Sweet Home,' to the admiration of all who heard it."

David Bonebraker was a stage driver of good reputation, and a general favorite. While his name would import otherwise, he was a careful driver and never during his whole service did he break a bone of man or beast. He was a large, fine looking man, and drove between Somerfield and Mt. Washington as early as 1831, and for a number of years thereafter.

Hanson Willison was early on the road as a stage driver, and none of his fellow drivers excelled him in skillfulness. He drove a brief period between Uniontown and Brownsville, but for the most part in and out from Cumberland. He is still living in Cumberland, proprietor of the American House livery stables, and doing a profitable business. He retains the habits of the early days of the road, generous almost to a fault, perfectly familiar with the roads history, his memory is well stored with its exciting incidents and accidents. Hanson Willison and Ashael Willison before mentioned, are brothers.

The few remaining old folks who witnessed the exciting scenes of the National Road in its palmy days, will readily recall the following old stage drivers: John Griffith, William Witham, George Lukens, Wash Alters, Hank Smith, John Heinselman, Barney Strader, John Munson, West Crawford, James Chair, William Roberts, Vin Huffman, John Windell, a small, thin faced man, with rings in his ears, one of the earliest drivers, William Saint, who was also a blacksmith, and worked, occasionally, at his trade in Uniontown. He went to Texas before the civil war, and died there. Lewis Gribble, son of John, the old wagoner and tavern keeper. He went to Virginia, drove stage in that State, and died there. John Sparker, John Snell, David Oller, Joseph Henderson, a steady-going man, mentioned among the old tavern keepers in connection with the "Gals house," David Armor, William Armor, Samuel Oller, and William Dickey. The Ollers, the Armors, Dickey and Henderson were of Washington, Pa. Jacob Sny-

HANSON WILLISON.

der, subsequently manager and proprietor of the Shipley house, in
Cumberland. William and George Grim, John Zane, James Schaverns,
Joseph Vanhorn, John McIlree, Jesse Boring, John Munson, John
Ruth, David Jones, Benjamin Miller, subsequently tavern keeper in
the old Mannypenny house, Uniontown. An early line of stages
stopped at Miller's. James Mannypenny, Thomas Fee, Walter Head,
educated for the ministry, Thomas and Edward McVenus, William
Totten, William Vanhorn, Spencer Motherspaw, James Griffith, Abram
Dedrick, William Fowler, Thomas Chilson, William Jones, Andrew
Heck, John Fink, William Irwin, James Sampey, subsequently and for
many years owner and manager of the tavern at Mt. Washington,
where the Good Intent line changed horses and passengers often
stopped for meals; Isaac Newton, Robert Jackson, a young man of
diminutive size, from one of the New England States, whose father
came and took him home; James Dennison, subsequently tavern
keeper at Claysville and at Hopwood; Isaac Newton, died at Mt.
Washington when John Foster kept the tavern at that point; Matthew
Byers, Hugh Drum, John Hendrix, Alexander Thompson, William
Hart, Charles Kemp, Ben Watkins, Ben Watson, John and Andrew
Shaffer, Garret Clark, Garret Minster, John Ferrell, James Lynch,
John Seaman, James Reynolds, John Bunting, Lindy Adams, Lean-
der Fisk, James Derlin, Aaron Wyatt, James Andrews, Alfred Haney.
Wash Bodkin, William Crawford, Charles Cherry, William Hammers,
Addis Lynn, Harry, Nelse and Jack Hammers, Nimrod, Joseph,
Jack and William Sopher, John and Joseph Pomroy, William and
Watt Whisson, John McCollough, William Miller, son of Charley, the
old tavern keeper west of Hillsborough; Robert McIlheney, John
McMack, Thomas, Joshua and William Boyd, John Parsons, Matthew
Davis, one of the oldest, and still living at Brownsville; John W.
Boyce, George Wiggins, brother of Harrison, the old fox hunter of
the mountains; Robert Bennett, William White, David Reynolds,
James McIllree, Fred Buckingham, Thomas and William Noble.

William Noble died in Washington, Pennsylvania, Jan. 26, 1894.

Robert McIlheny, after relinquishing the reins and whip, became
an agent for the sale of the celebrated Hayes buggies, of Washington.

John Parsons left the road to take charge of a hotel in Bridge-
ville, Allegheny county, Pennsylvania. Alfred Haney went South,
became baggagemaster on a Southern railroad, and was killed in an
accident. Charley Cherry had the manners of a savage, and was
called "the big savage man," but it is not known that he ever wan-
tonly shed the blood of a fellow being.

James McIlree drove between Washington and Wheeling.

Hugh Drum was called "Mickey Murray." He lingered for a
while on the road after its glory departed, and pushed out for New
York, where he engaged to drive an omnibus. What became of him
in the subsequent shifting sands of time is not known, but presumably
he has gone to the unknown world.

William McCleary, who died recently near Claysville leaving an estate valued at $50,000; Daniel Dawson, subsequently kept a tavern near Limestone, Marshall county, West Virginia, and died there; Samuel Rowalt, Robert Bell, William Watkins, John Ford, still living in Monongahela city; George Freiger, Barney and Samuel Nunemaker, Thomas Cox, John Ruth, Abram Boyce, Charles Oulitt, James Dean, William ("Boggy") Moore, when a boy a rider on the pony express; John Schenck, Thomas Hager, Joseph Ruff, Dandy Jack, James Fisk, Joseph Drake, Andrew Ferrell, John Fouch, George Walker, George Banford, Joseph Lewis, Larry Willard, Isaiah Fuller, Davy Crockett, Henry Wagner, John Foster, Henry Smith, James Foster, John Noble, Edward McGinnis, Thomas McGinnis, John Johnson (Old Sandy), John Horrell, William Grim, Elias Johnson, Daniel Boyer, James Bodkin, James Null, William Null, William Clark, David Brower, Richard Frantz, James Rowe, John Seaman, David Brennard, Henry Schuck, George Crow, James Andrews (Dutch Jim), drove in and out from Grantsville; John Huhn, drove in and out from Claysville; Moses Thornburg, Wylie Baily, James McClung, James, Abraham and Robert Devan, brothers; Thomas and George Henderson, Stephen Leggett, James Wilson, Henry Herrick, John Giddings, Ed Washburn, J. S. Beck, Frank White, Jesse Matthews, Robert Fenton, Jesse Hardin, David Johnson, Archy McGregor, Samuel Darby, James Moore, Joseph Drake, James Riley, William Matthews, Edward Hall, James Vancamp, Benjamin Miller, grandson of the old tavern keeper of Uniontown; Samuel Betts, Calvin Springer, ex-sheriff of Fayette county; James Noggle, Martin Stedler, William Wiley, John Wiley, William McGidigen, James McGidigen, Daniel Shriver, Jerome Heck, Frederic Zimmerman, Robert Bennett, Edward Kelley, John Clark, Samuel Blair, Ross Clark, George Butts, Beck Kelley, William Kelley, William Fisher, James and Thomas Bradley, Thomas Johnson, William Brower, Richard Frazee, Isaac Toner (Dumb Ike), Joseph Jenk, Evans Holton, Daniel Dean, Jesse Brennard, George Brennard, John Steep, John Cŏllier, Ben Tracy, George Moore, George Richmire, Charles Richmire, Thomas McMillen, Samuel Porter, Isaac Flagle, William and Ross Clark, Richard Butts, Garret and West Crawford, John Brown, subsequently a clerk in the Wheeling postoffice; Joseph Matthews, John Waugh, William Hickman, a circus man; George Robbins, Abram Boyce, Oliver Jackson, Joseph Bishop, Thomas McClelland, Elisha Stockwell, Isaac Denny, subsequently tavern keeper at the old Griffin house in the mountain, west of Somerfield; John Harris, drove on the Good Intent line, and died in Uniontown; Charles and Robert Marquis, James Moore, son-in-law of James Sampey, of Mount Washington; Perry Sheets, drove west of Washington; Elmer Budd, drove from Uniontown to Brownsville; Frank Watson, Bate Smith, Sam Jerome, James Downer, son of William, of the big water trough on Laurel Hill, when a boy a rider for the pony express; William Stewart, Caleb Crossland, of Uniontown; William Bogardus, who lost an eye by coming in contact with a pump handle

MATT. DAVIS.

on Morgantown street, Uniontown, on a dark night; John Robinson, a very large man; Samuel Youman, mentioned under the head of old wagoners, next to "Old Mount" the largest man on the road; Thomas Milligan, Joshua Boyd, Stephen Leonard, David Johnson, James Mc-Cauley, Thomas Boyd, Garret Clark, Henry Miller, Thomas Moore, William Wilkinson, Galloway Crawford, Samuel Jaco, Robert Wright, Fred. Buckingham, Jacob Rapp, killed at Brownsville about 1840 by his team running off; John Rush, Samuel Holsted, Sandy Connor, living as late as 1882, and carrying the mail in a two-horse vehicle from Frostburg to Grantsville; John Farrell, farming near Grantsville in 1882 and at that date eighty-five years old; Jacob Shock, Eph. Benjamin, William Bergoman, Upton Marlow, subsequently proprietor of the American and other leading hotels in Denver, Colorado; Archie Mc-Vicker, James Cameron, Charles Enox, Robert Amos, James Finnegan, drove a bob-tailed team from Somerfield to Keyser's Ridge; Squire Binch, of Brownsville, well remembered by the old folks of that place; Richard Harris, Joseph and David Strong, the former for many years a prominent citizen of Cumberland, and frequently honored by public trusts; Abe Walls, —— Bonum, called "Magnum Bonum;" James Gray, Henry Powell, Henry Bergoman, Rock Goodridge, Sherwood Mott, Daniel Boyer, Robert Dennis, David James, Thomas Grace, John Lidy, drove a dun team of bob-tails from Farmington to Somerfield, that formerly belonged to the Pioneer line; Isaac Frazee, James McLean, Thomas and Henry Mahany, Baptist Mullinix, Amariah Bonner, B. W. Earl, subsequently a stage agent, and tavern keeper at the Stone house near Fayette Springs, and at Brownsville; John and Matthias Vanhorn, Daniel Quinn, James Corbin, William Corman, of Braddee mail robbery fame; Atwood Merrill, a fiery partisan of the Good Intent line; William Willis, noted as a fast driver on the Old line. On one occasion Willis passed Peter Burdine, a fast driver as before stated of the Good Intent line, which prompted the partisans of the Old line to get up the little rhyme following to emphasize and signalize the event:

> "Said Billy Willis to Peter Burdine,
> You had better wait for the Oyster line."

The fares on the stage lines were as follows:

From Baltimore to Frederic...	$ 2 00
" Frederic to Hagerstown...	2 00
" Hagerstown to Cumberland	5 00
" Cumberland to Uniontown...................................	4 00
" Uniontown to Washington..................................	2 25
" Washington to Wheeling.......	2 00
Through fare..	$17 25

A paper was prepared by the agent of the line at the starting point of the coach in the nature of a bill of lading, called the "way bill." This bill was given to the driver, and by him delivered to the landlord at the station immediately upon the arrival of the coach. It

9

contained the name and destination of each passenger, and the several sums paid as fare. It also bore the time of departure from the starting point, and contained blanks for noting the time of the arrival and departure at every station. The time was noted by an agent of the line, if one were at the station, and in the absence of an agent, the noting was done by the landlord. If a passenger got on at a way station, and this was of daily occurrence, he paid his fare to the landlord or agent, which was duly noted on the way bill, together with the passenger's destination.

In addition to the stage lines hereinbefore mentioned, there was a line known as the "Landlords' Line," put on the road by tavern keepers, prominent among whom were William Willis (the old driver before mentiond), Joseph Dilly, and Samuel Luman. There was also a "Pilot Line" and a "Pioneer Line." These lines had but a short run. The railroad managers east of Cumberland favored the older lines, and gave them such advantages in rates that the new lines were compelled to retire from the competition. They sold out their stock to the old companies. James Reeside owned the "Pilot Line," and the "Pioneer Line" was owned by Peters, Moore & Co.

The compensation paid stage drivers was twelve dollars a month, with boarding and lodging. They took their meals and lodged at the stage houses, except the married men, who lodged in their own dwellings when chance threw them at home.

At Uniontown a number of contiguous frame buildings on Mill and South streets, in the rear of Brownfield's tavern, known as "Hopwood's Row," were occupied almost exclusively by the families of stage drivers. They were erected and owned by the late Rice G. Hopwood, Esquire, and hence the name given them. Two or three of these old houses are all that are left standing, and they are in a dilapidated condition. The spirit of improvement which in late years entered Uniontown, seems to have carefully avoided the neighborhood of "Hopwood's Row."

The Good Intent and Stockton lines were taken from the National Road in 1851, and placed on the plank road from Cumberland to West Newton. From the latter point passengers were conveyed by steamboat to Pittsburg by way of the Youghiogheny river, which was made navigable at that date by a system of locks and dams like that of the Monongahela. Upon the withdrawal of the lines mentioned, a line was put on the National Road by Redding Bunting and Joshua Marshe, and ran as far west as Washington, Pennsylvania. William Hall subsequently purchased the interest of Mr. Marshe in this line, which was kept on the road until about the close of the year 1852, when the era of four-horse coaches ended.

Mr. Ensley, before quoted, furnishes his juvenile opinion of stages and stage drivers, which was shared in by all the boys of the road, as follows:

"My earliest recollections are intimately associated with coaches, teams and drivers, and like most boys raised in an old stage tavern, I

JOHN McILREE.

longed to be a man when I could aspire to the greatness and dignity of a professional stage driver. In my boyish eyes no position in life had so many attractions as that of driving a stage team. A Judge, a Congressman, even Henry Clay or President Jackson, did not measure up to the character of John Mills and Charley Howell, in my juvenile fancy."

The picture of the stage coach era herein drawn may be lacking in vigor and perspicuity of style, but it contains no exaggeration. Much more could be written concerning it, and the story would still be incomplete. It is sad to think that nearly all the old drivers, so full of life and hope and promise when pursuing their favorite calling on the nation's great highway, have answered the summons that awaits the whole human family, and of the vast multitude that witnessed and admired the dashing exploits of the old drivers, but few remain to relate the story. When the old pike was superseded by the railroad, many of the stage drivers went west and continued their calling on stage lines occupying ground in advance of the approaching railway. Others lingered on the confines of the familiar road, and fell into various pursuits of common life. Of these, some achieved success. As drivers they had opportunity for making acquaintances and friends. Hanson Willison was eminently successful as a local politician, and achieved the distinction of being twice elected sheriff of Alleghany county, Maryland.

CHAPTER XXV.

The most conspicuous of all the old stage proprietors of the National Road was Lucius Witham Stockton. James Reeside was probably an older stage man, and may have owned and operated more stage lines; but Mr. Stockton was longer and more prominently identified with the business on the National Road. He was born at Flemington, New Jersey, September 1, 1799. He was a son of Lucius Stockton, and a grandson of the Rev. Philip Stockton, known in his day and among his countrymen as "The Revolutionary Preacher," who was a brother of Richard Stockton. a signer of the Declaration of Independence from the colony of New Jersey. L. W. Stockton appeared in Uniontown as a stage proprietor previous to the year 1824, the exact date not ascertainable. He was twice married. His first marriage occurred on November 24, 1824, and at that date he was a resident of Uniontown, and had been previous thereto. His first wife was Rebecca Moore, a daughter of Daniel Moore, an old stage proprietor who lived in Washington, Pennsylvania. By his first marriage he had six children, viz: Richard C., Daniel Moore, Elizabeth C., Lucius Witham, Margaret, and Rebecca. Richard, Daniel, and Elizabeth, by the first marriage, are dead; the last named died in infancy. Lucius Witham is living in Philadelphia. He married Ellen, the youngest daughter of Dr. John Wishart, an old and distinguished physician of Washington, Pennsylvania, grandfather on the maternal line of Hon. Ernest F. Acheson, late Republican nominee for Congress in the Twenty-fourth district of Pennsylvania. Margaret Stockton became the wife of Dr. Thomas McKennan, a leading physician at this time of Washington, Pennsylvania, and a member of the old and distinguished McKennan family of that place. Rebecca Stockton became the wife of Capt. Alexander Wishart, and is living in Newark, New Jersey, where her husband is executive officer of the Law and Order League. Captain Wishart was a gallant soldier of the Union army in the war between the States.

Mr. Stockton's second wife was Katharine Stockton, his first cousin. She is still living. making her home with her son-in-law,

L. W. STOCKTON.

Gen. Leiper, of Philadelphia. By his second marriage Mr. Stockton had four children, as follows : Katharine, Richard C., Elias Boudinot and Henrietta Maria. Of these all are dead but Henrietta Maria. She is the wife of Gen. Leiper, with whom her mother lives, as before stated, in Philadelphia.

It is related as an incident in the early career of Mr. Stockton that he had a race with a horse and buggy against a locomotive, between the Relay House and Baltimore, in which he came out ahead. The horse he drove on that occasion was a favorite gray. He had a pair of " Winflower " mares, which he drove frequently from Union-town to Wheeling between breakfast and tea time, tarrying two or three hours at mid-day in Washington. At the watering places he ordered a little whisky to be added to the water given these spirited and fleet animals, and they became so accustomed to it that, it is said, they refused to drink unless the water contained the stimulating element. He would also drive from Uniontown to Cumberland in a day, stopping at the stations to transact business, and from Cumberland to Hagerstown, sixty-six miles, was an ordinary day's drive for him. His private carriage was a long open vehicle which he called "The Flying Dutchman." Hanson Willison, who has a vivid recollection of Mr. Stockton and his lively trips over the road, says that the names of his sorrel mares (the " Winflowers") were " Bet " and "Sal," and that they once ran off. On that occasion Mr. Stockton was accompanied by his wife and a sister. Miss Stockton was much alarmed, and pulling the coat-tail of her brother cried out piteously, " Hold on, brother William, hold on, or we'll all be killed!" But Mr. Stockton heeded not the cries of his sister, and having no fear of horses, soon regained control of the runaways without sustaining loss or injury.

Mr. Stockton died at Uniontown on April 25th, 1844, at " Ben Lomond," the name he gave his residence, now the property of the widow and heirs of the late Judge Gilmore. A few years ago the remains of Mr. Stockton were removed from the old Methodist burying ground in Uniontown, under direction of his loving daughters, Mrs. Wishart and Mrs. Dr. McKennan, and deposited in the beautiful cemetery at Washington, Pa.

Mr. Stockton was of Episcopalian lineage, and active in establishing the services of the church in Uniontown. He brought out Bishop Stone, of Maryland, to baptize his daughter Rebecca, now Mrs. Wishart. He was a vestryman, and besides contributing liberally in money to support the church, donated to the parish of Uniontown the lot on which the new stone edifice of St. Peter's now stands.

James Reeside, the second son of Edward Reeside and his wife, Janet Alexander, was born near Paisley, Renfrew, Scotland, and was brought, when an infant, to Baltimore county, Md., in 1789, where he was raised. His parents being in humble circumstances, toil was his first estate. Poor in book learning and in earthly goods, he possessed genius, energy, executive ability, and an ambition that fitted him to be a leader of men.   Before the war of 1812 he was a wagoner, hauling merchandise from Baltimore and Philadelphia to Pittsburg and west to Zanesville and Columbus, Ohio.   His promptness and sagacity soon enabled him to own his own teams, which were employed in hauling artillery to Canada.   Commissioned a forage master under Gen. Winfield Scott, at Lundy's Lane, his Scottish blood prompted him to seize a musket, as a volunteer, from which hard fought battle he carried honorable scars.   On his return he settled at Hagerstown, Md., where, in 1816, he married Mary, the daughter of John Weis, a soldier of the Revolutionary war.   Abandoning wagoning, he ran a stage line, in 1816 to 1818, from Hagerstown *via* Greencastle and Mercersburg to McConnellstown, there connecting with the stage line then in operation from Chambersburg to Pittsburg by Bedford, Somerset and Mt. Pleasant.   In 1818, in connection with Stockton & Stokes, of Baltimore ; Joseph Boyd, of Hagerstown ; Kincaid, Beck & Evans, of Uniontown ; George Dawson, of Brownsville ; Stephen Hill, of Hillsboro ; and Simms & Pemberton, of Wheeling, he put on the first regular stage line, carrying the mail, between Baltimore and Wheeling, before the construction of the turnpikes between Hagerstown and Cumberland.   This division of the route being from Hancock to Frostburg, he removed to Cumberland, where, in conjunction with his stage line, he kept the " McKinley Tavern," at the corner of Baltimore and Mechanics streets, afterward kept by Jacob Fechtig, James Stoddard, John Edwards, and others, and now known as the " Elberon."   In 1820 he quit tavern keeping, and confined himself to mail contracting and the stage business.   In 1827 John McLean, Postmaster General, afterward one of the Justices of the Supreme Court of the United States, prevailed on him to take the mail contract between Philadelphia and New York, and he moved from Cumberland to Philadelphia.   In the first year he reduced the time for transporting the mail between the two cities from twenty-three to sixteen hours, and soon thereafter to twelve hours.   He soon became the owner of most of the lines running out of Philadelphia and New York, and the largest mail contractor in the United States. He employed in this service more than one thousand horses and four hundred men.   The wagoner soon became the " Land Admiral," a title given him by the press in recognition of his energy and ability.

The Postoffice Department at that time having to rely on its own resources, and under Major W. T. Barry, then Postmaster-General, the service had so increased in thinly settled sections it became deeply in debt.   Mr. Reeside raised, on his personal responsibility, large sums of money to relieve it.   His efforts were appreciated, and he was the esteemed friend of Andrew Jackson, Henry Clay, and other distinguished men, without regard to politics, although he was a pronounced Democrat.   Of massive frame, six feet five inches in height, yet spare in flesh, clear cut features, sparkling, clear blue-gray eyes, fair complexion, with dark, sandy, curly hair, he was a true Highlander in appearance, genial in disposition, with quick and ready wit.

JAMES REESIDE.

Fond of song and story, kind, yet strict, with all in his employment, and generous to a fault, no words can more appropriately describe him than those of his favorite poet and countryman, Robert Burns:

> " For thus the royal mandate ran,
> When first the human race began,
> The social, friendly, honest man
> Where 'er he be,
> 'Tis he fulfills great nature's plan,
> An' none but he."

Controversies arising between Amos Kendall, the successor of Barry, and all the old mail contractors, their pay was suspended upon frivolous grounds, compelling them to bring suits, among the most celebrated of which were those of Reeside and Stockton & Stokes. The latter's case was referred to Virgil Maxy, who found in their favor about $140,000. Mr. Reeside's claim was tried before Justice Baldwin and a jury in 1841, and resulted in a verdict for plaintiff of $196,496.06, which, after seventeen years, was paid, with interest. As soon as his contracts under Kendall expired he quit the mail service, after putting the Philadelphia and New York mail on the Camden & Amboy railroad during the residue of his contract term.

In 1836 he bought the interest of John W. Weaver between Cumberland and Wheeling, then a tri-weekly line; increased it to a daily, then twice daily, and added another tri-weekly line, and named the lines " Good Intent," which was the name he had previously given the fast mail line between Philadelphia and Pittsburg. In 1839 he sold his entire interest in the National Road lines, and gave his attention to his suit against the United States. His health being impaired, he spent the winter of 1842 in New Orleans. Returning in the ensuing spring, without benefit to his health, he died in Philadelphia on the 3d of September, 1842.

Mr. Reeside attracted attention by reason of the peculiar garb he appeared in. In the winter season he always wore a long drab overcoat and a fur cap. Once in passing along a street in Philadelphia in company with Col. Richard M. Johnson, of Kentucky, Vice-President of the United States, some scarlet cloth was observed in a tailor's window, which prompted Col. Johnson to say: "Reeside, as your coaches are all red, you ought to wear a red vest." Mr. Reeside replied: "I will get one if you will." "Agreed," said Johnson, and straightway both ordered red vests and red neckties, and from that time as long as they lived continued to wear vests and neckties of scarlet colors. James Reeside aided in an early day to develop the mighty resources of our country, with such agencies as were then available, and his name and good work deserve to be perpetuated in history.

Dr. Howard Kennedy, an owner of stock in the National Road Stage Company, and for a brief period a trustee of the road under the provisions of a Pennsylvania law, enacted in 1848, repealed in 1856, was born in Washington county, Maryland, September 15th, 1809. His father was the Hon. Thomas Kennedy, an illustrious citizen, who figured conspicuously in the history of Maryland in the olden time. Dr. Kennedy was a graduate of the Medical University of Baltimore, and a thoroughly educated physician, but the practice of medicine not proving congenial to his tastes, he soon abandoned it and embarked in other pursuits. About the year 1840, or a little before that time, he was appointed a special, confidential agent of the general postoffice department, in which relation he achieved distinction by detecting numerous mail robberies, and bringing the perpetrators before the courts for trial and punishment. It was through the vigilance of Dr. Kennedy that the mail robberies of the Haldeman brothers, Pete and Abe, and Pate Sides, at Negro Mountain, were discovered, and the offenders apprehended and punished.

The Haldemans and Sides were stage drivers, and their calling through the dismal shades of death and other dark regions in the mountains with big, tempting, mail bags in their charge, no doubt turned their minds to what they considered a speedy, if not altogether a safe method of getting money. Whispers of suspicion growing out of the vigilance of Dr. Kennedy in pushing his investigations, reached the ears of the suspected ones, and they fled to Canada, but not to be thwarted in his purposes, Dr. Kennedy pursued them thither, had them arrested and brought back to Baltimore for trial. Abe Haldeman was acquitted, but Pete and Pate Sides were convicted and sent to the penitentiary. Dr. Kennedy was also the prime mover in bringing to light the noted mail robberies of Dr. John F. Braddee, of Uniontown, as will be seen by the following affidavits:

Pennsylvania, Fayette County, ss.:

The testimony of Dr. Howard Kennedy taken before N. Ewing, president judge of the 14th Judicial district of Pennsylvania, the 8th day of January, 1841, in reference to the amount of bail to be required of John F. Braddee, Peter Mills Strayer and William Purnell. The said Dr. Howard Kennedy being first by me duly sworn according to law, deposeth and saith: "There will be difficulty in ascertaining the amount of money stolen from the mails. There have been six mail pouches or bags stolen, which would average twenty to thirty thousand dollars each. The whole would, I am satisfied, amount to one hundred thousand dollars. I saw the money alleged to have been found in the stable of John F. Braddee. The amount thus found was $10,098.60. The amount of cash stolen is probably about $50,000.

"HOWARD KENNEDY."

Taken and subscribed before me, January 8th, 1841.

N. EWING,
P. Judge, 14th Judicial District.

PITTSBURG, January 25, 1841.

"Howard Kennedy, special agent of the postoffice department, in addition to the testimony given by him before his Honor, Judge Ewing, further deposes that since that time he has received reports

WILLIAM H. STELLE.

from various persons and places in the West of letters mailed at dates which would have, by due course of mail, been in the bags stolen, containing bank notes, scrip, certificates, drafts, and checks, amounting to $102,000 and upwards; that every mail brings him additional reports of losses, and that he believes the amounts reported will not constitute more than one-half of what has been lost in the mails between the 16th of November and the 18th of December, 1840, on the route from Wheeling to New York.

"HOWARD KENNEDY,
"Special Agent Postoffice Department."

Sworn and subscribed before me the 25th day of January, 1841.

T. IRWIN, District Judge.

As before stated, Dr. Kennedy was one of the owners of the line of coaches known as the National Road Stage Company. This was popularly known as the Stockton line, called "the old line," because it was the oldest on the road. Dr. Kennedy managed all the business of this line relating to the transportation of the mails. He was also one of the original members of the Western Express Company, doing business between Cumberland and Wheeling and Pittsburg *via* the Monongahela river. L. W. Stockton dying in the spring of 1844, in the fall of that year Dr. Kennedy brought his family from Hagerstown, Maryland, to Uniontown, and established his residence in the old Stockton mansion, called "Ben Lomond," now the home of Mrs. Judge Gilmore. Here Dr. Kennedy resided until the year 1851, when he returned to Hagerstown, where he died on the 12th of June, 1855. He was of medium height and delicate form, of pleasant address, and a gentleman by birth, education, association and aspiration; in religion an Episcopalian, and in politics a Democrat. His widow, a sister of the late Alfred Howell, of Uniontown, survives him. She is enjoying the sunset of a gentle life in Hagerstown, the central figure of a remnant of that polite and refined society which in the palmy days of the National Road distinguished all the old towns along its line.

William H. Stelle was born in New Jersey, and it will be noted that many of the stage owners, agents, and drivers came out from that State. Two of Mr. Stelle's partners in the stage business, John A. Wirt and Mr. Hutchinson, were likewise Jersey men. It is related that Mr. Stelle and Mr. Acheson were both desirous of selling their interests in the stage lines, the former being an owner in the Good Intent, and the latter in the Stockton line. Mr. Stelle one day approached Mr. Acheson in Wheeling, and told him he would give him five hundred dollars, if he would sell or buy at a price to be mutually named. Mr. Acheson named a price which he would give or take, and Mr. Stelle elected to sell, and promptly paid Mr. Acheson five hundred dollars for acceding to his proposition. Mr. Stelle located in Wheeling about the year 1841, and died at Elm Grove, Ohio county, West Virginia, on the 26th of September, 1854, aged about fifty years. He left a son, William H., and a daughter, Mrs. Susan R. Hamilton, both living in Wheeling.

9a

Agents of the stage lines possessed functions somewhat, but not altogether, like those of railroad conductors. Some agents passed constantly over the road, paying bills, providing horses and equipage, and giving general direction to the running of the lines. Others were stationary, attending to local business. These agents were prominent characters of the road, and popularly esteemed as men of high position. One of the earliest agents was Charles Rettig, who subsequently kept the tavern two and one-half miles east of Washington, and referred to in a chapter on taverns and tavern keepers. John Risly, of Frederic, Md., and William Biddle and James Coudy, of Hancock, were old agents of lines east of Cumberland. Redding Bunting, Edward Lane, Theodore Granger and Charles Danforth were agents of the Old line west of Cumberland, with authority extending to Wheeling. Bunting also kept the National House in Uniontown, and Lane kept the National House in Washington, which were headquarters at those points respectively for their line. Charles Danforth was a leading local agent of the Stockton line at Uniontown. He was a large, fine looking man, with florid complexion, heavy black whiskers, and possessed of popular manners. He was a native of New York State, and died at Bedford, Pa., in 1853. His remains were brought to Uniontown, and interred in the old Methodist cemetery, near Beeson's old mill. His widow is living in Chicago. Edward Lane was a man of average size, of reddish complexion, energetic in motion, and affable in manner. His tavern in Washington, Pa., was one of the best eating houses on the road. Granger was a large, dark complexioned man, not well liked by the people, but a favorite of Mr. Stockton. After the stage lines were taken from the road, Granger went to Cincinnati, procured employment at a livery stable, and died in that city in indigent circumstances. Jacob Beck was an agent for Weaver's line, which was on the road a short time, and went with that line to Ohio and Kentucky. He returned from the West, and was a barkeeper for John N. Dagg, of Washington, Pa., and subsequently, as elsewhere stated, kept tavern at Rony's Point, Va., and died there. He was an old stage driver, a good one, and esteemed as an honest man. Daniel Brown, mentioned among the old tavern keepers, was an agent of the Good Intent line, and a very competent one. He was a native of New Jersey, and his sad ending has been alluded to in another chapter. William Scott, familiarly called " Billy," was a well-known agent of the Good Intent line. He had been a driver, and was promoted to an agency on account of his competency and fidelity. He was a master of his business, a man of small stature, dark hair and complexion, and a little given to brusqueness of manner, but on the whole rather a popular agent. He remained an agent of the Good Intent line until business ceased on the road, when he went to Iowa, and became an agent of a stage line in that State. From Iowa he went to Texas, and died at Jefferson in that State. It is said that he was descended from a good family on both sides, who were wealthy, and that he engaged in stage driving from choice, rather than necessity, and his friends were disappointed in his career. Lemuel Cross was an agent of the Old line. He also kept tavern at Piny Grove, as elsewhere stated, and is well remembered. His jurisdiction as agent was mainly on the mountain division of the road, and he thoroughly understood his business, and was familiar with all the haunts, hills, and hollows of the mountains. B. W. Earl was likewise an agent for a while of the Good Intent line. He commenced a driver, was advanced to an agency, and ended a tavern keeper. John Foster, Andrew Cable, William F. Cowdery, Levi Rose and William Terry were agents at Wheeling. The latter had charge in part of Neil, Moore & Company's line in Ohio.

THE PONY EXPRESS.

In the year 1835 or 6, Amos Kendall, being Postmaster-General, placed on the road a line of couriers, called the "Pony Express." It was intended to carry light mails with more speed than the general mail was carried by the coaches. The Pony Express was a single horse and a boy rider, with a leather mail pouch thrown over the horse's back, something after the style of the old-fashioned saddle-bags. The route for each horse covered a distance of about six miles on the average. The horse was put to his utmost speed, and the rider carried a tin horn which was vigorously blown when approaching a station. William Moore, Thomas Wooley, subsequently stage drivers, William Meredith, Frank Holly and James Neese were among the riders on the Pony Express east of Cumberland, and Sandy Conner, Pate Sides and Thomas A. Wiley, all three afterward stage drivers, and William Conn rode west of Cumberland. Wiley rode from Uniontown to Washington, Pennsylvania, and also between Washington and Wheeling. He went with the log cabin boys from Uniontown to Baltimore in 1840 as a driver of one of the stage teams employed on that occasion. He is still living, an employe of the Baltimore & Ohio Railroad Company at Camden Station, Baltimore, in the service of which he has been employed since 1852. He was an attendant at the bedside of L. W. Stockton during that gentleman's last illness. Calvin Morris, a son of William Morris, the old tavern keeper on the hill west of Monroe, and William Downer, a son of the old gentleman who lived at and maintained the big water trough on Laurel Hill, were also riders on the Pony Express. William Morris was one of the contractors for carrying this fast mail, and his house was one of the relays of the line. The relay next west was the old toll house near Searights. Luther Morris, a brother of Calvin, the Pony Express rider, went to Iowa previous to the civil war, and was elected State Treasurer on two or three occasions. John Gilfillan, now, or recently, of Parkersburg, West Virginia, was a rider on the Pony Express between West Alexander and Wheeling. Bryant and Craven, of West Alexander, were among the contractors of the Pony Express line. "The Pony Express" did not remain long on the road, but when it was on, old pike boys say "it kicked up a dust."

CHAPTER XXVI.

"CALDWELL'S TAVERN: We did not use the high sounding *hotel*, but the good old Anglo-Saxon *tavern*, with its wide open fire in the cheerful bar room, and the bountiful spread in the dining room, and the long porch for summer loafers, and the immense stabling with its wealth of horse-flesh, and the great open yard for the road wagons. How real and vivid it all seems to me this moment! All the reminiscences of the old pike, for which you are an enthusiast, are heartily shared by me."— JAMES G. BLAINE.

Caldwell's tavern, mentioned by Mr. Blaine, is seven miles west of Washington, Pennsylvania, and will be referred to hereafter in its proper place. Mr. Blaine's description is appropriate to nearly all the old taverns of the road.

The outward appearance of an old tavern of the National Road was no index to the quality of the entertainment it afforded. Many of the least pretentious houses furnished the best meals, and paid the most agreeable attention to guests and patrons. It was not unusual to see the wagon yard attached to a small wooden and apparently decaying tavern crowded with teams and wagons, while the inviting grounds of the imposing brick tavern near by were without an occupant.

The May Pole tavern in Baltimore was a favorite stopping place for old wagoners. It is located on the southwest corner of Paca and German streets, and still standing, an object of much interest to the old people of the road. In front of it stands a tall, slim, granite column, representative of a pole, and preservative of the ancient name. The May Pole was kept in 1833 by Henry Clark, and in 1836 by James Adams, who remained in charge until his death. His successor was Isaac Willison, a Virginian, and before assuming control of the May Pole, an agent of the Baltimore & Ohio Railroad company. at Frederic City. George Elliott, subsequently manager for

Mrs. Adams, at the Mountain City house in Cumberland, was at one time a clerk in the May Pole tavern.

The "Hand in Hand" tavern on Paca, between Lexington and Saratoga streets, and the "White Swan" on Howard street, were likewise old wagon stands in Baltimore, well patronized in the early days of the National Road. Thomas Elliott also kept a wagon stand in Baltimore, and enjoyed a fair share of patronage. He was the father of George Elliott, above mentioned. The May Pole, however, was the favorite tavern of the old wagoners of the National Road. The "Three Ton" and "Gen. Wayne" taverns had each extensive stabling, and furnished accommodations for droves and drovers. The National Road entered the city of Baltimore by way of West Baltimore street.

The first wagon stand west of Baltimore, fifty years ago, was kept by a man whose name was Hawes. It was seven miles from the city, and wagoners often left it in the morning, drove to Baltimore, unloaded, reloaded, and returned to it in the evening of the same day, and the next morning proceeded on the long journey to their western destination. The Hawes tavern ceased to do business after 1840.

At Ellicott's Mills, ten miles west of Baltimore, there was no wagon stand, but stage houses were located there, where stage teams were kept and exchanged.

One mile west of Ellicott's, Frank Earlocker kept a wagon stand, that was largely patronized. He was rather of an economical turn of mind, and old wagoners were wont to say of him that he concealed the whisky bottle behind the counter, against the custom of the road, which was to expose it to full view; and it is said that the miserly Earlocker lost more than he gained by his habit, since it induced wagoners to inquire for a drink, more to worry the landlord than to appease the appetite.

A short distance west of Earlocker's is "Pine Orchard," where a tavern was kept by one Goslin. He was a goslin only in name. Otherwise, he was a square man, and knew how to treat strangers and travelers, especially wagoners, who largely favored him with their patronage. His house was a brick structure, and stood on the north side of the road, and for aught known to the contrary, is still standing, a monument commemorative of the many good old taverns which studded the road in the days of its glory.

James Dehoff kept a tavern at Pine Orchard as early as 1835. His house was a wagoners' resort, and stood on the south side of the road.

An old tavern, known as the "Brown Stand," four miles west of "Pine Orchard," was a popular stopping place for wagoners in its day. In 1838 Levi Chambers took charge of this house, and continued to conduct it until 1842. He was called "Nullifier" Chambers, because of his adherence to the nullification doctrine, announced and advocated by John C. Calhoun. He, however, knew how to keep a tavern, and was a sober and intelligent man. On the first of January, 1841, John Crampton and William Orr, old wagoners before mentioned, drove out from Baltimore with full loads, and put up at the "Brown Stand." During the night a box of silk goods was stolen from Orr's wagon. The loss was discovered early in the morning, and Orr and Chambers each mounted a horse and pushed out in the direction of Baltimore, in search of the stolen goods and the thief. There was a light snow on the road, and tracks were visible, indicative of rapid steps toward the east. Reaching Baltimore, Messrs. Orr and Chambers entered the bar room of the May Pole tavern, in which a number of persons were drinking, and among them one, who, from his actions, was suspected as the thief. He was arrested, tried, convicted, and sent to the penitentiary.

Four miles west of the "Nullifier's," John Whalen kept a wagon stand, and one of the best on the road. Old wagoners entertain pleasant recollections of John Whalen, and delight in recounting the good cheer that abounded and abided in his old tavern. He kept the tavern at this point up to the year 1842.

One Warfield kept a tavern a short distance west of Whalen's as early as 1835, and had a good wagon custom. Old wagoners had a rough distich on this section of the road, running something like this:

> "Old Wheeler's sunfish,
> Bob Fowler's roast goose,
> Warfield's ham,
> Ain't that jam!"

New Lisbon was an aspiring village, twenty-six miles west of Baltimore, and the first point of note west of Whalen's. Stages stopped and teams were changed at New Lisbon, but it had no wagon stand.

At Poplar Springs, one mile west of New Lisbon, there was a wagon stand kept by Allen Dorsie. Near the old tavern is a large, gushing spring, in the midst of tall poplar trees, and hence the name "Poplar Springs." Such was the situation at this point fifty years ago, but alas, fifty years is a long time, and the "Poplar Springs" may present a different appearance now. Allen Dorsie, the old proprietor of the tavern here, was likewise and for many years superintendent of the Maryland division of the road. He was a very large man, six feet in height, and rounded out in proportion. He was besides a man of admitted integrity and good intellect. He ceased keeping tavern at Poplar Springs in 1842.

Seven miles west of Poplar Springs Van McPherson kept a tavern, which did an extensive business. The proprietor was half Dutch and half Irish, as his name imports, and he had the faculty of pleasing everybody. His house was a brick structure on the north side of the road, and is probably still standing. Van McPherson kept this house from 1836 to 1842, and made money in it.

New Market is a village west of McPherson's old tavern, and in Frederic county, Maryland. Here the stages stopped and changed teams, and an old wagon stand was kept by one Shell. It is said of Shell that his name differed from his table, in that the latter contained no shells, but the best of savory viands.

Three miles west of New Market, Frank Wharton kept a tavern, and a good one. He was rough in manner, and could swear longer and louder than Wilse Clement, but he kept his house in good shape and did an extensive business.

One mile west of Wharton's the widow Dean kept a tavern. Her house was a brick structure on the south side of the road, and she owned it and the ground whereon it stood, in fee simple. She was largely patronized by wagoners.

Next after passing Mrs. Dean's old stand, the city of Frederic is reached, which fifty years ago was the largest town on the road between Wheeling and Baltimore. James Dehoof and John Lambert kept old wagon stands in Frederic City. Lambert died about 1840, and was succeeded by John Miller, who kept the house down to the year 1853.

Four miles west of Frederic City the old wagoners encountered Cotockton mountain, and here was a fine old tavern kept by Getzendanner, a German. His house was a stone building, on the south side of the road, presumably standing to this day. Getzendanner, true to his native traits, was the owner of the property. Old wagoners unite in saying that the old German kept a good house, barring a little too much garlic in his sausages.

Peter Hagan played the part of host at an old tavern, one mile west of Getzendanner's. His house was a log building, and stood on the south side of the road. As before stated, the outward appearance of an old tavern on the National Road was no index to affairs within; and though Peter Hagan's house was small and made with logs, the cheer within was exhilarating. His meals were simple and but little varied, yet so manipulated in the kitchen, and spread upon the table so tastefully, and withal so clean, that they were tempting even to an epicure. Peter Hagan's patrons were for the most part wagoners, and the old wagoners of the National Road knew what good living was, and "put up" only where the fare was inviting. Peter Hagan was an uncle of Robert Hagan, a local politician of South Union township, Fayette county, Pennsylvania.

Proceeding westward from Hagan's old tavern, the next point is the village of Middletown, which hoped to become a city, and might have succeeded, had not the steam railway eclipsed the glory of the old pike. At Middletown the stages had relays of horses. One of the stage houses at this point was kept by —— Titlow, a relative of F. B. Titlow, of Uniontown. Here also there was a wagon stand, kept by Samuel Riddlemoser. This was in 1840. In the spring of 1841 Riddlemoser moved to the Widow McGruder house, one mile west of Middletown. The McGruder house was well conducted, and enjoyed a large patronage.

South Mountain comes next, and here a tavern was kept by one

Miller. It was a wagon stand, a stone building, on the north side of the road. The battle of South Mountain was fought here, but the roar of the cannon failed to awaken the departed glories of the old Miller tavern.

One mile west of South Mountain, Petter Zettle, a German, kept a tavern. It was a wagon stand, and a popular one. The house was of brick, and stood on the south side of the road. The old landlord was accustomed to join in the merry-making of the old wagoners, and as the jokes went around in the old bar room, the German spice was plainly discernible as well as agreeable, in unison with the familiar notes of the native pike boys.

One mile west of Zettle's, Robert Fowler kept a wagon stand. Fowler quit in 1839, and was succeeded by Emanuel Harr, who conducted the house for many years. Joe Garver, a noted blacksmith, had a shop at this point. Garver, it is said, could cut and replace as many as a dozen wagon tires in a single night. It was not an uncommon thing for the old blacksmiths of the road to work all night at shoeing horses and repairing wagons.

CHAPTER XXVII.

> " It stands all alone like a goblin in gray,
> The old-fashioned inn of a pioneer day,
> In a land so forlorn and forgotten, it seems
> Like a wraith of the past rising into our dreams;
> Its glories have vanished, and only the ghost
> Of a sign-board now creaks on its desolate post,
> Recalling a time when all hearts were akin
> As they rested at night in that welcoming inn."
>
> JAMES NEWTON MATTHEWS.

Boonsboro is a small town at the foot of South Mountain in Maryland, and in the palmy days of the National Road was a lively village. Old wagoners and stage drivers spread its fame, but railroad conductors are silent as to its memory. The Slifer Brothers kept tavern in Boonsboro in the olden time. Their house was not a wagon stand. One of the Slifer brothers, as before stated, claimed to be the inventor of the " rubber," brake, as it is commonly called. At the west end of Boonsboro the widow Galwix kept a wagon stand and did a large business. She was the widow of John Galwix, hereinbefore mentioned as a fancy wagoner. Robert Fowler kept a tavern in Boonsboro as early as 1835 and a wagon stand on the north side of the road.

Three and a half miles west of Boonsboro Henry and Jacob Fosnock, Germans, kept a wagon stand, which was well patronized. The property was owned by the Fosnocks, and they made money with their tavern. They were bachelors, but had an unmarried sister, Susan, who acted in the capacity of hostess. She subsequently became the wife of the old wagoner, Joseph Crampton. The Fosnocks were at the point mentioned as late as 1842.

Funkstown appears next in sight. Funkstown, another old village identified with the by-gone glories of the old pike. The name of this village brings to mind the once familiar form of John Funk, an old wagoner. John lived at or near Funkstown, and his family may have given the name to the village. Funkstown is located on Little Antietam creek, about seventy miles west of Baltimore. Fifty years ago there was a paper mill and a grist mill at Funkstown, and they may be there yet, and others in addition. At the east end of Funkstown, Joseph Watts kept a wagon stand, and competed for the custom of the wagoners with William Ashton, who kept a similar tavern at the west end of the town. Each did a good business. Ashton will be remembered as the athletic wagoner, who leaped over the top of a road wagon at Petersburg. He knew the wants of wagoners and served them well at his old tavern. He was the owner of two fine six-horse teams, and kept them constantly on the road.

After Funkstown, come the classic shades and handsome streets of Hagerstown. Hagerstown was always a prominent point on the road. It ranked with Wheeling, Washington, Brownsville, Uniontown, Cumberland, and Frederic. Hagerstown was a station for the stage lines. It outlived the road, and flourishes as one of the best towns of Maryland. The only old wagon stand in Hagerstown was that of John B. Wrench. But Hagerstown was rather too stylish a place for old wagoners, and Wrench gave up his house there in 1842, and removed to Piney Grove, where he found a more congenial atmosphere. He subsequently kept one of the old taverns at Grantsville, from which point he emigrated to Iowa, and died there.

Four and a half miles west of Hagerstown, an old wagon stand was kept by David Newcomer. It was a stone house, on the north side of the road. Newcomer furnished good entertainment, and was well favored with customers, mostly wagoners. He was a Quaker, and a money maker. He dealt in horses, in addition to tavern keeping. When offering a horse for sale, his wife was accustomed to say in the hearing of the person proposing to buy: "Now, David, thee must not sell that favorite horse." This, old wagoners say, was a "set-up job" between David and his spouse to gain a good price. Newcomer was the owner of the property, and as the house was of stone, is probably standing yet; but the ring of the old pike has gone from it long since.

Three miles westward from Newcomer's was the imposing and well-remembered tavern kept by John Miller. It was of brick, a large and commodious building, situate on the north side of the road. Miller owned the property, and it may be in the possession of his descendants to this day. There were large rooms in this house, adapted to dancing purposes, and young men and maidens of the vicinity frequently tripped to the notes of the old time music in its spacious halls. The waltz was unknown, and the figures varied from the "hoe down" to the cotillion, closing always with the "Virginia Reel." The old wagoners were invariably invited to participate in these festivities, and engaged in them with a gusto not excelled by the lads and lasses of the surrounding neighborhood. Alfred Bailes, the old pike boy of Dunbar, drove a line team from John S. Miller's to the Nicodemus House, two miles west of Hancock, as early as the year 1836, and is probably the only survivor of the young folks who participated in the gayeties of Miller's old tavern.

One mile west of Miller's is "Shady Bower." There a tavern was kept by Conrod Wolsey. His house was well favored by wagoners, who sought his generous board in goodly numbers, and while well liked by his customers, he got the name of "Dirty Spigot," because the spigot of a whisky barrel in his house was once besmeared with filth. There was a large distillery near Wolsey's tavern, operated by Barnes Mason. Mason had two teams on the road, driven by William Keefer and Joseph Myers.

Clear Spring comes next, and derives its name from the existence of a large, gushing spring of clear water, in volume sufficient to propel a mill. An old wagon stand was kept at Clear Spring by Andrew Kershaw, who died the proprietor of the house, and was succeeded by his son Jonathan. The house was a large brick building, on the south side of the road. Stages stopped and exchanged teams at Clear Spring, but not at Kershaw's. His house, as stated, was a wagon stand. Gusty Mitchell is a well-remembered character of Clear Spring. He used to steal and drink the wagoners' whisky, and "bum" around their teams in all sorts of ways. One night the wagoners poured turpentine over Gusty and set fire to him, which so frightened him that he never afterward had anything to do with wagoners.

The next old tavern was on the top of North Mountain, two miles west of Clear Spring, kept by Joseph Kensel. It was a log house, and on the north side of the road. Kensel owned the property. While this old tavern was humble in outward appearance, the fires burned brightly within, and its patrons, who were numerous, highly extolled the quality of the viands it spread before them.

Indian Spring comes next, four and a half miles west from Clear Spring. Here a wagon stand was kept by David Miller. The house is a stone structure, on the north side of the road, and Miller owned it in fee simple. This old house was a favorite resort of wagoners, and night after night echoed the once familiar notes of the great highway, in the days of its glory.

Three miles west from David Miller's, Anthony Snider, a distant relative of John Snider of happy momory, kept a wagon stand. It was a frame building on the north side of the road. Peter Hawes once lived at this house, and hauled stone for an aqueduct on the adjacent canal.

Four miles west of Snider's, on the north side of the road, stood the old frame tavern of Widow Bevans. She owned the property, and her house was a popular stopping place. It will be noted that in many instances widows kept the best taverns along the road. There is no record of a widow making a failure as a tavern keeper.

Two miles further on to the westward, and before the once familiar tavern of Widow Bevans entirely recedes from view, the old wagon stand of David Barnett is reached. His house was a large log building, on the north side of the road. Here the first transportation line of six-horse teams, John Bradfield agent, had relays, its next relay eastward being the house of John Miller, before mentioned. Barnett was a jolly old landlord, fond of exchanging jokes with old wagoners and other patrons. He had a manner and a method of pleasing his guests, and did a large and profitable business.

Westward, two miles from Barnett's, is the historic town of Hancock, named in honor of the man who wrote his name in letters so large and legible, that they were read all round the world. There was no old wagon stand tavern in Hancock, except for a short time about the year 1838. John Shane established it, but was not successful, and removed to Cumberland, where he set up a confectionery shop. Wagoners preferred country before town taverns, as a rule. Stages stopped and exchanged horses in Hancock.

Two miles west of Hancock, one Nicodemus kept an old wagon stand. His first name has not been preserved, owing probably to the sublimity of his surname. He was known all along the road, but mentioned only as Nicodemus. His house was a frame building on the north side of the road, and he owned it, and died in it. He kept a good tavern, and was well patronized. Widow Downer kept this house before the time of Nicodemus.

Two miles west of the house of Nicodemus is Sideling Hill, so called from the sloping character of the ground upon which the road is laid. At the eastern foot of this hill Jacob Brosius kept an old wagon stand, and had a good share of custom. His house was a frame building and stood on the south side of the road. The distance from the foot to the summit of Sideling Hill is four miles, and it is the longest hill on the road. In 1837 Jacob Anderson, an old wagoner, was killed on Sideling Hill. His team became frightened on the summit and ran down the western slope, coming in contact with a large tree on the roadside with such force as to break it down, and falling on Anderson, he was instantly killed. Isaac Browning, Caleb Langley and Black Westley, with their teams and wagons, were on the road with Anderson at the time of this accident. Anderson was a citizen of Loudon county, Virginia. Langley, Browning and Westley belonged to Fayette county, Pennsylvania. The road crosses a stream at Sideling Hill, called Sideling Hill creek. There was a covered bridge over this creek. In 1841 John Moss and Billy George, old wagoners, drove their teams on this bridge. and stopping a while to rest under the shade afforded by the roof. the bridge broke down, precipitating horses, wagons and drivers a distance of fourteen feet to the water, causing considerable damage to the wagons and the goods therein, but strange to say inflicting but slight injuries upon the drivers and teams. The teams and wagons belonged to Robert Newlove, of Wheeling.

Two miles from the foot of Sideling Hill, and on the north side of the road, John H. Mann kept a wagon stand. His house was a frame building. Mann was a citizen of some prominence, and at one time represented his county (Washington) in the Maryland Legislature. It is not known that his proclivities in the line of statesmanship impaired in any wise his talent for tavern keeping.

On the western slope of Sideling Hill, about midway between the summit and the foot, Thomas Norris kept a tavern, which was a favorite resort of wagoners. His house was a large stone building, on the north side of the road. There was a picturesqueness about the location of this old tavern that imparted a peculiar spice to the ordinary rounds of entertainment enjoyed by its guests. Samuel Cessna kept this house at one time.

One mile west of Sideling Hill creek, a wagon stand was kept by the widow Ashkettle, another widow, and she no exception to the rule before stated, that the widows all kept good houses. Her name is not inappropriate to some of the duties of housekeeping, but Mrs. Ashkettle's forte was not in making lye, but in setting a good, clean table. She had a son, David, who managed the business of the house for her. Her house was a frame building, and stood on the north side of the road.

Two miles west of Mrs. Ashkettle's the wayfarer struck the point bearing the homely name of "Snib Hollow." These old names never wear out, no matter how ugly they are, and it is well they do not. They all have a significance and an interest, local or otherwise, which would be lost by a change of name. Quidnuncs in history and literature have exerted their restless talents in efforts to obliterate these seemingly rude, old names, and substitute fancy ones in their stead, but they have failed, and their failure is a pleasant tribute to the supremacy of common sense. As early as 1825 the widow Turnbull kept a tavern at Snib Hollow. Later, an old wagon stand was kept there by John Alder, who had a large run of customers. His house was a log building, on the north side of the road.

Town Hill comes next, a half a mile west of Snib Hollow, at the foot of which Dennis Hoblitzell kept a tavern as early as the year 1830, and probably earlier. The house was on the east side of the road, and the locality is often called Piney Plains. Mrs. McClelland, of the McClelland House, Uniontown, is a daughter of Dennis Hoblitzell. Samuel Cessna subsequently kept this house, and stage lines and wagon lines all stopped at it. It was here, and in Cessna's time, that Governor Corwin, of Ohio, was treated as a negro servant, mention of which is made in another chapter. In 1836 John Snider stopped over night at this house, with a load of emigrants, while Cessna was keeping it, and had to clean the oats he fed to his horses with an ordinary bed sheet, the windmill not having reached this point at that early day.

At the foot of Town Hill, on the west side, Henry Bevans kept a tavern. It was a wagon stand, and likewise a station for one of the stage lines. The house stood on the north side of the road, and enjoyed a good trade. Samuel Luman, the old stage driver, kept this house in 1839.

Two miles west from the Bevans house is Green Ridge, where an old wagon stand was kept by Elisha Collins. His house was a log building, and stood on the north side of the road. Although this house was humble in appearance, old wagoners are unstinted in bestowing praises on its ancient good cheer.

Trudging onward, two miles further to the westward, the old wagoner, and many a weary traveler, found a pleasant resting place at "Pratt's Hollow," where Samuel Hamilton kept a cozy old tavern. It was a frame house, on the north side of the road. Hamilton was a planter as well as tavern keeper, and raised tobacco and owned and worked negro slaves. Levi McGruder succeeded Hamilton as the keeper of this house. This locality derived its name from Pratt, who owned the property at an early day, and, upon authority of the veteran David Mahaney, kept the first tavern there. An incident occurred at Pratt's Hollow in the year 1842, which brings to memory the state of public society in *ante bellum* times. Among the old wagoners of the road, was Richard Shadburn. He was a native of Virginia, and born a slave, while his complexion was so fair, and his hair so straight, that he readily passed for a white man. When quite young he escaped from his master and struck out for liberty among the enlivening scenes of the great highway of the Republic. On a certain evening of the year mentioned, he drove into McGruder's wagon yard along with a number of other wagoners, to rest for the night. The sun had not yet disappeared behind the western hills, and a stage coach pulled up in front of McGruder's tavern, and stopped for water, as was the custom at that point. Among the passengers in that coach was the owner of the slave, Shadburn. Looking out through the window of the coach he observed and recognized Shadburn, and calling to his aid a fellow passenger, emerged from the coach with a determination to reclaim his property. Dick was seized, but being a man of great muscular power, succeeded in releasing himself from the clutches of his assailants and fled. The disappointed master fired at Dick with a pistol, as he ran, but he made good his escape. The team driven by Shadburn belonged to Parson's of Ohio, who shortly after the escapade mentioned, sent another driver to McGruder's to take charge of it. Shadburn never afterward reappeared on the road, and it is believed that he found a home and at last a grave in Canada.

It was near Pratt's Hollow that the Cotrells, father and two sons, murdered a peddler in 1822, the perpetrators of which crime were all hung from the same scaffold in Frederic. The old tavern at Pratt's Hollow was destroyed by fire many years ago, and was never rebuilt.

Two miles west from Pratt's Hollow, John S. Miller conducted an old tavern, and a good one. His house was a frame building, and stood on the north side of the road. It was a popular stopping place for wagoners. Miller kept this house as early as 1836, and subsequently became the proprietor of the old tavern, five miles west of Washington, Pennsylvania, where he died.

"Polish Mountain" is reached next, one mile west of the old Miller stand. On the summit of this little, but picturesque mountain, Philip Fletcher kept an old tavern, and greeted and treated thousands of old wagoners and other travelers. His house stood on the north side of the road, and was made of logs, but the table it furnished was equal to the best on the road.

And next comes Flintstone, four miles west of Fletcher's. All old pike boys remember Flintstone. The name has a familiar ring. The stages stopped at Flintstone, and Thomas Robinson kept the leading tavern there, in the olden time. His house was a stage station, and a wagon stand as well. Robinson, the good old landlord. got into a difficulty, many years ago, with one Silas Twigg, and was killed outright by his assailant. As early as 1835 Jonathan Huddleson kept a tavern in Flintstone, and had the patronage of one of the stage lines. He subsequently kept the old Tomlinson tavern at the Little Meadows. John Piper was an old tavern keeper at Flintstone. His house was a favorite summer resort, and also enjoyed the patronage of old wagoners. The Piper house is a large brick building, and stands on the north side of the road. John Piper died about the year 1872. The house is continued as a tavern under the joint management of John Howard, a son-in-law, and an unmarried daughter of the old proprietor. Henry B. Elbon also kept a tavern in Flintstone for many years, but his career began after that of the old road ended. Elbon died about four or five years ago. Fairweather and Ladew, of New York, own and operate a large tannery at Flintstone.

Two miles west of Flintstone, Martin's Mountain is encountered. at the foot of which, on the east, Thomas Streets presided over an old tavern, and welcomed and cared for many a guest. His house was a frame structure, on the south side of the road.

Two miles further on the westward tramp the widow Osford kept a regular old wagon stand. She was assisted by her son, Joseph. It is needless to state that her house was popular. She was a widow. Her house was a log building, on the south side of the road, with a large wagon yard attached. Her dining room occupied the greater portion of the ground floor of her house, and her table was always crowded with hungry guests. Kitchen and bar room made up the remainder of the first story, and wagoners' beds covered every inch of the bar room floor at night. Mrs. Osford retired from this house after a long season of prosperity, and was succeeded by Peter Hager. an old wagoner, who at one time drove a team for William Searight.

Two miles west from widow Osford's, Henry Miller kept an old tavern. It was a brick house, on the south side of the road. It will be noted that Miller is the leading name among the old tavern keepers of the road. The Smiths don't figure much in this line.

Two miles west of Henry Miller's an old tavern was kept by Slifer, whose first name is lost to memory. It is probable he was of the family of Slifers who kept at Boonsboro. It is said of this Slifer that he was a good, square dealing landlord, kept a good house and enjoyed a fair share of patronage.

CHAPTER XXVIII.

Old Taverns and Tavern Keepers continued — Cumberland to Little Crossings — The City of Cumberland — Everstine's — The Six Mile House and Bridge — Clary's — Tragedy in Frostburg — Thomas Beall — Sand Springs — Big Savage — Little Savage — Thomas Johnson — The Shades of Death — John Recknor — Piney Grove — Mortimer Cade — Tomlinson's — Widow Wooding.

The city of Cumberland is the initial point, as before stated, of that portion of the National Road which was constructed by authority of Congress, and paid for with funds drawn from the public treasury of the United States. In 1835 James Black kept the leading tavern in Cumberland. It was a stage house. In 1836 John and Emory Edwards, of Boonsboro, leased the Black House, and conducted it as a tavern for many years thereafter. John Snider, the old pike boy of pleasant memory, hauled a portion of the household goods of the Edwards' from their old home in Boonsboro to their new location at Cumberland. At the date last mentioned there were two wagon stands in Cumberland. One of them was kept by Thomas Plumer. Plumer had teams on the road. The other was kept by George Mattingly. Frederic Shipley kept a tavern in Cumberland previous to the year 1840. It was located on Baltimore street, near the site of the station first established by the Baltimore & Ohio Railroad Company. This house was subsequently conducted by George W. Gump, and after him, in 1857, by David Mahaney. One Kaig, of Bedford county, Pennsylvania, succeeded Mahaney in the control of this house. It was called "The American," and entertained wagoners and the traveling public at large. In 1844 and later, the widow Adams kept a wagon stand in Cumberland, on the site of the present rolling mill. George Elliott was manager for Mrs. Adams. The house was a large brick structure, and known in its day as the "Mountain City House." Lewis Smith kept "The Blue Springs House" on Mechanics street, and was largely patronized by old wagoners. Frederic Shipley also kept a tavern on Mechanics street, after he left the American. John Kelso, the old wagoner, kept a tavern for a short time on Mechanics street, and was well patronized; and Otho Barcus, another old wagoner, kept the "Pennsylvania House" on Mechanics street in 1843, and for a period of three years thereafter. The road when first laid out, as seen in a previous chapter, passed over Wills Mountain. In 1834 this location was changed for a better grade, up the valleys of Wills creek and Braddock's run. To make

(204)

JOHN KELSO.

this change it was necessary to first obtain the consent of the State of Maryland, which was granted by an act of her Legislature in 1832. The old Plumer tavern stood at the eastern end of the old location, and the old Mattingly tavern at the same end of the new location. George Evans kept a tavern, also, near the eastern end of the original location.

Five miles west of Cumberland, on the new location, a wagon stand was kept by Joseph Everstine. This was a frame house, and stood on the north side of the road. It was well conducted, but owing to its proximity to Cumberland, did not do as large a business as other taverns of the road, more advantageously located.

Six miles west from Cumberland there was an old tavern known as the "Six Mile House." It belonged to the Bruces, an old and wealthy family of Alleghany county, Maryland, and many years ago was destroyed by fire. A new building was erected on the old site, and remains to this day in the occupancy of a nephew of the old tavern keeper, Aden Clary. This house is near the junction of the old and new locations above referred to, and near the stone bridge over Braddock's run. The sixth mile post from Cumberland stands on the north wall of this bridge, firm and unshaken. The bridge is well preserved, and a polished stone thereof bears this inscription: "1835 — Built by Thomas Fealy, Lieut. Jno. Pickell, U. S. Engineer. H. M, Petitt, Ass't Supt'd."

Eight miles west from Cumberland Aden Clary kept. His house was a large and commodious brick building on the south side of the road, and is still standing. There was not a more popular house on the road than Aden Clary's.

Frostburg is next reached. This was always a prominent point on the road. It did not derive its name, as many suppose, from the crisp atmosphere in which it was located, but from the original owner of the land on which it stands, whose name was Frost. Frostburg was the first stage station west of Cumberland. The leading taverns of Frostburg in the palmy days of the road were the "Franklin House" and the "Highland Hall House." The Franklin House was kept for many years by Thomas Beall, the father of the Bealls of Uniontown. It was headquarters of the Good Intent stage line. The Highland Hall House was conducted at different times by George W. Claybaugh, George Evans, Samuel Cessna and Thomas Porter. It was the headquarters of the Stockton line of coaches. During Cessna's time at this house he was the principal actor in a tragedy which produced considerable commotion in the vicinity. A negro servant employed by Cessna addressed some insulting remark to his wife, and immediately upon being informed thereof, Cessna proceeded to dispatch the negro without ceremony. He was tried in Cumberland for murder and acquitted, public sentiment very generally acquiescing in the verdict of the jury. About the year 1850 the Highland Hall House was purchased by the authorities of the Catholic church, remodeled, improved and converted to ecclesiastical uses.

10

About one mile west of Frostburg, and at the foot of Big Savage mountain, is Sand Springs, so called from the gurgling water in the sand at that point. In 1836 the widow Ward kept a wagon stand tavern at Sand Springs. Her house was a favorite resort for old wagoners. On the night of October 3, 1836, snow fell to the depth of a foot at Sand Springs, breaking down the timber all through the surrounding mountains. Mrs. Ward's wagon yard was crowded with teams and wagons that night, and the snow was so deep the next day that the wagoners deemed it inexpedient to turn out, and remained at Mrs. Ward's until the following morning. John Snider was among the wagoners at Mrs. Ward's on the occasion mentioned, and is authority for the occurrence of the October snow storm. The tavern at Sand Springs was subsequently kept by John Welsh, an old stage driver, Hiram Sutton and Jacob Conrod, in the order named. Hiram Sutton was a son-in-law of Jared Clary. He kept the Sand Springs tavern down to the year 1852, when he moved to Parkersburg, West Virginia, and may be living there yet. Philip Spiker, the old blacksmith at Sand Springs, it is said could shoe more horses in a given time than any other blacksmith on the road. He had a rival, however, in A. Brice Devan, now of Dunbar, who, in the palmy days of the road, carried on a shop in Hopwood, and shod horses for old wagoners all night long on many occasions. Devan's backers will not concede that Spiker was a speedier shoer than he.

A short distance west of Sand Springs, on the side of Big Savage mountain, an old wagon stand was kept by one Cheney, afterward by Jacob Conrod. It is a stone house, on the south side of the road. In Cheeny's time at this house, Henry Clay Rush, who was an old wagoner, says that metalic mugs were used for drinking purposes, instead of glasses. He further states that the mugs were clean, and probably used through deference to the pure whisky of that day. Big Savage mountain is two thousand five hundred and eighty feet above the Atlantic.

Two miles west from Cheney's, and at the foot of Little Savage mountain, Thomas Beall kept a tavern as early as 1830. William E. Beall, superintendent of the Uniontown rolling mill, was born at this old tavern. Thomas Beall removed from this place to Missouri, but after a short absence, returned to Western Maryland, and took charge of the Franklin House in Frostburg. Thomas Johnson succeeded Thomas Beall in the management of this house. It was a noted place, and Johnson was a noted character. He was a good fiddler and a good dancer. He owned a negro named Dennis, who was also a good dancer, and night after night in the cheerful bar room of the old tavern, Dennis performed the "double shuffle," responsive to lively music furnished by his old master. Johnson was small in stature, weighing but little over a hundred pounds. Although he participated freely in the fun of the old road, he was not unmindful or neglectful of his business. He owned the old tavern-stand mentioned and the lands adjacent, and dying, left a comfortable inheritance to his descendants. Little Savage mountain has an elevation of two thousand four hundred and eighty feet above the Atlantic, being one hundred feet lower than Big Savage.

Three miles further westward, and at the eastern approach to the Shades of Death, John Recknor kept an old wagon stand, well known, and in its day well patronized. Recknor kept this house as early as 1830, and ended his days in it. It was a log and frame structure on the north side of the road, with a commodious wagon yard attached. The thick branches of the pine trees growing on Shade Hill, hung over this old house, imparting to it a romantic, as well as an attractive perspective. The fame of Mrs. Recknor as a purveyor of hot biscuits was co-extensive with the line of the road. Now,

> "The kitchen is cold and the hall is as still,
> As the heart of the hostess out there on the hill."

Piney Grove comes next, two miles from Recknor's, so called from the numerous pine trees growing in the locality in the olden time. At an early day Joshua Johnson, a wealthy man of Frederic City, owned fifteen thousand acres of land, embracing Piney Grove and the Shades of Death, which he held for many years for speculative purposes. Portions of this large area, it is said, continue in the possession of Johnson's descendants to this day. The pine trees were cut down many years ago, sawed up and shipped to market. William Frost, of Frostburg, erected the first extensive saw mill in the vicinity. At Piney Grove there was an old tavern, kept at different times by Truman Fairall, Mortimer Cade, Lemuel Cross, John Wrench and David Mahaney. All the stage lines of the road stopped at this old tavern, and wagoners in goodly numbers also congregated there. It was a large frame building on the north side of the road, and on the opposite side large stables and sheds were erected for sheltering horses and vehicles.

West of Piney Grove about one-fourth of a mile, an old wagon stand was kept by a man whose name was Wagoner, and subsequently by Isaac Bell, and later by Mortimer Cade. Cade kept this house in 1840, and died in it. His widow continued to keep it as a tavern for a number of years, and until she became the wife of William Fear, who kept a tavern on Keyser's Ridge. A daughter of Mrs. Cade is living in Uniontown at this time.

Two miles west of Piney Grove the celebrated old Tomlinson tavern at Little Meadows is reached. This is an old stand; as old as the National Road. Here the lines of the National and the old Braddock roads coincide. Jesse Tomlinson owned the land at this point, and kept a tavern on the old Braddock road, before the National Road was made. Upon the opening of the latter he abandoned his old house and erected a new one on the new road, which he conducted as a tavern for many years. After his death the property passed to the hands of Jacob Sides. W. M. F. Magraw, as before stated, married a daughter of Jacob Sides. This place is referred to as the Little

Meadows in the official record of Braddock's unfortunate march through the mountains in 1755. The region at and about Mt. Washington, further westward on the line of the road, where the conflict between Washington and the French and Indians occurred, in 1754, is designated by Washington, in his official report of that engagement, as the Great Meadows. Tomlinson's tavern is a large stone house, on the north side of the road. After Tomlinson, it was kept by Thomas Endsley, who was succeeded by Thomas Thistle, Thomas Thistle by James Stoddard, and he, in turn, by Jesse Huddleson, Truman Fairall, Lemuel Cross and David Mahaney, all before the railroad was continued west of Cumberland. It was kept by George Layman after the railroad absorbed the trade. Layman was afterward sheriff of Alleghany county, Maryland. In the year 1862, while the property was under the control of Mr. Magraw, the old Tomlinson tavern was remodeled and much improved. The contract for the improvements was undertaken by George W. Wyning, a well known carpenter of Uniontown, who superintended the work in person, and during its progress he and Magraw together, spent many a pleasant hour amid the exhilarating atmosphere of the mountains, in the society of the old pike boys. James K. Polk dined at the Tomlinson house in the spring of 1845, on his way to Washington to be inaugurated President. Huddleson was keeping the house at that time. The occasion brought together a large concourse of mountain people, who were addressed by the President-elect.

One mile west from Tomlinson's the widow Wooding kept a tavern as early as 1842, and for some time thereafter. Her house was a frame building, on the north side of the road, and was largely patronized by old wagoners. Mrs. Wooding growing old, and wearied by the onerous duties of tavern keeping, gave up the business, and turned her house over to her son-in-law, Peter Yeast, who conducted it for a season, and in turn surrendered it to John Wright.

One mile west of Mrs. Wooding's old stand the traveler reaches the Little Crossings, a name given to the locality from the circumstance that here the road crosses the Castleman river, and the prefix "little" is used because the Castleman is a smaller stream than the Youghiogheny, which is crossed a few miles further westward, and called the Big Crossings. There was no tavern at the Little Crossings previous to the year 1836. Subsequent to that date a tavern was established there by Alexander Carlisle, who entertained the traveling public in a satisfactory manner. His house was a large frame structure, on the south side of the road, subsequently kept by John and Samuel McCurdy, and later, at different times, by David Johnson, William Dawson, Elisha Brown, Jacob Conrod and David Mahaney. Although nearly twenty years elapsed from the building of the road before any old landlord at Little Crossings beckoned the weary traveler to rest and refreshment, nevertheless, thereafter, and until business ceased on the line, that locality presented many and rare attractions, as all old pike boys are ready to verify.

CHAPTER XXIX.

Old Tavern and Tavern Keepers continued — Little Crossings to Winding Ridge — Grantsville — The Old Shultz, Steiner and Fuller Houses — The Veteran, David Mahaney — Thomas Thistle, Widow Haldeman, Death of Mrs. Reckner, Negro Mountain, Keyser's Ridge, Log Cabin Boys of 1840, James Stoddard, Dennis Hoblitzell, The Fears, The McCurdys, Adam Yeast, David Johnson, Perry Shultz, Truman Fairall, John Woods, The Bane House, Wooing and Wedding of an Old Tavern Keeper, James Reynolds, Henry Walters.

Next after leaving the Little Crossings on the westward march, comes Grantsville, a romantic little mountain village in Garrett, formerly Alleghany, county, Maryland, named long before the hero of Appomattox was known to fame, and therefore not in his honor. In 1833 Samuel Gillis kept a tavern in the east end of Grantsville, on the south side of the road, the same house that in later years was kept by John Slicer. It was a wagon stand in the time of Gillis, and Slicer did not take charge of it until business had ceased on the road. John Lehman kept a tavern in Grantsville in 1836. He was a son-in-law, as was Peter Yeast, of the good old widow Wooding, before mentioned.

The Lehman House was subsequently kept by Henry Fuller, and after him by George Smouse. It was a frame building near the center of the village, on the south side of the street and road. In 1843 Henry Fuller demolished this old house, and erected a new one in its place. Adam Shultz kept a tavern at the east end of Grantsville back in the forties, and dying in charge, was succeeded by his son Perry, who continued it down to the year 1852, when the ancient glories of the old pike began to weaken and wane. The Shultz House was an imposing brick structure, on the south side of the road, and was kept for a while by the veteran David Mahaney, and at one time by Jesse King. Perry Shultz was subsequently elected sheriff of Alleghany county, Maryland. Solomon Steiner also kept a tavern in Grantsville during a portion of the prosperous era of the road. Grantsville seems to have been a favorite locality for tavern keepers of German names and antecedents. Steiner's tavern was a brick building, and stood on the opposite side of the road from the old Shultz House. Steiner built it, owned it, and died in it, and his son, Archibald, conducted it for a number of years after his father's death. It was a wagon stand. The Fuller House was kept at different times by John

D. Wrench, Bazil Garletts, Barney Brown, John Slicer, William Slicer, William Beffler, John Millinger, and Nathaniel Slicer. Christian M. Livengood is the present proprietor. Archibald Steiner was succeeded in his father's old house, first, by William Shaw, and thereafter in turn by John Millinger and Jonas E. Canagy, the present proprietor, and it is now called the Farmer's House.

David Mahaney, whose name frequently appears in these pages, is a remarkable man. A boy when the National Road was made, he has lived on and near it all his life. His present residence is Dunbar, Fayette county, Pa., but he is a familiar figure on the streets of Uniontown. He is the father of Lloyd Mahaney, the well known enterprising owner and manager of the handsome new Mahaney house in Uniontown, and of George Mahaney, also a popular hotel man, who at one time kept the Dixon house in Greensburg, afterward a hotel in Pittsburg, and at the present time is conducting a house in Latrobe. David Mahaney was born in Washington county, Md., near Hagerstown, in 1807, and is therefore in his eighty-sixth year, while he has the appearance of a man not over sixty. His complexion is swarthy, step elastic, and his memory but slightly impaired by the inroads of time. His father was a native of Culpeper county, Va., who met with a melancholy death by drowning in the Potomac river, on the night of the presidential election of 1856. His polling place was eight miles from his residence, in Maryland, and to reach it and vote involved the crossing of the Potomac. It was late in the evening when he left the polls to return home, and upon reaching the river, by some untoward accident fell into the water and perished. David Mahaney's first venture in tavern keeping on his own account was at the old Shultz house in Grantsville. He was personally acquainted with Henry Clay, Thomas H. Benton, Lewis Cass, and others of the old time statesmen, and frequently entertained them.

As early as 1836 Thomas Thistle kept a tavern at the foot of Negro Mountain, two miles west of Grantsville. With a name somewhat rasping in its import, Thistle had a smooth tongue, a mild manner, and furnished excellent entertainment for the traveling public. He was one of the oldest and best known tavern keepers on the road. His house was a long, frame wooden building, on the south side of the road, at times a stage station, and throughout its entire existence a wagon stand. Here the National Road crosses the line of the old Braddock road. In 1844 William Dehaven kept the old Thistle tavern, and later it was kept by Levi Dean.

One and a half miles west from the old Thistle house, and on the eastern slope of Negro Mountain, the widow Haldeman kept a tavern as early as 1840, and like all the widows, had a large patronage. While conducting this house, Mrs. Haldeman became the wife of Daniel Smouse, who thereafter took charge of it. The house was a log building, on the south side of the road, and the spacious grounds surrounding it were crowded, night after night, with six-horse teams and big, broad wheeled wagons, covered with canvass, presenting the

DAVID MAHANY.

appearance of a military encampment. This old house was subsequently kept by George Smouse, and later by John Wright. The widow Recknor, of savory memory, before mentioned, died a boarder in this old tavern, much lamented.

Onward, westward and upward, the crest of Negro Mountain is reached. There are several versions of the origin of the name of this mountain. Probably the one most worthy of acceptance is that in the early collisions between the whites and the Indians, a negro appeared as an ally of the Indians in a conflict on this mountain, and was among the slain. Negro Mountain is two thousand eight hundred and twenty-five feet above the level of the Atlantic ocean, and the second highest elevation on the line of the road. The old commissioners give the height of the mountain as two thousand three hundred and twenty-eight and twelve one-hundredths feet, from their base of measurement in the Potomac, near Cumberland, and as before stated, make no mention of Keyser's Ridge. In the year 1836 Dennis Hoblitzell kept a tavern near the summit of Negro Mountain, on the eastern slope. He was the father of Mrs. McClelland, of the McClelland house in Uniontown. This old tavern is a stone building, on the north side of the road, and the same that in after years became celebrated as a resort for hog drovers, under the management of William Sheets. It was kept as a tavern after Hoblitzell left it, and before the time of Sheets, by Thomas Beall.

Two miles west from Negro Mountain Keyser's Ridge looms up in view. This was a famous locality in the prosperous days of the road. It is a bald, bleak range, not inaptly described as the back-bone of the mountains. It is two thousand eight hundred and forty-three feet above sea level, and the highest point on the road. In the olden time snow drifts often accumulated to the depth of twenty feet on Keyser's Ridge, and stages and wagons were compelled to take to the skirting glades to avoid them. Francis McCambridge kept a tavern here as early as 1820, and was succeeded by Robert Hunter, and he by James Stoddard, some time previous to 1840. Hunter went from this house to Petersburg. James Stoddard was the grandfather of Mrs. McClelland, of the McClelland house, Uniontown. Stages stopped at Stoddard's, as well as wagoners and travelers of every description. The log cabin boys of Uniontown stopped at Stoddard's the first night out on their memorable trip to Baltimore, in 1840, to attend the great Whig mass meeting of that year in that city. They had with them, on wheels, a regular log cabin, well stored with refreshments of every kind, and the very best; and every mile of their long journey resounded with lusty shouts for "Tippecanoe and Tyler, too." E. B. Dawson, esq., and Lucien B. Bowie, of Uniontown, are the only survivors of that unique pilgrimage, so far as can be ascertained. The party consisted of such distinguished and well remembered Whigs, of Uniontown, as James Veech, Alfred Patterson, Rice G. Hopwood, Thomas R. Davidson, Lee Haymaker, John Harvey, William McDonald, Robert L. Barry, James Endsley, William E. Austin, E. B.

Dawson and Lucien B. Bowie.   There were doubtless others, but owing to the long lapse of time their names are not recalled.   Redding Bunting drove the team that hauled the cabin, and Thomas A. Wiley was with the party as an employe of the Stockton stage line, which furnished four coaches for the transportation of the political pilgrims.   James Endsley was of the Somerfield family of Endsleys, and died in that place in July, 1893.   At Middletown, a short distance east of South Mountain, in Maryland, the log cabin boys were confronted with a petticoat suspended from a pole, which excited them to rage.   A collision and a fight ensued.   John Harvey, the muscular man of the log cabin boys, engaged a like representative of the other side, and it is claimed, by the friends of Harvey, that he vanquished his antagonist.   It is not improbable that both sides claimed a victory. The party reached Baltimore safely and on time, and were received in that city with great enthusiasm.   They were tendered a reception speech, which was delivered by "The Milford Bard," a celebrated Baltimore poet and orator of that day, and the speech responsive was made by William E. Austin, who was a graceful orator, and his effort on this occasion was one of his best.   The Stoddard House, at Keyser's Ridge, was subsequently and successively kept by Dennis Hoblitzell, William Fear, one of the McCurdys, Adam Yeast and David Johnson, the latter the stepfather of Mrs. McClelland, of the McClelland House, Uniontown, before mentioned, who was born in this house when it was kept by her father, Dennis Hoblitzell.   William Fear owned the old Stoddard House, and sold it to Perry Shultz, who conducted it as a tavern for a number of years, in addition to the parties above named.   William and Daniel Fear were brothers. William, upon quitting the road, removed to Virginia, where he lived to an old age and died.   Daniel exchanged the mountains for the rich valley of the Monongahela, and ended his days in Brownsville.   In 1840 Truman Fairall built a house on Keyser's Ridge, and conducted it as a tavern to the year 1853, and a short time thereafter moved to the State of Iowa, where he spent the remainder of his life. The Stockton line of coaches stopped at Fairall's.   Fairall was a native of Old Virginia.   Samuel Fairall, a son of Truman, the old tavern keeper, at one time a student in the Dunlap's Creek Academy, near Merrittstown, Fayette county, Pennsylvania, is a law judge in one of the courts of Iowa.

About half a mile west of Keyser's Ridge, and in the year 1850, John Woods built a house and conducted it as a tavern until the close of business on the road.   He was an uncle of Henry, Thomas and Alexander Woods, of Uniontown, and an old wagoner.   Sandy Connor, the old blacksmith of Keyser's Ridge, and occasionally a stage driver, retired to an humble dwelling on the road side, opposite the Woods House, and there in the depths of the mountains took final leave of the old road and all its endearing memories.

Two miles west of Keyser's Ridge an old wagon stand tavern was kept by Daniel Fear, before mentioned, who was the father of

John G. Fear, who kept the old Workman House, in Brownsville, a few years ago, George W. Fear, formerly a wholesale liquor merchant in the same place, and Frank Fear, who once kept the Yough House in Connellsville. The old Fear tavern referred to was also at one time kept by Harvey Bane and by William Carlisle, and later by David Johnson. It was a frame house on the north side of the road. Within the venerable walls of this old tavern, and amid the romantic walks about it, when it was kept by David Johnson, Alfred McClelland, the renowned old tavern keeper of Uniontown, wooed and won his bride, and here in 1856 was happily married to Miss Sarah E. Hoblitzell, now, and for many years, a widow, and reigning mistress of the old McClelland House, in Uniontown, one of the most famous of all the far famed hostelries of the road.

About three-fourths of a mile west from the old Fear House, in later years better known as the Bane House, James Reynolds established a tavern as early as the year 1818, and continued to preside over it and entertain the traveling public until the year 1843. It was a popular wagon stand in its day. James Reynolds, its old proprietor, was the father of William Reynolds, elsewhere mentioned as an old wagoner, tavern keeper and express agent. Daniel Fear succeeded James Reynolds in the old house mentioned, and conducted it for a term of four years. He next moved to a wooden house about three hundred yards to the westward, and kept it as a tavern for two years. This old house was built by Jacob Frederic Augustine, and known as the Augustine House. From this old house Daniel Fear moved to Sand Springs, and kept the old Hiram Sutton house at that point for a term of two years, at the end of which he moved to Brownsville, and died suddenly in Uniontown on July 7, 1854, while on a business errand to that place. John Woods succeeded Fear in the Augustine House.

Within a distance of one hundred yards westward from the old Reynolds House, and in the year 1845, Henry Walters erected a wooden building and embarked in the business of tavern keeping. After a brief experience in this line, he removed to Hopwood, where he operated a blacksmith shop. While in Hopwood, and from the savings of tavern keeping and blacksmithing, he purchased the land on Dunbar's Camp, occupied it a number of years, sold it at an advance to Dr. Waters, of the Soldiers' Orphans' School, and with his added accumulations, bought the old Grier-Brown farm on Redstone creek, in Franklin township, Fayette county, Pennsylvania, founded the village of Waltersburg, and about two years ago died, leaving his family a comfortable inheritance. He is well remembered as an amiable, industrious and money accumulating citizen of German origin.

CHAPTER XXX.

From Baltimore to the point last mentioned in the preceding chapter, all the old taverns on the road are in the State of Maryland. The road crosses the dividing line between the States of Maryland and Pennsylvania, near the eastern foot of Winding Ridge. The crossing point is marked by a metal slab shaped like the ordinary mile post, and bears this inscription on one side: "State Line, Md. 96¾ to Wheeling, to Petersburg, 2¾." On the other side: "State Line, Penna. 34¼ to Cumberland, to Frostburg, 23¼."

Near the top of Winding Ridge, and in Somerset county, Pa., there is an old stone tavern which was built as early as the year 1819, and by John Welsh, who occupied it and conducted it down to the year 1821, when it passed to the management of Samuel Dennison, who was succeeded in turn by M. J. Clark, Isaac Ochletree, Peter Yeast, Maj. William Paul, Michael Cresap, Robert Boice and William Lenhart. John Welsh, who built this house and first occupied it, was the father-in-law of Aden Clary, well known in the early history of the road. Major Paul kept this house in 1836, and for some time thereafter. He subsequently kept a tavern in Washington, Pa., on Maiden street, opposite the female seminary, and later in West Brownsville, where he died more than forty years ago. He was familiarly known from one end of the road to the other. Voluble in speech, rotund in form, and ruddy in complexion, Major Paul was a fine type of the jolly landlord of the old road. He had a daughter, the wife of Aaron Wyatt, an old tavern keeper of the road, who always enjoyed the reputation of keeping a good house, owing in all probability to the early and practical training of his wife. Mrs. Patrick at one time owned and occupied the old stone house on top of Winding Ridge. She was the mother of W. W. Patrick, now, and for many years, the intelligent head of the old reputable and successful banking house of R. Patrick & Co., of Pittsburg. About the year 1850 the stables,

JOHN RISLER.

appurtenant to the old stone tavern, above mentioned, and when it was kept by William Lenhart, were destroyed by fire, supposed to have been the incendiary work of a disreputable woman. The loss was serious, and included two fine horses, the property of William Hall, the typical old regular wagoner, hereinbefore mentioned. Winding Ridge derives its name from the tortuous course of the old Braddock road up the mountain, at that point.

At the foot of Winding Ridge, on the north side of the road, an old wagon and drove stand was kept as early as the year 1820, by John Wable. This old tavern keeper was probably well advanced in years when he first put out his sign, and from this old house he was summoned to his last account. He had two sons, John and Jacob, who succeeded him in the management of the old tavern, as tenants in common. The sons applied themselves assiduously to the business of entertaining the public, and after a brief experience, concluded that their father's old house was too small to meet the demands of the increasing trade and travel of the road, and accordingly tore it down and erected a new and larger one in its place. The new house attracted a paying business, and remains a well known landmark of the road. In course of time the Wables left this house, and their successor was Edward C. Jones, the grandfather, on the maternal line, of Caleb and Noble McCormick, of Uniontown. This was more than fifty years ago. Mr. Jones moved from this old house to Searights, where he resided for a time, and subsequently located in New Salem, where he died. The old Wable house next passed to the hands of Jonas Augustine, who became its owner and conducted it as a tavern for many years, doing a good business. While in charge of this old tavern he was elected a member of the legislature of Pennsylvania for Somerset county, and represented his constituents with recognized fidelity. He died soon after his legislative career ended, and the old tavern was purchased by his brother, Daniel Augustine, who kept it for many years, and until tavern keeping on the road ceased to be profitable. Previous to the occupancy of Daniel Augustine, this house was kept for brief periods between 1840 and 1845, first by Michael Cresap, and after him by Joseph Whetstone. Cresap went from this house to the stone house on Winding Ridge. The widow of Jonas Augustine, well advanced in years, occupies this old house at the present time, as a private residence, and Daniel Augustine is a resident of Petersburg, and regarded as the richest man in that town.

One mile west of Augustine's, Daniel Blucher kept a tavern as early as 1828. He was a German, and his custom consisted mainly of the patronage of old wagoners. This house dropped from the roll of taverns long before the great travel on the road ceased.

The ancient and picturesque village of Petersburg is the next point reached on the westward march. Petersburg is noted for its healthful location and the beauty of the surrounding scenery. It has always been a popular resort for summer tourists seeking exemption from the stifling heat of crowded cities. Here lives * Gen. Moses A. Ross, a retired merchant, who did business in the village for fifty years, and gained the confidence and enjoys the esteem of all his neighbors. A number of years ago his fellow citizens elected him to the legislature, and he served them intelligently, faithfully and honestly. He is a christian gentleman, and his long and honest business career on the road entitles him to be classed as a pike boy, well worthy of honorable mention. General Ross was born in Masontown, Fayette Co., Pa., in the year 1810. Here also lived for many years, and died, William Roddy, who was at one time a superintendent of the road, and a gentleman of unquestioned integrity. The first tavern ever kept in Petersburg was by Gabriel Abrams, father of the late Judge Abrams, of Brownsville. It was a frame house, on the south side of the road, and built by Gabriel Abrams, aforesaid. This house did a large business throughout the entire career of the road, as a national highway. Subsequent to the time of Abrams it was conducted successively and successfully by John Skinner, Daniel Clary (in 1830), William Reynolds, Thomas Brownfield, James Marlow, Michael Cresap, Peter Turney, Joseph Hendrickson and Henry Magee. A frame house on the north side, erected by Henry Wentling, was conducted by him as a tavern from 1820 to 1829, when he leased it to John Risler, a celebrated old tavern keeper, who kept at various points on the road in the days of its glory. Mr. Risler was the father-in-law of the venerable Harrison Wiggins, Brown Hadden, and the late Stephen W. Snyder, and it is the tradition of the road that wherever a kitchen and a dining room were controlled by a female member of the Risler family, there a well cooked and relishable meal was sure to be obtained. Mr. Risler was succeeded in the old Wentling house by James Connelly, and he, in 1835, by the stalwart and popular old wagoner, Matthias Fry. Fry remained in charge until the spring of 1838, when he turned it over to John Bell, who was succeeded by his son-in-law, Col. Samuel Elder, who remained in charge until some time late in the forties, when he moved to Uniontown and took the management of the National house in that place. In the year 1832 Robert Hunter opened a tavern in a brick house, on the south side of the road and street, in Petersburg, and conducted it for many years with marked success. Mrs. Hunter, the old and amiable hostess of this house, is remembered as well for her good qualities as a housekeeper as for her immense size. She weighed two hundred and fifty pounds. This old house was subsequently kept by John A. Walker, John McMullin, Alfred Newlon and Lott Watson, in the order given, and was always well kept. The stage coaches of one of the early lines stopped at this house, and it has been extensively patronized by summer visitors and pleasure seekers. It was one of the very best eating houses on the road, and is continued as a tavern to this day by Mr. Mitchell, who holds a license and keeps a good house. John E. Reeside married a step-daughter of John McMullin.

* Died December 12, 1893.

THE TEMPLE OF JUNO.

At a very early period in the road's history, John Mitchell kept a tavern one mile west of Petersburg, on the north side. Besides doing a general business, this old house was a station for the first line of stages on the road. It was destoyed by fire on the 31st day of October, 1828, and supplied by a new log structure, which was kept as a tavern for many years by John Mitchell, jr., who erected near the old site the present large and substantial brick building in which he is now living, one of the oldest men on the road. On the opposite side of the road from this house immense stabling was erected, in after years supplemented by cattle and hay scales, all of which are still standing, tending slightly towards dilapidation and decay, but in a much better state of preservation than most of the old stables of the road. There is a large and fertile farm connected with this old tavern stand, well managed, under the direction of its venerable owner, *John Mitchell.

A short distance west from Mitchell's, a large brick house on the north side of the road, was kept as a tavern by John Bradfield in 1840, and later. The locality was known as Newbury. John Bradfield was the general agent of the first heavy freight line put on the road, moved by six horse teams, stationed at intervals of fifteen miles. He was an old wagoner, and a good business man, and before going to Newbury kept a tavern in Wheeling and in Washington, Pennsylvania. After Bradfield's retirement the Newbury house was continued as a tavern by Moses Jennings.

Less than a mile west of Newbury, on the north side of the road, an old building once used as a tavern, attracts special attention by reason of the singular style of its architecture. It is a wooden structure, commonly called a frame, with an unusually high portico in front, supported by four round and tall wooden columns, tapering upward and and downward from the centers. It reminds one of the old pictures of the temple of Juno, and possibly the designer had that ancient temple in view when he planned this old tavern. He is said to have been a native of the vicinity, not likely versed in the classic orders of architecture, but the style he adopted in this instance might reasonably be regarded as the Monogynous. Two immense stables appurtenant to this old tavern, one log, the other frame, both still standing, weather beaten, empty, and useless, bear silent, but impressive testimony to the thrift of other days, and impart a tinge of melancholy to the memories of the old pike. Daniel Show was the original owner of the quaint old building above described, and its first occupant. He sold it to Samuel Easter, who conducted it for a brief period, and was succeeded by Peter Lenhart, mentioned hereinafter as "Shellbark." Samuel Thompson succeeded Lenhart, and he in 1846 was succeeded by Mrs. Metzgar, who subsequently became the wife of John Olwine.

And now the hills that skirt the Youghiogheny river rise to view, and Somerfield is reached, an ancient little town, which the old metal

* Died in 1892.

mile posts on the road persist in calling Smithfield. That this town was once called Smithfield there can be no doubt, and that it now is Somerfield is equally clear. It was originally called Smithfield, because its founder's name was Smith, but the postoffice department changed it to Somerfield on account of the great multitude of Smiths and Smithfields in all portions of the universe. Somerfield has been the scene of many a lively incident of the old road. Here light feet, impelled by lighter hearts, tripped to the notes of merry music, and the ringing laugh and sprightly jokes of the old stage driver and wagoner, enlivened the now dull halls of the old taverns. The most noted old tavern keeper of Somerfield was Capt. Thomas Endsley. Somerfield was always a stage station, the second relay east of Uniontown. The Endsley House was the headquarters of Stockton's line. It is a stone building, and stands near the bank of the river at the western end of the town, and was erected in the year 1818 by Kinkead, Beck & Evans, the old bridge builders, and occupied and conducted as a tavern by James Kinkead, the senior member of the firm, from the date of its completion to the year 1822. John Campbell was its next occupant, who kept it for a term of two years, and until 1824. Capt. Endsley then took charge of it, and conducted it down to the year 1829. John Shaffer kept it from 1829 to 1831, when Capt. Endsley again took charge and continued down to 1834, when Redding Bunting was installed, and conducted it down to the year 1837. He was succeeded by John Richards, who remained in charge until 1840. Squire Hagan conducted it from 1840 to 1842, and Aaron Wyatt from 1842 to 1847, when Capt. Endsley, the third time, reentered, and remained in charge until 1852, when he gave place to his son William, the present incumbent. This old house is as solid as when first constructed. Its foundation walls are not the least impaired, and its mortar pointings are as hard as the stones, while the wood work, and notably the doors, casings and mantel pieces, are in a perfect state of preservation, attesting the skill of the mechanics at the early period in which the house was built. Near the center of the town, on the south side of the street, an old log tavern was kept by John Campbell, as early as the year 1824, and immediately after his retirement from the Endsley House. He was succeeded in turn at this house by L. C. Dunn, Samuel Frazee, Moses Jennings, and John Bradfield. The June Bug line of stages stopped at this house, and for a while the Good Intent line. It went out of business in 1853, was remodeled and improved, and is now the private residence of James Watson. Prior to 1837 and down to 1849 a tavern was kept on the north side of the street in Somerfield, by Daniel Blucher, J. Tantlinger, Capt. Morrow, Aaron Wyatt, Andrew Craig, Samuel Thompson and P. R. Sides, in the order given. This house ceased to do business in 1849, and was pulled down in 1883, and never rebuilt. In 1823 James Kinkead, the old bridge builder, kept a tavern in a brick house on the south side of the street in Somerfield. This house was afterward and successively kept by William Imhoff, James

THE ENDSLEY HOUSE.

Watson, Lot Watson, John Irvin and Ephraim Vansickle. Vansickle was a blind man and engaged in tavern keeping when the glory of the road was fading away. He had many of the elements of a successful tavern keeper, and furnished satisfactory entertainment to the few travelers and strangers who sought shelter and refreshment under his kindly roof; but he was too late. Tavern keeping on the National Road was but a legend when he embarked in the business, and he was constrained to listen day after day, and night after night to the glowing recitals of the good times in bygone years, and reconcile himself as best he could to the existing situation. At Somerfield the road crosses the Youghiogheny river over a large, handsome and substantial stone bridge, three hundred and seventy-five feet in length, with three symmetrical arches, and appropriately named by old pike boys the Big Crossings. A large dressed stone in the wall of this bridge above the surface of the road, and near the eastern end, bears the inscription; "Kinkead, Beck & Evans, builders, July 4th, 1818." The day of the month, the anniversary of Independence, is given because on that day the bridge was finished, and the occasion was celebrated with great eclat. The inhabitants of the mountains for miles around, male and female, old and young, with old fashioned banners and old fashioned music, turned out in great numbers, inspired by that genuine patriotism which characterized the early period of our country's independence, while yet many of the soldiers of the revolution were living, and were addressed in eloquent terms by the Hon. Andrew Stewart, Col. Samuel Evans, Hon. John Dawson and John M. Austin, of Uniontown.

CHAPTER XXXI.

The first old tavern west of the "Big Crossings," and the first in
Fayette county, Pa. (for the river here is the boundary line between
the counties of Fayette and Somerset), is that which for many years
was kept by Peter Lenhart, commonly known as "Shellbark." This
is a two-story house, originally built with logs, but subsequently
weather-boarded and painted red. The red, however, has long since
disappeared, and it now wears the dingy, dark colored hue that
settles upon all ancient buildings. A man named Ebert built this
house and occupied it as a private residence. He was a tanner by
trade, and a justice of the peace. He sold out to Peter Lenhart's
father, who occupied the house also as a private residence until his
death, when his son Peter succeeded him and opened up the house
as a tavern, and soon after added a distillery. The house had a good
custom and "Shellbark" was prosperous. He was an eccentric man,
and like Orator Puff, had two tones to his voice. He had a habit,
upon rising every morning, of cutting a large slice from a loaf of
bread, spreading it with butter, and eating it in connection with a
glass of whiskey. He enjoyed this matutinal habit for many years,
and rarely omitted it. Why he was called "Shellbark" is not accurately known. He was in early life an old-line Democrat, but in
later years got "mixed up," and seemed to have lost his political
moorings. He died a few years ago, and his widow and daughter
remain in the old house, occasionally entertaining strangers and travelers in very satisfactory style.

The next old tavern stand is about half a mile from Lenhart's,
on the south side of the road. The line of the National Road
here is the same as that of the old Braddock road, and this
house was kept as a tavern by Andrew Flenniken, before the
National Road was constructed. Jacob Probasco succeeded Flenniken in this house. Besides keeping a tavern, Probasco had teams
on the road, was a contractor for repairs, operated a store, put up
and operated a grist and saw mill, and engaged in many other en-
terprises. One of his contracts was for taking up a portion of the
old road bed. At first, as elsewhere noted, the road was paved with
large boulders, which were subsequently taken up and their places
supplied by stones broken into small pieces. There are points along

THE BIG CROSSINGS.

the road where the old bed remains, and here the road is in better condition than elsewhere, which has started the belief that it was a mistake to take up the original bed; but this is a disputed and unsettled question. Prominent among those who thought it was a mistake to take up the original road bed was Capt. Thomas Endsley, the old tavern keeper of Somerfield. He argued the question on many occasions with the engineers, and after the work was done adhered to his opinion, and characterized the plan as a foolish notion of inexperienced young cadets. Probasco got into trouble in attempting to collect a claim by attachment, was indicted for perjury, and soon after left the State, settling in Ohio, and there became prominent and wealthy. It was a relative, probably a son of Jacob Probasco, who donated the money for the erection of the celebrated fountains in the city of Cincinnati. Probasco sold out to Peter Baker, who kept the house a number of years, and he was succeeded in turn by John Irvin, Jacob Richards, Charles Kemp, Aaron Wyatt, Morris Mauler, Aden Clary and Alexander Speers. It was a stage house, and passengers by one of the coach lines took meals there. John Conway now occupies the property, and it is owned by Aden Clary, of Frostburg, Maryland. The house is long and narrow, made up of different structures erected at different times, one part stone, another log, and a third frame, all now, and for a long time heretofore, joined together and enclosed by weather-boarding. The intervening space between this and the Youghiogheny river is called "Jockey Hollow," a level piece of road upon which horses were run and cock-fighting practiced. Hence the name Jockey Hollow. Ephriam Vansickle, "Blind Eph," as he was called, kept a tavern many years in an old log house in Jockey Hollow, and did a good business. This house was never kept as a tavern by any other person than Vansickle. He subsequently kept a tavern in Somerfield. Nicholas Bradley, who died a few years ago, was an old denizen of Jockey Hollow. He was a contractor on the original construction of the road, and as his name implies, an Irishman. His son, Daniel, still lives here, an active business man and an influential Democratic politician. *Jeremiah Easter, esq., Democratic Jury Commissioner, also lives here. John Conway once kept a tavern in the "bend of the road" near the foot of the hill, about half a mile west of Jockey Hollow. This house was a log structure, long since demolished, and a small frame now stands on the old site. John Conway was Daniel Bradley's grandfather, long since dead, and therefore not the man at present occupying the old Probasco tavern.

Next is the old tavern of Thomas Brown. This is a large stone house, built by Mr. Brown about the time the road was made. It stands on the south side of the road. Brown kept it as a tavern from the time it was built until the time of his death. Col. Ben Brownfield and Gen. Henry W. Beeson were wont to come here on their sleighing excursions in the olden time, often remaining many nights

* Now deceased.

and days enjoying themselves in dancing and feasting. Brown was a good fiddler, and furnished his guests with music, as well as other means of entertainment. He was a large man with a shrill voice, and considered a popular landlord. The property remained in the Brown family a few years after the death of the old proprietor, and ultimately fell into the hands of Jacob Umberson, the present occupant. The elections of Henry Clay township were formerly held at this house, and many exciting scenes have been witnessed here on election day.

The next old tavern site is Mt. Augusta. (Site is used because the old brick tavern house that stood here for so many years was burned down some time ago, and has not been rebuilt.) It was one of the largest and most commodious houses on the road, with two large water troughs and extensive stabling among the appurtenances. In the palmy days of the road it did a large business. John Collier was the original owner and occupant of this property. At his death it fell into the hands of his son, Daniel, who kept it for a number of years and sold out to Thomas Brownfield. Brownfield kept tavern here for thirty years, and sold out to John O'Hegarty, the present owner and occupant. Daniel Collier moved from here to Georges township, where he died a few years ago, the owner of a large estate. Brownfield became successively commissioner and sheriff of Fayette county, Pennsylvania, and at the close of his term as sheriff removed to the State of Missouri, where he died. The sale of this property by Brownfield to O'Hegarty, was effected through the agency of the celebrated Henry Clay Dean. O'Hegarty lived in Lebanon county, Pennsylvania, when he became the purchaser. The old tavern house was burnt during the occupancy of Mr. O'Hegarty. After the fire he moved into a frame tenant house, on the opposite side of the road, a little to the east, where he lives now. He is an acting justice of the peace, esteemed for his honesty and probity, and wields great influence among his neighbors.

Next is a stone house on the south side of the road, first kept as a tavern by William Shaw, and afterward by William Griffin, Charles Kemp, Isaac Denny and William A. Stone, in the order given. It did a good business, and was regarded as a good house.

Next comes the old Marlow House. This is a large two-story brick building, near the summit of a long hill. On the opposite side of the road a large stable was erected, capable of sheltering a hundred horses, and now in a decaying condition. The indispensable water-trough was here also. This house was built and kept as a tavern by Benjamin Miller, the grandfather of Ben, Jeff and Sam Miller, of Uniontown. Miller sold the property to James Marlow. Marlow kept it a long time, and died in it. At the time of his death he was superintendent of the road. He was a short, heavy set, quiet man, and came from Maryland. He had several sons, all of whom went west many years ago, and one of them is now the proprietor of the "American hotel," in the city of Denver. Benjamin Miller was

DANIEL COLLIER.

once a candidate for the Legislature, and pending his canvass declared, "By the Eternal, if the people did not elect him he would go up on the hill overlooking Harrisburg, and look down with contempt upon the Capitol." He was not elected.

At the foot of the hill, below the Marlow House, stood, in the olden time, a cluster of small log cabins, three in number, which constituted a tavern stand known as the "Bush House," or "Three Cabins." This quaint old tavern was kept by one Leonard Clark, who entertained a great many strangers and travelers, especially such as were in quest of something to slake their thirst. Its best business days were during the time the road was undergoing construction, and upon its completion the "Three Cabins" succumbed to more pretentious inns. These cabins were covered with clap-boards; the chimneys built of rough stones, and "topped out" with mud and sticks. Clark, the old proprietor, retired from public life soon after the completion of the road, went west, left his cabins to the tender mercies of the elements, and scarcely a trace of them can be seen at this day. That jolly times occurred at this old tavern, among the early pike boys, there can be no question.

The next house is a two-story stone building with portico in front, known in recent years as the "Old McCollough Stand." It was built and first kept as a tavern by a man named Bryant. James Sampey, Isaac Nixon, Morris Mauler and Nicholas McCartney, each kept this house for shorter or longer terms before McCollough went into it. Col. John W. McCollough, who became the owner of the property, kept tavern here for many years, and died the proprietor. He was a man of stalwart size, a talking man and a politician. He was likewise a contractor, and did much work on the road. He left a widow and several children. *Jim and Nick, two of his sons, are well known pike boys. His † widow married 'Squire Burke, who now occupies the house, and there is no place on the road where a better meal can be obtained. A tragedy was enacted at this house which forms a memorable event in the history of the old pike, and served as a good text for the old anti-slavery agitators. It was on the 4th of July, 1845. Early in the morning of that day, while a number of wagoners were engaged in feeding and cleaning their teams, as they stood in the wagon yard, a negro passed along the road, and William King, one of the wagoners aforesaid, cried out in a loud voice to Nicholas McCartney, who was then keeping the house, "There goes a runaway nigger." "Are you sure of that?" inquired McCartney, "I am," replied King, whereupon McCartney darted after the negro and captured him a short distance south of the house, the rocks and brush in that locality having impeded the progress of the fugitive. McCartney led him into the house, and informed him that he was going to take him back to his master in Maryland. The negro seemed submissive, and McCartney placed him in charge of one Atwell Holland, his brother-in-law, while he went for a horse to carry

* Both now dead.   † Now dead.

out his purpose of taking him back to Maryland. During McCartney's absence the negro ran out of the house, and Atwell and others
pursued him. Atwell being more fleet than any of the other pur-
suers, soon overtook the negro, whereupon he wheeled upon Holland,
drew a dirk knife from his pocket, struck it into his pursuer's heart,
and made good his escape. Holland immediately fell to the ground,
and expired while being borne to the house by his companions.
Among the persons present on this tragic occasion, was one Lewis
Mitchell, who was a great hunter and an occasional preacher. While
Holland was lying on the ground dying, Mitchell placed wild grape
leaves on his wound, and prayed for him. Mitchell was preaching
once in this neighborhood, and in one of his most earnest passages,
heard the yelping of hounds. He immediately ceased preaching, and
exclaimed, "There are the hounds, and d—d if Lead ain't ahead,"
and straightway dashed out of the meeting house to join the sportsmen.

The next old tavern is about four hundred yards from the last
one, and was also built by Bryant, above mentioned, but not for a
tavern. This house was kept successively by John McCollough,
Morris Mauler and Adam Yeast, and is now kept by *Nick McCollough.
There were times when it had a "good run" of patronage. Adam
Yeast, one of its old occupants, was an eccentric character, and ultimately became a lunatic.

Next we come to Charley Rush's old stand. This was a famous
stopping place. Charles Rush settled here in the woods in 1838,
built the house, which he occupied as a tavern until he died in 1846,
in the prime of life. He always kept a big team on the road,
under the management of a hired driver. He was a brother of Boss
Rush, and the father of Henry Clay Rush, a prominent and influential citizen of Uniontown. He was fond of horse racing, and always
kept fast horses. His son Henry Clay was his favorite rider, who,
when a small boy, appeared on the race course arrayed in the jockey
outfit, and exactly filling the regulation weight. He would cut a
sorry figure now, on the back of a race horse. Charles Rush was
kind and charitable in disposition, but when exigencies required,
would not decline a fisticuff. Many an overbearing bully has felt the
damaging effects of his well-aimed blows. He entertained strangers
and travelers at his hospitable board, whether they had the means
of paying their bills or not, but always preferred that impecunious
guests should inform him of their condition before engaging accommodations. On one occasion an Irishman tarried with him over
night, and in the morning, after breakfast, informed him that he had
no money to pay his bill. "Why didn't you tell me that last night?"
sharply inquired Mr. Rush. "And faith, sir," replied the Irishman,
"I'm very sorry to tell you of it this morning." Rush, pleased with
his wit, absolved him from his bill, gave him a parting drink, and allowed him to go "Scot free." † William L. Smith, esq., ex-county
commissioner, married the widow Rush, and occupies the old stand as

---

* Since deceased.   † Now dead.

SEBASTIAN RUSH.

a private residence. Samuel Rush, a farmer, and brother of Charles, lived about three miles from here, back in the country. He was a contractor on the road, and an energetic, honest and highly respected citizen. He was the father of *Marker Rush, the proprietor of the well known "Rush House," near the Union Depot, in Pittsburg. Marker must have inherited his fondness for the sports of the day through his uncle Charles, as his father was not given to worldly indulgences.

There was a little log house a short distance west of Charley Rush's old stand, which was kept as a tavern for a few years by Edward Dean. It was not one of the original taverns, and not considered "regular." The pike boys of the neighborhood called it the "Sheep's Ear." Its chief business consisted in selling whisky at three cents a drink, which was the price of whisky all along the road. F. H. Oliphant, the well known iron manufacturer, probably the oldest in the State, once put a line of wagons on the road to carry goods and merchandise from Brownsville to Cumberland. The wagons were drawn by mules, and the teams changed at fixed points along the road. This old Dean House was one of the stopping places of this line. One night some mischievous person, or persons, cut the harness of one of the teams into shreds, so that Oliphant's line did not move out the next morning from the "Sheep's Ear." Another house of similar proportions and character near by, was kept by Thomas Dean. It was known in the neighborhood as the "Bull's Head." It was the custom of the pike boys of the neighborhood to collect together in these old houses, when they were kept as taverns, now at one and then at the other, to "while away" the long winter evenings, and enjoy themselves in dancing and revelry. Nicholas McCartney often attended these festive gatherings when a young man, and could relate many interesting incidents and anecdotes connected twih the "Sheep's Ear" and "Bull's Head" inns.

We next come to the old Inks House, now owned and occupied by Nicholas McCartney. This is a large frame, weather-boarded house, with a spacious wagon yard attached, a large stable and a number of sheds and other outbuildings. The house was built by George Inks, and kept by him as a tavern for many years. A man named Heckrote kept here once, and so also did John Risler, and Samuel M. Clement, for many years a prosperous farmer on Redstone creek, near Uniontown, entertained the traveling public for a brief period, in his early manhood, and proved himself a competent landlord. The house enjoyed a large share of patronage during the prosperous times on the road. †Mr. McCartney, present occupant and owner, has been in feeble health for many months. Previous to his present illness he was a man of robust health and great energy. He is a son-in-law of Thomas Brownfield, the old proprietor of the Mt. Augusta House. He is universally esteemed among his neighbors, and general sympathy is manifested on account of his illness.

* Since deceased.　† Now dead.

We next reach the celebrated house of *Sebastian Rush, invariably called "Boss." It is not a wagon stand, but an old stage house. Here stage passengers took meals, which were invariably gotten up in the best style. The house was built in 1837 by Hon. Nathaniel Ewing, who then owned it. Rush moved into it soon after it was finished, as lessee of Judge Ewing, and not long after purchased it, and occupied it uninterruptedly to the present time. Here, also, is a store, postoffice and other improvements, constituting a little village called Farmington, and considered the grand commercial and business center of the mountains. Sebastian Rush is widely known as an influential Republican politician, has been superintendent of the road by appointment of the Governor, and nominated by his party for Associate Judge, but defeated by reason of the decided and long existing preponderance of the Democracy in the county. When a young man, and living in a small log house near the tavern stand of his brother, Charles, he was elected constable of his township, and, being too poor to own a horse, performed the functions of his office on foot. Since then he has made constables and other officers, and owned horses without number. Previous to 1837 the widow Tantlinger kept tavern in an old wooden house, on the ground now covered by the Rush house. The store here, before Rush came to the property, was conducted by Peter T. Laishley, an old and well known Methodist preacher, still living. He was then a Free Will Baptist. Morgan Jones also once kept store at this point. He is now a real estate broker in Philadelphia, and said to be wealthy. He had several brothers, among them David, John and Samuel E., who were well known. David settled in Wisconsin, and became Lieutenant Governor. John went to Kentucky, and became a prominent iron manufacturer. Samuel E. is a Probate Judge in southern Colorado. Allen Crane also once kept store here.*

The house now owned and occupied by Washington Hensel, was once kept as a tavern by Samuel Frazer. Its public career terminated about the time Sebastian Rush located at Farmington. A short distance over the hill, west, there is a frame house, built by John Rush, and by him kept as a tavern for a number of years. Henry Clay Rush also kept this house for a short time. It is not classed among the old taverns, but during its short public career enjoyed a high degree of popularity. Boss Rush, jr., lives here now in the capacity of a private citizen. John Rush was one of the most popular landlords along the road. He is a brother of Boss, and is still living, somewhere in the west. This old house was destroyed by fire a few years ago, and nothing remains of it but two tall chimneys, standing erect at this day.

* Deceased.

RUINS OF THE OLD JOHN RUSH HOUSE.

CHAPTER XXXII.

Old Taverns and Tavern Keepers continued — Fort Necessity, Washington's First Battle Field, Monroe Springs, Reception to President Monroe, Gate Bob Mc-Dowell, Braddock's Run and Grave, Fayette Springs, A Trio of Old Fiddlers, Chalk Hill, Snyders, Old Squire Price, The Summit of Laurel Hill, Molly Calhoun, Ephriam McLean, The Big Water Trough on Laurel Hill, The Goat Pen, The Turkey's Nest, Monroe, known now mostly as Hopwood, Matthias Fry, German D. Hair, The Old Morris House, Widow Sands, Harry Gilbert.

Mt. Washington is a point replete with historic interest. Here Washington first measured swords with an enemy, and fought his first battle. It is the site of Fort Necessity, and known in colonial times as the Great Meadows. Gen. Washington subsequently became the owner of this property, and held it until his death. It was no doubt owing to the fact that his first engagement with an armed foe took place on this ground he resolved to buy it. In his last will he directed it to be sold by his executors, together with other real estate he held, and the proceeds divided among parties he named. The tract, when owned by Washington, contained two hundred and thirty-four acres, and he valued it at six dollars an acre. He thus refers to it in a note appended to his will:

"This land is valuable on account of its local situation. It affords an exceeding good stand on Braddock's road, from Ft. Cumberland to Pittsburg, and besides a fertile soil, possesses a large quantity of natural meadow, fit for the scythe. It is distinguished by the appellation of the Great Meadows, where the first action with the French, in 1754, was fought."

Previous to 1835, and by divers good conveyances and assurances, down from Washington, this estate passed into the hands of the late Hon. Nathaniel Ewing, who caused to be erected on the property the large brick house, still standing, and one of the most noted old taverns on the road. Judge Ewing subsequently sold and conveyed the property to James Sampey, who went into possession and kept the tavern for many years, and until his death. The first year after Mr. Sampey's death the management of the tavern and farm was placed in charge of Robert Hogsett, who turned over to the representative of the estate the sum of four thousand dollars, as the profits of one year. The Good Intent line of stages stopped at Sampey's, and as showing the extent of the business of the house, Mr.

Hogsett mentions that on one morning seventy-two stage passengers took breakfast there. John Foster and James Moore subsequently kept this house. They were sons-in-law of James Sampey, and Moore was an old stage driver. At the close of business on the road, Ellis Y. Beggs purchased the property and the tavern was closed. William D. Beggs, the father of Ellis, died in this house. He had collected the tolls for many years at the gate near Searights, was likewise a school teacher, and a good one, and was, for a number of years, Steward of the County Home. His eldest daughter, Jane, was the second wife of Dr. Smith Fuller, the eminent Uniontown physician. Godfrey Fazenbaker succeeded Beggs in the ownership, and engaged extensively in farming and stock raising. Mr. Fazenbaker died in possession, and the property descended to his heirs, who are the present occupants. The big water-trough still remains on the opposite side of the road from this old tavern, but all else has changed since the days when the proud stage driver cracked his long silken-ended whip over the backs of his four spanking steeds.

The next old tavern was at Monroe Springs, on the hillside, a short distance west of one of the old round toll houses. This house was built by Charles McKinney, and opened up by him as a tavern. It was a log house, weather-boarded, of small dimensions, now entirely obliterated. Boss Rush commenced his career as a tavern keeper in the old honse at this point, and it was kept at various times by such well known men as Wm. S. Gaither, German D. Hair, Wm. Dillon, Morris Mauler, John Rush, John Foster and David Ogg. It was essentially a wagon stand, and night after night, in the prosperous era of the road, the ground all around it was crowded with big wagons and teams, and the old bar room rang out with the songs and jokes of the jolly wagoner. Opposite the house a large water-trough was erected, kept full and overflowing from a spring near by, called "The Monroe Spring," in honor of President Monroe. When McKinney kept this house President Monroe passed along the road, and a public dinner was given him here. John Hagan, then a contractor on the original construction of the road, was prominently connected with the bestowal of this compliment upon the old-time President. The few old folks who have personal recollections of this event, speak of it as a memorable and exciting occasion. The dinner was substantial and superb, and highly enjoyed by all participating, including the illustrious guest. John Hagan was the father of Robert Hagan, esq., ex-commissioner of Fayette county, Pennsylvania.

One of the old stone toll houses stood a short distance east of the Monroe Springs, and remained until 1893, when it was torn down. Hiram Seaton was one of the early collectors at this point. He was the father of *C. S. Seaton, the well known banker of Uniontown. He subsequently served two terms as County Treasurer. He had a wooden leg, and was esteemed as an honest man. He went west, settled in Missouri, and died there. He was succeeded as toll collector

* Now dead.

HON. SAMUEL SHIPLEY.

by Robert McDowell, always thereafter called "Gate Bob," to distinguish him from a number of other well known citizens bearing the same name. Robert McDowell was also an honest man, a popular man and a fighting man. He was tall, thin and muscular. His fingers were distorted by rheumatism, but he could use them in a fight with terrible effect. He was the Democratic candidate for county commissioner of Fayette county, Pennsylvania, in 1854, but beaten by the Know Nothings. He died a few years ago at Dunbar, very greatly lamented. The memory of "Gate Bob" will long remain fresh in the recollection of the pike boys, old and young.

The next old tavern stand is the "Braddock's Run House." Gen. Braddock was buried near this house, a day or two after his disastrous defeat by the French and Indians, at Braddock's Field, near Pittsburg. The exact spot where he was buried is still pointed out, and can be seen from the road. This circumstance gave name to the brook here, and the tavern. The house was built by Charles McKinney, the same person who built the "Monroe Springs House." He kept tavern here for many years. The house is a large two-story stone structure. It was subsequently and successively kept by Robert Shaw, Noble McCormick and William Shaw. This property is now owned by the heirs of James Dixon, and is not a public house.

Next we come to the "Fayette Springs Hotel," a large stone house built at an early day by the Hon. Andrew Stewart, who owned the property, and remained its owner until the day of his death. It was recently sold by his heirs to Capt. John Messmore, of Uniontown. This house was a favorite resort for visitors to the Fayette Springs, situate about three-quarters of a mile distant. In its halcyon days it had its ten-pin alley, billiard tables, swing, and other appliances of pleasure and comfort, but they have all passed away, and probably by reason of hard times, and the abatement of interest in the Springs may never again be brought into requisition. Here merry parties of young folks from Uniontown and elsewhere were accustomed to assemble and enjoy a hearty supper, engage in the dizzy mazes of the dance, and when it was all over "go home with the girls in the morning." Mahlon Fell and Tom Collins were the old-time fiddlers, and furnished the music, which in its line was of superior excellence. They were occasionally reinforced by Jacob B. Miller, esq., who tendered his services without pecuniary reward, and in the language of the day, "could make a fiddle talk." Collins is dead. *Fell and Miller are both living. The former has joined the church and abandoned the fiddle, while the latter still retains his taste and talent for music, and often entertains his friends in a private manner, with many of the popular tunes of the olden time. The "Fayette Springs House" has been kept in turn by Cuthbert Wiggins, John Risler, B. W. Earl, Samuel Lewis, William Snyder, William Darlington, John Rush, Major Swearingen, Redding Bunting, Cuthbert Downer, and perhaps others.

* All now dead.

I I

We next reach "Chalk Hill," so called from the circumstance of white clay adhering to the shovels of the workmen engaged in digging the foundation of the road. The tavern house was built here in 1823 by Jonathan Downer, who was its first host. He was succeeded by Boss Rush, and he in turn by Springer Downer, Samuel Shipley, William Shipley and Milford Shipley. *John Olwine now owns the property, and keeps tavern here. It is a two-story frame, with commodious stabling attached. Boss Rush went from this house to Farmington. Samuel Shipley bought this property at an Orphans' Court sale, in 1846, for $1,405, and paid for it in gold. Westley Frost was the sheriff and trustee to sell. Shipley subsequently became an associate judge. He was more fortunate than his neighbor and fellow inn keeper, Boss Rush, in belonging to the strong side. Rush was one of his competitors on the Republican side.

Next comes the old tavern stand of James Snyder. Snyder seems to have been here always, and is here yet. He did vacate a short time for William Shaw, but not long enough to change the tradition that this is, and always was, Snyder's. The house looks old and dingy, and no wonder, for it has withstood the wild dashes of numberless mountain storms. It is situate at the foot of the eastern slope of Laurel Hill, and on the head waters of Sandy Creek. The old stable is decaying, and will soon be gone. The old host, too, is showing the marks of time and age. He has already passed beyond the age defined by the Psalmist. His three score and ten are supplemented by well nigh half a score.† He is the only old landmark left along the road, that has not shifted from original ground, except Natty Brownfield. A few years ago he was elected county commissioner on the Democratic ticket, but practically without opposition. He is universally esteemed for his honesty. As a tavern keeper he enjoyed an excellent reputation, and many a weary traveler has found consolation and comfort under his hospitable roof. The best wishes of all his neighbors attend the old gentleman in his declining years, and heaven's choicest blessings are invoked upon his venerable head.

Near the top of Laurel Hill on the eastern slope, once lived a noted character named Benjamin Price. His house, a log structure, was built near the roadside, but below its surface, so that the upper story was about on a level with the road. He kept a cake shop, was an acting justice of the peace, and a strict Methodist, and was in the habit of annoying wagoners and hog drovers by fining them for swearing, and they in turn annoyed him by throwing billets of wood and disabled hogs down his chimney. Price is long since dead, and the last vestige of his old house has disappeared. The stable near by it remained longer, but it has gone, too. A few apple trees planted by the hands of the 'Squire, now encroached upon by the mountain undergrowth, are all that remain to indicate the spot where the old house stood.

We next reach the "Summit House." This is not a wagon

* Now dead.   † Now deceased.

STONE HOUSE, DARLINGTON'S.

stand, nor strictly an old tavern, but rather a fashionable and popular summer resort. It is on the apex of Laurel Hill, and has the advantage of pure air, and an extensive and charming view of the surrounding and underlying country. At this point large finger boards were erected, indicating distances and routes to the Washington Springs, Dulaney's Cave and Jumonville's Grave, which are landmarks indelibly impressed upon the memories of surviving wagoners and stage drivers. The property here belongs to *Col. Samuel Evans, a wealthy and well known citizen of Fayette county. † Ephraim McClean kept the house here for many years, and made it famous by the excellence and style of his entertainment. His flannel cakes and spring chickens have passed into history, as unrivalled productions of culinary art and tempters of the appetite. There is a large spring and bath house here. This has ever been a favorite resort of parties in pursuit of pleasure. Here the youth, beauty and fashion of Uniontown were wont to come to while away an evening in eating, dancing and other diversions. The rooms were small, but the pleasure was unbounded. Here also the yeomanry of the county came to make a harvest home, or celebrate an anniversary. The drive, up and down the mountain, is delightful, and formed no small share of the pleasure incident to the old time parties at this popular place of resort.

Ephraim McClean left this house many years ago and settled in Illinois. He was succeeded by Henry Clay Rush, who maintained the reputation of the house during his occupancy, but left it in 1856 to go to Searights. Brown Hadden came in after Rush, and after Hadden the house was successively kept by Stephen W. Snyder, John Snyder, William Boyd and Webb Barnet, the present occupant. Anterior to the erection of the present buildings, and many years ago, one Molly Calhoun kept a small cake shop at this point, and displayed upon her sign-board the following quaint legend:

"Out of this rock, runs water clear,
'Tis soon changed into good beer,
Stop, traveler, stop, if you see fit,
And quench your thirst for a fippennybit."

About a mile down the western slope of Laurel Hill we come to the famous watering trough. Here William Downard lived for many years in a stone house built against the hillside. He did not keep a tavern, for he had no ground for teams to stand upon, and no stabling that was accessible, but he always maintained the big water-trough in good condition *pro bono publico*, and it would be almost impossible for big teams to make the ascent of Laurel Hill, in hot weather without water. Downard was eccentric and cross, and begrudged the use of his water to persons he did not like, although the supply was inexhaustible. He was born near Uniontown of English parentage, a Federalist in politics, and a skeptic in religion. He was endowed

* Deceased.　† Deceased.

with strong sense, and could argue with considerable force. He has been dead many years.

A little over a mile below the big water trough the romantic spot known as the "Turkey's Nest" is reached. The road crosses a small stream here, which, owing to the peculiar formation of the ground, required the erection of a bridge, supported on the south side by an immense stone wall. This is one of the largest stone structures on the road, and is in a good state of preservation. It is a fine specimen of workmanship, and a grand monument to the skill of the old time stonemasons. This locality has always been invested with much interest, and admired by the lovers of picturesque beauty. Until recently it wore its primitive colorings. Now it is changed. Its primitive appearance has disappeared before the advancing forces of progress and improvement. The native trees have been cut down and a little hamlet occupies their places with attendant stables, cribs, coops and other out-houses. The old massive curved stone wall remains, but all about it so changed in appearance that the spot is scarcely recognized as the "Turkey's Nest." It is the popular belief that this locality derived its name from the discovery here of a wild turkey's nest, by workmen engaged on the original construction of the road.

An old long log house, near the foot of the hill, was called the "Goat Pen," and why is not accurately known, but this name it bore from one end of the road to the other.

We now reach the ancient and celebrated village of Monroe, a name it took in honor of the President hereinbefore mentioned. Approached from the east, the first old tavern and the first house in the place is the "Deford House," in the olden time and by old people called the General Wayne House. It appears that at an early day General Wayne had occasion to pass this way, and tarried over night with John Deford, who kept tavern in a small log house a short distance in the rear of the present building. Deford at this time was contemplating the erection of a new and more imposing edifice, and applied to his distinguished guest for a plan. It was furnished, and the present stone structure is the outcome of it, which shows plainly enough that General Wayne was a much better soldier than architect. Deford kept tavern here for a long time, and was succeeded first by Henry Fisher and next by Matthias Fry. Samuel Magie is now the owner of the property, and its career as a tavern is ended.

A frame house a short distance below and on the opposite side of the street from the Deford House was once kept by James Dennison, who had a considerable trade. It was afterward kept by Matthias Fry, but business then had greatly decreased. Fry, in his prime, was one of the best men on the road, and a great favorite among the wagoners. He had been a wagoner himself for many years, and was at one time general agent for a transportation line from Baltimore to Wheeling, which made him the disburser of large sums of money, and he discharged his office with scrupulous fidelity. He was a large,

JAMES SNYDER.

fine looking man, stoutly built, and possessing great physical power. Although amiable and good natured, he was occasionally drawn into a fight, and on one occasion, at Petersburg, in Somerset county, Pennsylvania, whipped three reputed bullies, one after another, who entered his house when he lived there, and proposed to "clean him out," as evidence of their prowess. He died a few years ago in Monroe, where his widow is still living.*

The next old tavern in Monroe is the stone house built by Andrew McMasters, and subsequently owned and kept for many years by German D. Hair. He was the only man that ever kept this house, and he died in it a few years ago, aged about eighty years. He was a native of Chester county, Pennsylvania, and came to the vicinity of Uniontown about the time the road was made. He was a stone-mason by trade, and worked on many of the bridges of the road, including the eastern and western bridges at Uniontown.

Next we come to the "Shipley House." Like all the tavern houses in Monroe, and nearly all the private houses, this is a stone building, and is two stories high. It was erected by E. W. Clement, and good workmanship displayed in its construction. It was kept awhile by Clement, and after him at different times by John Wallace, Archibald Skiles, Samuel Shipley, Redding Bunting, and Lindsey Messmore.

Next is the "Monroe House," one of the oldest in the place. It was built by Andrew McMasters, and subsequently and successively kept by E.W. Clement, Thomas Acklin, James Shafer, A. Skiles, John Worthington, M. Fry, and Calvin Springer. This was a popular house in the golden era of the road, and did an extensive business. Monroe was a thriving village when the pike flourished, and the center of fun and frolic. It began to decline when the trade left the road, but is now reviving and wearing an air of prosperity by reason of the coal developments in the vicinity.

On the hill above Monroe stands an old two-story brick house, fast sinking into decay, which was once a well known and popular tavern stand. It was owned and kept by William Morris. He put up an imposing sign, inscribed on the west side with the words, "Welcome from the West," and on the east side the words, "Welcome from the East." This was no false lure, and travelers from the east and west crowded into the old house to enjoy its good cheer. Alonzo L. Little, for many years editor and proprietor of the *Genius of Liberty*, was a son-in-law of William Morris, and he had a son (Luther) who settled in Iowa and was elected State Treasurer there.

Harry Gilbert once kept a tavern in the house where Charles Livingston now has a grocery, at the east end of Uniontown, and in later years it was kept by M. Fry and J. Allen Messmore.

Many years ago the Widow Sands kept tavern in the frame house at the point where the Connellsville and Cool Spring Furnace roads lead off from the pike.

* Now dead.

CHAPTER XXXIII.

Old Taverns and Tavern Keepers continued — Uniontown — The Town as it Appeared to Gen. Douglass in 1784 — Its Subsequent Growth and Improvement — The First Tavern — Other Early Taverns — An Old Chief Justice and an Old Landlady wrangle over a Roasted Pig — Anecdote of George Manypenny and President ,Jefferson — The Swan, The McClelland, The Seaton, The National, The Clinton, The Moran, The Mahaney.

At the east end of Uniontown the road crosses Redstone creek, over a massive and extensive stone bridge, one of the best and most expensive samples of masonry on the whole line, built by Kinkead, Beck and Evans in 1818. Gen. Ephraim Douglass, the first prothonotary of Fayette county, Pennsylvania, in a letter to Gen. James Irvine, in 1784, describes Uniontown in the following vigorous and graphic style:

"*My Dear General* — If my promise were not engaged to write to you, my inclinations are sufficiently so to embrace with alacrity any opportunity of expressing the gratitude so justly due to your valuable friendship, of declaring the friendship of mine. This Uniontown is the most obscure spot on the face of the globe. I have been here seven or eight weeks, without one opportunity of writing to the land of the living, and though considerably south of you, so cold that a person not knowing the latitude, would conclude we were placed near one of the poles. Pray have you had a severe winter below? We have been frozen up here for more than a month past, but a great many of us having been bred in another State, the eating of hominy is as natural to us as the drinking of whisky in the morning. The town and its appurtenances consist of our president and a lovely little family, a court house and school house in one, a mill and consequently a miller, four taverns, three smith shops, five retail shops, two tan yards, one of them only occupied, one saddler's shop, two hatter's shops, one mason, one cake woman (we had two, but one of them having committed a petit larceny is upon banishment), two widows and some reputed maids, to which may be added a distillery. The upper part of this edifice is the habitation at will of your humble servant, who, beside the smoke of his own chimney, which is intolerable enough, is fumigated by that of two stills below, exclusive of the other effluvia that arises from the dirty vessels in which they prepare the materials for the stills. The upper floor of my parlor,

GEN. EPHRAIM DOUGLASS.

which is also my chamber and office, is laid with loose clap-boards, or puncheons, and the gable ends entirely open ; and yet this is the best place in my power to procure, till the weather will permit me to build, and even this I am subject to be turned out of the moment the owner, who is at Kentuck, and hourly expected, returns. I can say little of the country in general, but that it is very poor in everything but its soil, which is excellent, and that part contiguous to the town is really beautiful, being level and prettily situate, accommodated with good water, and excellent meadow ground. But money we have not, nor any practicable way of making it. How taxes are collected, debts paid, or fees discharged, I know not; and yet the good people appear willing enough to run in debt and go to law. I shall be able to give you a better account of this hereafter. Col. McClean received me with a degree of generous friendship, that does honor to the goodness of his heart, and continues to show every mark of satisfaction at my appointment. He is determined to act under the commission sent him by council, and though the fees would, had he declined it, have been a considerable addition to my profits, I cannot say that I regret his keeping them. He has a numerous small family, and though of an ample fortune in lands, has no cash at command. The general curse of the country, disunion, rages in this little mud hole with as much fury, as if they had each pursuits of the utmost importance, and the most opposed to each other, when in truth, they have no pursuits at all that deserve the name, except that of obtaining food and whisky, for raiment they scarcely use any. The commissioners — trustees, I should say — having fixed on a spot in one end of the town for the public buildings, which was by far the most proper, in every point of view, exclusive of the saving of expense, the other end took the alarm and charged them with partiality, and have been ever since uttering their complaints. And at the late election for justices, two having been carried in this end of the town, and none in the other, has made them quite outrageous. This trash is not worth troubling you with, therefore I beg your pardon, and am with unfeigned esteem, dear general, your very humble servant.

"EPHRAIM DOUGLASS."

That was a long time ago, and a great change has come over the face of things. Gen. Douglass lived to see Uniontown arise from the mud hole and become a flourishing county seat. His mortal remains lie buried within the sound of the court house bell, and could he come forth now, and see Uniontown, he would be startled. Instead of a mud hole, he would see finely paved streets, studded with handsome buildings, lighted by electricity, enlivened by electric cars, telegraphs, telephones and railroads, and where the old distilleries stood, beautiful and staunch church edifices with spires pointing to the skies, and in fact he would behold all the evidences of a flourishing city, inhabited by active, intelligent and Christian people.

The first tavern in Uniontown was kept by John Collins in 1781. It was a log house on the north side of the main street, the site of which is now covered by "Commercial Row." This old house remained standing until 1839, when it was torn down by its owner of that date, Isaac Beeson, who erected the buildings thereafter known as "Commercial Row." John Collins kept this old tavern down to the year 1799. It was subsequently kept at different times by Samuel Salter, Cuthbert Wiggins, William Salter, John Hoge and Andrew Byers. William Salter was an old sheriff. Byers went from this house to the old Walker House, now the "Central," and afterward to the "Clinton House."

Jonathan Rowland, Daniel Culp and Matthew Campbell each kept a tavern in Uniontown as early as 1783. The location of Rowland's tavern is not accurately known, but the best evidence available, points to the lot now owned by Daniel Downer, esq., and occupied by law offices, near the court house, as the site. Jonathan Rowland subsequently became a justice of the peace, and a leader in public affairs. Culp's old tavern was a log house on the lot now owned and occupied by Justice Willson, corner of Main street and Gallatin avenue. Matthew Campbell's old tavern, stood on the western side of the lot now covered by the Moran House, formerly and for many years known as the "Fulton."

Colin Campbell as early as 1785 kept a tavern in a house that stood on the lot now covered by the Bryan building, on Main street, near the center of the town. This old tavern was subsequently owned and presided over by Samuel Salter, father of William Salter, the old sheriff.

Margaret Allen kept a tavern in the east end of town, a little above and opposite the Madison College buildings, in the year 1788, and for some time thereafter. She died in 1810, at the age of ninety-one years.

Dr. Robert McClure opened a tavern in December, 1792, a short distance west of the court house, on the south side of the street, and kept it down to the year 1813. It does not appear that any other person kept this house. It was in close proximity to the "Jolly Irishman," hereafter mentioned.

Thomas Collins, son of John Collins, before mentioned, kept a tavern as early as 1794 in an old house on the lot, corner of Morgantown and Main streets, now occupied by the Tremont buildings. Thomas Collins was sheriff of Fayette county from 1796 to 1799, and commanded a company of soldiers from Uniontown and vicinity in the war of 1812, locally called the "Madison Rowdies." A number of his descendants are still living in the neighborhood of Uniontown.

Previous to the opening of the present century the veteran of Laurel Hill, John Slack, before mentioned, kept a tavern in the old Shelcut house, on the south side of Main street, opposite the old Gregg house, and afterward kept the "Spread Eagle," the exact location of which is involved in doubt, but the best information available assigns it to the Weniger corner, opposite the old Walker house, hereinafter mentioned.

William Downard, subsequently proprietor of the big watertrough house on Laurel Hill, kept tavern in the Shelcut house from 1801 until probably 1808, when he retired to the pine covered slope of Laurel Hill, where he spent the remainder of his life. He served as County Commissioner from 1802 to 1805.

The Gregg house, situate on the north side of Main street, on the lot now covered by the residence of Dr. J. B. Ewing, was in existence as a tavern as early as 1798, and continued as late as 1865. It was a small house of brick and frame united, but had a large patronage. In early times travelers and other guests at taverns did not desire or expect separate rooms, and hence a small tavern like the Gregg house could accommodate as many persons as the more pretentious hotel of the present day; and at wagon stands the bar room, as before stated, was the only bed chamber for wagoners. James Gregg was the first proprietor of the Gregg house, and was succeeded by his widow, Nancy Gregg, in 1810. After her time it was kept in turn by William Medkirk, Matthew Allen, Simeon Houser, Amos Howell, Philip D. Stentz, and Thomas Moxley. James Gregg, the old proprietor of this house, was the father-in-law of the late Hon. Daniel Sturgeon, who was a United States Senator in the days of Clay, Webster and Calhoun.

In 1779, and for a number of years thereafter, Pierson Sayers kept a tavern in the house now occupied by Mrs. Ruby, on the north side of Main street, a short distance west of the court house. While keeping this house Sayers was elected Sheriff, and turned over his tavern to Jacob Harbaugh, who conducted it for three years, when, singularly enough, he was elected to succeed Sayers as Sheriff. Ellis Baily, the grandfather of Mrs. Ruby, bought this property from Pierson Sayers, and subsequently, and for many years, it was the private residence of the late Hon. John Dawson.

James Piper kept the "Jolly Irishman" as early as 1801. This bustling old tavern was located on Main street, opposite the residence of the late Hon. Daniel Kaine. James Piper, a son of the old proprietor, was a prominent and influential citizen of the town and county for many years. He was a member of the bar, a Justice of the Peace, Register of Wills, and Recorder of Deeds. He left Uniontown about 1850, went west, and died soon after.

William Merriman kept a tavern near Margaret Allen's old stand as early as 1802. But little is known at this date of Merriman or his old tavern. Its existence was brief and its patronage limited.

At and before the beginning of the present century Samuel Salter kept a tavern in an old log and frame house that stood on the lot now occupied by the handsome residence of the Hon. John K. Ewing. Chief Justice Thomas McKean "put up" at this old tavern on his visits to Uniontown to hold the courts of Fayette county, and was frequently regaled with roast pig. The pig was well prepared, cooked

11ª

and dressed, and in all respects savory, but its frequent appearance on the table moved the old Chief Justice to believe that he was getting "too much of a good thing," and accordingly one day, in peremptory terms, he commanded the dining room girl to remove the offensive dish, which she did with trembling hands. This of course raised a storm in the old hostelry. Mrs. Salter became indignant, and, bringing back the pig, replaced it on the table, at the same time addressing the Judge thus: "You are Chief Justice and run the court; I am chief cook and run this dining room. That pig must stay," and it did. Upon the withdrawal of Salter, in the year 1811, this old tavern came under the management and control of Jacob Harbaugh, the old Sheriff before mentioned. After Harbaugh's time it was kept by George Ewing down to a period as late probably as 1830. Hugh Espey, a well remembered old County Treasurer, and straightgoing Presbyterian elder, married a daughter of George Ewing.

Opposite the old Gregg house, and adjoining the Shelcut house, George Manypenny kept a tavern as early as the year 1814, and probably before that date. This was a leading tavern of the town, subsequently conducted by Benjamin Miller, and after him by Harry Gilbert. One of the old stage lines stopped at this house. George Manypenny, the old proprietor, was the father of the late Hon. George W. Manypenny, who was for many years a prominent and popular political leader and officeholder of the State of Ohio. He was born in Uniontown, and most likely in his father's old tavern. George Manypenny, sr., is described by those who remember him as a vigorous, pushing and witty Irishman. He called once to see President Jefferson, and was invited by His Excellency to take a glass of wine with him, which he did without hesitancy, and to obtain a second glass, this story is told of him: As he was about to withdraw from the executive mansion he remarked to Mr. Jefferson that he was going home, and would tell his friends that he had the honor of taking TWO glasses with the President of the United States, and hoped His Excellency would not let him go home with a lie in his mouth. As the story goes, the old President saw the point of the ingenious suggestion, and again brought forward the wine.

The Walker house, corner of Broadway and Main streets, was kept as a tavern as early as 1816 by Zadoc Walker, who owned the property. General LaFayette was entertained at this house in 1825, and Santa Anna, the renowned Mexican warrior, stopped over night in it on his way to Washington City, about sixty years ago. This house has been kept at different times since by Andrew Byers, William Byers, Redding Bunting, and others. When Bunting kept it, it was called the "United States." It has recently been enlarged and improved, and its name changed to the "Central." Its first host under the new name was James I. Feather, who subsequently became associated with William A. McHugh. Its present lessees and managers are Messrs. Frock and Mitchell. The Spottsylvania house, for

AARON WYATT.

many years conducted prosperously by John Manaway, and afterward, until it closed, by Lloyd Mahaney, adjoined the Walker house on the west, and used a number of rooms belonging to that old hostelry.

The McCleary house ranked high as an old-time inn or tavern. It is situate on the corner of Main and Arch streets, a substantial brick building, recently enlarged, embellished and improved, and at present catering to the public under the historic name of "Brunswick," and conducted by Russell W. Beall, a gentleman admirably equipped for the business. Ewing McCleary owned and kept this old tavern as early as the year 1819, and many years thereafter. Upon his death, which occurred in this house, it was continued as a tavern under the management of his widow, until she became the wife of William Hart, when he took charge of it and kept it down to the year 1840, or thereabout, when he fell into disgrace and retired under a storm of popular reprobation. This house was a favorite stopping place of General Jackson. On an occasion a committee of citizens met Jackson on the road near town and tendered him the freedom of the municipality. Among other things made known to him by the committee, he was informed that quarters had been provided for his accommodation at the Walker House. He replied that he "always stopped at Hart's." "But," rejoined the chairman of the committee, "Hart is a Whig, and his tavern a Whig house." The old warrior answered back by saying that "Hart always treated him well, and he would go to his house," and to Hart's he went, reluctantly escorted by the Democratic committee. After Hart's precipitate withdrawal from this old house, it was leased by S. B. Hays, subsequently of the Mansion and other old taverns in Washington, Pennsylvania. Hays conducted it for a brief period when it went into the possession of Joshua Marsh, who remained in charge not longer than a year or two, and left it to take charge of the National House. Its next occupant was the veteran Redding Bunting. After Bunting came Aaron Stone, then William Beatty, and after him William Gans. After Gans, Peter Uriah Hook was installed as landlord, who named the house "The Eagle," and remained in charge a number of years. Hook was an eccentric man, given to redundancy of speech, a merchant, auctioneer, and for two years a member of the lower branch of the State legislature. He died in Uniontown, a number of years ago, but will not soon be forgotten. Aaron Wyatt succeeded Hook, and kept the house until his death. His widow and son James succeeded to the management, and James dying in the house, it passed to the hands of his widow, Mrs. Kate Wyatt, and from her to Russell W. Beall, the present occupant.

The before-mentioned old taverns were of the town, rather than of the road. Most of them were in existence and doing business before the road was made. The remaining old taverns of Uniontown, hereafter mentioned, were essentially taverns of the National Road, and derived their principal patronage from it.

The Swan, Nathaniel Brownfield proprietor, is an old, long frame building, at the west end of town, supplemented some years after it commenced business, by a brick addition to the eastern end. Thomas Brownfield, father of Nathaniel, the present proprietor, and grandfather on the maternal side, of the author of this volume, kept this old tavern as early as 1805, and down to the year 1829. When the National Road was opened for business, this house became a wagon stand, and continued such until the last crack of a Battelly White whip was heard on the road. It was provided with two commodious wagon yards, one at the front, on the roadside opposite the house, and the other between the house and the large stable in the rear. With the exception of one year that this old tavern was kept by William Cox, Nathaniel Brownfield, who was born under its roof, has kept it, uninterruptedly, from the date of his father's death, and "holds the fort" to this day, "with none to molest or make him afraid." Upwards of eighty, and in vigorous health, he has witnessed and participated in the exciting scenes of the road from the beginning to the end thereof. At an early period he became the owner of a farm consisting of one hundred acres adjacent to town, which he managed advantageously in connection with his tavern, and within the past year sold for the sum of one thousand and five dollars per acre, retaining his old tavern stand, to which he is attached by so many memories. His wife and good helpmate survives with him, and together they occupy the old tavern and recount with varied emotions the stirring scenes of the eventful past.

The McClelland House, as has been elsewhere stated, is one of the best known old taverns on the National Road. It is located on the north side of the Main street, and in the western end of town. As early as 1795, Richard Weaver kept a tavern in a wooden building on the lot now covered by the McClelland House, and was succeeded by William McClelland. William McClelland was keeping this old tavern in 1802, and owned the lot on which it stood at that date in fee simple. After the death of William McClelland his son, Alfred, came into possession, tore down the old building, and erected in its stead the present brick building, known always thereafter as the McClelland House. This house was the headquarters of the Good Intent line of stages, from the time it was put on the road until it was withdrawn at the end of the road's career as a national highway. Alfred McClelland presided over this house and controlled it from the date of its erection until he died, with the exception of brief intervals mentioned below. He was a large, raw-boned man, of agreeable, though somewhat awkward manners, and had complete knowledge of the mysterious art of keeping a tavern. He had for his main clerk and bar-keeper, Macon W. Rine, a confidential and loyal friend, well remembered by the older citizens of Uniontown, as a thoroughly competent man for his employment. Alfred McClelland died on the 8th of September, 1862. In the intervals before mentioned, the McClelland House was kept for a short time previous

THE BROWNFIELD HOUSE.

to 1840 by S. B. Hays, before he took control of the old McCleary House. Thereafter, at different times, the house was kept by Jerry Colflesh, Lewis D. Beall, William and Thomas Swan, J.W. Kissinger, Calvin Springer, William Wyatt, Kim Frey, Russell Frey, Frey and Swan, Joseph C. Stacy and Charles H. Rush, in the order named. It is at present conducted, as elsewhere stated, by Mrs. Sarah E. McClelland, widow of the old proprietor, and retains all its ancient prestige, under her admirable management.

The Seaton House was a familiar hostelry in the olden time. It was founded by James C. Seaton in the year 1820, or thereabout. It is located on the northeast corner of Main and Arch streets, diagonally opposite the old McCleary House, and is now known as the West End Hotel. Mr. Seaton, the old proprietor, came to Uniontown from Virginia, and died in this old house many years ago. The house was built in sections at different times until it reached its present large proportions. During its occupancy by Mr. Seaton it was a wagon stand of the National Road, and extensively patronized. It was provided with ample grounds for wagons and teams to stand on, which are now covered by the Lingo block and other buildings in the vicinity. Mr. Seaton had three sons: Hiram, James, and John. Hiram was the old toll collector before mentioned, and James was a pike boy in a general way. He drove stage occasionally, and also the express; led horses from station to station on the road, and made himself useful in many other ways. He died at his father's old tavern in the meridian of the bright era of the road, and before he had reached middle age. John Seaton, the other son, went west, and died recently in Nebraska. Daniel Collier, before mentioned as keeper of the old tavern at Mount Augusta, was a son-in-law of James C. Seaton; and Charles H. Seaton, the well known insurance agent of Uniontown, is a great-grandson of the old proprietor, and others of his descendants are still living in Uniontown and vicinity. After Mr. Seaton's death this old tavern was continued a number of years by his widow, and growing old she leased it to James Swan, who conducted it for a brief period, Mrs. Seaton boarding with him in the house. Mr. Swan was succeeded by Philip D. Stentz, and he in turn by J. W. Kissinger, Kim Frey, David G. Sperry, John Messmore and Henry Jennings. The late James T. Redburn bought the property from the Seaton heirs and sold it to John Messmore, who in turn sold it to Henry Jennings. It is now owned and kept by George Titlow, under the name of the West End Hotel, as before stated, well conducted and well patronized.

The old National House is located on the northwest corner of Morgantown and Fayette streets. It was built for a private residence by the late Hon. Thomas Irwin, and occupied by him as such until he was appointed Judge of the United States District Court for the Western district of Pennsylvania, when he moved to Pittsburg. Judge Irwin sold the property to the celebrated Dr. John F. Braddee, of mail robbing notoriety, and he occupied it during the period covered by his depredations upon the mail bags. Its situation for such operations was convenient, as it adjoined the old Stockton stage yard hereinbefore described.. After Braddee's conviction L.W. Stockton acquired title to the property, and subsequently sold and conveyed it to Joshua Marsh, who opened it as a tavern. It was the headquarters of the Stockton line of stages from the time it was opened until all stage lines were withdrawn from the road. James K. Polk, with his family and traveling companions, stopped over night at The National when on his way to the capital to be inaugurated President, in the spring of 1845. A large number of citizens assembled on the occasion to meet the coming President, and were addressed by him from the high steps in front of the house. The National was a well kept house. Situate a distance from the main street, it was comparatively exempt from the ordinary street noises, and conducted in a quiet manner, disturbed only by the arrival and departure of the stage coaches. Mr. Marsh, its old proprietor, was a man of retiring disposition, gentle manners, and feeble health. He visited Washington when Mr. Buchanan was inaugurated President, and was one of the unfortunates who were poisoned on that occasion at the National Hotel of that place. He returned home, but never fully recovered from the effects of the poison, and died in Uniontown. Among others who kept the National were George Evans and Col. Samuel Elder. The latter is still living, a hale octogenarian, at Ligonier Westmoreland county, Pa.

The Clinton House, which stood on a lot adjoining the old Court House, was a popular house throughout its whole career. It was demolished in 1890 by condemnation proceedings, and the lot on which it stood taken by the county for the use of the new Court House. It was erected in 1835 by the late Hon. Andrew Stewart, who occupied it as a private residence and kept his law office in it for a number of years. It was first kept as a tavern by Andrew Byers, and after him, from time to time, until its demolition, by Stephen W. Snyder, whose wife was a Risler, Zadoc Cracraft, Isaac Kerr, Jesse B. Gardner, John Bierer, Calvin Springer, Springer & Renshaw, Bernard Winslow, William Springer, Joseph Wright, J. R. Thornton, and James I. Feather. General Taylor stopped over night at the Clinton House in 1849, *en route* to Washington to assume the office of President of the United States. It was kept at that time by Andrew Byers.

The Moran House is the old Fulton House, opposite the Court House, on Elbow or Main street. Like the old Seaton House, the Fulton was built in sections, some of them by Seth Howell and others by his predecessors. Seth Howell kept this house a long time. He was called "Flinger," because he had a habit of flinging disorderly persons out of the house, as he termed the process of ejecting. Howell was succeeded by Calvin Springer, and he by William Thorndell, who became the owner of the property. David Mahaney came in after Thorndell, Michael Carter after Mahaney, and it next passed

COL. SAMUEL ELDER.

to the hands of James Moran, its present occupant and owner, who gave it the name of the Moran House. This old tavern was always well patronized, and continues to be under its present proprietor, who has added many improvements, and the house is in better shape now than at any time heretofore.

The name Mahaney has long been identified with the National Road. The Mahaney House was built and is conducted by Lloyd Mahaney, a son of David, elsewhere mentioned. It is the newest hotel in Uniontown, and the finest in architectural display. It is a hotel, having come into existence after the old inns and taverns had been relegated to the dead past. It is located on a lot formerly owned and occupied by George Ebbert, adjoining the present National Bank of Fayette County on the east, and is on the south side of Main street. It is well managed and does a large business, and is likewise one of the best of the many recent improvements in Uniontown, and reflects credit on its proprietor.

CHAPTER XXXIV.

Old Taverns and Tavern Keepers continued — Uniontown to Searights — Anecdote of John Slack — Slack at Night and Tight in the Morning — Old Roads — Parting Tribute to the Old Taverns of the Mountains — Henry Clay Extols the Virtue of Buckwheat Cakes — Boss Rush and his Poker — Moxleys — The Old Hunter House — Searights — The Grays and the Gray Meeting — Jackson Men and Adams Men Meet and Count Noses — Old Political Leaders — Barnacles of the Road.

The tavern keepers on the "old road," as it is called, were as earnestly opposed to the building of the National Road, as those on the latter were to the building of the railroad, and for like reasons. The following anecdote serves as an illustration : John Slack kept a tavern for many years at the summit of Laurel Hill on the old road, in a house near the Washington Springs. Before the National Road was opened said Slack, in a complaining manner, "Wagons coming up Laurel Hill would stick in the mud a mile or so below my house, when the drivers would unhitch, leave their wagons in the mud, and bring their teams to my house and stay with me all night. In the morning they would return to their stranded wagons, dig and haul them out, and get back to my house and stay with me another night. Thus counting the wagons going east and west, I got four night's bills from the same set of wagoners." "Now," concluded Slack (since the completion of the National Road), with indignation, "the wagoners whiff by without stopping." Old wagoners were accustomed to say of Slack that he was "Slack at night and tight in the morning," meaning that he was clever and cheerful when they "put up" with him in the evening, and close and exacting in the morning when bills were payable.

The old road referred to was the Braddock road, which from the summit of Laurel Hill, turned northwardly, as before stated, to Gists (Mt. Braddock), Stewart's Crossing (Connellsville), Braddock's Field and Fort Pitt (Pittsburg).

An old road between Uniontown and Brownsville was laid out in 1774 by viewers appointed by the court of Westmoreland county, Pennsylvania, before Fayette county was established, upon a petition signed mainly by inhabitants of Brownsville and vicinity, who complained that "they had to carry their corn twenty miles to the mill of Henry Beeson at Uniontown." The distance of twenty miles complained of was by way of the old road known as "Burd's," from

THE SEARIGHT HOUSE.

the mouth of Redstone creek to Gists, where it intersected Braddock's road. The road between Uniontown and Brownsville, above mentioned, was carried east of Uniontown, to intersect the Braddock road, which it did, near Slack's tavern. The line of the National Road closely follows that of the old road between Uniontown and Brownsville. Marks of the old road are plainly visible to this day, and some of the old buildings, which were erected along its line, are still standing, notably the dwelling of Thomas B. Graham, esq., three miles west of Uniontown, which was an old tavern. This old house was the first residence of the Hon. Andrew Stewart after his marriage, and his oldest son, David Shriver, was born in it.

John Slack, the old tavern keeper before mentioned, was the father of Mrs. McClean, wife of Ephraim McClean, who for many years kept the Cottage tavern on the summit of Laurel Hill, and no doubt the fame of this house under the management of the McCleans is attributable in great measure to the early training of Mrs. McClean in her father's old tavern, where she was reared.

Heretofore in these pages the reader has been introduced to old taverns and old tavern keepers on the mountain division of the road, a long division covering two hundred miles, including the intervening glades and valleys. Surprise is often expressed that there were so many good taverns in the mountains, remote from fertile fields and needed markets. That they were equal to the best on the road is conceded; and that the old taverns of the National Road have never been surpassed for bounteous entertainment and good cheer, is likewise conceded; in fact, has never been disputed. It may seem a trifling thing to be written down in serious history, that the old taverns of the mountains excelled all others in the matter of serving buckwheat cakes; but it is germane and true. To relieve this statement from the imputation of being a trifling one, it may be added that there are men and women still living on the line of the National Road who often heard the great statesman, orator and patriot, Henry Clay, praising the good qualities of the buckwheat cakes furnished by the old mountain taverns with as much fervor and more enthusiasm than he ever exhibited in commending his favorite measure, the Protective Tariff. And, as a matter of fact, it might be stated in this connection, that the making of buckwheat cakes is essentially a home industry, not, however, of the infantile order, and while it may not need protection, is certainly deserving of encouragement. Another memorable feature of the mountain taverns was the immense fires kept constantly burning in the old bar rooms during the old-time winters. In many instances the grates were seven feet in length, with corresponding width and depth, and would contain an ordinary wagon load of coal; and when the fires were stirred up in these immense grates, and set to roaring, the jolly old wagoners occupying the bar rooms paid little heed to the eagerness of the howling mountain weather. The old landlord of the mountains took special pride in keeping up his bar room fire. He kept a poker from six to eight feet long, and would not allow it to be used by any one but himself. Boss Rush, not inaptly termed "the prince of landlords," was so careful and punctilious about the management of his bar room fire that he kept his big poker under lock and key, so that no one could use it but himself, always using it at the right time, and keeping up a uniform and proper temperature for the comfort of his guests. With this parting tribute to the memory of the old taverns and tavern keepers of the mountains, the attention of the reader is now invited to those on the line of the road through the rich valleys of the tributaries of the Ohio. Monroe and Uniontown, and the intervening space of two miles between these points, are covered in a previous chapter.

Three miles west of Uniontown is an old tavern stand known in late years as the Moxley House. It is a long log and frame building, situate on the south side of the road, with a porch extending along its entire frontage. This house was first kept as a tavern by Bazil Wiggins, an uncle of Harrison Wiggins, the old fox hunter before mentioned, next by John Gray, grandfather of the old and popular conductor from Uniontown to Pittsburg on the Baltimore & Ohio Railroad, now and for many years deceased. Its next occupant, and from 1836 to 1838, was William Cox, a brother-in-law of E. W. Clement, the famous swearer. In 1838 the property was purchased by Thomas Moxley, who went into possession and continued it as a tavern stand down to the year 1863, when Henry Clay Rush bought it and occupied it until the year 1865, when he sold it to Edmund Leonard, its present occupant. When Moxley took charge of this old tavern he gave it the name of "The Half-way House," for the reason that its location is about midway between Cumberland and Wheeling. It was always a well conducted tavern, and did a large business, mainly in the line of wagon custom.

Less than a mile west of the old Moxley House, on the south side, and back a few yards from the road, is a fine brick building, which, during a portion of the prosperous era of the road, was a well known and popular tavern stand. The house was built by Robert Hunter, who occupied it for several years, but did not seem inclined to court patronage, and, as a consequence, did not do much business. He leased the house to William Darlington, and moved to Ohio. Darlington, as before stated, had been an old wagoner, was a man of amiable temper, and did a large business at this house. He remained in it until the year 1848, when he moved to the mountain and took charge of the Stone House, then known as the Fayette Springs House, now Dean's. There he remained until he became the occupant of the Mansion House on the estate of the late Col. Samuel Evans, near Uniontown, where he died. When Darlington vacated the old Hunter House it was turned over to Peter Colley, whose father, Abel Colley, had previously bought it from Hunter. Peter Colley kept the house a number of years, and died in possession. He was a man of quiet deportment, attentive to strangers and travelers, and

JOSEPH GRAY.

enjoyed an extensive line of custom, until the termination of the road's high career. The old tavern is now the private residence of A. A. Taggart, son-in-law of Peter Colley, proprietor of one of the planing mills of Uniontown, and a successful contractor and builder.

Next, two miles further west, is Searights. Here is the old half-way house between Uniontown and Brownsville, a large stone building on the north side of the road, at the crossing of the great drovers' road of other days leading from the Flats of Grave Creek, Virginia, to Bedford, Pennsylvania. The large stables connected with this house, on the opposite side of the road, are still standing, and in a good state of preservation. In the olden time, in addition to the ordinary travel on the road, sleighing and other parties from Uniontown and Brownsville were accustomed to go to this old tavern for a night's dancing, and the attending festivities. This is also the battle-ground of the memorable "Gray Meeting" in 1828, where the opposing hosts between Jackson and Adams went into an open field and measured strength by "counting off," the Jacksonians outnumbering their adversaries by a decided preponderance, greatly to the mortification of the weaker column. This meeting was called the "Gray meeting," because the tavern there was then kept by John Gray, formerly of the Moxley House, before mentioned. The leaders on the occasion of this trial of strength were as follows: On the Jackson side, Gen. Henry W. Beeson, Col. Ben Brownfield, John Fuller, David Gilmore, Larkin S. Dearth, Alexander Johnson, Provance McCormick, William F. Coplan, Henry J. Rigdon, William Hatfield and William Searight. On the Adams side: Andrew Stewart, John Dawson, John M. Austin, Israel Miller, E. P. Oliphant, Chads Chalfant, Stokely Conwell, Levi Springer, Dennis Springer, and William Colvin. Prior to 1840 many of the Democratic county meetings and conventions were held at Searights. Before the era of railroads it was a central point for Uniontown, Connellsville and Brownsville. A large water-trough was always maintained at this old tavern, where teams attached to all kinds of wagons, coaches and other vehicles, as well as horses and mules led in droves, were halted for refreshment. At times relays of stage horses for extra occasions were stationed here, and it was always a relay for the line teams moving merchandise. An old sign-board was displayed at the front of the house for many years, bearing in large gilt letters the legend SEARIGHTS. The old tavern at Searights was built by Josiah Frost, about the time the National Road was constructed, and in the year 1821 William Searight acquired it by purchase from Frost. Joseph T. Noble as lessee of William Searight kept the tavern first after it was vacated by Frost. It was kept for a brief period at intervals by William Searight, but owing to his absence from home, being a contractor on public works, he did not give the management his personal attention, but placed it in the hands of James Allison, a well remembered and highly esteemed citizen, subsequently and for many years postmaster at Searights. John Gray, as has been stated, kept this house in 1828.

He was succeeded by John Risler, the noted old tavern keeper, before mentioned. Mrs. Risler's mother died at this house. Her name was Marsh. After Mr. Risler left, and about 1840, Matthias Fry went into possession, and conducted the house for a number of years. He had been a popular old wagoner, and drew a large wagon trade. He was succeeded by Joseph Gray, son of John, before mentioned, and father of John Gray, the old railroad conducter. Joseph Gray died in this house in January, 1851. He was a worthy citizen, well deserving of honorable mention. After the death of Joseph Gray the house was kept first by William Shaw, known as "Tavern Keeper Billy," and after him by William Shaw, known as "Wagoner Billy." These two Shaws were not of kin. In 1856 Henry Clay Rush took charge of the house and remained in it until 1863, when he purchased the Moxley property and removed to that point, as before stated. Rush was a popular man, and was liberally patronized by the traveling public. In the fall of 1862, or winter of 1863, the mansion house of Ewing Searight was destroyed by fire, and he moved to the old tavern when Rush vacated it, remained for a while, and subsequently from time to time leased it to James Frost, Alfred McCormick, Thomas Allen, C. W. Downer, Robert Moxley, Lewis Fry and James W. Claybaugh. During the terms of the last mentioned persons the patronage of the house was mostly local. The house is now the private residence of William Searight, a son of Ewing Searight, owner of the property, and late superintendent of the road. William Searight, the old proprietor, was superintendent of the road for many years, during its flourishing era.

The National Road had its contingent of quaint characters, eccentric men, philosophers in one sense, and loafers in another. They were indigenous to the road, could not live away from it, and enjoyed the precarious subsistence they obtained on it. The load-stone that attracted them and attached them to the road, probably above all other influences, was the pure whisky, before mentioned. It was plentiful and cheap, and could be obtained almost for the mere asking. It did not contain the elements of modern whisky, which excites men to revolution, insurrection, violence and insanity. Of the characters alluded to, whose haunts were at the old taverns along the road between Searights and Brownsville, the reader familiar with that portion of the line will readily recall Marion Smith, (Logan) George Ducket, Jonathan Crawford, John W. Dougherty, Gideon Lehman and Billy Bluebaker. Logan's forte was imitating the crowing of a rooster. Ducket had no pronounced trait, but under a patriotic impulse volunteered as a soldier in the Mexican war, and marched with Major Gardner, Daniel Hazard and the other heroes to the halls of the Montezumas. Crawford was a tailor, and worked at his trade as little as possible, but quietly enjoyed his potations. He had nothing to say. Dougherty was a walking arsenal, savage in appearance and gesticulation. He carried knives, pistols and a general assortment of deadly weapons, but was never known to use them on an adversary.

WILLIAM SHAW.

"WAGONER BILLY."

Lehman was also a tailor and bass drummer. He had a bronzed complexion, and a stolid temperament. Billy Bluebaker was elastic in motion, but lacking in brain. He wore the smallest hat of any individual on the road, and was happy in doing little jobs for old wagoners at his uncle's tavern. These odd characters have all gone with the majority of the men of the road. They witnessed and in their way participated in the enlivening scenes of the great highway, and are entitled to a place in its history.

CHAPTER XXXV.

Old Taverns and Tavern Keepers, continued — Searights to Brownsville — Abel Col-
ley's, Johnson's, known later as Hatfield's — William Hatfield, his Good Name
and Melancholy Death — An old and odd Indenture — The old Peter Colley House
— A Tavern with a Brief Career, the Red Tavern, Wilkes Brown, Brubaker's —
Brownsville — Anecdotes of Jackson and Clay — James Workman and Doctor
Stoy — Ham and Eggs — Bazil Brashear, James C. Beckley, William Reynolds,
the Monongahela House, the Clark House, the Iron Bridge, Bridgeport, John
Riley, the Monongahela Bridge.

Over the hill from Searights is the old Abel Colley stand. The
old tavern here, in the flourishing era of the road, did a large business, mainly in the line of entertaining wagoners. While all the
taverns of the road were more or less patronized by wagoners, excepting a few which were exclusively stage houses, they had favorite
stopping places, and the Abel Colley tavern was one of these. The
old proprietor and his family had methods and manners which were
agreeable to wagoners, and they made it a point to stop at this house
in great numbers. The bills were moderate, yet the patronage was
so extensive and continued so long that Abel Colley accumulated a
considerable fortune at this old tavern, and when trade and travel
ceased built a fine brick residence on the roadside opposite, where he
retired with his family to private life, and in a few years thereafter
died. Nancy, the wife of the old tavern keeper, is well remembered
as a large, amiable woman, who habitually wore an expansive cap of
the Queen Anne style. She long since passed to the life beyond. W.
Searight Colley, a son of Abel, now occupies and owns the brick
dwelling mentioned, with a fine farm adjacent. Peter Colley, of the
old Hunter tavern before mentioned, was likewise a son of Abel, and
he had a son, Levi, a farmer and freeholder, who died a number of
years ago on the old Covert farm, near Moxley's, now in the occupancy of one of his sons. The Abel Colley tavern is still standing, a
monument, like many others, of the faded glories of the old pike.
This old house was kept as early as the year 1825 by Darius Grimes,
and after him by Thomas Moxley. In Moxley's time it was called
the "Green Tree," and the writer remembers the picture of the green
tree which appeared on the sign board that hung and swung for
many years in front of this old tavern. Abel Colley took charge
after Moxley left. According to the recollection of Ebenezer Finley,
as appears by his letter in the Appendix to this volume, the Abel

ABEL COLLEY.

Colley tavern was kept by Samuel Wolverton and by Hugh Thompson, and this must have been previous to the time of Darius Grimes. It was certainly before Moxley's time.

About one mile west of the Abel Colley house there is an old stone tavern on the north side of the road, known in early days as Johnson's, later as Hatfield's. This house was built in 1817 by Randolph Dearth for Robert Johnson, who kept it as a tavern down to the year 1841, when he retired to a farm in Franklin township, Fayette county, Pennsylvania, where he died, leaving behind him a good name, which is better than great riches, of which latter he had a goodly share. He was the father-in-law of Thomas Brownfield, who, in 1862, was Sheriff of Fayette county, Pennsylvania, and previously a tavern keeper on the road. Henry L. Murphy, a well known and thrifty farmer of Jefferson township, Fayette county, Pennsylvania, likewise married a daughter of Robert Johnson. This tavern, under the guidance of Robert Johnson, did a large business, and the old proprietor made money by conducting it. The successor of Robert Johnson in the management of this house was Arthur Wallace, who remained in it for a single year. He was a brother of John Wallace, who once kept the Wilse Clement house in Hopwood, and subsequently removed to Morgantown, Virginia, and an uncle of James Wallace, present proprietor of the Wallace House in Morgantown. Peter Frasher, the old wagoner and tavern keeper before mentioned, married a daughter of Arthur Wallace. Charles Guttery succeeded Arthur Wallace in the Johnson House. * Guttery was an old wagoner, and is now keeping a tavern in Beallsville, Washington county, Pennsylvania, and probably the oldest man in the business. He was at the Johnson House in 1844, and a wagoner many years before that date. From 1849 to 1851 John Foster kept the Johnson House. He was a brother of the first wife of Robert Hogsett. Foster was succeeded by Hiram Holmes, who kept the house one year. In 1852 William Hatfield, who had previously bought the property, went into the house and kept it as a tavern until the year 1855, when he closed it as a public house, but continued to occupy it as a private residence until his melancholy death. Before engaging in tavern keeping, William Hatfield served many years as a Justice of the Peace, and subsequent to 1855 served a term as Associate Judge. He was a blacksmith by trade, and made the old iron gates of the road. He was industrious and honest, and likewise noted for his kindness to his fellow men. It was while engaged in doing a favor for an old neighbor, in the year 1871, that he lost his life. His neighbor, John C. Craft, had purchased a patent pump, and called on Judge Hatfield to assist him in placing it in his well. The Judge, as was his habit, promptly responded, and, going down to the bottom of the well, called to his neighbor, who stood at the surface, to send him down a saw or an ax. The needed tool was placed in a heavy iron-bound tub and started down, but, through neglect, the cable slipped, and the

* Deceased.

tub was precipitated a great depth upon Judge Hatfield's head, fatally injuring him. He was extricated from his perilous position in an unconscious state, carried home, and lingering only a few hours, died. His remains were interred in the beautiful cemetery near Brownsville, attended by a large concourse of sorrowing citizens, including the Judges of the Courts and the members of the bar of Fayette county, Pennsylvania.

Following is an exact copy of the indenture which bound William Hatfield to learn the trade of a blacksmith:

This Indenture Witnesseth: That William Hatfield, of the township of Union, in the county of Fayette, State of Pennsylvania, hath put himself by the approbation of his guardian, JOHN WITHROW, and by these presents doth voluntarily put himself an apprentice to GEORGE WINTERMUTE, of the township of Redstone, county and State aforesaid, blacksmith, to learn his art, trade or mystery he now occupieth or followeth, and after the manner of an apprentice to serve him from the day of the date hereof, for and during the full end and term of five years next ensuing, during all which time he, the said apprentice, his said master shall faithfully serve, his secrets keep, his lawful commands every where gladly obey; he shall do no damage to his said master, nor suffer it to be done without giving notice to his said master; he shall not waste his master's goods, nor lend them unlawfully to others; he shall not absent himself day or night from his master's service without his leave; he shall not commit any unlawful deed, whereby his said master shall sustain damage, nor contract matrimony within the said term; he shall not buy nor sell, nor make any contract whatsomever, whereby his master receive damage, but in all things behave himself as a faithful apprentice ought to do during the said term. And the said George Wintermute shall use the utmost of his endeavors to teach, or cause to be taught and instructed, the said apprentice the trade or mystery he now occupieth or followeth, and procure and provide for him, the said apprentice, sufficient meat, drink, common working apparel, washing, and lodging, fitting for an apprentice during the said term; and further, he the said master, doth agree to give unto the said apprentice, ten month's schooling within the said term, and also the said master doth agree to give unto the said apprentice two weeks in harvest in each and every year that he, the said apprentice, shall stay with his said master; also the said George Wintermute, doth agree to give unto the said apprentice one good freedom suit of clothes. And for the true performance of all and every the said covenants and agreements, either of the said parties binds themselves to each other by these presents.

In witness thereof, they have interchangeably put their hands and seals, this first day of April, one thousand eight hundred and sixteen.

GEORGE WINTERMUTE. [Seal.]
WILLIAM HATFIELD. [Seal.]
JOHN WITHROW. [Seal.]

Witness present,
BENJAMIN ROBERTS.

HON. WILLIAM HATFIELD.

Fayette County, ss.:

May the 29th, one thousand eight hundred and sixteen, before me the subscriber, one of the justices of peace in and for the said county, came the parties to the within indenture and severally acknowledged it as their act and deed. Given under my hand and seal the day and year above mentioned.

BENJAMIN ROBERTS. [Seal.]

All the covenants and agreements of this quaint document were faithfully kept on the part of William Hatfield. Benjamin Roberts, the Justice of the Peace, before whom the instrument was acknowledged, was the father of William B. Roberts, who led the company from Uniontown to engage in the Mexican war, and upon the organization of the second regiment of Pennsylvania volunteers was elected colonel, and served as such until his death, which occurred in the city of Mexico. The old justice lived on a small farm in Menallen township, Fayette county, Pennsylvania, north of and adjoining the Searight farm, and Col. Roberts, his distinguished son, was born there.

One mile west of Hatfield's is the old Peter Colley stand. It is a stone house on the south side of the road. Peter Colley was the father of Abel Colley, and an early settler. He kept a tavern on the old road before the National Road was made. He was a money maker, and owned the land on which his tavern was erected, in fee. He was probably the first man on the National Road who acquired the fame of having a barrel of money. Old pike boys said he kept his money in a barrel. Peter Colley was well advanced in years when the National Road was made, and did not long enjoy the profits of the new highway. At his death his tavern passed to the hands of his son George, who kept it for many years, and until he followed his father to the unknown world. George Colley lived to see and lament the decline of business on the road, and after his death his house was discontinued as a tavern. The hills on either side of this old house are among the highest on the road, the summit of the western range being twelve hundred and seventy-four feet above the level of the sea. In the olden time, as before stated, extra horses, called "the postilion," were required to aid the stage coaches in ascending these hills.

A little over a mile further west a plastered stone house, on the north side of the road, was kept as a tavern at intervals, during the prosperous era of the road. It is not, however, to be classed among the old taverns of the road. It was first kept as a tavern previous to 1840 by Arthur Wallace. Isaac Baily subsequently kept it for a brief period, and enjoyed a good measure of patronage. Baily afterward became postmaster at Brownsville, and finally a member of the Fayette county, Pennsylvania, bar. He was a shrewd Yankee, and an active local politician. His wife was a daughter of Solomon Colley, of the large family of Colleys of the vicinity. George Craft once lived in this house, and occasionally entertained strangers and travelers, but was not a regular tavern keeper. This was also the

12

residence at one time of "Jackey Craft," known as an eccentric character, who was in the habit of starting out over the road in a sleigh with bells, when there was no snow on the ground. Before his mind became unbalanced, "Jackey" was a pushing, money making citizen, but his life went out under a cloud of mental derangement, causing deep regret among his many friends,

A few hundred yards further west on the south side of the road, is the red tavern, so called, because in early days it was painted red. It is a wooden building, weather-boarded. This house had a large wagon custom, and, what may be considered strange without explanation, was more largely patronized by wagoners going west than east. This was owing to the means of ingress to and egress from the house. It is located near the summit of a hill, a short distance from the road, and immediately in front of it, adjoining the road, is a steep embankment. To drive to the house going west, a way leads off from the summit of the hill, which is level, but to drive out to the road the descent is steep, and wagoners coming east could not reach the wagon yard without driving up this steep grade, and, in many instances, preferred driving on to Colley's rather than pressing their teams against such an obstacle. Despite the disadvantage mentioned, this tavern, as before stated was a popular resort for wagoners. It was first kept by Cuthbert Wiggins, father of Harrison Wiggins, and at this house Harrison Wiggins was born. It was next kept by George Richards, whose widow became the wife of John Gadd. Cuthbert Wiggins was at this house as early as 1812. John Gribble succeeded Richards as early as 1836, and continued to keep this house for many years, making money in the business, and ultimately buying a farm in the neighborhood, ceased tavern keeping and became a successful farmer. He has been dead many years, but is well remembered as a worthy citizen. Upon the retirement of Gribble, this house passed to the management of Fielding Frasher, a steady-going man, who had been a wagoner on the road, and knew how to keep a tavern. He was an uncle of Capt. L. H. Frasher, of Uniontown, ex-District Attorney of Fayette county. Fielding Frasher had a good custom while keeping this house, but did not continue long in the business, and was succeeded by Huston Todd, a well known citizen in his day. He was a brother-in-law of Judge Hatfield, father of Ewing Todd, for many years a leading citizen of Brownsville, now deceased, and grandfather of William Hatfield Todd, a popular and efficient postal clerk on the route between Pittsburg and New York. Peter Williams, oldest son of the late Gen. William W. Williams, married a daughter of Huston Todd. The reputation of this old house was fully maintained while under the control of Huston Todd. Peter Frasher next took charge of this house. He was a brother of Fielding Frasher, and a typical pike boy, bright, active, and popular. He had been a wagoner, and knew the road from Baltimore to Wheeling. The house, while he kept it, was crowded with guests, but his generous nature prevented him from exacting full payment of bills at all

JOHNSON-HATFIELD HOUSE.

times, and as a consequence his coffers were not as much swollen as those of many of the tavern keepers, more mindful of the chief end of tavern keeping. George Friend succeeded Peter Frasher, but remained only a short time, when he gave way to Parker McDonald. McDonald was the last man who conducted this house as a tavern. He was active, attentive, and popular, but the glory of the road had departed, and the business of tavern keeping was a thing of the past. The old red tavern and the farm adjacent belong to the old and wealthy Bowman family, of Brownsville.

A short distance west of the red tavern a stone house was kept by Wilkes Brown, before the National Road was made, and derived its trade for the most part from the old road. It is still standing, but not immediately on the National Road. Wilkes Brown was of the family of Thomas Brown, the founder of Brownsville.

The next old tavern stand on the westward tramp is Brubaker's, a fine brick building on the north side near Brownsville. Daniel Brubaker purchased this property from David Auld, and went into possession in the year 1826, and from that date until his death was its constant occupant, with the exception of a very brief period that it was occupied and kept as a tavern by Alexander R. Watson. Mr. Brubaker survived the business era of the road, and died in his old tavern. He was a Pennsylvania Dutchman, born in Somerset county, and possessed the thrift characteristic of his race. Although economical and saving, he was not stinted in providing for the comfortable entertainment of his guests, and enjoyed a large patronage, especially in the line of wagon custom. After ascending the long hill out from Brownsville, going east, old wagoners found a pleasant resting place at Brubaker's. Alex. R. Watson will be remembered by the old folks of the road as a man of small stature, but considerable energy, who, about forty-five years ago, ran an omnibus line between Brownsville and Uniontown for the conveyance of passengers.

The next point is Brownsville, for many years the head of steamboat navigation on the Monongahela river. Here many passengers were transferred from the stage lines to the steamboats plying between this point and Pittsburg. It is shown by official figures that from 1844, the date at which the slack water improvement was completed to Brownsville, to 1852, when through business ceased on the National Road, covering a period of eight years, more than two hundred thousand passengers left the stage lines at Brownsville and took passage on the Monongahela steamers. West-going passengers were "ticketed through" from Cumberland, Baltimore and other points east, to Pittsburg and other points west, via the National Road, and the Monongahela river route. A movement was set on foot as early as the year 1814, looking to the improvement of the navigation of the Monongahela river, by means of locks and dams, followed by later spasmodic efforts, but nothing of a practical nature was accomplished in this direction until 1836, when a company was incorporated to carry forward and complete the work. The act of incorporation designated a number of prominent citizens to solicit and receive subscriptions of stock, among whom where Ephraim L. Blaine, father of James G. Blaine, of Washington county; William Hopkins, of the same county, and Andrew Stewart and Samuel Evans, of Fayette county. Of all the gentlemen designated for this purpose, and there was quite a large number, not one is living at this day. There were no wagon stand taverns in Brownsville. Wagoners "put up" at the old Riley and Bar houses in Bridgeport, and at Brubaker's, east of town. The old Workman House, at the upper end of Market street, was a famous stage house. It had the patronage of the Stockton line. This house is a stone structure, on the north side of the street, with a spacious porch in front. James Workman, the old proprietor, will be remembered as a gentleman of ruddy complexion, gray hair, slim, but erect stature, elastic step and curt speech. He presided at this house for many years, and had a wide reputation for serving good meals. This old house was built by John McClure Hezlop in 1797, who first kept it as a tavern. James Beckley afterwards kept it, and after his decease, it was continued as a tavern by his widow. James Workman took charge of it in 1843. After Workman, and since the decline of travel on the road, it has been kept at different times by William Garrett, Aaron Wyatt, William Wyatt, Jacob Marks, John G. Fear, and probably others. It is continued as a tavern, and kept at the present time by Fred Chalfant.

The late George E. Hogg, for many years a leading and wealthy citizen of Brownsville, is authority for the following amusing story concerning James Workman, the old tavern keeper, and General Jackson. On an occasion of one of General Jackson's frequent trips over the National Road, the citizens of Brownsville resolved to give him a public reception. All the usual arrangements for such an event were made, including a dinner at Workman's tavern. The hero, upon reaching town, was taken to the Presbyterian church to listen to a reception speech and receive the greetings of the people. Soon after the audience had settled down Mr. Workman entered the building, and forcing himself down the main aisle, and to a front pew occupied by General Jackson, accosted him thus: "General Jackson, I have been commissioned by the committee of arrangements to provide your dinner, and have come to inquire if there is any particular article of diet you prefer above another, that I may have the pleasure of gratifying your taste." The old General gravely responded, "Ham and eggs." This seemed rather confusing to the old landlord, who, supposing the General was joking, repeated his inquiry, when the same response came a second time and in an emphatic tone, "HAM AND EGGS." The old landlord then hastily withdrew, hurried home, and commanded his cook to prepare ham and eggs for General Jackson's dinner. The ham of that day was a different thing from the flabby, flavorless so-called "sugar cured" counterfeit of the present day, and thousands of other well meaning citizens besides General Jackson were fond of the ham of the olden time. Eggs, of course,

WORKMAN HOUSE.

are the same now as of yore, but simply and solely because modern food corrupters have not discovered any method of debauching them.

Mr. Hogg, above quoted, is responsible also for the following story: An Old Line coach in which Henry Clay was a passenger was upset on the iron bridge, and he was slightly injured and conveyed to the Workman house. Dr. Stoy, an old practitioner of the place, was summoned, and hastened to the relief of the distinguished sufferer. The old physician was given to loquacity, and not a little elated by being called to see so distinguished a patient. He prescribed brandy, and to vary the prescription and assuage the patient's apprehension, began the recital of an old joke, meanwhile holding in his hand a glass of brandy. Mr. Clay, perceiving that the story was going to be a long one, interrupted the doctor by suggesting that he be permitted to drink the brandy without further delay, and rub the glass over his wounds.

A few steps below the Workman House an old tavern was kept by Bazil Brashear, and subsequently by James Searight, who left it in 1836, to take charge of the "National House" in Washington, Pennsylvania. The Brashear House was a station for many years of one or more of the early stage lines, and in 1825 Gen. Lafayette dined at this house while on his way from Washington, Pennsylvania, to Uniontown. This old house, built of stone, is still standing, owned and occupied as a private residence by the widow of the late Westley Frost. Bazil Brashear was a brother-in-law of Thomas Brown, the founder of Brownsville, and the grandfather of Prof. Brashear, the distinguished astronomer of Pittsburg.

James C. Beckley kept a tavern in a frame house at the head of old Front street, for a number of years. He was a local politician of much shrewdness, commanding a considerable following, a close friend of the late Hon. John L. Dawson, and served that old-time, able and distinguished statesman in many trying contests.

Further down the main street and on the south side near the present location of the old Monongahela Bank, was the Marshall House. This house was first kept as a tavern by William Reynolds, who was an agent of the Adams Express Company. Mr. Reynolds previously kept the old Abrams House in Petersburg. He did a good business at the Marshall House, which was headquarters for the Express Company. This house was subsequently kept at different times by Hiram Holmes, Isaac Vance, Harvey Schroyer, J.W. Kisinger and William Garrett. After Reynolds left it the name was changed, and it was known as the Petroleum House. It has not been used as a tavern for a number of years.

William Reynolds was a native of Brownsville, born in 1804, and drove his father's team between Baltimore and Wheeling, before reaching his majority. He kept tavern in Petersburg five years, and moved from that place to Brandonville, Virginia, where he engaged in a mercantile venture, as a partner of his uncle, Zalmon Ludington, esq. After a brief experience as a merchant, he returned to his father's old tavern west of Keyser's Ridge, and afterward resumed tavern keeping in Petersburg. From Petersburg he went to Brownsville. He was killed in a railroad accident near Pittsburg in 1856, while in the service of the Adams Express Company. His son John is postmaster at Confluence, Somerset county, Pennsylvania, and William Hartman, the unfortunate brakeman who was shot and killed on the Baltimore & Ohio Railroad, near Dunbar, in August, 1893, was a grandson of William Reynolds.

The old Clark mansion, located at the east end of "the neck" in Brownsville, was converted to a tavern about forty-five years ago, and became the headquarters of the Good Intent stage line. It was first opened up as a tavern by Andrew Byers, who had previously kept the Clinton House in Uniontown. When Byers left it Daniel Brown, the old stage agent, took charge of it and conducted it for a brief period. Daniel Brown's reputatation as a model tavern keeper has been adverted to in another chapter. After Brown's time the patronage of this house was mostly of a local character. The Clark House was kept for a while after Brown left it by Capt. Morgan Mason, who subsequently located in St. Louis, where he still resides, a leading citizen, and an ex-sheriff of that city. The widow Schroyer also kept this house, and Matthew Story, and it is at present kept by the Theakston Brothers.

The Monongahela House, a short distance west of the Clark House, on the south side, was originally and for many years the private residence of Samuel J. Krepps. It has been probably fifty years since this house was thrown open to the public as a tavern. One of the McCurdy's was first installed as landlord of this house. He was succeeded by Jesse Hardin, an old stage driver, and Isaac Bailey, William Gans, Ephraim H. Bar, Cyrus L. Conner and John B. Krepps, son of the owner, kept this house nearly, if not exactly, in the order given. It was a stage house, and had a large run of general custom. It continues to be one of the leading hotels of Brownsville, under the management of David Provins.

Thomas Brown, James Auld, Amos Wilson and James C. Beckley were tavern keepers in Brownsville prior to the construction of the National Road. Auld preceded Beckley in the old house at the head of Front street, above mentioned. Amos Wilson kept the old "Black Horse" tavern on Front street.

A few yards westward from the Monongahela House the road crosses Dunlap's creek over a handsome and expensive iron bridge, erected in 1835, and the first of the kind west of the Allegheny mountains. The vicissitudes attending the construction of this bridge have been alluded to in a previous chapter. The stone work of this bridge, which is a fine specimen of heavy masonry, was let by contract to William Searight, who pushed it forward and completed it with his characteristic energy. David Chipps, a well remembered old citizen of the vicinity of Uniontown, and an expert stone mason, was a boss workman on this bridge, and the late Gen. William W. Williams, who

BRIDGE OVER THE MONONGAHELA.

in the prime ot his life was an excellent mason, also worked on its walls and abutments. The work was done under authority of the War Department of the general government.

After crossing the iron bridge the traveler is in the ancient borough of Bridgeport. Here Jack Arnold kept a tavern at a very early period. He was succeeded by John Riley, who for many years kept a wagon stand. Riley was a staunch citizen, and participated in the public affairs of his town. His tavern was near the market house, and was a popular resort in the olden time. Isaac Kimber, Robert Patterson and John Neelan kept taverns in Bridgeport before the National Road was made. The present Bar House is on the site of the old Kimber House. The Bar House is owned by Ephraim H. Bar, who conducted it as a tavern for many years. It was a wagon stand, and had a good trade. Robert Carter, old wagoner before mentioned, was one of the men who for a time successfully conducted the Bar House. Thornton Young, George Garrard, Matthew Story and Eli Bar kept this house in recent years at different times, and it is now conducted by W. F. Higinbotham.

It is but a short distance from the iron bridge before mentioned to the long wooden bridge over the Monongahela river. This bridge, although a link of the National Road, was not built by the government. It is a private enterprise, and was erected in 1833. In 1810 an act was passed by the Legislature of Pennsylvania, authorizing the Governor to incorporate a company to build and operate a bridge at this point; but for some cause the company was not organized, and in 1830 a company was incorporated by the Legislature. Ephraim L. Blaine, father of the brilliant and popular statesman, was an incorporator under the provisions of the act of 1830, and the company authorized by that act promptly organized, and completed the bridge at the date above mentioned. Neil Gillespie, the grandfather of James G. Blaine, was named in the act of 1810, above mentioned, as one of the commissioners to solicit and receive subscriptions of stock for the bridge.

CHAPTER XXXVI.

*Old Taverns and Tavern Keepers continued — Brownsville to Beallsville — West Browns-
ville, the Birthplace of James G. Blaine — Indian Hill, later known as Krepps'
Knob — Indian Peter and Neil Gillespie — The Adams House, John Cummins,
Vincent Owens — An Old and Mysterious Murder — Malden, Bry Taylor —
Tragic Death of a Beautiful Girl — Centreville, John Rogers, Zeph Riggle,
Battelly White, the whip-maker, Mrs. Dutton, Eli Railley, The Old Constitution,
Beallsville, David Mitchell, Andrew and Thomas Keys, Robert Cluggage, William
Greenfield, Mrs. Chambers, Charles Guttery.*

From the Big Crossings to the Monongahela river at Brownsville
the road passes through Fayette county, Pennsylvania. After crossing the river bridge at Brownsville, going west, the traveler reaches
the soil of Washington county, and plants his feet in the ancient
village of West Brownsville. From the hill tops on the road, as far
west as Hillsboro, glimpses are had of the receding mountains. West
Brownsville has the great distinction of being the birth place of
James G. Blaine, the foremost and most popular of all American
statesmen of the present day. It is related in Crumrine's valuable
and well written history of Washington county, that the land upon
which West Brownsville stands was originally owned by Indian Peter.
This Indian Peter, at a very early day, lived on lands in the vicinity
of Uniontown, and gave name to Peter's street, the oldest street of
that town. He had a neighbor whose name was Philip Shute, with
whom he was not on friendly terms. Prior to 1769 Indian Peter
wrote to the authorities of the proprietary government, that "he
could not get along with the damned Dutchman, and wished to give
up his land for another tract." His request was promptly complied
with, and he was given a tract of three hundred and thirty-nine acres,
situate on the west side of the Monongahela river, which was surveyed
and called "Indian Hill," and upon this tract stands the town of West
Brownsville. It embraces Krepps' Knob, which together with the
character of the old owner, accounts for the name given the tract.
Krepps' Knob is ten hundred and forty feet above the level of the
Atlantic ocean. Indian Peter, it seems, died in possession of the
Indian Hill tract, and it passed to his widow Mary, a white woman,
and his oldest son William. In 1784 the widow and son aforesaid,
sold the tract to Neil Gillespie, the great-grandfather of James G.
Blaine. The price agreed upon between the parties was forty shillings
per acre, payable in instalments of money, iron and one negro. This

OLD TAVERN AT MALDEN.

tract of land remained in the Gillespie family for many years. Philip Shute, the old German neighbor of Indian Peter, lived in Union township, Fayette county, now North Union, near the late residence of Colonel Evans, and gave name to the gushing mountain stream which flows through the lands of that vicinity. The bridge over the Monongahela river stands on an almost direct north and south line, and a short distance from its northern end the road makes a sharp angle to the westward. On the south side of this angle a tavern was kept by Samuel Adams, as early as the year 1820. Samuel Adams was the father of Estep Adams, the present polite and popular postmaster at West Brownsville. John Huston succeeded Samuel Adams in this old house. In the early days of the road this house was constantly crowded with guests. At the close of Huston's term, the old house, which was a wooden structure, was torn down, and the present brick building was erected on its site, and continued as a tavern throughout the whole period of the road's prosperous era, and for many years thereafter. Joshua Armstrong was the first occupant of the new building. His term was prior to the year 1840. Morris Purcell came in, after Armstrong. Dr. Adams, the postmaster before mentioned, when a boy, counted fifty road wagons standing around this old tavern, in one night, when it was kept by Morris Purcell. The wagon yard, which was large and commodious, was located on the west side, and in the rear of the house. Major William Paul, hereinbefore mentioned, succeeded Purcell in this house, about the year 1842, and retained the extensive line of wagon custom with which his predecessor was favored. James Watkins, an old stage driver of Washington, Pennsylvania, was Maj. Paul's bar keeper at this house, and his son-in-law, Thomas Hamen Hopkins, was the successor of Maj. Paul in this house. His widow is still keeping a tavern in West Brownsville. She is well up in years, but her memory is clear and well stored with interesting reminiscences of the road. Greenberry Millburn next had charge of this house, and kept it for a brief period, when he retired, and his name does not subsequently appear on the roll of old tavern keepers. John Cummins was the next occupant of this house. He purchased the property, and held it until his death, which occurred near the close of the prosperous era of the road. He was an Irishman, thrifty and energetic, and besides tavern keeping, took contracts on public works. About the year 1859 this house passed to the control of Moses Bennington, who conducted it during the era of the civil war. He was succeeded by William Dawson, whose successor was James B. Dorsie. Doc Bar kept the house for a brief period, and one of its occupants was Robert Miller. Upon the expiration of Miller's term Thomas H. Hopkins again took charge, and it was subsequently kept for short periods, at different times, by Solomon Watkins, James Nichols and John Taylor. The house is at present owned by the Pittsburg, Virginia and Charleston railroad company, and used as a passenger and freight station.

A few hundred yards west of the old Adams stand, and near the

12a

foot of the river hill, on the river side, an old stone house was kept as a tavern when the road was first opened, and for a number of years thereafter. The first man who catered to the wants of the traveling public at this old tavern was Vincent Owens, who had been a faithful soldier in Washington's army in the war of the Revolution. The property belonged to the old Krepps family of the vicinity, and the old tavern stood at the northwest landing of the old Krepps ferry. Owens was succeeded at this old tavern by Samuel Acklin, and Acklin by John Krepps, a brother of Samuel J. Krepps. Morris Purcell succeeded Krepps, and went from here to the old Adams House, before mentioned. The Krepps ferry was operated in connection with the management of this old tavern, and the ferry was continued down to the year 1845. The tavern was closed here long before the decline of travel on the road. The father of Vincent Owens was murdered in this old tavern while his son was conducting it. The crime was an atrocious one, causing great excitement and indignation in the neighborhood at the time, and the manner and motives of the act seem to be shrouded in mystery. Two persons who lodged in the house over night were suspected of the crime, but they fled before the light of the morning and were never apprehended.

About two and one-half miles west of Krepps' Ferry an ancient hamlet called by old pike boys Malden is reached. Here on the north side of the road stands an old stone tavern, which in the palmy days of the road was a popular stopping point. It belonged originally to the old Krepps family, of Brownsville, and was designed and erected for a tavern. It was evidently the belief of the old owners that a town would grow up on this site, as they caused a stone in the front wall of the old tavern, near the top, to be dressed and inscribed in cut letters with the name Kreppsville. This name, however, was not adopted by the public, but the place was, and continues to be known as Malden. The origin of this name is not positively known, but tradition has it that a party of emigrants encamping on the ground one night, fancying that it resembled the place of their nativity, Malden, probably in the State of Massachusetts, gave it that name. Be this as it may, Malden is the popular name of the locality. The old tavern here was built in two sections and at different dates. The original, which is now the western section, was built in 1822, and a dressed stone in its front wall bears that date. The second, or eastern section, was built in 1830. It is the second section that bears the name Kreppsville, above mentioned; and, in addition, the stone slab disclosing this name shows the date 1830, also the word "Liberty," and the figure of a plow and sheaf of wheat. Bry Taylor was the first person who kept the old tavern at Malden, and he was constantly busy while there in attending to the wants of the traveling public. He had an amiable and beautiful daughter, Kizzie, who was accidentally killed in this house, causing great sorrow in the neighborhood. Her brother, James, had been out hunting one day, and returning, placed his gun negligently on a table. His sister, Miss Kizzie, be-

WILLIAM GREENFIELD.

sought him to put the gun in a safe place, which he declined to do, remarking that "it wouldn't hurt anybody where it was." Miss Kizzie did not share his confidence in regard to the absence of danger, and proceeded to remove the gun herself. Her brother interfered to prevent the gun's removal, when a scuffle ensued between the parties, during which the gun was discharged, and Miss Kizzie was fatally shot. The room in which this sad affair occurred is still pointed out to visitors. As if by the law of compensation, James Taylor, the brother, many years afterward was himself shot. He became a river man, and gradually made his way to points down the Ohio and Mississippi, and was finally shot and killed by a United States Marshal near Memphis. Samuel Acklin followed Taylor in the old tavern at Malden, and was favored with a large patronage, consisting mainly of wagoners and drovers. Acklin was at this house as early as 1836. Samuel Bailey succeeded Acklin, and Bailey was succeeded in turn by William Pepper and William Garrett. James Britton, now and for thirty years past, has owned this property. He occupies the old tavern as a private residence, and operates the fertile farm attached to it.

The next point west, distant about three miles, is Centreville. Moving onward towards Centreville the traveler passes the old farms and residences of Jonathan Knight, the famous civil engineer of other days, and Nathan Pusey, father of Hon. W. H. M. Pusey, a leading banker, Democratic politician and ex-member of Congress, of Council Bluffs, Iowa. Another point of interest on this part of the line, is the old historic Taylor church, which stands on the north side of the road, a monument of the religious tendencies of the good old inhabitants of the vicinity. Centreville was laid out in 1821, soon after the road was completed, and with special reference to its completion, and the anticipated prosperity to ensue by reason thereof. It is equidistant between Uniontown and Washington. The first old tavern kept in Centreville was by John Rogers, father of the venerable Joseph T. Rogers, of Bridgeport. It is a brick house, on the north side of the road, still standing. Robert Rogers succeeded his father in this house and kept it for many years, and died in possession. At brief intervals in the lifetime of Robert Rogers this house was conducted by Solomon Bracken, son-in-law of Mr. Rogers, and a Mr. Wilson, the latter occupying it but for one year. The Rogers House was known and noted throughout the entire period of the road's prosperous era as a quiet, orderly, well kept tavern. The leading wagon stand in Centreville was on the hill at the west end of town, a brick house, on the south side of the road. The wagon yard was in the rear. Zephania Riggle kept this house at an early day, and was succeeded in 1845 by Peter Colley, a nephew of Abel Colley, before mentioned. Henry Whitsett came in after Colley, and next Jacob Marks, who was followed by William Garrett, and Jesse Quail succeeded Garrett. The property is now owned by Joseph B. Jeffreys who keeps the old tavern open for the accommodation of strangers and travelers. The house kept by Zeph Riggle on this site was destroyed by fire during his incumbency, and promptly rebuilt. Battley White, the celebrated manufacturer of the wagoner's black snake whip, before mentioned, lived in Centreville. The house now occupied by Morris Cleaver, on the hill west of Centreville, was at one time a tavern. It was first kept by Charley Miller, then by Zeph Riggle, and next, in 1836, by Mrs. Dutton, mother of John R. Dutton, the well known, reputable and prosperous merchant of Brownsville. Mrs. Dutton owned the property, and moved from here to Brownsville, after which this old tavern closed. Its career was somewhat brief, but it was a well kept tavern, and had a good line of custom in its day.

About half a mile west from Mrs. Dutton's an old frame tavern, on the north side of the road, as early as 1824, displayed the sign of the CONSTITUTION, and entertained primitive travelers of the road. This old house was kept for a while by one Johnson, but it long since disappeared from view.

Eli Railley kept a tavern as early as 1830 in a brick house on the north side of the road, about one and a half miles west of Centreville, and was succeeded by the widow Welsh, who conducted it as a tavern as late as 1850. This house is still standing, owned by Amos Cleaver, and occupied by his son as a private residence.

Beallsville, distant one and a half miles from the old Railley tavern, is next reached. In proceeding to Beallsville the traveler passes one of the old toll houses, all of which, as before stated, are still standing, and in good condition, except the one near Mt. Washington and the one on Big Savage mountain. David Mitchell, the old collector at the gate near Beallsville, is well remembered as a straightforward, honest and intelligent citizen. Beallsville, like Centreville as a town, was the outgrowth of the National Road. It was laid out in 1821, and incorporated as a borough in 1852. Jonathan Knight, the old engineer before mentioned, surveyed the site of the town and made the plat. The National Road forms the main street of this town, as it does that of Centreville. The first old tavern reached in Beallsville, going west, was on the north side, at the east end of the town. This house was first kept by Andrew Keys, and after him by Thomas Keys. This was previous to 1840. It was next kept by Robert Cluggage, and after Cluggage, James Dennison kept it. Dennison was succeeded by Moses Bennington, who afterwards kept the old Adams House at West Brownsville. Charles Guttery also kept this house in 1854. Dennison was a Claysville man, and after keeping tavern for short terms, at different points on the road, returned to Claysville, where he died. He was an old wagoner, as well as a tavern keeper, and well and favorably known on the road. He had an interest by marriage, or birth-right, in some real estate at or near Claysville, and this is doubtless the chord that drew him at last back to that point. The old Keys tavern had a commodious wagon yard attached, and entertained many old wagoners.

CHARLES GUTTERY.

About the center of the town of Beallsville, and on the south or west side, Wm. Greenfield kept a famous old tavern, and he was in many other respects a famous old man. He was tall and spare, with a brown complexion, a defective eye, and a philosophic turn of mind. It was his fortune to have a good wife, and to her, in great measure, was attributed the high grade of this old tavern. The traveler could always get a good cup of coffee at Greenfield's, a rare thing in a tavern and utterly unknown in a hotel. In addition to keeping tavern, William Greenfield was a banker, and established the "Beallsville Savings Bank." His bank was in his tavern, and his safe was his pocket. He issued notes of small denominations, which were handsomely printed and engraved, and they acquired some credit, and a limited circulation. The pressure of redemption, however, was more than the old banker-tavern keeeper could withstand, and he was forced to close business as a banker, but continued his tavern successfully. It is due to the memory of the old gentleman to state, that no serious losses were sustained by the note holders of his bank. He continued to keep tavern at the old stand until his death, which occurred many years ago, and all the old pike boys, from one end of the road to the other, have a kind word for the memory of William Greenfield.

Charley Miller kept a tavern as early as 1830, and probably before that date, in the brick house on the corner opposite Greenfield's, and this house was subsequently, and for many years kept by Mrs. Chambers. It was a quiet, orderly, and aristocratic old tavern, especially when under the management of Mrs. Chambers, and enjoyed a good reputation as an eating house. Benjamin Demon took charge of this house after the retirement of Mrs. Chambers, and kept it for a while. Moses Bennington succeeded Demon, and Charles Guttery succeeded Bennington. Guttery was the last of the old line of tavern keepers, at this house. Beallsville was a station for the line wagons, and John Cook, an old wagoner whose home was there, drove a line team for many years.

CHAPTER XXXVII.

Old Taverns and Tavern Keepers continued — Beallsville to Washington — Hillsboro — The Old Hill House — Samuel Youman, next to Old Mount the biggest man of the Road — George Ringland, John Noble, Billy Robinson, Charley Miller's, The Gals House, Daniel Ward, Egg Nog Hill, The Long Stretch, Thomas Hastings, The Upland House, Joseph Doak, The Mount Vernon House, Maj. Dunlap, Charles Rettig, Pancake, Jonathan Martin, The Sample House.

Three miles west from Beallsville the traveler reaches the village of Hillsboro. This little town is another outgrowth of the National Road, and as at Beallsville and Centreville, the road forms its main street. The grade from Beallsvile to Hillsboro is for the most part ascending, the hill going out west from Beallsville being one of the longest on the road, and Hillsboro is situate on a lofty eminence overlooking a wide range of hills, and many fertile slopes and valleys. On the summit above Hillsboro, the traveler coming east, gets the first glimpses of Laurel Hill, thirty miles distant in the mountains. Crumrine's history of Washington county, before quoted, informs us that Hillsboro was laid out in the year 1819, a date coincident with the completion of the road. The proprietors of the town were Stephen Hill and Thomas McGiffin, and Crumrine's history contains the following notice of the first public sale of lots:

"The public are informed that a town has been laid off, to be called Hillsboro, adjoining Hill's stone tavern, about equal distance from Washington to Brownsville, and that lots will be sold on the premises on Monday, the 19th day of August, at public auction. Sale to commence at 10 o'clock A. M.   Stephen Hill,
        July 19, 1819.   Thomas McGiffin,
                                                          Proprietors."

Accompanying the plat of the town as recorded, says Crumrine, were these remarks: "The above is a plan of the town of Hillsboro, nearly equi-distant between Brownsville and Washington, Pennsylvania, on the United States road." Signed by the proprietors. Stephen Hill belonged to an old family of that name, which was among the early settlers of the region, and Thomas McGiffin was an old and prominent lawyer of Washington, and a contractor on the original construction of the road, father of Col. Norton McGiffin, a soldier of two wars, and Sheriff and member of the Legislature for Washington

BILLY ROBINSON.

county. Hill's stone tavern was in existence as early as 1794. In the early history of the National Road, and for a number of years, it was the leading tavern of Hillsboro, kept by Thomas Hill, who was not a son, but a near relative, probably a nephew, of Stephen Hill, the old proprietor. Samuel Youman kept this house fifty years ago, after the retirement of Hill. Youman was a stage driver as well as a tavern keeper, and next to "Old Mount," as before stated, the biggest man on the road. One of the stage lines, that on which Youman was a driver, stopped at this house, and it was the only stage house on the road that was largely patronized by old wagoners, and their favor was obtained probably by reason of the spacious and commodious wagon yard in front of the house. John Hampson, John Gibson, William Dawson and Oliver Lacock each in turn kept this house since Youman's time, and it is at present continued as a tavern by Mr. Lacock's son.

In the year 1827 James Beck kept a tavern in Hillsboro. He was a member of the old bridge builders firm of Kinkead, Beck & Evans, and moved from the "Vance farm," near Uniontown, which he once owned, to Hillsboro, at the date named. He remained in Hillsboro but one year, and his successor in the tavern there was George Ringland. Ringland was a citizen of some prominence in his day, a brother of Col. Thomas Ringland, an old soldier, and a leading man in the public affairs of Washington county more than half a century ago. David Railly succeeded Ringland in this house about the year 1840. It was a stage house, but did a general business. After Railly this house was kept at different times by John Noble, who married Railly's widow, John Taylor, Henry Taylor, Jesse Core and William Robinson. Noble and Robinson were both old stage drivers, Noble before, as well as after his experience as a tavern keeper. Robinson died a tavern keeper, and in the house last mentioned. "Billy" Robinson was one of the best known and most popular men of the road. He was short in stature, with reddish complexion, dark hair, and an amiable disposition. He hauled many an old-time statesman safely in his nimble coach, and afterward dined him sumptuously in his bountiful tavern. There was an old tavern in Hillsboro, near the centre of the town, on the south side of the road, kept first by John Wilson, and after his time by Stephen Phelps, and next and last by David Powell. Its career was not as long as many other old taverns of the road, but in its time it was a lively house and had a large run of custom. Zeph Riggle kept a tavern in what is known as the Dr. Clark house, on the south side, in Hillsboro, at an early day, and as at other points on the road where he catered to the wants of the traveling public, drew a good trade. He was the only person that ever kept this house as a tavern.

About two miles west of Hillsboro the famous old tavern of Charley Miller is reached. It is a large and handsome brick building on the south side of the road, and was kept before Miller's time by Henry Taylor. Miller did a large business, and had all sorts of customers, with a capacity to adapt himself to the wants and whims of every variety. He was accustomed to say, in commendation of his whisky, that it was a hundred years old; that he could vouch for its age, for he helped to make it. Parties of young folks were accustomed to drive out from Washington, a distance of ten miles, to take a meal and have a dance at Charley Miller's. His meals were sumptuous and savory, and gave his house a reputation from which he did not fail to profit. One of his specialties was fine peach brandy, which is graciously remembered and frequently spoken of by the survivors of the old pike boys with a glow of enthusiasm. Miller died in this house, and it passed to the hands of David Ullery.

> "No longer the host hobbles down from his rest
> In the porch's cool shadow, to welcome his guest
> With a smile of delight and a grasp of the hand,
> And a glance of the eye that no heart could withstand,"

One and a half miles west of Charley Miller's, on the south side of the road, a tavern was kept in a wooden building many years ago by William Plymire. This old tavern furnished good entertainment, and its old host was attentive and polite to his patrons. Plymire was succeeded in this house by Henry Yorty, who kept it going as a tavern until his death, and for some time thereafter it was kept by his widow, but was never kept as a tavern after Mrs. Yorty's time.

The next old wagon stand on the westward tramp is the "Gals House." This house is situate on the north side of the road, about two miles west of Charley Miller's. It is a frame building, and once was painted red, but the red all wore off many years ago, and was not replaced. It was called the "Gals House," because it was owned and conducted by three maiden women of the family name of Dague. The grounds around this old house, night after night, throughout the entire period of the road's prosperity, were crowded with teams and wagons, and the reputation of the place was excellent in every particular. The Dague girls were the owners of the house, and of about eighty acres of rich land surrounding it, and after business closed on the road, they sold and conveyed the property to Joseph Henderson, a well remembered and worthy old stage driver, who went into possession and made this place his home for many years.

One mile further west is Ward's. Here a well known tavern was kept by Daniel Ward, all through the flourishing era of the road, and it was well kept and well patronized. Ward was rich, the owner of his tavern stand, and a fine farm in addition, and therefore unlike many other old tavern keepers of the road who leased their houses from year to year, and changed from point to point at different times. Ward's tavern is a large frame house, on the north side of the road, with a spacious porch in front, and a large wagon yard conveniently attached, and was a favorite stopping place for old wagoners. The old house is still standing, unused, because not needed as a tavern, but it remains a prominent landmark of the road, carrying the mind

DANIEL WARD.

back to the period of its enlivening scenes and moving pageants. Daniel Ward was a pronounced type of the old tavern keeper. He was rather a large man, not fleshy, but broad shouldered, with a slight stoop. His complexion was reddish, and he always had a pleasant smile wherewith to greet a guest. He wore a broad-rimmed, high-crowned, brown-colored fur hat, with long, soft nap, the style of hat worn by all old tavern keepers and wagoners when dressed for special occasions. Mrs. Ward was an admirable help-mate for her husband. She was a large woman, of florid complexion, and full of energy and zeal in her occupation. The meals she spread before her numerous guests in all seasons were bountiful and relishable, and gave her husband's old tavern a wide reputation. What a change? Once all was life and animation at this old tavern, now

"The wind whistles shrill, through the wide open doors,
      And lizards keep house, on the mouldering floors."

Four miles west from Ward's the old and popular wagon stand of Thomas Hastings is reached. In proceeding onward toward the Hastings House a celebrated point is passed, known in the peculiar vocabulary of the road as "Egg Nog Hill." On this hill for many years lived in retirement Samuel Flowers, one of the oldest, steadiest and best known wagoners of the road. William D. Evans, residing in Malvern, Iowa, a son of Gabriel Evans, of the old firm of Kinkead, Beck & Evans, contractors and bridge builders, before mentioned, furnishes the following story as to the origin of the name of this hill : The engineers in locating the line of the road were much exercised in fixing the grade at this point, and before arriving at conclusions the sun went down, and with a view probably of stimulating their minds to clearer conceptions, they ordered a bucket of egg-nog to be served in their shanty. Partaking freely of this ancient, agreeable and strong beverage during the night, they proceeded next morning with the work in hand, and established the grade without further embarrassment. The chain carriers and other employees were called in to the rough, roadside banquet, and the region all around echoed the notes of that night's revelry, and ever thereafter the locality has been known as "Egg Nog Hill." If this is a true account of the origin of the name, and the authority quoted is respectable and credible, there are many persons willing to aver that the influence of the egg nog was anything but propitious, since the grade of the road at this point is nothing to boast of. At the foot of Egg Nog Hill a valley is reached over which the road passes for a distance of two miles on a level grade, varied by slight undulations, terminating at or near the old Buchanan postoffice. This portion of the road was called by old stage drivers "The Long Stretch," and over its favorable grade stage teams sped with more than ordinary rapidity. It is considered germaine to state in this connection, that the general grade of the road has been much and sharply criticised, and by many condemned outright. The main point of objection urged against the grade is, that it involves many long and steep hills, which could have been avoided by making side cuts and occupying the valleys, and this is true, but any other location would have lengthened the line and increased the cost of construction and maintenance. David Shriver, of Cumberland, was the chief engineer in charge of the location, and instructed by the Government to make the line as straight as practicable, within the limit of a five degree elevation. Besides, there was a popular theory when the line was located, that a road over hills was not as fatiguing to horses as a road with a uniform grade. It was argued that a horse is provided with two sets of muscles, one of which is used in going up and the other in going down a hill, and the conclusion was that horses were relieved and rested by a change from an up to a down grade. After this digression, the reader's attention is invited back to the old tavern of Thomas Hastings. It is situate on the summit of a hill of average length and grade on the south side, and a short distance back from the road. The location of this house, with reference to the road, is similar to that of the old red tavern, two miles east of Brownsville. The Hastings House was a leading tavern of the road, all through its prosperous era. The large patronage it enjoyed is the best evidence that it was well kept.

John W. McDowell, of Uniontown, an ex-County Commissioner of Fayette county, Pennsylvania, was working on the road in 1844 under the superintendency of William Searight, and boarding at the Hastings House. On the morning of the election of that year he rose "bright and early," took his breakfast "before the break of day," mounted a horse, and rode to Mt. Washington, the polling place for Wharton township, which was his home, in time to vote for Polk and Dallas. McDowell frequently relates this incident of his life, when recounting his party services, and lays particular stress on the circumstance that the dining room girls gladly furnished him his breakfast and cheered him on his mission. The distance from the old Hastings tavern to Mt. Washington is forty-two miles.

While the road was undergoing construction, there was a tavern about midway of the "Long Stretch," and on the south side of the road. It was kept by one Smith, of the extensive American family of that name. At times there was great disorder and much tumult, amounting almost to riot, at this old tavern, and on one of these occasions the old militia of Washington county was ordered to the scene to enforce the keeping of the peace. These disorders, like similar outbreaks of the present day, were no doubt attributable to the immoderate use of intoxicants.

Within a few hundred feet, and west of the old Hastings house, Samuel Hughes kept a tavern in 1844 and before, and probably a short time after that date. His house was a large and imposing frame building on the north side of the road, and known in its day as the "Upland House." This name appeared on the sign board. The surroundings of this house were attractive. It had an aristocratic air about it, and enjoyed an aristocratic patronage. While old

JOHN W. McDOWELL.

wagoners crowded the Hastings House, travelers in chaises and fine carriages stopped at the Upland. By some means, and many years ago, this old house was demolished, and a fine brick building erected on its site, owned and occupied by Joseph Doak, who was at one time a superintendent of the road.

About one and a half miles west of the Upland House, Major James Dunlap, at a very early period of the road's history, kept a tavern on the south side, on an elevation and a little distance back from the roadside. It was called the "Mt. Vernon House," and was doing business as early as the year 1816, two years before the road was completed as far west as Washington. Major Dunlap was a prominent man of his day, and brigade inspector of the Washington county (Pennsylvania) militia, an office of no little consequence in the early history of Pennsylvania. Major Dunlap subsequently kept the Jackson House in Washington, Pennsylvania. Before reaching the Mt. Vernon House, an old round toll house is passed, where William Hill collected tolls for many years from the throngs of travelers on the road. The old Mt. Vernon House was supplanted by a new one, under the direction of Charles Rettig, who became the owner of the property. The new house is a brick structure, and was a wagon stand. There was an abundant water supply at this house, and old stage drivers and wagoners halted upon reaching it to refresh their teams. Charles Rettig died about the year 1860. He was a staunch and sturdy citizen, and possessed the confidence and enjoyed the respect of all his neighbors.

The next point west, but a short distance, is invested with more than ordinary interest. It is Pancake, sometimes called Martinsburg, and in later years, to a limited extent, known as Laboratory. But Pancake was the original, and remains the popular name. It is almost within eyesight of Washington. The first tavern here was kept by George Pancake, and hence the name given the place. His house was a small log building, erected near the beginning of the present century, and probably the first house in the village. Pancake did well with the means at his command, but his old house was not equal to the growing wants of the road, and after it was removed, and the old proprietor called to his final reckoning, Jonathan Martin appeared on the scene. Martin was a discerning man, and foreseeing the future of the National Road as a great highway, built a large brick house for use as a tavern. It is situate on the north side of the road, two stories, twelve large and comfortable rooms, and was erected in the year 1825. A spacious porch runs the entire length of the house and approaches the edge of the road. Jonathan Martin kept this tavern from the date of its erection until business closed on the road, with the exception of one year that it was in charge of J. W. Holland, back in the forties. Since the close of its career as a tavern it has been occupied as a quiet farm house. Martin was a genial landlord, and made money at tavern keeping. A short distance back from the tavern he had a horse-power grist mill and a carding machine which he operated for a number of years, thus supplementing his gains as a tavern keeper. General Jackson was on one occasion a guest of Martin's tavern, and the celebrated theologian, Alexander Campbell, frequently lodged within its venerable walls and sat at its bounteous table.

As early as 1824 George Ringland kept a wagon stand tavern within a short distance of the borough limits of Washington. His old house, a commodious brick building, is still standing, situate on the north, or at this point rather, east side of the road, with sufficient ground intervening to form a good wagon yard. John Sample succeeded Ringland at this old stand, and became the owner of the property. It is now the private residence of William Workman, esq., and has not been kept as a tavern since 1844.

CHAPTER XXXVIII.

Old Taverns and Tavern Keepers continued — Washington — Washington and Jeffer-son College — The Female Seminary — James Wilson, first Tavern Keeper in Washington — The two Dodds — Major McCormick's — The White Goose and the Golden Swan — Hallam's Old Wagon Stand — The Valentine — The Buck — The Gen. Andrew Jackson — The Globe — The Cross Keys — The Indian Queen — The Mermaid — The Rising Sun — The Gen. Brown — The Fountain — Billy Brown and Jimmy Brown — The Mansion — John N. Dagg — A Giant Boot Jack — The American — The Fulton — The National — Surratt's — The Greene House.

Washington became a point on the National Road by force of a provision in the act of Assembly of Pennsylvania, approved April 9th, 1807, before recited. In a retrospective view that seems to have been a wise provision. Washington, it is true, is older than the road, but without the road it would be difficult to conjecture what the history of the town would have been from 1818 down to 1852. That the road had much to do in promoting the growth and prosperity of the town, there can be no question, and it must also be conceded that the town contributed in good round measure to the life and prosperity of the road. Washington is one of the largest and prettiest towns on the road, not as well favored by location as Uniontown. While Washington possesses many very important advantages, it has at the same time, like other towns, its disadvantages. For example, it is a dry town. It was not dry in the palmy days of the old pike. No liquor can at this time be lawfully sold in Washington as a beverage, and the town is not over abundantly supplied with good water. On the other hand, the town is justly distinguished for the superiority of its educational institutions. Washington and Jefferson college is one of the best in the land. Its graduates include many of the ablest men of the country, both of the present and the past. Everywhere, at every leading point in our widely extended Republic, the graduates of Washington and Jefferson College are pushing ahead at the front, in all the learned professions, in the judiciary, and in every line of honorable industry. It is not a dude college, as many more preten-tious colleges are, but a working college, sending out workers, equip-ped like men, to run the race set before them. The Female Seminary is another institution of which the citizens of Washington are justly proud. It stands in the front rank of similar institutions, and for more than half a century, year after year, has sent out its graduates to cheer and brighten the world.

The writer of these lines confesses to an affection for Washington, which no vicissitude of life or time can alienate. He was educated at her college, and if he failed in obtaining a thorough education, it was not the fault of his venerable *alma mater*. Dr. David McConoughy, who presided over the college, when the writer was a student within its halls, deserves to be classed among the Saints. A purer man never lived. He was a Christian, who never entertained a doubt, and a scholar in the broadest sense; and it is most gratifying to the thousands of graduates and friends of the college scattered broadcast throughout the land, to know that Dr. Moffatt, the present head of the institution, is a worthy successor of that venerated president. The writer also retains the sweetest recollections of the old citizens of Washington, and cherishes with deepest feeling his associations at college with James G. Blaine, who subsequently became the most illustrious statesman of his generation, and many others who have written their names high on the scroll of fame.

There may be some readers inclined to think that the blending of stage drivers and wagoners with doctors, teachers and statesmen, is a strange commingling; but it is not. History is literature, and stage drivers and wagoners, like other classes, and occupations of men, enter into the web and woof of history.

James Wilson hung out the first tavern sign in Washington. His house was a log structure, and stood at the northwest corner of Main and Beau streets, now covered by Smith's store. He opened up business in 1781, and was licensed by the court to dispense the ardent at "Catfish Camp." He continued business in this house down to the year 1792. The old Supreme Judges stopped at Wilson's tavern when they went to Washington to hold the courts of Oyer and Terminer. Whether they were fed on roast pig, as Chief Justice McKean at Salter's old tavern in Uniontown, does not appear of record. After Wilson's time this house was enlarged and otherwise improved, and continued as a tavern by Michael Ocheltree, who remained in charge down to the year 1812, when a man of the name of Rotroff was installed as host. Rotroff gave way to John Kline, who came up from the Cross Roads, nine miles west of Brownsville, and took charge of the house, under the sign of "Gen. Wayne." Capt. John McCluney followed Kline, and he in turn was followed by Joseph Teeters and Joseph Hallam. Hallam kept the house until probably 1840, when he went down town to take charge of the old wagon stand on the site of the present Valentine House. When Hallam left it the old Wilson House ceased to be a tavern.

As early as 1782 John Dodd kept tavern in a log house on the east side of Main street, nearly opposite the court house, and remained its host until his death in 1795. He died while returning home from a trading trip to New Orleans. John Wilson next took charge, and conducted its affairs for many years, associated with stirring events, down to a period as late probably as 1835, when the house disappeared as a tavern. John Dodd was an ancestor of the numerous Dodds now of Washington and vicinity, most of whom have taken to the ministry and other learned professions.

Charles Dodd, a brother of John, above mentioned, kept a tavern on Main street in 1782, in a log house, recently occupied by Robert Strean's hardware store. The first courts of Washington county were held in this old tavern, and the county jail was a log stable in the rear of the lot on which it stood. Charles Dodd kept this tavern for ten years, and sold out to Daniel Kehr, who continued it a short time, but finding it unprofitable, took down his sign and went to shoemaking.

John Adams kept a tavern from 1783 to 1789. Its location is not accurately known, and so in the case of John Colwell, a tavern keeper of 1784. In 1785 Hugh Means, Samuel Acklin and William Falconer, were tavern keepers in Washington. Acklin continued in the business until 1788, and Falconer until 1791. William Meetkirk, who was subsequently a justice of the peace for many years, kept a tavern on Main street from 1786 to 1793, in the house until recently occupied by Mrs. McFarland, and it is not unlikely that this is the house kept by Colwell and Means.

Maj. George McCormick kept a tavern in 1788, and Col. John May's journal compliments it by this entry: "Thursday, Aug. 7, 1788, set out from the hotel at four o'clock, and at half-past eight arrived at Maj. George McCormick's in Washington, where we breakfasted. This is an excellent house, where New England men put up." The writer regrets his failure to ascertain the exact location of this old tavern.

Hugh Wilson (son of James) kept a tavern in Washington in 1789, and John McMichael in 1790, the locations of which are not now ascertainable.

Charles Valentine kept the "White Goose" in 1791. This house stood on the lot now covered by the Valentine House. The name Valentine is prominently identified with the National Road from the date of its construction to the present time. The "White Goose" was the symbol under which this old tavern sailed until the year 1806, when it assumed the more poetic name of "Golden Swan," under the management of John Rettigg. Rettigg was relieved from its cares and responsibilities in 1810 by Juliana Valentine, who presided over its destinies down to the year 1819. It next passed to the control and management of James Sargeant, who kept it for a brief period, and turned it over to John Valentine and Lewis Valentine, who continued it down to 1825. It was next kept for two years by John Hays. In 1827 it was kept by Isaac Sumny, under the sign of the "Washington Hall." It was kept by Samuel Donley and various other persons, down to about the year 1840, when as before stated, it passed to the control of Joseph Hallam. In Hallam's time it was a popular wagon stand, and did a large business. Hallam was a man below the medium size, a little stooped, and of quiet demeanor. He had a good wagon yard, and catered to the tastes of old wagoners in an agreeable manner. The happiest moments of Amos Waltz were those in which he inserted the gear pole between the spokes of the hind wheel of a road wagon, as it stood on Hallam's yard, and afterward took a drink with the jolly wagoners in Hallam's old bar-room. In 1847 or 1848 the present Valentine House was built, and kept for many years thereafter by Maj. Geo. T. Hammond. It was also kept a while by ex-Sheriff Andrew Bruce, afterward by ex-Sheriff Hugh Keys, and later and until a recent date by William F. Dickey, and is now called the "Allison House."

In 1791 Michael Kuntz kept a tavern where Vowell's drug store stands. This house was kept in 1797 by John Scott, under the sign of the "Spread Eagle." I. Neilson, John Fisher, Samuel McMillen, and John Ferguson, were all old tavern keepers of Washington.

Joseph Huston kept the "Buck Tavern" as early as 1796. This is a stone house on the east side of Main street, below Maiden. Huston kept this house until 1812, and died in it. His widow succeeded him for a brief period, and leased the house to James Sargeant, who kept it until 1815, when Mrs. Huston again went in, and kept it until 1820. She afterward re-married, lost her second husband, and was keeping this house in 1838 as Elizabeth Fleming, and it was continued after that date by her son, William B. Huston. The old Buck is still standing, one of the landmarks of the town.

In 1797 James Workman kept a tavern, the site of which is not known. He continued until 1813, when he went to farming. After three years' experience in farming he returned to town, and opened a tavern under the sign of "Gen. Andrew Jackson." This old tavern stood on the west side of Main street, below the "Globe Inn." It was subsequently kept by Maj. James Dunlap of the old Mt. Vernon House, east of Pancake.

From 1798 to 1806 Dr. John J. Lemoyne kept a tavern on the south side of Main street, where an old road came down over Gallows Hill. This house was afterward kept by Jacob Good, and continued for a number of years by his widow.

The "Globe Inn" was one of the most famous old taverns in Washington. It was located on the west side of Main street, at the corner of Strawberry alley. This house was opened as a tavern in 1797, and in the next year passed to the hands of David Morris, and was kept by him, continuously, until his death in 1834. General La-Fayette was entertained at this house in 1825, and it was a favorite stopping place of Henry Clay, and many other statesmen and heroes of the olden time. This old tavern was a frame building, and remained standing until 1891. Rev. William P. Alrich, an old and popular professor of mathematics in Washington college, married a daughter of David Morris.

One Fox kept a tavern, at an early period, in a house that stood on the east side of Main street, where the Morgan Block now stands.

The "Cross Keys" was a popular tavern of the olden time. It stood on the southeast corner of Main and Wheeling streets, opposite the Valentine House. It was opened in 1801 by James McCamant, who kept it until his death, which occurred in 1813. Tradition has it that he died from the effects of a bite by a mad wolf. His widow continued it for about two years, when she quit it to take charge of the "General Washington House," nearly opposite the court house. She returned, however, after a time to the "Cross Keys," and was keeping that house as late as 1831. In the year last named she caused to be inserted in a town paper a notice that she furnished dinner and horse feed for twenty-five cents, and boarding and lodging for jurors and others attending court for two dollars a week. The "Cross Keys" was kept afterward at different dates by James Sargeant, Charles Rettig, John Bradfield, William Blakely and Otho Hartzell. It closed as a tavern previous to 1844. James McCamant, the first proprietor of the "Cross Keys" tavern, was the father-in-law of Joseph Henderson, esq., a prominent and popular old lawyer of Washington.

Christian Keiffer kept a tavern in 1805 at the sign of "Washington." Keiffer's career as a tavern keeper must have been a brief and an uninteresting one, since old inhabitants are unable to locate his house, although it bore a name that should and does survive, in every other form except in its application to Keiffer's old tavern.

John Kirk kept a tavern about the beginning of the present century in a house that stood on Wheeling street, west of Main. This house was painted red and penciled to imitate brick. After Kirk left it William Wilson became its proprietor. He was known as "Center Billy." He did not find tavern keeping sufficiently profitable, and quitting the business, turned his attention to blacksmithing and wagon making. The old name of Wheeling street was "Belle," and the present name was given it by the old stage drivers and wagoners, because it intersected the old road leading to Wheeling.

The "Indian Queen" was an old and well remembered tavern on Main street, opposite the court house. It was opened in 1808 by John McCluny. In 1815 it changed its location and solicited public patronage on Main street, above Chestnut, where Justice Donehoe's residence now is, under the auspices of its old founder, John McCluny aforesaid. In its new location it became the headquarters of the Jackson Democracy. This house was kept by Thomas Officer, and was known as the "Green Tree," before McCluny placed it under the shield of the "Indian Queen." It was afterward occupied by John Johnson, who kept it for a number of years, and it ceased to do business as a tavern during his occupancy.

About the year 1820 John Manuel kept a tavern in a white frame house on the west side of Main street, immediately below the present depot of the Baltimore & Ohio railroad.

There was an old tavern in Washington at an early day kept by Jacob Moler, and known as "The Mermaid." It was located on the

13

south side of West Wheeling street, and on the lot now owned by Charles Driehorst. It was the headquarters of the Hibernians, and while it did not aspire to rival the "Globe" or the "Rising Sun," it was not lacking in patronage. It does not appear to have been continued as a tavern after the time of Moler.

The "Rising Sun," a leading tavern in its day, occupied a lot near the corner of Main and Chestnut streets, almost directly opposite the house subsequently known as "The Mansion." The first proprietor of the "Rising Sun" was James Garrett, and he remained in charge until 1822. He was active in his business, and accustomed to say, "Walk in, walk in, gentlemen; I keep a decent house, and provide sweetened bitters." James Briceland kept this house for one year, after which he turned it back to Garrett, who continued to keep it until it passed to the hands of John N. Dagg, who kept it until he purchased the "Mansion House," on the opposite corner. It is said that one hundred teams have been seen standing around the "Rising Sun" in a single night. Briceland went down to the lower end of town and took charge of the house subsequently known as "The National." In 1823 while Dagg was keeping the "Rising Sun," a townsman and an old wagoner had an altercation in the bar-room, and Dagg pitched them both out into the street. In the descent the wagoner's head struck the curb-stone, fatally injuring him. Mr. Dagg was prosecuted and arraigned for murder in consequence, but acquitted by the jury on the ground that the homicide was more the result of accident, than any intention to kill. During the brief term of Mr. Briceland at the "Rising Sun" he had as guests on one occasion, Gen. Andrew Jackson, family and suite. The distinguished party were *en route* to Washington City, and upon departing from the "Rising Sun" were honored by an escort of citizens of Washington as far east as Hillsboro.

In 1821 Enoch Miller opened a tavern in a large brick house at the west end of town, nearly opposite the old Methodist church, which stood on Chestnut street, a little below Franklin. He called his house the "General Brown," and it was well patronized. Richard Donaldson kept this house after Miller's time. Upon quitting the "General Brown" Enoch Miller opened the "Fountain Inn," a brick building nearly opposite and a few doors east of the "General Brown," on Chestnut street, and he was succeeded in this house in 1825 by George Ringland. William P. Byles was an old proprietor of this house also.

William J. Brown, called "Old Billy," kept a tavern as early as 1832, and for many years thereafter, on the east side of Main street near the center of town. It was a frame building and had a fair paying custom. It was known for a time as the "Farmers' Inn," and later as the "Black Bear." The old proprietor was a quaint character, and much pestered by the boys of the town. With all his troubles and tribulations he managed to lay aside a sufficiency of worldly goods to protect himself against the requirements of a rainy day.

S. B. HAYS.

And there was old "Jimmy Brown," another odd character, not a relation of "Billy." Jimmy was an Irishman, and knew how to make and keep money. He kept a tavern for many years in a white frame house opposite the court house, and near the "Fulton." He called his house "The Franklin." His savings were sufficient to warrant him in tearing down his old house and erecting in its stead a fine new brick structure, which he did. After building his new house he married a wife, and was warmly congratulated by his numerous friends. With the assistance of his wife he continued to entertain the public until his death, leaving the cares and anxieties of his business to his bereaved widow, who soon after remarried and retired to private life. The house is now used for mercantile purposes, one of the best locations in town. Jimmy Brown, when occupying his old house, was accustomed to say to his friends: "I have some nice *fesh*, come away to the cellar with me, and see my *fesh*." He had no license then.

The Mansion House was a leading tavern in Washington from the time it commenced business until it was destroyed by fire, which occurred after the National Road ceased to be a great thoroughfare. It was located on the northeast corner of Main and Chestnut streets. Before the "Mansion House" was built an old red frame house stood on this corner, which was kept as a tavern by a man whose surname was Scott. John N. Dagg bought this property prior to his withdrawal from the "Rising Sun," on the opposite corner, and commenced to improve it. The outcome of his enterprise was the erection of a large brick building, known as the Mansion House, with extensive sheds and stables in the rear. About the year 1834 Mr. Dagg leased the premises to John Irons, who conducted the house for a period of two years, after which Mr. Dagg returned as landlord, and continued to keep it down to the year 1844, or thereabout, when he leased it to S. B. and C. Hayes, who conducted it for a brief period, and were succeeded by Bryson and Shirls, subsequently of the St. Charles Hotel, Pittsburgh. The Good Intent line of stages gave its patronage to the "American," when that house was kept by the Messrs. Hayes, and to the "Greene House," when it was kept by Daniel Brown. Thereafter the headquarters of that line were at the Mansion House, and it was headquarters for the Pilot line when the Good Intent stopped at the "American." The Mansion House had a large country trade, as well as that derived from the National Road. The old bar room was of immense size, and the old proprietor, John N. Dagg, was one of the largest men on the road. He was not fat, but tall, and widely proportioned. He provided for his country guests a large upright boot jack, with side bars, which acted as levers, designed to steady the toe in the operation of drawing off a boot. Half cut, cheap leather slippers were also provided, and upon pulling their boots, guests put on these slippers, and in the mornings, piles of boots, nicely polished, were placed in a corner of the bar room, to await the return of their owners from the slumbers of the night. It was not an uncommon thing to see scores of country people sitting about in the big bar room after supper, talking over the events of the day, all wearing the slippers referred to, preparatory to going to rest for the night, at the early bed time of that happy period.   James K. Polk, wife and suite, stopped at the Mansion House on the inaugural trip in 1845. The "Examiner," under date of February 15, 1845, gave the following account of the reception of the distinguished party: "President Polk arrived in our borough on Monday evening last, about 5 o'clock, escorted by quite a respectable number of our citizens.   The President was accompanied by his lady, J. Knox Walker, his private secretary, and Master Marshall Polk, comprising the President's family; also Colonel Butler, of Kentucky, Judge Hubbard, of Alabama, and Messrs. T. K. Stevenson, J. G. Harris and J. N. Esselman.   The arrival of the President having been sooner than was anticipated, and intelligence of the same having reached us on Sabbath last, the arrangements on the part of our citizens were not so complete or extensive as they would have been under other and more favorable circumstances.   Upon the arrival of the President at the Mansion House he was addressed by Dr. Wishart, as chairman of the committee of reception, in a spirited and appropriate manner, to which the President responded, to the evident gratification of the large assembly of persons who were present.   In the course of his remarks Colonel Polk alluded to the unbounded feeling of gratitude which filled his bosom for the distinguished partiality which had been extended toward him by his fellow citizens; to the great responsibility which that partiality had devolved upon him; to his implicit confidence in that power which controls the destinies of individuals as well as nations; to his determination to act for the best interests of our beloved country, and the vital importance of freedom of opinion and contrariety of sentiment among a Republican people. In concluding his remarks, the President expressed a strong desire to interchange congratulations with as many of our citizens, of all parties, as time and circumstances would permit.   After the formal reception was completed the President was conducted into the Mansion House, and during the evening was waited upon by many hundreds of our citizens, from town and country, without party distinction.   Many of the ladies of our borough, with the Principal, assistant teachers and young ladies of our Female Seminary, also, called upon Mrs. Polk, whose plain, dignified and fascinating deportment and intelligent conversation rendered her company exceedingly pleasant. Mrs. Polk has certainly not been too highly complimented, by the many notices which have been bestowed upon her, as a lady most admirably suited to the discharge of the peculiar duties which await her as the wife of the President-elect.   On Tuesday morning at 9 o'clock the President and suite left our borough, in good health and spirits, for Uniontown, at which place they remained over night."

The Fulton House was a prominent house of entertainment in Washington for many years. It is located on the corner of Main and

GEORGE T. HAMMOND.

Beau streets, nearly opposite the court house. John Purviance kept a tavern on the Fulton House site from 1790 to 1805, and three years thereafter went to Claysville, as stated elsewhere in these pages. Richard Donaldson succeeded Purviance in this old house. John Fleming kept a tavern on this corner in 1820, called "The Philadelphia and Kentucky Inn." In January, 1821, a fire occurred in this house, on occasion of the marriage of a daughter of Mr. Fleming, which partially destroyed the building, and saddest of all, burnt to death one of the old proprietor's daughters. After the present large brick building was erected on this corner, it was called "The American House," and was kept by S. B. and C. Hayes previous to 1840, and after them by John Huey. In 1846 or 1847 it was leased by Henry Fulton, who came from Westmoreland county, Pennsylvania, and under his management it took the name of the "Fulton House," which it retained, and under which it became widely and favorably known, until it was given the absurd name of "Hotel Maine." The Fulton House was admirably conducted and extensively patronized.

The National House was the headquarters of the Stockton line of stages. It is located on the northwest corner of Main and Maiden streets. The firm name of the Stockton line of stages was "The National Road Stage Company," and it has been seen that this line bestowed its favor upon public houses bearing the name "National." In 1821 Samuel Dennison, who came from Greensburg, Pennsylvania, kept an old tavern that stood on the site of the "National House." It was then known as "The Travelers' Inn and Stage Office." It was subsequently enlarged and improved, and in 1823 passed to the control of James Briceland, under the name of the "National House." Its next occupant was John Irons, who was succeeded by James Searight, in 1836, and he in turn by Daniel Valentine, George T. Hammond, Edward Lane, Adam C. Morrow and Elliot Seaburn. It was an elegant eating house in the days of staging, and at its best under the management of Hammond and Lane, respectively. It is now called the "Auld House," and, as in many other instances, its old prestige departed with its old name. James Searight went from the "National House" to Zanesville, Ohio, and kept a tavern there for a short time, and returning to Washington, leased the "Greene House," which was managed by his son, William. These Searights were of a Cumberland, Maryland, family.

As early as 1815 Richard Donaldson kept a tavern on Maiden street, opposite the Female Seminary. This old house was surrounded by spacious grounds, and there was a ball alley in the rear of it, which afforded means of exercise and amusement for the town boys of the olden time. James Workman succeeded Donaldson in this old tavern, and he, in 1830, was succeeded by Samuel Surratt, father of James F. Surratt, the popular postmaster of Steubenville, Ohio. Major William Paull kept this house previous to 1840, and for a time thereafter, and at the close of his term it was purchased by the trustees of the Female Seminary, since which time it has formed a portion of the real estate belonging to that institution. Major Paull came to this house from the old stone house on Winding Ridge, and kept it as a wagon stand. It had good facilities for the accommodation of wagoners, by reason of the spacious grounds before mentioned, and these, in connection with the fact that Major Paull was an experienced tavern keeper of the road, attracted a large and profitable patronage.

The "Greene House," a popular tavern, was located on the east side of Main street, south of the Mansion House, and on a lot formerly owned by John L. Gow, esq. It was kept in 1842 by William Searight, before mentioned, who was succeeded by S. B. and C. Hayes, whose occupancy was brief, and about 1846 it came under the control of Daniel Brown, one of the most competent landlords of his day and generation. During Brown's incumbency it had the patronage of the Good Intent Stage company. Brown's bar-keeper was Benjamin White, who wore his hair long and had a scar on his face. His employer always addressed him as "Benny," and confided in his integrity to the fullest extent, and in very truth "Benny" was entirely worthy of his employer's confidence. Whither this quaint old bar-keeper drifted, when the eclipse came over the sunshine of the road, is not known, but his name deserves to be perpetuated in history.

Most of the facts contained in this chapter rest on authority of Crumrine's history of Washington county, Pennsylvania.

THE RANKIN HOUSE.

CHAPTER XXXIX.

After passing Washington the ancient little village of Rankintown is reached. It is situated a short distance over the top of the hill leading up from Catfish, and a little over a mile from Washington. Here a tavern was kept in early times by one Spalding, who seems to have failed in impressing his name on the locality. His successor was John Rankin, who dying, left his name behind him. His house was a large frame building on the south side of the road, with the customary wagon yard attached. While this old tavern did a large wagoner's trade, its agreeable old host ministered largely to the wants of the traveling public without distinction. As before intimated wagoners as a rule preferred country taverns, and this is probably the reason so many of them halted at Rankin's rather than proceeding on to Washington, going east, where a number of good taverns were located, but being in a large town, more or less under the ban of "tony places." John Rankin owned the old tavern stand at Rankintown, and after conducting it for many years during the flourishing era of the road, to use a common phrase of the road, "died with the harness on." His widow continued to keep tavern at the old stand until about the year 1847, when growing old and tired of the cares and responsibilities of tavern keeping, concluded to retire to private life, and leased the premises to a Mr. Johnson, who conducted the house down to the fifties, when he was succeeded by Andrew McDonald, who remained in charge until the activities of the road ceased. The private residence of the late Hon. William Montgomery was for a number of years on the roadside near the old Rankin tavern. He was an illustrious old pike boy and championed the glories of the road on many an occasion. Rankintown is now an incorporated borough, under the name and style of West Washington, but the glories of the old pike all rest and abide behind the present municipality.

In 1844 and subsequent to that date, Alpheus Murphy, a wagon-maker, lived and operated a shop near the old Rankin tavern. He gained a local notoriety for proclaiming in a loud voice in season and out of season, his sentiments on current topics, and especially polit-ical issues. He was a man of great physical strength, and a skillful workman. He had no scruples against taking an occasional glass of the pure whisky that abounded on the road in his day, and was a fre-quent visitor to Washington. Prompted possibly by the influence of the active element mentioned, he was accustomed to ascend the cupola of the Washington court house and from the balustrade near its summit give vent to his feelings, mainly of a Democratic tendency, in stentorian tones that startled the whole community. Notwith-standing the boisterous fits that marked and may have marred his life, he passed quietly away from the scenes of earth, and will be long and kindly remembered by those who knew him.

Two miles west of Rankintown Robert Smith kept a tavern as early as the year 1818. At this point the National Road crossed an ancient roadway leading from Washington to Wheeling, and Robert Smith kept a tavern here on the old road. It was a frame house on the south side of the road, and in after years became the homestead and private residence of Jacob Weirich, who also did its possessor.

Less than a mile west of Smith's John Coulson kept a tavern as early as 1820, and probably before that date. His house was a frame building, on the south side of the road. The old building was torn down many years ago, and a brick structure erected in its place. Coulson, the old proprietor, has been dead fifty years, and at his death his tavern was closed, and not again re-opened as a public house. The old wagoners and stage drivers who were familiar with Coulson's tavern long since passed to other scenes, along with its old proprietor.

About one mile west of the old Coulson House the well remem-bered and popular wagon stand of John Miller is reached. Miller moved to this point in 1836 from a stand two miles west of Pratt's Hollow, and east of Cumberland, as before stated. The Miller house here is a large brick building, with all the necessary outbuildings for a tavern, and a good wagon yard. It is situate on the north side of the road. To gain the wagon yard going west, old wagoners as-cended a steep grade, but on the other side the way was level. Miller had a good custom at his tavern east of Cumberland, and his old friends followed him to his new location. He had long experience as a tavern keeper, and furnished satisfactory entertainment to the traveling public. Previous to 1836 Levi Wilson kept this house, and entertained the first crop of wagoners on the road, and tradition at-tributes to him a good fame as a tavern keeper. Miller died in this house. A son of Levi Wilson married a daughter of John Miller, and since the death of the latter has been occupying this old tavern-stand as a private residence.

At the foot of the hill west of Miller's, and on the north side of the road, is the old Bedillion tavern. This house was kept as early

THE JOHN MILLER HOUSE.

as 1830 by one Scott, and as late as 1848 by Christly Wolf, and later by George Boyd, but owing to a usage, in some instances difficult to account for, it is better known as Bedillion's, especially among old wagoners, than by any other name. Bedillion was a German, and his first name was Abraham, and he probably possessed German traits and practices which made an impression on old wagoners not to be forgotten. He kept this house in 1836. Wolf also was of German origin, but his manners and methods were of the American type. He was a man of prominence in his neighborhood, and wielded considerable local influence, and was likewise a member of the firm of Buck, Lyon and Wolf, contractors, before mentioned. The old Bedillion tavern is a large frame building, with a high porch in front. George Boyd took charge of this house in the early fifties. He exchanged the shoe business in Washington for what he no doubt considered the more profitable pursuit of tavern keeping on the old pike. In this he seems to have been disappointed. His career as a tavern keeper was not successful, and there were two reasons for it. First, he began too late, and second, he was not a pike boy, and therefore not familiar with the wants and ways of the road.

On the north side of the road, about one mile west of the S Bridge, and as far back in the past as seventy years, one Andrew Caldwell (not a relative of James, hereinafter mentioned), kept a small wooden tavern and entertained primitive travelers and neighborhood callers in primitive style. An old blacksmith, bearing the surname McSwiggin, was found dead near this old tavern, and there was an undercurrent of suspicion in the neighborhood that Andrew Caldwell, aforesaid, had, in some manner and for some purpose, taken the old blacksmith's life. However, no prosecution was instituted, and, in fact, no legal investigation made as to the cause of the mysterious death; and it is to be hoped, for the reputation of the early pike boys, that the suspicions whispered against the old tavern keeper were groundless.

The next noted old tavern on the westward march is Mrs. Caldwell's, seven miles from Washington. Before reaching Mrs. Caldwell's, the celebrated S Bridge is passed. This bridge takes its name from its shape, which resembles the letter S. It is a large stone bridge over a branch of Buffalo creek. Near this bridge a county road leads to Taylorstown, celebrated in recent years for its oil developments, and in this vicinity reside James Noble and John Thompson, two old wagoners of the road, mentioned in a previous chapter. There is a postoffice here called "S Bridge," which affords postal facilities for a rich and populous neighborhood. In early times there was a tavern at the eastern end of the S Bridge, and one at its western end. These old taverns accommodated the public in their day, but their facilities were limited, and they ceased to entertain strangers and travelers previous to 1840. Caldwell's is the tavern mentioned by Mr. Blaine, in the opening chapter of this volume on old taverns. James Caldwell owned and conducted this old tavern from the time the road was opened up for travel, or very soon thereafter, until the

13a

year 1838, when he died, and his widow, Hester Caldwell, kept it going as a tavern from that date until 1873, so that she was one of the oldest tavern keepers of the road. The house is a large and handsome structure, near the summit of a long hill, and on the south side of the road. It is, at the present time, occupied by J. A. Gordon, who entertains the public, and as of old, the house is a favorite resort of pleasure seeking parties.

A half a mile west from Caldwell's, the widow Brownlee kept a tavern in the early history of the road. Her house was a frame building on the south side of the road. Robert Hall afterwards kept this house, and upon his retirement it ceased to do business as a tavern.

On the top of the hill west of Mrs. Brownlee's the widow McClelland kept a tavern sixty years ago. She was not of the famous tavern keeping family of McClelland, of Uniontown. This widow McClelland was keeping tavern at the point mentioned before the widow McClelland of the McClelland House in Uniontown was born. The Baltimore & Ohio railroad at this day passes through a tunnel near the old tavern of widow McClelland.

Claysville is next reached. It is stated in Crumrine's history of Washington county, that John Purviance was the first tavern keeper in Claysville, and that he was the founder of the town. "When it became certain," says Crumrine, "that the National Road would pass through the place, Purviance caused the following notice to be inserted in the Washington *Reporter:*

"The subscriber having laid off a number of building lots in the new town of Claysville, will offer the same at public sale on the premises, on Thursday, the 8th day of March, next. Claysville is distant ten miles from Washington, westward, and about eighteen east of Wheeling, and six from Alexandria. The great NATIONAL ROAD from Cumberland to Wheeling as located by Col. Williams and confirmed by the President, and now rapidly progressing towards its completion, passes directly through the town.

Washington, April 21, 1817.   JOHN PURVIANCE."

It goes without saying that this town was named in honor of Henry Clay, the unrivaled champion of the road. As at other towns mentioned, the road forms the main street of Claysville. In 1821 James Sargent kept a tavern in Claysville, at the sign of the Black Horse. He moved to Claysville from Washington, and the house he kept in Claysville was a brick building, occupied formerly by John Porter. Claysville was a stage station, as before stated. Bazil Brown kept a tavern in Claysville as early as 1836, and probably before that date. He kept a wagon stand and had a large patronage. Some time during the forties, Dan Rice, after his circus stranded, was exhibiting a "learned pig" to the people of Claysville, and in Bazil Brown's tavern. On the night of the entertainment Brown lost an overcoat, and charged Dan Rice with stealing it, and had him sent up to Washing-

THE "S" BRIDGE.

ton jail to await trial. Dan employed Seth T. Hurd to defend him, and was acquitted. Soon after Dan appeared in Claysville with a new circus, and sang an original song in the ring intended to embody his recollections of the overcoat escapade, and to lampoon Brown for prosecuting him. The song was smooth, as all Dan's were, and the thrusts at Brown sarcastic and severe, and much enjoyed by the local hearers. Despite this unfortunate occurrence Bazil Brown was a popular landlord, and kept a good house. The old circus man is still living, and has probably forgotten and forgiven the old tavern keeper for accusing him of felony, but the old tavern keeper long since passed beyond the dark waters, and entered upon the realities of another and unknown realm. James Dennison kept a tavern in Claysville as early as 1840. He subsequently kept at Beallsville and at Hopwood as before stated. He was an old wagoner and kept a wagon stand, but had the patronage of one of the stage lines in Claysville, as well as a wagon custom. Old wagoners felt themselves entirely at home at Dennison's tavern, and thoroughly enjoyed his agreeable entertainment. David Bell, John Walker, James Kelley, Stephen Conkling and John McIlree were all old tavern keepers at Claysville, and kept stage houses.

There was also a Watkins who kept tavern in Claysville. The house he kept was destroyed by fire previous to 1850. It had the patronage of the Good Intent stage line. David Bell was an old stage driver. His house in Claysville was a brick building on the south side, diagonally opposite the old Walker House. He subsequently kept the Fulton House in Washington in 1862 and 1863. The Walker House was a frame building, on the north side. Walker subsequently located at Wheeling and kept a tavern there. Conkling kept the Walker House. McIlree kept the Brown House. Kelley also kept the Walker House, and it was in this house, and in Kelley's time, that Jim Burr, the noted stage driver, "knocked out" the Cincinnati buffer, before mentioned. The Stockton line of coaches stopped at the old Brown House, and the Good Intent line at the Walker and Watkins Houses.

The widow Calahan kept a tavern in Claysville prior to 1840. Jonathan D. Leet married her daughter. Leet was a pike boy of no little distinction in his day. His discernment and good taste in wedding the fair daughter of an old tavern keeper were not the only proofs of his wit and worth. He was a lawyer of ability, a major of militia, postmaster of Washington during the presidency of President Polk, and member of the Legislature for Washington county. A large man with prominent features, and somewhat awkward in manner, he was the personification of Mars, when arrayed in the elaborate uniform of the old militia system. The great gilt rolls of the ponderous epaulette, and the immense three cornered and sharp pointed chapeau produced a feeling of awe among all beholders, and struck terror to the hearts of young folks. Major Leet being a lawyer was Judge Advocate at all courts martial during the time he was in commission. These courts were frequently held in Washington, and their members were required to sit, hear and determine in full uniform. On such occasions Major Leet was "the observed of all observers," and elicited the admiration of his many friends. There was an old silversmith in Washington by the name of Galt, a man of acute intelligence, given to the amusing side of life, and a close friend of the philosopher Dr. Creigh, of the same place. These old worthies were warm friends of Major Leet, and their enthusiasm knew no bounds in expressing delight over the triumphs of the Major, in conducting these courts martial. In 1848, when Major Leet was postmaster, he was an ardent advocate of the election of General Cass to the presidency, and accustomed to allude with emphasis to the fact that his favorite was "a brave old volunteer." His candidate, however, was defeated, and under the rule of partisanship, he was superseded in the postoffice by a friend of the victorious columns. Subsequently he was elected to the Legislature, and after serving his term did not return to live among his constituents. He was essentially a pike boy, devoted to the memories of the road, and fond of its associations, yet he died in a strange land, and his is not the only instance wherein a seat in the Legislature has led a man from the gentle paths and innocent pastimes of his early days.

Three miles west from Claysville, at the foot of a long hill, the romantic, not to say classic spot of Coon Island is reached. Here was an old tavern stand, for many years kept by John Canode previous to 1840. It was on the north side of the road, and a wagon stand. The stages stopped here also at times, and it was a regular relay for the express wagons. After Canode's time the tavern here was kept by John Brotherton and sons. It was a prominent point during the flourishing era of the road. As late as 1853 a Mr. Reed kept the old tavern at Coon Island. The old stage and wagon lines, however, were withdrawn previous to that date, and some small local lines substituted, as if to prevent an abrupt termination to the high prosperity which the road enjoyed for so long a period. The origin of the name Coon Island is presumably unascertainable, else Crumrine in his history of Washington county would have given it, as the locality is within the limits of that county. That coons existed and flourished in the neighborhood from time immemorial, there is scarcely a doubt, but an island has never been witnessed there since the subsidence of the great flood in Noah's time. The point is now a station on the Baltimore & Ohio railroad, and the name is changed to Vienna. The old name is more appropriate, albeit the island is absent. It is more appropriate, because it is familiar to the people, but it seems to be the inevitable doom of many old familiar names to fall before the advance of modern fancies. Think of an old wagoner going back to Coon Island after an absence of half a century, to find himself "a mere looker on in Vienna!" Shades of the old pike, hide this ruthless and senseless innovation from the eyes of mankind.

DAVID BELL.

Two miles west from Coon Island and a short distance beyond the site of the old Catholic church, an old tavern was kept in early days by one Rogers, and subsequently by Jacob and Michael Dougherty. It was a frame house, on the north side of the road. A good water trough was maintained at this old stand, and travelers halted here for water. In 1830 this old tavern was kept by Jacob Jones, the father of the distinguished iron manufacturer and politician, B. F. Jones, of Pittsburg. The old church mentioned, which will be remembered by all who are familiar with this section of the road, was taken down a few years ago, and rebuilt at Claysville, a more central point for the parishioners. Before reaching Dougherty's another old round toll house is passed, the last one on the road in Pennsylvania. Here William McCleary collected the tolls for many years.

A few hundred yards further west the old and popular tavern of John Valentine is reached. It is a frame house, on the north side of the road, large and commodious, and was a favorite resort of wagoners. Valentine kept this tavern a great many years. If he had a predecessor or a successor in this house, his name is totally eclipsed by that of John Valentine. He possessed the talent for tavern keeping in a rare degree, and was a brother of Daniel Valentine, the old and popular tavern keeper of Washington, and of Charles Valentine, an old wagoner of that place.

CHAPTER XL.

Crumrine's history of Washington county states that West Alexander was first laid out in 1796 by Robert Humphreys, that most of the lots were subsequently acquired by Charles D. Hass, who in the year 1817 sold them by public outcry; that the National Road at the last mentioned date was in process of construction, and had been actually opened for travel from Cumberland to the Big Crossings, and it was believed that all the towns upon its route would become places of prosperity and importance; that the town of West Alexander was destroyed by fire on May 4, 1831, but slowly recovered from the disaster, and in the succeeding twenty years became a thriving village, by reason of the prosperity of the great thoroughfare on which it was located. A house called the "American Eagle" was the first tavern in West Alexander, established by Duncan Morrison in 1796, and kept by him for a number of years. Subsequent tavern keepers in West Alexander were Charles Mayes, Zebulon Warner, John Gooding, John Woodburn, William McCall, Solomon Cook, James Sargent, Charles Hallam, Mary Warner, James Bell, Silver Gilfillan, Samuel Beamer, James Matthers, John Irons, Moses Thornburg, Samuel Doak, Joseph Lawson, Joseph Dowdal, William F. Gordon, William McCutcheon, and perhaps others. Joseph Lawson was probably the best known of all these old tavern keepers. He kept a wagon stand for a long time during the prosperous era of the road, and was extensively patronized. He had been an old wagoner himself, and knew the secret of agreeably entertaining old wagoners. He is mentioned in a previous chapter as a "fancy wagoner" of the road. His tavern in West Alexander was a large and commodious frame building at the western end of the town, on the south side of the road, with a large and well arranged wagon yard attached. He owned the property, and died in possession. Beside being a successful wagoner and tavern keeper, Joseph Lawson was a staunch citizen, a man of influence and

JOSEPH F. MAYES.

(OLD JUSTICE OF THE PEACE.)

highly esteemed. He was at one time, for a brief period, Superintendent of the road from Brownsville to the Virginia line.

There was, during the prosperous era of the road, an academy at West Alexander under the management of the Rev. Dr. John McCluskey, where many boys were trained for entrance to Washington college. Dr. McCluskey was an eminent scholar, an able preacher, a successful educator and a worthy man in all the walks of life. He devoted a long and laborious life here, to gain a better one hereafter, and let us hope he is now realizing its enjoyment. West Alexander is also noted as a rival of the celebrated Gretna Green, of Scotland, by reason of the many clandestine marriages which have taken place there. Joseph F. Mayes, an old justice of the peace of the place, married nineteen hundred and eighteen couples from 1862 to 1881, more than nine-tenths of whom were elopers. It is estimated that from 1835 to 1885, the date of the enactment of the Pennsylvania marriage license law, over five thousand eloping couples were married in West Alexander.

One mile distant from West Alexander on the north side of the road, Abram Carr kept a tavern as early as 1836. It was a frame building, and a wagon stand. After Carr this old tavern was kept by Silver Gilfillan, before mentioned in the list of tavern keepers at West Alexander. Carr and Gilfillan well knew the ways of the road, and were competent men in their line. Old wagoners were accustomed to lay aside their coin, to pay bills at Gilfillan's tavern, under a belief that he coveted silver because of his Christian name. This was the first tavern located in Old Virginia on the westward march, being less than a mile from the Pennsylvania State line.

Two miles further west a large frame tavern on the north side of the road, was kept by Mrs. Sarah Beck as early as 1832. It was a station for the Stockton line of coaches. Mrs. Beck was succeeded in this house by Samuel Knode, who retained the good will and patronage extended to his predecessor. Mrs. Beck was the widow of James Beck, of the old bridge building firm of Kinkead, Beck & Evans, frequently mentioned in these pages. Her son, William G. Beck, still living in Fairfield, Iowa, was the hero of the exciting race between two coaches from Cumberland to Piney Grove, mentioned in a previous chapter. James Beck, the husband of Sarah Beck, died in Wheeling in 1829, while keeping a tavern in that place. His widow was of a heroic mold, and resolved to carry on the battle of life on her own account, and continued in the business of tavern keeping. She kept tavern at various points, and finally about the year 1847 bade a last adieu to the scenes of the road, amid which she had been reared, and emigrated to the then far west. Leasing a house in Springfield, Illinois, she resumed the business of tavern keeping. While a member of the Illinois Legislature, Abraham Lincoln was a boarder in Mrs. Beck's house, and Robert T. Lincoln, the late United States minister at London, was born under her roof. Thus an old tavern keeper of the National Road was closely associated with, and enjoyed the confidence of, one of the most illustrious personages of his time or of any time.

A short distance, less than a mile further west, the widow Rhodes kept a popular wagon stand as early as 1830. Another widow, and no exception to the rule, before stated. Her house was a frame building, on the south side of the road, and a busy, bustling hostelry. Abram Beagle, an old wagoner, became the husband of the widow Rhodes, as elsewhere in these pages stated, and relieved her of many of the active cares of tavern keeping, until his death, which occurred in this house, leaving his wife a second time a widow, and she continued the business of tavern keeping as the widow Beagle, with her usual success. Abram Beagle was likewise, and before he married Mrs. Rhodes, a contractor on the road. His work was near the Little Crossings.

The next old tavern on the west, and a short distance from the widow Rhodes' house, was kept as early as 1830 by John White. It was a frame house on the north side of the road. Mrs. Beck, before mentioned, subsequently bought this property, improved it in many details, and especially by the erection of a substantial new stable, with a capacity for sheltering one hundred horses. She conducted this tavern in 1833, and kept the stock and boarded the drivers and other employes of the Stockton line of coaches. She was a favorite of that line, and patronized by it at all points of the road where she kept a tavern, except at the Greene House in Washington, where she had the favor and patronage of the Good Intent line. The old White stand was kept by the widow Miller and her son, after Mrs. Beck left it, and they were succeeded by Peter Perkins, and he in turn by John Brotherton.

One mile further west Isaac Jones kept a tavern as early as 1835, and probably before that date. His house was a frame building on the north side of the road. He was not active in soliciting patronage, and after a brief and not very successful career as a tavern keeper, closed his house to the public and continued to occupy it as a private residence, and it was never thereafter opened as a tavern.

Roney's Point is next reached, a stage station ten miles from Wheeling. The original owner of the land here was Roney, and its peculiar conformation, a high ridge ending in a point on the south side of the road, gave it the name of Roney's Point. It is a familiar name, and was a lively place during the palmy days of the road. On the north side of the road, at Roney's Point, a large stone tavern was kept by one Ninian Bell, prior to the year 1828. He was succeeded by James Beck, Mrs. Sarah Beck, Moses Thornburg, and Jacob Beck, in the order named. James and Jacob Beck were not relatives. The old Simms line of stages stopped at this house when it was kept by James Beck, and it was the stopping place of the Good Intent line, when kept by Jacob Beck.

One mile west of Roney's Point, on the south side, stood an old frame tavern, which, in the eventful days of the road gathered in its

MRS. SARAH BECK.

share of glory. It was kept first by John Bentley, and after him by James Kimberly. In addition to the custom it gained from the road, this house was a favorite resort of the young rural residents, male and female, of that portion of Old Virginia, and here they were accustomed to go for a night's festivity, always confining themselves within the bounds of propriety, but within those bounds enjoying themselves in a high degree. There is many a gray-haired veteran living in the vicinity now, of both sexes, whose memories revert with pleasure to the exciting and exhilarating scenes they witnessed and participated in, at John Bentley's old tavern.

One mile further west, Triadelphia is reached, a small village, and like many others, the outgrowth of the National Road. Here John D. Foster kept a tavern at an early day, and very old pike boys say it was a good one. It was a frame building on the north side of the road. The old landlord is said to have been courteous in deportment, given to hospitality, and scrupulously observant of the proprieties of life. His daughter, Mary, became the wife of C. S. Maltby, the celebrated oyster dealer of Baltimore. The first parties who shipped oysters over the road by express were Nicholas Roe, Edward Wright, and Holt and Maltby. The latter firm soon obtained entire control of the business, and made a fortune in it. Maltby died within the past two years in Connecticut, and Holt was killed in a railroad accident in Virginia in 1852. Colonel Thompson also kept a tavern in Triadelphia in an early day. His house was a frame building, on the north side. Colonel Thompson was a gentleman of the old Virginia school, and a fine type of the genial landlord. He ceased keeping this house previous to 1840, and was succeeded by William Barnes, who in turn was succeeded by Edward Lane, and Lane by Frank Lawson. This house was largely patronized by pleasure seekers from Wheeling and other places, beside doing an extensive road business, and enjoyed an excellent reputation as a hostelry.

Three miles further west the old tavern of Mrs. Gooding, another widow, is reached. The site of this old tavern is now covered by the flourishing village of Elm Grove. Mrs. Gooding had a wide fame as a hostess, and her house was crowded by patrons. It is a stone building, still standing, situate on the south side of the road. Old wagoners to this day, enthuse over the sumptuousness of the widow Gooding's table. Sleighing parties from Wheeling frequented this old tavern in the halcyon days of the road, and were handsomely entertained.

"Oh, the songs they would sing, and the tales they would spin,
As they lounged in the light of the old country inn.
But a day came at last when the stage brought no load
To the gate, as it rolled up the long, dusty road.
And lo! at the sunrise a shrill whistle blew
O'er the hills — and the old yielded place to the new —
And a merciless age with its discord and din
Made wreck, as it passed, of the pioneer inn."

Before reaching Mrs. Gooding's the Clay Monument is passed. This monument was erected by Moses Shepherd and Lydia, his wife, under an inspiration of personal admiration of the great statesman, and with a further view of commemorating his distinguished public services in behalf of the road. It is of free stone, located upon a level piece of ground about fifty feet south of the east end of a stone bridge of three arches, over Wheeling creek. At its base its circumference is twenty-four feet, towering to a height of twenty feet, and surmounted by a chiseled figure of the Goddess of Liberty, at this date bearing plain evidences of the ravages of time and storm. Originally each of the four sides of the base column revealed an elaborate inscription, but all are totally effaced now, except the one on the east side, which is as follows: "TIME will bring every amelioration and refinement, most gratifying to rational man, and the humblest flower freely plucked under the shelter of the Tree of Liberty, is more to be desired than all the trappings of royalty; 44th year of American Independence, Anno Domini, 1820." The word TIME stands out in bold relief over the other words quoted. John Aery, of Claysville, and Alexander Ramsey, of Washington, two old and well remembered stone-cutters, worked on this monument. The former did most of the carving, in which he was an expert, and the latter much of the fine chiseling. Ramsey was the father-in-law of William G. Beck, the old stage driver previously mentioned.

On a picturesque eminence, near the monument, overlooking Big Wheeling creek, stands the ancient and historic Shepherd mansion, a stone building erected in 1798, and now known as "Monument Place," the delightful and hospitable home of Maj. Alonzo Loring. In the olden time, when the National Road was the bustling highway of the Republic, the handsome and luxurious stage coaches of the period, frequently bore Henry Clay and other eminent men of his day to the Shepherd mansion, where they reveled in Old Virginia hospitality.

Near the old Shepherd mansion stands an antiquated sun dial, covered with the marks of time, and bearing on its south face this inscription:

> "The noiseless foot of TIME steals softly by,
> And ere we think of MANHOOD age draws nigh."

On the north face of this dial appear the names and the figures: "Moses and Lydia Shepherd, 1820." Col. Moses Shepherd died in 1832, and his widow subsequently married Gen. Daniel Cruger, whom she also survived many years. They are all now dead, and their mortal remains mingle with their native dust, in the cemetery attached to the "Stone Church," near Elm Grove. A handsome monument stands at their graves bearing the following inscriptions: On one side, "*Sic Transit Gloria Mundi :* Sacred to the memory of Col. Moses Shepherd, who departed this life April 29th, 1832, in the 69th year of his age." "To him the country owes a large debt of gratitude, as well for his defense of it, when a frontier settlement, as for his recent public ser-

COL. MOSES SHEPHERD.

MRS. LYDIA SHEPHERD.

vices in aiding the extension and construction of the CUMBERLAND ROAD through Virginia." The obverse side tells the story of the second husband, as follows: "*Sic Transit Gloria Mundi:* Sacred to the memory of Gen. Daniel Cruger, who died July 12th, 1843, in the 64th year of his age." A third side perpetuates the memory of the twice bereaved widow as follows: "*Sic Transit Gloria Mundi:* Lydia S. Cruger, wife of Gen. Daniel Cruger, formerly Lydia S. Boggs, first married Col. Moses Shepherd: Born Feb. 26th, 1766: Died Sept. 26th, 1867, in the 102d year of her age." High up on the granite shaft is chiseled on two sides the picture of a log cabin, and at the door appears a female figure in sitting posture, with a dog in repose at the feet, while in the back ground is seen the representation of a martial group, with branches of a palm tree overhanging the whole design.

A short distance west from widow Goodings, Samuel Carter kept a tavern as early as 1830. It was a brick house on the south side of the road, a resort for pleasure seekers from Wheeling, and a well kept house. This house was subsequently kept by William Strawn.

About one mile west of Carter's, Michael Blackburn kept a tavern in the olden time, and was well favored with custom. It was a stone house on the north side of the road.

Next comes Steenrod's, two miles out from Wheeling, a brick and stone building on the south side of the road, and a widely known old tavern. Daniel Steenrod, the old landlord, owned the property, and was a man of intelligence and much influence. His son, Lewis, represented the Wheeling district in Congress during the prosperous era of the road, and, as before stated, was one of its most zealous champions. Lewis Steenrod, a grandson of the old landlord, is at this time (1892), High Sheriff of Ohio county, West Virginia, and on November 18th of this year, executed Maier, the murderer. Daniel Steenrod kept the old tavern last mentioned as early as 1825, and probably before that date, and continued throughout the whole period of the road's great career as a national highway. He died April 27th, 1864, aged eighty years. The property still remains in the Steenrod family.

A short distance from Steenrod's, on the north side, was "Good's Bottom," now called Pleasant Valley, doubtless by reason of the frantic iconoclasm, which has lain its ruthless hands on so many old and familiar names. At Good's Bottom there was a race course in early times, and it was here, and previous to 1840, that the celebrated horse "Tariff" lost his laurels. "Tariff" was owned by Thomas Porter, a farmer and stockman of Claysville. Joseph White, the well known marble dealer of Uniontown, a native of the vicinity of Claysville, was a witness of the discomfiture of "Tariff" on the old race course at Good's Bottom.

And now, after a long journey of two hundred and sixty miles, the city of Wheeling is reached. Wheeling was the western terminus of the road, in contemplation of the Act of Congress of March 29th, 1806, given in a previous chapter. John McCortney kept the most

noted wagon stand in Wheeling. He was likewise a commission merchant, which further identified him with old wagoners, enabling him
to furnish them with back loads. His tavern was located on Main
street, running back east on Fourteenth to alley B, parallel with, and
between Main and Market, with ample grounds surrounding it for
wagons and teams to stand on. These grounds were so extensive
that they accommodated the old time circus, in addition to wagons
and teams of the road, and two distinct circuses have been known to
exhibit on them at the same time. They were not of the modern
"triple ring" order, but of the Dan Rice design. McCortney was a
man of agreeable manners, and managed his extensive business with
marked success. He died in Wheeling on December 10th, 1872, aged
seventy-nine years. He was three times married. His last wife was
the widow of William H. Stelle, one of the proprietors of the Good
Intent stage line. Martin Bugher was McCortney's bar-keeper for
many years, and is remembered by old wagoners as a rival of Wilse
Clement in hard swearing. On lower Water street, Robert Newlove
kept a wagon stand, and was well liked by old wagoners, and well
patronized by them. He was the owner of wagons and teams, which
he kept on the road, in charge of hired drivers. In 1829 Richard
Simms, the old stage proprietor, kept the United States hotel, and
was its owner. James Beck kept this house after Simms, and James
Dennison after Beck. James McCreary kept it next after Dennison,
and Mordecai Yarnell next after McCreary. The Monroe House, on
Monroe, now Tenth street, was kept in 1830 by John McLure, and
subsequently by James Matthers. The Virginia House was kept in
1830 by John Graham, and afterward by one Beltzhoover, and later
by Jacob Kline. Beltzhoover and Kline came out from Baltimore.
The United States, the Monroe and the Virginia, were stage stations.
On upper Main street, in 1830, Moses Mosier kept a tavern, and on
the same street, and at the same time, a tavern was kept by Mrs.
Beymer, widow of Captain Frederic Beymer, assisted by her son,
Samuel, who was a soldier of 1812. Capt. Frederic Beymer kept a
tavern in Wheeling as early as the year 1802, at the sign of the
Wagon, and took boarders at two piasters a week. The town council
of Wheeling met in Capt. Beymer's tavern in 1806. The house that
Widow Beymer presided over as hostess, is a brick building, on the
southwest corner of Main and Ninth streets, on a lot bordering the
river. This house is still standing, but has not been used as a tavern
for many years. Beymer's old Landing was at the foot of Ninth
street, where the National Road approached the Ohio river. In 1830
Joseph Teeters kept a wagon stand in Wheeling, below McCortney's,
and John Bradfield kept a similar stand on Water street in 1837–8.
The mysterious disappearance of a man by the name of Cooper from
the Mosier House about 1840, produced a local sensation, followed by
an accusation of foul play and a charge of murder. Cooper, in company with a friend and neighbor by the name of Long, put up together one evening at the Mosier House, and on the next morning

JOHN McCORTNEY.

Cooper was missing. The two had come in from Ohio, and were going to Washington county, Pennsylvania, where they were born and raised, to visit relatives and old friends. It appears that Cooper rose early and took an outgoing coach back to Ohio without notifying his traveling companion or any one else. A dead body was found in the river and identified as that of Cooper; and Long, after reaching his destination, was arrested for murder and lodged in the Washington jail. The Virginia authorities made no requisition for him, and he was finally discharged, and settled in Michigan. A few years afterward, Cooper was discovered in Indianapolis, sound and well.

The Forsythes of Wheeling, James H. and his son Leonard, were prominently identified with the destinies of the National Road. The commission house of James H. Forsythe & Co. was a leading establishment of its kind. James H. Forsythe, the senior member of this old firm, was noted for his energy and clear-headedness. He could converse with any number of persons, and indite a letter at the same time, without being in any wise confused. His son, Leonard, was also well known on the road. He conducted commission houses at Brownsville and Cumberland, and very often passed over the road, in the management of his business. He is now living in Texas near Austin, and feels a deep interest in the history of the road.

W. L. McNeely, of Wheeling, when a young man, had a brief experience as a wagoner. He drove several trips for Thomas Drakely, who was a merchant with stores in Baltimore and Wheeling, and is well remembered by old pike boys. McNeely "put up" at Natty Brownfield's, in Uniontown, when driving Drakely's team, a half a century and longer ago, and has never forgotten the good entertainment he enjoyed at that old tavern.

The old tavern keepers of the National Road were a remarkable body of men. In many instances they were free holders, men well posted in current affairs, and influential in their respective neighborhoods. They were honorable in their dealings, and believed that every man's word should be as good as his bond. As caterers they made no display. They had no bills of fare, printed on gilt edged paper, or fine linen, and it is doubtful if any one of them ever heard the modern word *Menu*, yet the spreads of their generous boards would almost kindle exhilaration in the heart of a misanthrope. The thought may be attributable to change of time or circumstance, or taste, or all together, but there is an unmovable conviction in the mind of the writer of these pages, that the viands of modern hotels, lack the savoriness of those of the old taverns of the National Road.

CHAPTER XLI.

*West of Wheeling — Old Stage Lines Beyond the Ohio River — William Neil —
Gen. N. P. Talmadge — Stage Stations — Old Taverns and Tavern Keepers—
Rev. Doctor Sinsabaugh and "Sunset" Cox were old Pike Boys — Lively Times
in Guernsey — Crossing another State line — Sycamore Valley — Old Taverns in
Richmond — A link out — Centerville — Dublin — Through Indiana — The Road
Disappears among the Prairies of Illinois.*

It is estimated that two-fifths of the trade and travel of the
road were diverted at Brownsville, and fell into the channel furnished
at that point by the slack water improvement of the Monongahela
river, and a like proportion descended the Ohio from Wheeling, and
the remaining fifth continued on the road to Columbus, Ohio, and
points further west. The travel west of Wheeling was chiefly local,
and the road presented scarcely a tithe of the thrift, push, whirl and
excitement which characterized it, east of that point; and there was a
corresponding lack of incident, accident and anecdote on the extreme
western division. The distance from Wheeling to Columbus is one
hundred and twenty-nine miles, and the road enters the capital of
Ohio by way of High street. Before the era of railroads Columbus
derived its chief business from the National Road.

Neil, Moore & Co. operated a line of stage coaches between Wheeling and Columbus prior to, and for some time after, the year 1840,
and their line extended west as far as Springfield. Daniel Moore, of
Washington, Pennsylvania, and his son Henry, composed the Moore
end of this old Ohio Stage Company. Henry Moore subsequently
located in Baltimore, and died there. His father died in Washington,
Pennsylvania, more than half a century ago. John Scott, of Washington, Pennsylvania, antedates Daniel Moore as a stage proprietor.
He ran a line of coaches between Washington and Wheeling as early
as the year 1810, on an old road between those points, which was
used previous to the construction of the National Road, and had the
contract for carrying the United States mails.

William Neil, the old stage proprietor, was the projector and
owner of the Neil House, the leading hotel of Columbus. He was
the possessor of large means, enhanced by holdings of large tracts
of fertile land near Columbus, which he acquired at low figures in an
early day. It is said his manners were not of the *suave* order, but
he was noted for energy and shrewdness. One who knew him says
of him, that "he was honest in his dealings, somewhat rough in his

(298)

ways, but an energetic, pushing man, who made things move." This description fits many of the old pike boys.

Gen. N. P. Talmadge, of whom further mention is made hereafter, owned and operated a line of coaches also between Wheeling and Columbus, and made things lively along the road. He called his line the "Good Intent."

John Weaver, as before stated, transferred his old line of coaches called the "Peoples," from the eastern to the Ohio portion of the road. There was considerable competition between these old lines, but not comparable to that of the old lines east of Wheeling. The stage stations between Wheeling and Columbus were: St. Clairsville, Morristown, Fairview, Washington, Cambridge, Concord, Zanesville, Gratiot, named in honor of Brig. Gen. Gratiot, before mentioned; Jackson, Etna and Reynoldsburg.

Among the old tavern keepers west of Wheeling, the following were prominent and well known in the olden time: Moses Rhodes kept at Bridgeport, and hailed the west-bound traveler on his entrance to the borders of the State of Ohio. A short distance further west, one Cusic, and after him Nicols, in the same old tavern, ministered to the wants of the traveler on the nation's old highway. A short drive from Nicols' brought the wayfarer to the house of Chambers, ever ready to wait upon the public, and a little beyond was the Woodmancy house, kept by Isaac Gleaves, who afterward hung up his sign at a house further west. Passing Woodmancy's, the next old tavern was McMahon's, a veritable son of Erin, overflowing with native generosity. This part of the road seems to have been an Irish row, since the next old tavern, after passing McMahon's, was kept by one McCaffrey. A short distance west of McCaffrey's the town of St. Clairsville comes in view, one of the oldest towns of Ohio, the seat of justice for Belmont county, and named in honor of the illustrious old Westmoreland county, Pennsylvania, soldier and patriot, Gen. Arthur St. Clair.

In St. Clairsville, James Smith kept the stage office, and bowed in genuine old pike style to the coming and going passengers. One mile west of St. Clairsville, an old German, or Swede, bearing the non-musical name of Neiswanger, or something like it, kept a tavern, and, according to tradition, a good one. His house was a fine brick building, on the north side of the road. One mile further west, one Hoover entertained the traveling public, and beyond him, one Chamberlin presided over a good old tavern.

The village of Sloysville is next reached, which, of course, had its tavern, as all villages have, and probably more than one; but the old wagoner who furnished most of the data for this chapter could not recall the names of the old proprietors thereof. It was a long time ago that he drove a team on the road, and he is verging upon his ninetieth year, and therefore not to be censured for forgetfulness.

The writer found more difficulty in obtaining information concerning this portion of the road than any other. In fact, he admits his failure to obtain the necessary data for producing an accurate history of it. He wrote to all the postmasters on the Ohio line east of Columbus, for information concerning the road, and no response came, except in one instance. and that was to a letter which reached a wrong destination. It was addressed to the postmaster at Jackson, a village on the road, called "Jacktown" by the old pike boys, and found its way to the postmaster of Jackson, Jackson county, a considerable distance south of the National Road. It happened that the postmaster who received this letter was a native of Brownsville, Fayette county, Pennsylvania, a member of the old Sloan family of that place, but he was so far away from the road that he could furnish no information concerning it. He, at least, was courteous, a trait for which he is indebted, probably, to the circumstance of his nativity. A self-important postmaster, especially of a little town, like the political carpet-bagger, has no respect for ancient landmarks.

Moving on westwardly, the next point reached is Morristown, the second stage station west of Wheeling. This town was at its best when the National Road was the leading avenue of trade and travel. John Bynum and John Lippincott were the old tavern keepers of Morristown, and took pride in scanning the old way bills, and catering to the wants of hungry stage passengers.

One mile west of Morristown Christopher Hoover hung out his old sign board in front of a substantial brick house, on the south side of the road, and a short distance beyond, Noble Taylor, a combination of familiar old pike names, entertained the traveling public.

The village of Hendrysburg is next reached. This place is on the dividing line between Belmont and Guernsey counties. It is not and never was a pretentious town, but its old inhabitants derived much comfort, and not a little pleasure, from advantages afforded by the National Road.

Passing one or more old taverns whose occupants and owners cannot be recalled, the traveler comes upon the town of Fairview, a stirring place in the palmy days of the road. There William Bradshaw was a popular tavern keeper. He and Isaac Gleaves, formerly of the Woodmancy House, near Wheeling, were the leading tavern keepers in Fairview fifty years ago.

West of Fairview the old tavern keepers were: William Armstrong, Joseph Ferrell and Alexander Taylor.

Middletown is next reached, and here Thomas Hays and one Thompson each kept a tavern in the olden time, and gladdened the heart of many a weary traveler.

West of Middletown the roll bears the names of Alter Briggs and Alexander Speers.

Samuel Smith kept the old tavern at Elizabethtown. West of Elizabethtown, one Crayton kept a tavern, and beyond him Widow Drake. The widows never surrender.

The village of Washington is next reached. Here Simon Beymer kept at the sign of the "Black Bear," and Peter Colley, formerly of Centreville, kept a tavern in Washington as late as 1854.

West of Washington the old traveler on the road found rest and refreshment first at the tavern of Widow Slams, and before reaching Cambridge, excellent entertainment was furnished by Joseph Griffith, James Smith, John Shaw, Mr. Slater, Mr. McCuen, John Nice, Robert McMurry, Mr. Waterhouse, and Joshua Davis.

Cambridge comes next on the line. This is the capital of Guernsey county, one of the liveliest towns on the road, and surviving its decline, remains prosperous. The old tavern keepers in Cambridge were William Ferguson, Wyatt Hutchinson, Bazil Brown, Mr. Needam, Mr. Pollard, Joseph Bute, Elijah Grimes, John Cook, James B. Moore, Captain Hersing, John Tingle and George Metcalf. The latter kept one of the stage houses.

Three miles west of Cambridge, Thomas Carran kept an old tavern. Further west, taverns were kept by Jacob Sunefrank, Mr. Laird, Alex. Leeper, Ichabod Grummon, Mr. Sutton, Frank Dixon, William McDonald and Lewis McDonald. Lewis McDonald's old tavern was near the dividing line between Guernsey and Muskingum counties.

After entering the county of Muskingum the first old tavern reached was kept by William McKinney, and next in line comes the old tavern of William Wilson, still doing business under the management of Edward McCloud.

At Norwich Mr. Sinsabaugh kept a tavern. He was the father of Rev. Hiram Sinsabaugh, D. D., for many years a leading member of the Pittsburg Conference of the Methodist Episcopal church, a man of much learning and genuine piety, pure in thought, and upright in conduct. The author of these pages knew him well, and in the whole range of his acquaintance never met a sincerer friend, or a more just man. He died in Los Angeles, California, a few years ago. Lightly rest the sod that covers his grave. He is numbered among the pike boys, as in early life he led horses from his father's house in Ohio to eastern markets.

Further westward on the road Jacob Probasco hung up his sign in front of an old tavern, he of Jockey Hollow fame before mentioned. His tavern at this point was known as the "Ten Mile House," being distant ten miles from Zanesville.

One mile west of Probasco's one McNutt, of Irish extraction, and good fame as a landlord, kept a tavern, and next beyond, on the westward trend, John Livengood, whose name imports old Pennsylvania Dutch stock, ministered to the wants of strangers and travelers.

Zanesville is next reached. Zanesville is the county seat of Muskingum county. It is situate on the Muskingum river, fifty-nine miles east from Columbus. Mr. Leslie kept a tavern in Zanesville in the olden time, and entertained the public in a highly satisfactory manner. His house was a brick building on the north side of the street and road, and at the west end of the town. When Leslie kept

14

tavern in Zanesville, the town contained a population of about 7,000. Its population at this date exceeds 25,000. It survived the decline of the road, and grew rapidly in population and wealth, but it may be doubted whether its present money making inhabitants experience as much of the real pleasures and enjoyments of life as their predecessors of fifty years ago, when the dashing stage coach woke up the echoes of the dull town, and the heavy tread of the ponderous broad wheeled wagon told the whole story of commerce and trade. The illustrious Samuel S. Cox was born and reared in Zanesville, and therefore, under a definition given in a previous chapter, a pike boy. He was called "Sunset," by reason of a gushing description he wrote of the Setting Sun, when a young man, and there is no doubt that the views which so deeply impressed his youthful mind were had from points on the National Road, in the vicinity of his native town. He was one of the brightest stars in the galaxy of American statesmen.

A writer in a Guernsey county paper gives the following lively description of scenes on the road in that locality:

"Isaac Gleaves was one of the old tavern keepers in Fairview. His house was the stage office, where a halt was made for exchange of horses, and to discharge and take on passengers. The stage offices were places of public resort, and around the bar-rooms gathered the topers and loafers, by day and by night. The old stage drivers were full of fun and frolic, and could entertain the curious with

> 'Tales fearful and awful,
> E'en to name would be unlawful.
> Fast by an ingle blinking bonnily,
> W'ie recanning swats that drank divinely,
> These souters told their queerest stories,
> And the landlord's laugh was ready chorus.'

"There was Nat Smith, Sam Smith, Jim Smith, Bate Smith, Jo Smith, Quil Smith, Bill Smith, and more of the Smith family, and Sam Crouse, Jake Crouse, Sylvester Root, Sam Kirk, Tom Kirk, Tom Bryan, Andy Caster, Tom Carter, Jim Bryan, Bony Shelden, Wash Cranford, Jim Bayless, Mart Houck, Henry Hight, Tom Crawford, John McIllvaine, Ross Briggs, and a host of others of the ' knights of the whip and reins,' of those old coaching days.

> ' When hand to hand they cut and strive,
> Devil take the hindmost of the drive.'

"Near by stood the old 'smithy' of Capt. John G. Bell's father, whose bellows flapped, and red sparks flew, and anvil rang, night and day, to keep the horses feet in trim, so that down the slope to Hendrysburgh, and on to Boden's hill and Taylor's hill, and o'er Salt Fork's long stretch, through ice and sleet, these Jehus could safely, and on time, move on their load of living freight and the mails sent out by ' Uncle Sam.' John Miskimmins, one of the early settlers at the mouth of Wills Creek, was the general agent from Columbus to Wheeling, of the great Neil, Moore & Co., whose lines cobwebbed the State of Ohio. Otho Hinton was the United States mail agent to look after the mail robbers. He turned out to be one himself, and was placed under arrest for opening the mails between Cambridge and Washington. He was indicted and arraigned before the United States court at Columbus, released on bail, and fled to Honolulu, where he died in 1856.

"Gen. N. P. Talmadge placed on the road what was called the opposition, or Good Intent, line of stages. This was just after the Washingtonian temperance movement. He made temperance speeches along the line, and required his drivers to take the pledge. He stopped at Cambridge and made a speech in the old Presbyterian church, and sang a song, his drivers taking up the chorus. We give in substance, if not in word, a verse :

'Our horses are true and coaches fine,
  No upsets or runaways ;
Nor drunken drivers to swear and curse,
  For its cold water all the days.

CHORUS.

For our agents and drivers
  Are all fully bent,
To go for cold water,
  On line Good Intent,
Sing, go it, my hearties,
  Cold water for me.'

"Isaac Gleaves was not behind as a caterer to the inner man, and a dinner or supper by the stage passengers, after being rocked and tossed at a six miles per hour rate, was relished even by Tippecanoe and Corwin, too, and Democrats did not starve nor turn up their noses because old Isaac was a Whig. He had a famous recipe for the cure of the ague, which for its queer compound he was often required to give, not so much for the ingredients; they were very simple; but for the first preparation for the compound. This was to boil down a quart of water to a pint. And to the inquiry, 'What is the water boiled down for, Uncle Isaac?' he would reply, 'to make it stronger.'

"A little further, and last, was Major William Bradshaw, just over in Belmont county. He was the soul of wit and humor, and gave out many expressions that have become noted. To all that he did not feel disposed to entertain, he gave the answer, 'Take the Barnesville road.' His toast drank in honor of the Fairview guards, a military company that had been parading 'with plumes and banners gay,' just after the close of the Mexican war, will live in the military history of Guernsey county — 'Soldiers in peace, civilians in war.'"

The Smiths above mentioned all drove stages on the road east of Wheeling, before going to Ohio, and lived in Brownsville. All the male members of the family were drivers, including Samuel, the father. His sons were, Samuel, jr., Gilbert, Quill, Bate and Nat, familiar names in the early history of the road.

The largest town on the line of the road west of Columbus, in the State of Ohio, is Springfield, the capital of Clark county. The distance between Columbus and Springfield is forty-five miles. Springfield enjoyed for a number of years the advantages of the road, and felt a pride in being on its line, but its growth and development, the result of other agencies, have thrown a mantle of oblivion over the time when the rattle of the stage coach and the rumble of road wagons furnished the chief excitement of her streets.

The road penetrated Indiana at the boundary line of Wayne county, in that State. The length of the line through Indiana is one hundred and forty-nine and one-fourth miles, and the sum of $513,099 was expended on it for bridges and masonry. Work was begun at Indianapolis and prosecuted east and west from that point, in obedience to an act of Congress given in the chapter on Appropriations. The road was completed through Wayne county in 1827. It was not macadamized or graveled, and in the year 1850 was absorbed by the Wayne County Turnpike Company, under a charter granted by State authority. The length of this pike is twenty-two miles.

The second section of the act incorporating the Wayne County Turnpike Company reads as follows:

"The capital stock of said company shall be one hundred thousand dollars, divided into shares of fifty dollars each, and shall be applied to the construction of a turnpike road in Wayne county, commencing at the western terminus of the Richmond turnpike, about three miles east of Richmond, and to be continued westward on the line of the National Road to the county line between the counties of Henry and Wayne; and the State of Indiana hereby relinquishes to said Wayne County Turnpike Company all the rights, interests, and claims in and to the line of said National Road in said county of Wayne; the grade, materials, bridges, constructions of all kinds she now has, or may hereafter acquire from the General Government, in and to the said National Road: *Provided*, That in case the Federal Government should, at any time hereafter, determine to resume the ownership and control of said road, said company shall relinquish the same to the General Government, on receiving from it the full cost of construction as expended by said company."

The section quoted discloses a point which the court of Somerset county, Pennsylvania, seems to have overlooked when it condemned that portion of the road lying within the borders of that county, took possession of its property, and decreed it free from tolls. The several acts of Congress ceding the road to Pennsylvania and the other States through which it passed, reserved the right of Congress at any subsequent time to resume ownership and control, and in case of the exercise of this reserved right, the question arises, what would become of the decree of the Somerset county court?

Prior to the construction of the National Road in Indiana, Robert Morrisson, the founder of the Morrisson Library, of Richmond, and one of the leading citizens of that place, was mainly instrumental in causing a gravel road to be made from Richmond to Dayton, Ohio, which was known as the "Richmond and Short Line Pike." The engineers of the National Road adopted the line of Morrisson's road in Indiana, with the exception of one mile from a point near Clawson's tavern to the Ohio State line. The Government survey carried the line east from Clawson's tavern, and north of Sycamore Valley, over two long and steep hills, separated by a deep valley. To avoid these hills on the Ohio side, travel dropped down over a good country road to the Richmond and Short Line Pike at the State line. This country road was afterwards macadamized, but the distance between the State line and Clawson's tavern has remained a gravel road until the present time, kept up and used as a portion of the National road, instead of the line over the hills north of Sycamore Valley.

Morrisson's company was merged in the Wayne County Turnpike Company in 1850. This company issued seven hundred and eighty shares of stock of the par value of fifty dollars each, and operated its road until the year 1890, when Jackson township, by virtue of a popular vote, purchased that portion of it lying within her boundaries for the sum of $4,500, and made it free of tolls. In 1893, Wayne township bought the road within her boundaries for $11,000, and made it free. The preliminary steps are now being taken by the citizens of Center township to take a vote on a proposition to purchase the road within her borders. If this measure carries the road will be free throughout its entire length in Wayne county.

The Presidents of the Wayne County Turnpike Company have been Robert Morrisson, Jacob Brooks, Edmund Laurence, William Parry, and Joseph C. Ratliff, the last named having served continuously from 1871 to the present time, a pleasant gentleman of fine executive abilities.

This company has always paid dividends of seven per cent. on its capital stock of $39,000, and for the last ten years a majority of its stockholders have been women.

The rate of toll was two cents a mile for horse and buggy and one-half cent per mile for each additional horse, one cent for a horse and rider per mile, and one-half cent for a led horse.

The toll houses were small frame structures and the gates simply heavy poles to raise and let down after the manner of the beam that lowered and lifted up "the old oaken bucket that hung in the well."

Going westwardly from the Ohio State line, in Indiana, the first tavern was that of James Neal, at Sycamore Valley. Of Neal but little can be gleaned beyond the fact that he kept tavern at this point for several years.

The next tavern was Clawson's, a brick building, erected about the year 1818 by Robert Hill. It stood a little distance north of the road, and near the western end of the line before mentioned, as having been located but not used, and was subsequently torn down and rebuilt on the traveled line. It is said that Robert Hill's daughters hauled the brick for their father's house in an ox cart. Clawson was a tall, muscular man, and beyond these facts concerning him, he is lost to the memory of the oldest inhabitant of Indiana. West of Clawson's the first toll gate in Indiana was encountered. It stood near Glen Miller Park and almost within the suburbs of Richmond. This gate was moved several times, but never over a mile from Richmond.

The city of Richmond is the first large town on the line of the road within the borders of the State of Indiana, and the road forms its Main street. It is four miles from the Ohio line, and the county seat of Wayne county. Its present population is 25,000.

The first tavern of the road in Richmond was kept by Charles W. Starr. It was a regular old pike tavern, with extensive stabling and drove yards attached, occupying one-fourth of a square on the northeast corner of Eighth, formerly Fifth street. The building was of brick, known in later years as the Tremont Hotel. It is still standing, but not used as a hotel or tavern. Charles W. Starr was a man of medium size and of Quaker faith. He wore the Quaker garb, had Quaker habits, and was esteemed a good citizen. Some of his descendants are still living at Richmond, and three of his sons are prominent and active business men of that place.

A short distance below Starr's, and between Sixth and Seventh streets, stood Sloan's brick stage house, and its proprietor, Daniel D. Sloan, was at one time postmaster of Richmond. This tavern was headquarters for two stage lines, one running to Indianapolis and the other to Cincinnati. The Cincinnati line had opposition, and by cutting rates the fare was reduced by the competition and during its continuance, from five dollars to fifty cents for the round trip, distance seventy miles direct. A portion of Sloan's old tavern still remains, and adjoins Roling's hardware store. Sloan was heavy set, fleshy, and well poised for a tavern keeper.

On the south side of the road, between Seventh and Eighth streets, William Nixon kept a tavern on the site of the present Huntington House. He was a spare, sinewy man, of the Quaker faith. He kept the tavern at the point named from 1840 to about 1843.

A noted tavern was Gilbert's, on the northeast corner of Sixth and Main streets. Joseph W. Gilbert kept this house for many years. It was a two-story frame building, pebble coated. Gilbert was tall and slim, polite and affable, and had many friends. He suffered the misfortune of going blind, and died at Richmond in 1890, in the ninety-second year of his age. When barely able to distinguish large objects he walked much up and down the streets, asking persons he met to tell him the time of day, always pulling out his watch and holding it up for inspection. At one time when Gilbert was moving a part of his tavern building, Charles Newman, on passing along, inquired of the old landlord, whose house was noted for its cleanliness, how many bed bugs he found. Gilbert replied with indignation, "Not a single one." "I believe you, Joseph," said Newman, "for they are married and have large families." Most of the early taverns of Richmond were in the western part of the town.

It is related in the latest history of Indiana, that Jeremiah Cox, one of the earliest settlers in Richmond, regarded with disfavor the scheme of building up the town; and is said to have remarked, that he would rather see a buck's tail than a tavern sign, and his sincerity was made evident by the fact, that he did not make his addition to the town plat until two years after the date of Smith's survey, or two years after Philip Harter had a tavern sign swinging near a log building on lot 6, South Fifth (Pearl) street.

Another early tavern of Richmond was kept at the northwest corner of Main and Fifth (Pearl), sign of the green tree, by Jonathan Bayles, and another, of later date, on Fourth (Front) street, near the southwest corner of Main, by Ephraim Lacey. Harter soon afterward kept a tavern at the corner of North Fifth (Pearl) and Main, where the Citizen's bank afterward stood, then called Harter's corner.

Another tavern was kept on Gilbert's corner, northwest corner of Main and Sixth (Marion), first, it is believed, by Abraham Jeffries, and continued afterward by several other persons at different times.

Richard Cheesman, an early settler, lived on South Fourth (Front) street, kept a tavern several years, and subsequently removed to Center township, where he died. William, a nephew, remained in Richmond, and married a Miss Moffitt. He died some years ago, but his widow is still living.

John Baldwin, an original Carolinian, kept a tavern and store at the Citizen's bank corner. He went west, and became a trader with the Indians. Their savage nature having at one time been excited by liquor which he had sold them, they scalped, or partially scalped him, but he survived the operation and returned to Wayne county, where he died, six miles north of Richmond, in 1869. After Baldwin, William H. Vaughan kept this tavern for several years, and until it ceased to entertain the public. Vaughan had previously kept the Lacey tavern on Fourth (Front) street.

Patrick Justice, at an early period, kept a tavern on North Fourth (Front) street, near Main. He afterward kept a public house which he built in 1827, near the extreme limits of the town, now the southeast corner of Main and Fifth streets.

Benjamin Paige, a New Englander, father of Ralph Paige, once a merchant on Main street, kept a tavern previous to 1830, at the corner originally owned by John C. Kibbey, an early inn-keeper, and known as Meek's corner, northeast of Main and Sixth (Marion).

Abraham Jeffries had a tavern on Gilbert's corner, which he kept a number of years, and was succeeded by Joseph Andrews, his brother-in-law, who died soon after taking charge.

The last westward tavern in Richmond was kept by Christian

Buhl, who came from Germany, and his house was a three story stone structure where Minck's brewery now is.

At the west end of Richmond the road crosses Whitewater river over a handsome and expensive bridge. This bridge has seven arches, and is a combination truss and arch design, capable of sustaining an immense weight. On the west side timbers and wool sacks were sunk into a quicksand upon which to rest the foundations of the abutment.

Toll-gate No. 7 was erected at the fifth mile post west of Richmond and afterwards moved to a point near Earlham college. This gate was kept by William Fagan for twenty-three years, and afterwards by Mr. Gardener for nearly ten years. Mr. Gardener is a New York man and was one of the best gate-keepers on the road. His wife is a cousin of the late Hon. William B. Windom, who was Secretary of the Treasury in President Harrison's administration.

There was a tavern between gate No. 7 and gate No. 8, which was near the Center township line and East Clear creek. West of this point there is a curve in the road caused by the refusal of Thomas Croft to remove his house, which was on the surveyed line. He was offered $500 to remove his house and declined to take it. The road was then of necessity made around his house, and so near it as to loosen its foundations, and it toppled and fell down, causing him to lose his house, and the sum offered him as damages besides.

At the seventh mile stone, a little beyond West Clear Creek bridge, stood the shop of Jeremy Mansur, who manufactured the first axes made in the county of Wayne. When Martin Van Buren made his trip through Indiana, many persons denounced him as an enemy of the road, and some one in Richmond, to inflict chastisement upon the distinguished statesman for his supposed unfriendliness, sawed a double-tree of the coach in which he was traveling nearly through, and it broke near Mansur's ax-shop, causing Mr. Van Buren to walk to the top of a hill through thick mud. The author of this mishap to Mr. Van Buren subsequently boasted that he had put a mud polish on Gentleman Martin's boots to give him a realizing sense of the importance of good roads.

Near the ninth mile stone from Richmond were two celebrated taverns, Eliason's and Estepp's. Both were brick houses and well kept. Joshua Eliason was a man of medium size, jovial disposition, remarkably industrious, and a zealous member of the Christian church. His tavern was on the north side of the road, and, in connection with it, he maintained two one-story emigrant houses to accommodate families moving west. The emigrants carried and cooked their own provisions, and paid Eliason a certain sum for the use of his buildings. Drove yards were also a profitable feature of Eliason's tavern. He sold grain to the drovers, and after the cattle were turned out, put his own hogs in the vacated field to eat up the remnants and refuse.

John Estepp's tavern was on the south side of the road, nearly opposite Eliason's. He had one emigrant house, and did an extensive

BRIDGE OVER WHITEWATER, RICHMOND, IND.

business. He was a man of the lean order, but always on the alert to turn an honest penny.

A short distance beyond Estepp's, Centerville comes in view, near where Daniel L. Lashley kept the principal tavern. He was a large man, and had a large patronage.

Centerville boasts of having been a nursery of great men. Here Oliver P. Morton, when a young man, worked as a hatter, and Gen. A. E. Burnside pursued the humble trade of a tailor. Gen. Lew Wallace and Gen. Noble went to school in Centerville, and possibly the germs of Ben Hur had their origin in this rural village. Hon. George W. Julian, of free soil notoriety, was at one time a resident of Centerville, and Judge Nimrod Johnson, of the State Supreme Court, and John S. Newman, ex-president of the Indiana Central Railroad Company, were among the noted personages who lived there. Centerville was for many years the county seat of Wayne county, and the removal of the offices and archives to Richmond produced a feeling of jealousy between the inhabitants of the places which lingers in a measure to this day, although Richmond has far outstripped her ancient rival in growth and improvements.

West of Centerville the road crosses Nolan's Fork, a small Indiana stream, and a short distance beyond, and near the Poor Farm, a toll-gate was established, and there was also a tavern at this point. One mile west of the Poor Farm, Crum Fork is crossed by means of a bridge, and between this stream and Germantown there was another toll-gate and also a tavern. There is a bridge over the stream between Germantown and Cambridge city. West of Cambridge City, and near Dublin, there was a toll-gate, and a short distance west of Dublin, the road passes out of Wayne county.

The road forms the main street of Dublin and is called Cumberland street, by reason of this fact. The first tavern established in Dublin was by Samuel Schoolfield, an old Virginian, pleasantly remembered on account of his staunch patriotism. He displayed on his sign-board the motto: "Our country, right or wrong."

The railroad absorbed all passenger and freight traffic in the year 1852, after which date and to the close of the civil war, outside of home travel, the main vehicles on the Indiana division were "Prairie Schooners," or semi-circular bedded, white-covered emigrant wagons, used by parties moving from Virginia and the Carolinas to Illinois.

Indianapolis as before stated is on the line of the road, but her proportions as a city are the outgrowth of other agencies. In the early days of Indiana's capital the National Road was her only commercial artery, and her pioneer citizens regarded it as a great advantage to their aspiring town. The railway era dawned so soon after the road was located through Indianapolis that but few memories cluster about its history in that locality like those east of the Ohio river.

The last and only remaining large town of Indiana on the road

14a

is Terre Haute, a city like Indianapolis that has outgrown the memories of the road, and is probably little mindful of the time when her early inhabitants deemed it a matter of high importance to be located on its line. Though remote from the active centres of the historic road, Terre Haute is more or less associated with its stirring scenes and former prestige.

There was a striking similarity in the habits, manners and pursuits of the old inhabitants of the towns along the National Road, notably between Baltimore and Wheeling. The road was a bond that drew them together and united them as neighbors. There are many persons still living who remember when Frederic, Hagerstown, Cumberland, Uniontown, Brownsville, Washington and Wheeling derived their main support from the road, and their chief distinction from their location on its line. This feature was also true of the towns on the Appian Way, on authority of the classic author, Anthon.

Any one familiar with the National Road in its prosperous era, whose business or other engagements required a divergence from it, invariably returned to it with a sense of security and a feeling of rest and relief. This feeling was universal and profound. An illustration is furnished by Hon. William H. Playford, of Uniontown, who was born and reared on the road. After his college graduation he went South to teach, as did many other graduates of northern colleges. When his term as a teacher ended his heart of course yearned for home, and homeward he set his sails. He struck the National Road at Terre Haute, and the moment his eyes flashed upon its familiar surface he felt that he was among old friends and nearly home. It was the first object he had witnessed since his departure from the paternal roof that brought him in touch again with home.

Before the road was completed beyond the western boundary of the State of Indiana, the steam railway had become the chief agency of transportation and travel, and our grand old national highway was practically lost amid the primitive prairies of Illinois, so that whereas its splendor was favored by the rising, it was dispelled beneath the Setting Sun.

GEN. GEORGE W. CASS.

CHAPTER XLII.

Down to the year 1834, as has been seen, the road was under the control and supervision of the War Department of the General Government. Brig.-Gen. Gratiot was the chief officer in immediate charge. The town of Gratiot on the line of the road in Muskingum county, Ohio, was named in his honor. Captains Delafield, McKee, Bliss, Bartlett, Hartzell, Williams, Colquit and Cass, and Lieuts. Mansfield, Vance and Pickell, all graduates of West Point, were more or less identified with the construction, management and repairs of the road. These army officers were all well known to the people along the road sixty years ago. Gen. Gratiot was probably dead before the beginning of the civil war, or too old for active service. Mansfield fell at Antietam, a major general of the Union forces. Williams was killed at the storming of Monterey in the Mexican war. McKee fell while gallantly leading a regiment in the hot fight at Buena Vista. Hartzell, promoted to the rank of major, fought through the Mexican war, and died soon after returning to his home in Lexington, Kentucky. Bliss and Delafield both died within the current decade. Colquit, a near relative of the Georgia Senator of that name, died in the Confederate service. Capt. Geo. W. Cass, while on the road as an engineer in charge of repairs, married a daughter of the late George Dawson, of Brownsville, located at that place, and transacted business there for a number of years. He subsequently went to Pittsburg as president of the Adams Express Company, and later became president of the Pittsburg, Ft. Wayne & Chicago Railway Company. He was prominent and influential in the politics of Pennsylvania, and on several occasions stood second in the ballotings for the Democratic nomination for Governor. He died in the city of New York. He was twice married. His widow surviving him, is a sister of his first wife.

The iron mile posts, so familiar to the traveler on the road, were turned out in foundries of Connellsville and Brownsville. Major James Francis had the contract for making and delivering those between Cumberland and Brownsville. His foundry was at Connellsville,

Pennsylvania. Col. Alex. J. Hill, a well known and popular coke operator, and Democratic politician of Fayette county, Pennsylvania, is a son-in-law of Major Francis, the old foundryman. Those between Brownsville and Wheeling were made at Snowden's old foundry, in Brownsville, John Snowden, contractor. They were hauled along the road for distribution in wagons drawn by six horse teams. Within the last two years they were re-set and re-painted, between Brownsville and the Maryland State line, under the direction of Commissioner Ewing Searight, and stand erect in their original sites, silent witnesses of the great procession that passed in front of them for so many years, and if they possessed the attributes of speech and memory, could narrate the story of a great highway, which in incident and interest is without a rival.

WILLIAM SEARIGHT was a commissioner of the road for a number of years in its prosperous era. His jurisdiction extended over the line within the limits of Pennsylvania. He was of Irish lineage, and Presbyterian faith. His parents located in Ligionier Valley, Westmoreland county, Pennsylvania, about the year 1780. Upon reaching his majority he came to Fayette county to work out his destiny. He learned the trade of fulling and dyeing, and started in business on his own account at Hammond's old mill on Dunlap's creek, long since demolished and forgotten. He subsequently pursued the same business at Cook's mill, on Redstone creek. His education was such only as could be procured in his boyhood by persons of slender means, but his natural endowments were of the highest and best order. He was honest and industrious. On March 26th, 1826, he married Rachel, a daughter of Thomas Brownfield, proprietor of the old Swan tavern in Uniontown. At Searights, on the National Road, he laid the foundation of a considerable fortune, and died in the sixty-first year of his age. He was a leading Democratic politician of his day in Fayette county, and in 1827 rode on horseback from Searights to Harrisburg, to aid in nominating General Jackson for the presidency. He was a trusted friend of the late Gen. Simon Cameron, when that unrivalled politician was a leader of the Democratic party in Pennsylvania. At the date of his death he was the nominee of his party for the important State office of Canal Commissioner, and would have been elected, had not death interposed and called him from the active duties of this life to the realities of another. William Hopkins, another old commissioner of the road, was nominated to the vacancy thus made, and elected by a large majority. The death of William Searight occurred at his home, near Searights, on August 12, 1852. He was a man of generous impulses and charitable disposition, ever ready to lend his counsel, his sympathies and his purse, to ameliorate the sufferings of his fellow men. Although death plucked him from the very threshold of earthly honors, it caused him no regret. His work was well done, and he was ready to go. The kingdom he was about to enter presented higher honors and purer enjoyments. In looking forward and upward he saw—

Engraved by James B. Rice & Sons, Phila.

Wm Searight

> "No midnight shade, no clouded sun,
> But sacred, high, eternal noon."

A more emphatic eulogy than pen could write, or tongue express, was furnished by the immense concourse that attended his funeral. The patriarchs and the youth of the country came to testify their appreciation of his worth. A few days after his death, a large meeting of citizens, irrespective of party, convened in the court house at Uniontown, to give expression to their sorrow for his death. Hon. Nathaniel Ewing presided. Hon. Daniel Sturgeon, then a United States Senator, and Zalmon Ludington, esq., were the vice presidents, and Hon. R. P. Flenniken and John B. Krepps, esq., secretaries. On motion of Hon. James Veech, a committee was appointed to formulate the feeling of the meeting, which reported through its distinguished chairman (Mr. Veech) the following preamble and resolutions, which were unanimously adopted:

"When a valuable citizen dies, it is meet that the community of which he was a member, mourn his loss. A public expression of their sorrow at such an event, is due as some solace to the grief of the bereaved family and friends, and as an incentive to others to earn for their death the same distinction. In the death of William Searight, this community has lost such a citizen. Such an event has called this public meeting, into which enter no schemes of political promotion, no partisan purposes of empty eulogy. Against all this, death has shut the door. While yet the tear hangs on the cheek of his stricken family, and the tidings of death are unread by many of his friends, we, his fellow citizens, neighbors, friends, of all parties, have assembled to speak to those who knew and loved him best, and to those who knew him not, the words of sorrow and truth, in sincerity and soberness. Therefore, as the sense of this meeting:

Resolved, That in the death of William Searight, Fayette county and the Commonwealth of Pennsylvania have lost one of their best and most useful citizens. The people at large may not realize their loss, but the community in which he lived, over whose comforts and interests were diffused the influence of his liberality and enterprise, feel it, while his friends of all classes, parties and professions, to whom he clung, and who clung to him, mourn it.

Resolved, While we would withhold our steps from the sanctuary of domestic grief, we may be allowed to express to the afflicted widow and children of the deceased, our unfeigned sorrow and sympathy in their great bereavement, and to tender them our assurance that while to their hearts the memory of the husband and father will ever be cherished, in ours will be kept the liveliest recollections of his virtues as a citizen and a friend.

Resolved, That among the elements that must enter into every truthful estimate of the character of William Searight, are a warm amenity of manner, combined with great dignity of deportment, which were not the less attractive by their plainness and lack of ostentation, elevated feelings more pure than passionless, high purposes with untiring energy in their accomplishment, an ennobling sense of honor and individual independence, which kept him always true to himself and to his engagements, unfaltering fidelity to his friends, a liberality which heeded no restraint, but means and merit; great promptness and fearlessness in the discharge of what he believed to be a duty, private or public, guided by a rigid integrity which stood all tests and scouted all temptations; honesty and truthfulness in word and deed, which no seductions could weaken, nor assaults overthrow, in all respects the architect of his own fortune and fame. These with the minor virtues in full proportion, are some of the outlines of character which stamped the man whose death we mourn, as one much above the ordinary level of his race.

Resolved, That while we have here nothing to do or say as to the loss sustained by the political party to which he belonged, and whose candidate he was for an office of great honor and responsibility, we may be allowed to say that had he lived and been successful, with a heart so rigidly set as was his, with feelings so high and integrity so firm, and withal an amount of practical intelligence so ample as he possessed, his election could have been regretted by no citizen who knew him and who placed the public interests beyond selfish ends and party success. As a politician we knew him to hold to his principles and party predilections with a tenacious grasp, yet he was ever courteous and liberal in his intercourse with political opponents.

Resolved, That in the life and character of William Searight we see a most instructive and encouraging example. Starting the struggle of life with an humble business, poor and unbefriended, with an honest aim and a true heart, with high purposes and unflagging industry, he gained friends and means, which never forsook him. He thus won for himself and family ample wealth and attained a position among his fellow men which those who have had the best advantages our country affords might well envy. That wealth and that position he used with a just liberality and influence for the benefit of all around and dependent upon him. Though dead he yet speaketh to every man in humble business: "Go thou and do likewise, and such shall be thy reward in life and in death."

WILLIAM HOPKINS was one of the best known of the old commissioners. He was born in Washington county, Pennsylvania, September 17th, 1804. He was of Scotch origin, on the paternal line, and his mother was a native of Ireland, so that he was a genuine Scotch-Irishman. He figured conspicuously in the public affairs of Pennsylvania, for many years. At the age of twenty-three he was a justice of the peace, holding a commission signed by Governor Shultze, one of the early German governors of the State. In 1831 he was a county auditor. In 1834 he was elected to the State Legislature, and re-elected four times, consecutively. He was speaker of the House in 1838, 1839 and 1840. In 1842 he was secretary of the land office of Pennsylvania. During his first term as speaker, the

COL. WILLIAM HOPKINS.

public commotion occurred, known as the "Buckshot War." Troops surrounded the State house, and a bloody collision seemed inevitable. Speaker Hopkins, on this trying occasion, behaved with distinguished wisdom and firmness, and he is credited with having averted the horrors of civil war. In 1852 Colonel Hopkins, as he was invariably called, was nominated and elected Canal Commissioner, as before stated. In this important office he fully sustained his high reputation for honesty and ability. In 1861 he was again elected to the State House of Representatives, and re-elected in 1862. In 1863 he was elected a State Senator. The experience of his previous legislative career gave him a great advantage over others less favored in this regard, and he became, by common consent, "the Nestor of the Senate." In 1872 he was elected a member of the convention to revise the Constitution of the State. He was chairman of the committee to devise and report amendments to the bill of rights, and author of the preamble that reads thus: "We, the people of the commonwealth of Pennsylvania, recognizing the sovereignty of God, and humbly invoking His guidance in our future destiny, ordain and establish this Constitution for its government." If there was nothing else to his credit, this alone would immortalize him. While a member of the Constitutional Convention, he made a visit to his home, and on the cars contracted a cold which developed into pneumonia, and terminated fatally, March 5th, 1873. His funeral was one of the largest and most impressive ever witnessed in Washington.

Rev. Doctor Brownson, the distinguished Presbyterian minister of Washington, grouped together the leading traits of Colonel Hopkins in the following terms: "Such a man could not but be extensively known and respected. In fact, his mental force, discriminating judgment, urbanity, integrity and kindness, joined with his facility as a writer and speaker, rising above the defects of early education, were a continual pledge of public favor and success. He was very firm in adhering to his own views, but considerate also of the feelings and opinions of others. In co-operation or in opposition, he commanded respect. In private life, also, it was impossible not to realize the power of his politeness, and his delicate regard to the sensibilities of all about him. His fondness for children seemed to increase with his years, showing itself both in a desire for their enjoyment and their good. His fine business capacity was often taxed for the benefit of others, especially widows and orphans. In the hallowed circle of home, he was the central object of uncommon reverence and affection, answering to his own peculiar love and tenderness within his domestic relations. But, better than all, is the witness he leaves behind him, in his confession and life as a disciple of Christ, and in the repose of his heart upon the divine promise, when called down into the valley and shadow of death."

The late Judge Black, one of the most eminent men of his day, spoke of Colonel Hopkins as follows: "I do not underestimate the very high qualities of my associates in this body (the Constitutional Convention). I do not think, indeed, that any man here appreciates their various abilities and virtues more than I do; but I devoutly believe that there is no man in this Convention, that we could not have spared better than him who has gone. I do not propose to give an analysis of his character, and it is not necessary to repeat his history. I may say, for I know it, that he was in all respects the best balanced man that it was ever my good fortune to know. His moral and personal courage were often tested; he was one of the most fearless men that ever lived, yet all his measures were in favor of peace, and every one who knew him testifies to the gentleness and kindness of his manner."

Mr. Biddle, a Philadelphia member of the Convention, said: "I well recollect being struck with the commanding figure and strongly marked countenance, in the lineaments of which were unmistakably written simplicity and directness of purpose, integrity and unswerving firmness. He has rounded off a life of great moral beauty, of great usefulness, of great dignity, by a fitting end, and he has fallen before decay had begun to impair his faculties."

One who stood very close and was very much endeared to Col. Hopkins, brings out his great character in form of metaphor, as follows: "There was a remark in your paper which has given me a great deal of mental exercise of a reminiscent character. The wheel of time turns only one way. At the moment I read this, and in the multitude of times it has since come into my head, my mind ran at once to a point in the revolution of that wheel which you never could guess. That point is marked with the year 1838. I had been turned up far enough out of the darkness of the wheel pit to get a view of the top of the wheel, where stood a group of men who have ever since been 'the heroes I loved and the chiefs I admired.' In the center of this group, and the most heroic figure in it, stood WILLIAM HOPKINS. The various members of that group have gone down beyond sight, as the wheel of time kept turning steadily, but their virtues and their public services remain fresh in my memory. They rendered Pennsylvania as great a service as Washington and his compeers rendered the United Colonies."

Such a man was William Hopkins, once a commissioner of the National Road, familiar with every mile along its line, and in daily touch with its moving masses. The writer of these pages had the honor of knowing Col. Hopkins personally and well, and can and does testify that no word of eulogy herein quoted concerning him is in the least overwrought.

An act of the Pennsylvania Legislature, approved April 4, 1831, named William F. Coplan and David Downer of Fayette county, Stephen Hill and Benjamin Anderson of Washington county, and Thomas Endsley of Somerset county, to be Commissioners of the Cumberland Road for the term of three years from the passage of the said act, after which time the right to appoint said Commissioners shall vest in the Governor of the Commonwealth. In 1834 the

Governor appointed these same gentlemen Commissioners for another term of three years. In 1835 an act was passed reducing the number of Commissioners to two, and under this act Stephen Hill of Washington, and Hugh Keys of Fayette county, were appointed on May 7th, 1835, until their appointments were suspended or annulled. On the 9th of January, 1836, the Governor appointed George Craft of Fayette county, and Benjamin Leonard of Washington county, to act in conjunction with the other Commissioners appointed in pursuance of an act approved April 1, 1835. Thompson McKean of Fayette county, and Robert Quail of Washington county, were appointed Commissioners by the Governor on the 29th day of January, 1839, until appointments were suspended or annulled. Robert Quail's appointment was suspended by an act of 1840. An act was approved March 28th, 1840, reducing the number of Commissioners to one, and William Hopkins was appointed for a term of three years, but served less than two years, and resigned, to take the position of secretary of the land office. William Searight was appointed by the Governor on May 3, 1842, for a term of three years, and on April 19th, 1845, William Hopkins was again appointed. On the 8th of April, 1848, an act was approved authorizing the courts of Somerset, Fayette and Washington counties to appoint trustees for the road, with power to appoint Commissioners. Under this act William Searight was again appointed, with jurisdiction limited to the line through the counties of Fayette and Somerset, and served until 1851, when David Hartzell of Somerset county was appointed. William Roddy of the same county succeeded Hartzell in 1852. James Marlow succeeded Roddy and died in commission. Robert McDowell was appointed in 1856. Under the act of 1848, above quoted, Joseph Lawson was appointed for Washington county, and was succeeded in 1852 by Mark Mitchell, in 1856 by Alexander Frasher, and in 1858 by John Long. In 1861 the act of 1848 was repealed in so far as it related to the appointment of Commissioners in Fayette and Somerset counties, but continued in force as to Washington county, stripped of the intervention of trustees. In 1862 John Long was appointed Commissioner for Washington county by the court. In 1864 G. W. Botkins was appointed; in 1866 John Long was restored, and continued until 1871, when T. W. Beatty was appointed. In 1872 Joseph Doak was appointed, and was succeeded in 1876 by George W. Smith. In 1877 the appointing power, as to Washington county, was restored to the Governor, and Samuel Kelley was appointed. In 1881 Peter Hickman was appointed, in 1887 James W. Hendrix, in 1890 Marshall Cox, in 1891 John McDowell, present incumbent. In 1862 the Governor of the State appointed Redding Bunting Commissioner for the counties of Fayette and Somerset. Bunting was the famous old stage driver and stage agent, mentioned in previous chapters. He served as Commissioner until 1864, when the Governor appointed Sebastian Rush, the old tavern keeper before referred to. Rush served until 1870, when Solomon Crumrine was appointed, and served until 1872, when Rush was restored.   In 1875 Charles H. Rush, a son of Sebastian, was appointed, and served until 1881, when William Endsley was appointed.   In 1883 George W. Daniels was appointed.   In 1887 David Johnson was appointed, and in 1891 Ewing Searight was appointed.

As before stated the road east of Cumberland was owned by associations or companies. Allen Darsie was one of the leading stockholders and general superintendent as early as 1835.   He lived at Poplar Springs, twenty-six miles west of Baltimore, was the proprietor of a large and fertile tract of land, and a slave owner.   Allen Darsie, jr., succeeded his father in the superintendency of the road, and remained in charge down to the date of the civil war.   Thomas Bevins of Hancock succeeded the younger Darsie, and Denton Oliver succeeded Bevins.   West of Cumberland, in the State of Maryland, the superintendents were: Thomas Thistle, the old tavern keeper near Grantsville; Jonathan Huddleson, another old tavern keeper, Nathan Dudley, John Swan, Benjamin R. Edwards, George Cady, Henry Atkinson, Robert Welsh, Edward Doneho and William Hall. William Otterson was an old Commissioner in charge of the road through Virginia, and among his successors appear the familiar names of Moses Thornburg, Lewis Lunsford and Abram Bedillion.

In the year 1888 the court of quarter sessions of Somerset county, Pennsylvania, condemned that portion of the road lying within the borders of said county, decreed it exempt from tolls, confiscated all its belongings, and turned it over to the tender care of the township supervisors, under authority supposed to be conferred by an act of assembly, approved June 2d, 1887.

CHAPTER XLIII.

The first contracts in sections for the first ten miles of the road west of Cumberland were signed April 16th and May 8th, 1811, and were finished in the fall of 1812. The next letting was in August, 1812, of eleven miles, extending west as far as Tomlinson's, and these contracts were completed early in 1815. The work was let from Tomlinson's to Smithfield, eighteen miles, in August, 1813, and completed in 1817. The delay was caused by the scarcity of laborers during the war, war prices, and apprehension of failure of some of the contractors. The next letting was in September, 1815, embracing the work six miles and a half westward from Smithfield. This was awarded in sections to John Hagen, Doherty, McLaughlin and Bradley, and Charles McKinney. In May, 1817, the work was let to Uniontown, the successful bidders being Hagan and McCann, Mordecai and James Cochran, Thompson McKean, and Thomas and Matthew Blakely. From Uniontown to Brownsville, portions were let in September, 1815, to Kinkead, Beck & Evans, who soon thereafter undertook the residue to Brubaker's. This firm sub-let many sections of the work. Bond and Gormley had the contract from Brubaker's to Brownsville, and their work was completed in 1818. George Dawson had the contract for the heavy stone walls in Brownsville. John Miller and John Kennedy, of Uniontown, took contracts in the mountains. Miller was a son-in-law of Jacob Beeson, one of the founders of Uniontown. Mr. Kennedy was the grandfather of Hon. John K. Ewing, of Uniontown, and after his experience as a contractor, one of the justices of the Supreme Court of Pennsylvania. The whole line of the road, for purposes of construction, was laid off in two divisions, called Eastern and Western. David Shriver was superintendent of the eastern, and Josias Thompson of the western division. The dividing line between the two divisions was Brubaker's, near, and east of, Brownsville. Mr. Shriver lived in Cumberland, and was the father-in-law of Hon. Andrew Stewart. Mr. Thompson was a Virginian.

In March, 1817, the greater part of the work, from a point two miles east of Washington to the Virginia line, was let to Thomas Mc-

Giffin, Thomas H. Baird and Parker Campbell, the latter one of the foremost lawyers of his time. In 1819 the same gentlemen contracted to do the work, from the point first above named, to a point two miles west of Brownsville. The work east of Hillsboro was turned over by the contractors above named, to William and John H. Ewing, who were returned to the authorities at Washington City as original contractors, and they finished the work for $6,000 per mile. The remainder of the work west of Hillsboro was sub-let by McGiffin, Baird and Campbell, to a number of small contractors.

The road was completed from Cumberland to Uniontown at a cost, including all expenses of survey and location, salaries, bridges, and some repairs, of $9,745 per mile. The average cost of the entire road to Wheeling was nearly $13,000 per mile, showing the Eastern division much less costly than the Western. This was charged to some prodigality of work and too liberal contracts, for which Superintendent Thompson was "investigated" and superseded.

Daniel Steenrod, the old tavern keeper, and Col. Moses Shepherd, were extensive contractors for construction on the Virginia line of the road. Colonel Shepherd built Feay's bridge, near Wheeling, one of the best on the road, and also the bridge over Wheeling creek, near Mrs. Gooding's old tavern. Capt. Valentine Giesey, a veteran of Brownsville, who is well remembered by the old citizens of that place, was a large contractor on the work of taking up the original road bed.

The foregoing were all contractors for work on the original construction of the road. Among the contractors for repairs, after the road was completed, and during its prosperous era, the following familiar names are recalled: Abram Beagle, James McIntyre, William Hastings, John Whitmire, James Dennison, Henry Masterson, Hiram Freeman, Thomas Egan, John Robinson, William Paull, Charles Stillwagon, Jacob Stillwagon, Jacob Dougherty, Anthony Rentz, Henry Murray, James Thompson, Thomas D. Miller, Daniel Canon, Hugh Graham, Morris Whalen, Perry White, Anthony Yarnell, John Whollery, Thomas McKean, John Risler, Isaac Nixon, Robert Brown, Thomas McGrath, Matthew McNeil, Edward Kerven, John Bennington, William H. Graham, Henry Showalter, John Dickey, John McDonough, Morris Purcell, Daniel Ward, Daniel Valentine, Jacob Probasco, John Bradfield, William Reynolds, Thomas Brownfield, Peter Lenhart, James Marlow, John W. McCollough, Nicholas McCartney, John W. McDowell, Robert McDowell, James Snyder, Lewis M. Snyder, Samuel Shipley, Elias Gilmore, Samuel Rush, German D. Hair, Jackson Brown, William C. Stevens, John Gadd, Robert S. Henderson, Joseph Lawson, Michael Thomas, Charles Rush, Nicholas Bradley, John Bradley, Daniel Bradley, Henry Show, William Griffin, Robert McDowell, esq., Adam Speers, James Speers, William Hatfield, Thomas Brown, Thomas Moxley, Hiram Miller, Matthias Fry, John Wallace, John Hardin, William Hardin, John G. Burnworth, Henry Sampey, Henry Clay Rush, Alex. McDowell, Benjamin Miller, Jeffer-

DANIEL STEENROD.

son Miller, John Worthington, E. W. Clement, John Snider, Hiram Mitchell, John Mitchell, William Endsley, Daniel Augustine, John M. Oliver, and many others, some of whose names appear in the accounts of the old Commissioners in the Appendix to this volume.

The average result of a stone breaker in a single day was eight perches, and the price paid was twelve and a half cents per perch. Tradition has it that Robert S. McDowell, still living in Dunbar, Fayette county, Pennsylvania, was the speediest stone breaker on the road. He is the eldest son of "Gate Bob," elsewhere mentioned. In the year 1848, when Colonel Hopkins was commissioner, Robert S. McDowell broke in one day sixteen perches and two feet. This was done on a bet, and in a contest with Capt. Elias Gilmore. A string of stones one rod in length made two perches, under the guage in use, and McDowell's string measured eight rods and two feet. Captain Gilmore, who was one of the most vigorous men on the road, gave up the contest about the middle of the afternoon, and yielded the palm to McDowell. Peter Kelley, who lived at Searights, was one of the best and speediest stone breakers on the road. His occupation, for many years, was breaking stone on the pike, and near the close of his life he became an actor in a tragedy, which lost him his liberty, as well as his former good name. He was not a vicious man, but on occasions would indulge in immoderate drinking. On one of these occasions he killed William Thornton, father of the Hon. J. Russell Thornton, member of the Legislature of Pennsylvania for the county of Fayette. Kelley and Thornton were returning from Brownsville after nightfall, and quarrelled. When near the old Brubaker tavern, Thornton was struck by Kelley, and killed. Kelley was tried, convicted and sent to the penitentiary for a long term, and never thereafter returned to the familiar scenes of the old pike. Alexander Campbell, of Somerfield, was one of the fastest stone breakers on the road, and Robert Hogsett, the well known millionaire of Fayette county, Pennsylvania, broke stones on the road when a boy.

In the early work on the road, there was a requirement that stone for the lower stratum or bed should be broken so that the pieces would pass through a seven-inch ring, and for the upper stratum, which was six inches in thickness, would pass through a three-inch ring. Old contractors provided rings of these dimensions, respectively, and enforced a strict compliance with the regulation mentioned. Subsequently the rings fell into disuse, and were ultimately abandoned, but the stones spread over the surface of the road were always broken to small pieces. The hammer of the stone breaker was a very simple contrivance. It was of iron, round as an apple, weighing probably one pound, with a hole through the center for the insertion of a handle. The handle was of hickory wood, slender in the middle, with a thick end for the grasp of the hand. There was also a larger hammer, with a longer and stouter handle, used for breaking stones thrown into holes. In using this hammer the breaker stood on his feet, and in using the smaller one, sat on the stone pile, moving his position as his work advanced. In hot weather the stone breaker, in many instances, used a ready-made, movable bower, to ward off the scorching rays of the sun. About the year 1848, some person whose name is forgotten, supposing himself endowed with inventive genius, constructed a machine for breaking stones. It was operated by horse power, proved a failure, and was laid aside to rot on the summit of Laurel Hill.

The following table showing the heights of mountains and hills on the road is copied from the sketch by Mr. Veech, accompanying the map of Fayette county, Pennsylvania, before mentioned. It will be seen that it differs somewhat from the measurement of the Commissioners who ran the original lines of the road, but it will be remembered that their measurement was from a point in the Potomac, near Cumberland, whereas the table below gives heights above the Atlantic and above Cumberland. This table also gives heights of hills, west of Uniontown, and the heights furnished by the old Commissioners, are of mountains and hills between Cumberland and Uniontown. As to the accuracy of, and authority for, this table, the author of this volume is not informed, but it seems to have been sanctioned and adopted by Mr. Veech, whose reputation as a local historian is unimpeachable.

THE TABLE.

	Above the Atlantic.	Above Cumberland.
Cumberland	537 feet	
Wills Mountain	1003 "	466
Frostburg	1792 "	1255
Big Savage Mountain	2580 "	2043
Little Savage Mountain	2480 "	1943
Red Hill	2437 "	1900
Meadow Mountain	2550 "	2013
Little Crossings	2000 "	1463
Negro Mountain	2825 "	2288
Keyser's Ridge	2843 "	2306
Winding Ridge	2534 "	1997
Smithfield	1405 "	868
Barren Hill	2450 "	1813
Woodcock Hill	2500 "	1963
Laurel Hill	2412 "	1875
Monroe	1065 "	528
Uniontown Court House	952 "	415
Colley's Hill	1274 "	737
Brownsville	833 "	296
Krepps' Knob	1040 "	503
Beallsville	1010 "	473
Hillsboro	1770 "	1233
Egg Nog Hill	1532 "	995
Washington	1406 "	869
West Alexander	1792 "	1255
Wheeling Hill	850 "	313
Wheeling City	748 "	211

CHAPTER XLIV.

Two Noted Old Tavern Keepers — Thomas Endsley and William Sheets — The Latter the Driver of the First Mail Coach Out from Cumberland — A Wedding Party Surprised, and a Marriage Prevented — William M. F. Magraw, a well known Man of the Road.

A prominent and widely known man of the road was Thomas Endsley. He was born near Richmond, Virginia, in 1787. He was the only child of parents who came from Switzerland and settled in Virginia at an early day. His mother was of an old family of Gilberts, who were Quakers, well known and much respected in their day and generation. His wife was Mary McCloy, to whom he was wedded in the year 1805. The offspring of his marriage consisted of eight children, five sons and three daughters. The sons were John, Thomas, James, William and Andrew Jackson. The three last named are still living, James and William in Somerfield, and Andrew Jackson in Somerset. The daughters were Mary Ann, who became the wife of Redding Bunting, the noted old pike boy heretofore mentioned; Nancy, who was the wife of J. Squire Hagan, another old pike boy; and Julia, who in 1842, married P. R. Sides, and is now living with a son in New Mexico. Her husband died in Missouri in 1877, or thereabout. Mrs. Hagan died in Uniontown in 1849, and Mrs. Bunting died in the same place about five years ago. Nancy Endsley and Squire Hagan were married in 1834. Mrs. Endsley, wife of Thomas, the subject of this sketch, died in the stone tavern at Somerfield in 1832, and her husband died in the same house in 1852.

Thomas Endsley was an old wagoner before the Cumberland Road was constructed. In the years 1812, 1813, 1814, 1815, 1816, 1817 and 1818, he hauled goods and merchandise from Baltimore to Nashville, Tennesse, to points in Ohio and to Brownsville, Pennsylvania. He owned two six-horse teams, one of which he drove himself, and placed the other in charge of a hired driver. In spring and fall he was frequently compelled to remain with his teams at the old Smith tavern, near the present town of Somerfield, for several days awaiting the subsidence of freshets in the Youghiogheny river, so that he could ford that stream, there being no other means of crossing at that time. The road was frequently in such condition by reason of mud, deep cuts, and other obstacles, that a whole day's progress did not cover a greater distance than three or four miles. To pass through Jockey Hollow it was often found necessary to attach twelve horses to one wagon.

(323)

In the year 1819 Thomas Endsley moved from Virginia to Frost burg, Maryland, and at that place commenced a career of tavern keeping, which terminated only with his death. He leased the old Frost House in Frostburg, and conducted it for three years. In 1822 he went to the Tomlinson House, a prominent old landmark twenty-one miles west of Cumberland. He occupied the Tomlinson House for two years, and while there enjoyed the patronage of one of the stage lines. In December, 1823, he bought the old Smith farm at Somerfield, lying on both sides of the road. On this farm was erected the large stone tavern house, at the eastern end of the big stone bridge which spans the Youghiogheny river. For this property he paid $8,000 cash down, which shows the enhanced value of the property at that day by reason of contiguity with the National Road. He took possession of this property on the first day of April, 1824. The land was poor, the fences were dilapidated, and the general outlook unpromising. But Mr. Endsley was a man of great energy and good judgment, and going to work with determination, soon changed the aspect of things, and had flowers blooming and grass and grain growing, where before the eye had rested on nothing but briars, weeds and rocks, with here and there a scant appearance of sickly oats and buckwheat. It is said that he was the first man who ever attempted to raise corn and wheat in the neighborhood of Somerfield, and old settlers jeered him for trying it. It was not long under his judicious management until his farm yielded thirty-five and forty bushels of wheat to the acre, and crops of corn equal to the best of the adjoining county of Fayette. This farm continues in the possession of the descendants of Thomas Endsley. The northern portion of it is owned and occupied by the heirs of Thomas Endsley, jr., deceased, except the stone tavern, which with the southern portion of the farm, is owned and occupied by William Endsley.

While assiduous in bringing up his farm, Thomas Endsley was by no means neglectful of his tavern. He was always attentive and courteous to guests. His table was spread with well cooked victuals, and his rooms were clean and neat, so that altogether his house was one of the most inviting on the whole line of the road. The Stockton line of coaches stopped at the Endsley House during its entire career on the road, with the exception of a short time, when it was withdrawn by reason of a temporary estrangement between Mr. Stockton and Mr. Endsley. Stockton was of a fiery temper, while Mr. Endsley was not slack in resenting a supposed wrong, and at one time in going over their accounts they disagreed, and each gave utterance to expressions not taught in the Sunday schools. As a result, Mr. Stockton removed his stock from Endsley's tavern and passed and repassed the house thereafter for awhile without casting a glance of recognition toward it. It was not long, however, until Mr. Endsley was surprised to see Mr. Stockton enter his house, extend his hand, and hear him say: "This foolishness has lasted long enough; my coaches must stop at this house." "When?" calmly queried

Mr. Endsley. "To-morrow," said Mr. Stockton, and the old terms of friendship between them were restored, and continued as long as Mr. Stockton lived. As stated in another chapter Mr. Endsley was a slave owner, and frequently aided in the capture and return of fugitives. Two of his slaves, Peter and Phebe Butler, after acquiring their freedom, settled in Brownsville, and died there. They were well known by the old people of Brownsville, and held in high esteem. Thomas Endsley, in 1834–'35, in connection with James Black, of Somerfield, had contracts for taking up the original road bed on Winding Ridge and Negro Mountain, and proved himself as efficient in this line as in every other line of business he engaged in. He was imposing in personal appearance, well up to six feet in height, and weighed about two hundred pounds. He was an habitual reader, and a subscriber for the *Cumberland Civilian* and the *National Intelligencer*, from the time he lived in Frostburg to the date of his death. He carefully and studiously read the long and prosy editorials of the *Intelligencer*, as well as the speeches it published of Henry Clay, Daniel Webster, John C. Calhoun, Thomas H. Benton, and other noted statesmen of that era.

In 1828 a military company called "The Addison Blues," was organized, drawing its members from Somerfield, Petersburg and the surrounding neighborhood, of which Thomas Endsley was elected captain, and ever thereafter known and hailed as Captain Endsley. At all the old battalion parades in Somerset, Bedford and Uniontown the "Addison Blues" bore off the palm for soldierly bearing, and especially for the stalwart size of its rank and file, all of whom were hardy mountaineers, and known and honored as "frosty sons of thunder."

WILLIAM SHEETS was a prominent character of the road, more widely known as a tavern keeper, than in any other relation. He was a remarkable man in many respects, and in none more than relates to his extreme longevity. He was born February 2d, 1798, near Martinsburg, Berkeley county, Virginia, and died May 4th, 1892, in Jefferson county, Iowa. He was a wagoner before the Cumberland Road was made, and hauled goods from Baltimore to points west, over the old Braddock road. He also had some experience as a stage driver. His first venture as a tavern keeper was at or near the Little Crossings, where he remained but a short time, and did not do a paying business. Leaving the Little Crossings, he went to Negro Mountain and took a house there. His first experience at Negro Mountain was attended by only limited success, and he abandoned tavern keeping and moved to a small house on Jennings' run, about two miles west of Uniontown, and near the old Moxley tavern, then kept by William Cox. In that vicinity he engaged in various pursuits, mostly of a precarious nature, with a downward tendency, accelerated by too much indulgence in drinking. This was between the years 1835 and 1840, and probably a little earlier. He seemed to realize that his fortune was on the wane, and resolved to retrieve himself. He

15

accordingly, by some means not ascertainable, secured a new lease on the Negro Mountain house which he had left, and returned to it. Beginning life anew, as it were, he quit drinking and devoted himself energetically to business. It was not long until he established a good reputation and did a large and profitable business. His house was a favorite stopping place for hog drovers, and in the latter part of his career on Negro Mountain, the number of barrels of corn he bought and sold would count up to hundreds of thousands. The weary and hungry hog drover (pig pelter the pike boys termed him), as he trudged along the road in snow and slush, urging forward the lagging, grunting porkers, apparently reluctant to move on to the sure slaughter awaiting them, would cry out at intervals, and in despairing tones: "Suboy, suboy, forty cents a day and no dinner; how far is it to Sheets'?" For many years William Sheets fed the hungry hogs, and their no less hungry owners and drivers, and while his profits were small, his business was so large that his accumulations in a few years aggregated a sum which made him a comfortable fortune. William G. Beck, the old stage driver living in Fairfield, Iowa, before referred to, avers that William Sheets drove the first mail coach out from Cumberland that ever passed over the National Road west of that place. This was in the year 1818, and on Kinkead's line of coaches. Kinkead was an uncle of William G. Beck, and a member of the old bridge building firm of Kinkead, Beck & Evans, and an owner of the first stage line on the road, as before stated. The wife of William Sheets was Sarah Wiggins, a sister of Isaac Wiggins, late of South Union township, Fayette county, Pennsylvania, deceased, and an aunt of James H. Wiggins, a prosperous and well known farmer of that township. She was an attractive girl, and had many suitors. One of her lovers was a man by the name of Bradley, an employe of Kinkead, before mentioned. She gave her hand to Bradley, and consented to become his wife, and went so far as to appear upon the floor with Bradley to have the knot tied by the Rev. William Brownfield. The relatives and friends of Miss Sarah were stoutly opposed to her alliance with Bradley, and a moment before the old and renowned Baptist parson began the ceremony of marriage, Col. Cuthbert Wiggins, an uncle of the would-be-bride, and father of Harrison Wiggins, the old fox hunter of the mountains, appeared on the scene and carried Miss Sarah from the floor, thus abruptly terminating the pending nuptials, to the great astonishment of those in attendance, and causing much comment and town gossip. This unusual incident happened in a house on Morgantown street, in Uniontown, about the year 1821. No subsequent effort was made by the parties most interested, to consummate the forbidden marriage, and the fair Sarah, in a short time thereafter, forgetting her affection for Bradley, became the wife of William Sheets. The after career of Bradley is unknown. He seems to have passed from the memory of men without making a sign. In the year 1855 William Sheets took final leave of Negro Mountain and the scenes of the National Road, and moved to Jefferson county, Iowa, where he made his

W. M. F. MAGRAW.

last settlement, and died at the date above given. At his death he was the possessor of a large estate, chiefly in lands, which descends to his two surviving sons, Isaac and Joseph, and to the heirs of deceased sons and a deceased daughter. He had six sons and one daughter. Bazil Sheets, one of his sons, was an old wagoner, well remembered by the old citizens along the line of the road.

One of the smartest, best known and most picturesque men of the road forty years ago was WILLIAM M. F. MAGRAW. He was probably little known west of Brownsville, as his business was for the most part on the line east of that point. He was a native of Maryland, and belonged to an old and influential family of that State. His brother, Harry, practiced law for several years in Pittsburg, and served a term as State Treasurer of Pennsylvania from 1856 to 1859. The Magraws were intimate friends of James Buchanan, and Harry was a leader in the movements that led up to the nomination and election of that old time statesman to the Presidency. W. M. F. Magraw became identified with the National Road as many others did, through a matrimonial alliance. His wife was a daughter of Jacob Sides, who owned the Tomlinson tavern. His first business engagement in the vicinity of Uniontown was with F. H. Oliphant, the old iron master of Fairchance. Soon after engaging with Mr. Oliphant that gentleman put on a line of teams and wagons hereinbefore mentioned, to haul freights between Brownsville and Cumberland, and Magraw was placed in charge of the line as its general road agent. This put him in communication with the people along the road, and established him in the ranks of the pike boys. He was a large, fine looking man, always well dressed, attracting attention wherever he appeared, and making friends by reason of his agreeable manners. He was not fleshy, but broad shouldered, tall and erect, of ruddy complexion, light hair, and habitually wore gold rimmed spectacles on account of some defect of vision. He was generous almost to a fault, and lavish in his personal expenditures. He spent much of his time in Uniontown, making his headquarters with his friend Joshua Marsh, of the National House. His habits of living were different from the majority of the old pike boys, especially in the matter of eating, and he enjoyed a good supper at midnight, better than any other hour. He brought in game of all kinds from the mountain and had it served in savory style at the National House. He kept a carriage, and often had it ordered out as early as three and four o'clock in the afternoon, to go to the mountain, but lingered about the town, chatting with friends, until nightfall. He seemed to delight in driving over the mountain in the night. Leaving Uniontown about the dusk of the evening, he would reach the Tomlinson tavern about daybreak the next morning. He called up the old tavern keepers along the road, all of whom knew him, chatted a while with them, took a mint julip, or something stiffer, and pushed on, and this was his habit as long as he remained on the road. He was a southern sympathizer during the war, and participated as a Confederate partisan, in some of the irregular skirmishes in Missouri, in the incipient stages of the long struggle. Notwithstanding his southern sentiments, he was well liked by his northern acquaintances, and had many warm friends among them. There was no bitterness in his heart. He was clever and courteous to all. He had no stauncher friend than Redding Bunting, the good old stage driver, who was a pronounced Union man. Sometime near the close of the war, Magraw appeared in Harrisburg. Upon being questioned as to the object of his mission, he said he had come to see the Governor on behalf of the appointment of his old friend, Red Bunting, to the office of Commissioner of the Cumberland Road. He knew the Governor (Curtin) personally. In fact, he knew nearly all the public men of his time. He called on the Governor, and was cordially received. "What brought you here," queried the Governor. "I came," said Magraw, "to solicit the appointment of Redding Butting as Commissioner of the Cumberland Road." "How does it come," further queried the Governor, "that all you copperheads are for Bunting?" "Oh!" said Magraw, "Bunting is a good man, the right man for the place, and a good Republican." "Well," said the Governor, "I guess I'll appoint him," and he did. Mr. Bunting was not aware that Magraw intended to go to Harrisburg in his behalf, which shows the disposition of the man. During the administration of President Pierce, Magraw had a contract for carrying the mails from the Missouri boundary to western points beyond the plains. He suffered much loss by reason of Indian invasions, and preferred a claim to Congress for a large sum of money to reimburse him. While his bill was undergoing consideration by the committee, he appeared before it and emptied upon the floor a number of bags of mules ears, as evidence of his losses. His bill was passed. Magraw died suddenly, in Baltimore, a number of years ago, much lamented. His wife is also dead. He had a daughter, Miss Sallie, well remembered by the older citizens of Uniontown, who is living in Kansas City, a widow, in affluent circumstances.

CHAPTER XLV.

Dumb Ike — Reminiscences of Uniontown — Isaac Johnson — Squire Hagan — A Musician Astride of a Hog — Anecdote of Judges Black and Williams — Morgan Miller, an Old Tavern Keeper — Philip Krishbaum, an Old Stone Cutter — Crazy Billy — Highway Robbery — Slaves Struggling for Liberty — William Willey, an old Friend of the Slaves — Unsuccessful Attempts at Suicide by an old Postmaster and an old Drover — Tom Marshall, of Kentucky, appears on the Road and amuses the boys.

The National Road had its variety, as all the ways of life have, and this variety added spice to it, and gave it much if not all of its flavor. There were high types, and low types, and queer types of life on the road. Every section of the road had its noted character. There was Marion Smith (Logan), who made his headquarters, for the most part, at Searights, but a familiar figure all along the line between Uniontown and Brownsville. He stood ever ready to fetch the gear pole and insert it between the spokes of the hind wheels of the big wagon, the moment it was driven upon the yard at the old tavern in the evening, to rest for the night. He was likewise prompt in carrying the hay and grain to feed the big six horses that stood with their heads to the long, strong trough supported by the wagon tongue, and when this little job was done, his compensation was replete, and his topmost ambition realized in the big drink he took with the driver at the bar. And Logan was further noted as an imitator of the rooster, and gave many a long, loud crow over Democratic victories in the olden time. Bill Hickman will be readily recalled by the reader who is familiar with the history and traditions of the road, as an eccentric character. He gravitated between Chalk Hill and Jockey Hollow, and Billy Brubaker afforded amusement for the men of the road near Brownsville. It would scarcely be doing justice to the nomenclature of the old road, without writing this name "Bluebaker." There were many others of this class, but time and space will not permit a reference to them, and besides, this sketch is devoted especially to "Dumb Ike." His name was Isaac Griffin, or Toner, and he belonged to the queer type in the above enumeration. He was not in fact dumb, but everybody called him "Dumb Ike." He was opaque and bright by turns. Dr. Hugh Campbell once asked him why they called him dumb, and he said "he didn't know, unless because they were dumb themselves."

Isaac was born and reared in Springhill township, Fayette county, Pennsylvania. The sound of the glories of the old pike reached his ears at his rural home, and he resolved to cast his lot upon it. It was previous to the year 1840 that he made his appearance in Uniontown, and for the first time beheld the National Road. When he shook the dust of Springhill from his feet, it was with a high resolve to never engage in hard labor, a resolution he never thereafter broke. His ambition was to become a stage driver and it was irrepressible. He reached his goal. He obtained employment as a driver on one of the stage lines and approved himself a good one. Not given to absolute steadiness of habit, his employment was not continuous, but he was held in reserve, as it were, to take the place of regular drivers in cases of accident or emergency. He could handle the reins and crack the whip equal to the best of drivers, and took good care of his team. He not only drove stage but was a driver on the express line, and perched on the high front seat of an express wagon, drawing the reins over four stout horses, was the personification of a proud and happy man. A little incident in the old National House on Morgantown street, when that popular old hostelry was kept by the kind-hearted and gentle Joshua Marsh, goes to illustrate the eccentric ways of Isaac. It was in the bar room. Samuel McDonald, a prominent citizen of the town, had occasion to call there, and among those in the room at the time was "Dumb Ike," with whom McDonald was well acquainted, as was every other citizen. McDonald invited Isaac to take a drink, a proposition quite agreeable to him, and which he promptly accepted. Standing at the bar with glass in hand, well filled, Isaac felt it a duty to compliment his entertainer, and said: "McDonald, I respect you," and hesitating, continued, "and probably I am the only man in town that does." Isaac intended to be complimentary, and McDonald knowing this, joined in the loud laughter of the bystanders over Isaac's bull.

During the prevalence of Asiatic cholera in Uniontown in 1850, some one was speaking to Isaac in reference to the fatality of the epidemic, and was much astounded to hear Isaac say it was not cholera. "What then is it?" queried the other party. "It is death," retorted Isaac. When Isaac wished to express indignation against a person he thought was putting on airs, he called him "The Great Nates," and of conceited persons he said they were "great in their own *estimashing*." The writer has in his possession a boot jack made and given to him by "Dumb Ike" in 1852. It is a clumsy specimen of mechanism, but prized on account of the maker and donor. Isaac's patriotism was accelerated by a drink, and often under its influence he exclaimed with emphasis of voice and violent gesticulation of his right arm, "I am going to the District of Columbia to see the Goddess of Liberty." When the war against the South assumed the shape of open and active hostilities, "Dumb Ike" volunteered as a soldier, and proudly marched to the front under the flag of the stars and stripes. He was assigned to duty in the transportation service, for which his experience eminently fitted him, and he died in the faithful discharge of duty, and was buried where he died, near the capitol of the Republic beneath the shadow of the Goddess of Liberty, at whose shrine he was a devoted worshipper. At his death a small sum of money was on deposit to his credit in the old bank of Fayette county, which was absorbed by claims for nursing and other services in his last illness. He left neither widow or heirs to survive him. His administrator was Nathaniel Brownfield, his old friend of the Swan tavern in Uniontown, where he made his headquarters for many years, and where he was living when he enlisted as a soldier. There were worse men and better men than "Dumb Ike," but no one who knew him will begrudge a good, kind word for his memory.

Isaac Johnson, a former well known and respected citizen, who died at his residence near Uniontown a number of years since, had occasion to visit the East in the year 1833, and on his return home walked the entire distance from Baltimore over the National Road. His mission carried him as far east as New Castle, Delaware, and from that point to Frenchtown he rode on the first passenger cars propelled by steam in the United States. He was a native of Greene county, Pennsylvania, and the father of David D. Johnson, of Fayette Springs, who was Commissioner of the road during the administration of Governor Beaver.

Squire Hagan, who died in Uniontown a few years ago, much lamented, father of Miss Maggie, the popular clerk in the Uniontown postoffice, was a "Green Mountain Boy," born in Vermont, near Montpelier, the capital of that State. The fame of the old National Road was carried on the wings of the wind to the snow-capped hills of his native land, and he yearned for a share of its glories. His first appearance on the road was at Somerfield, where, in the year 1834, he owned and conducted a general store. The leading trait in the character of Squire Hagan was amiability, and the trend of his mind was toward philosophy. He was widely known along the line of the road, and highly respected.

William Hunsucker was a hog drover from Greene county, Pennsylvania, and the boys called him "Suboy Bill." Upon being asked who owned the hogs he was driving, and where they came from, he replied in words that jingled thus:

> "Mr. Lindsey is the owner,
> They call me Suboy Bill,
> The hogs came out from Greene county,
> Near the village of Blacksville."

It is said that Joe Williams, a wit, musician, comedian, lawyer, and in his riper years Chief Justice of the Territorial Court of Iowa, once straddled a big black hog in a drove, and rode it through the main street of Uniontown, playing a clarionet. Judge Williams was born in Somerset county, Pennsylvania, and was a brother of Mrs. William Murphy, who lives near Uniontown. Hon. Jeremiah S. Black, of national fame, and Joe Williams were cronies in their boyhood days. Williams visited New York after he became Chief Justice, and it happened that Judge Black was in that city at the same time. A morning paper stated that Judge Black was a guest at the Astor House, and this falling under the eye of Williams, he proceeded hastily to the hotel to see his old friend. He walked into his room, to discover that he was out, and seeing writing material on the table, indited the following lines, which he left in the room for Judge Black's perusal, on his return:

"The salutations of the Chief Justice of Iowa, to the Chief Justice of Pennsylvania:

> "Oh, Jerry, dear Jerry, I have found you at last!
> How memory, burdened with scenes of the past,
> Restores me to Somerset's mountains of snow,
> When you were but Jerry, and I was but Joe."

Morgan Miller kept a tavern on Morgantown street, Uniontown, as early as 1830, and probably before that time. His house was a dingy frame structure, painted red, which time and storm made a dead red. The location was on the hill near the old Baptist church, in that day called "Prospect Hill." At this old tavern many persons of the neighborhood were accustomed to spend their evenings in drinking and gossipping. Among its patrons were Philip Krishbaum, a stone cutter, and Abram Brown, a farmer. Krishbaum had some aptitude in making rhymes, a talent he found useful in his business of chiseling tomb-stones. After spending an hour or two, one evening, in alternate drinking and gossipping with his friend Brown, he rose from his chair and remarked that he must take a drink and go, as he had to finish some lettering on a tomb-stone. "Stay awhile," said Brown, "and write an epitaph for my tomb-stone, and I will treat." "Agreed," said Krishbaum, who, taking up a pen, wrote this:

> "Here lies the body of Abram Brown,
> Who lived three miles from Uniontown.
> The more he got, the more he craved.
> Great God! can such a soul be saved!"

Brown paid for the drinks. Seeing that Krishbaum had made a success of the Brown epitaph, Miller, the landlord, requested him to write one for his tomb-stone, which he did, as follows:

> "Here lies the body of Morgan Miller,
> Who has drunk the whisky of many a 'stiller.
> He once lived up on Prospect Hill,
> And sold his whisky by the gill."

The well known character brought to mind by the name of "Crazy Billy," was at no time in his strange life engaged in any pursuit connected with the National Road, but his long stay at Uniontown, covering a period of fifty years and more, entitles him to a place in this history. He was well known to many of the stage drivers, wagoners and tavern keepers of the road, and to every man,

CRAZY BILLY.

woman and child in Uniontown. His name was William Stanford, and he was born in England. It was evident that he had been well bred, and had received some education. He was often heard quoting from the liturgy of the Church of England. He was brought to Uniontown about the year 1829, and closely confined in the county jail. His first appearance in Fayette county was in Springhill township, whither he wandered without any apparent object, and no one knew whence he came. On a certain day of the year above mentioned, he was discovered alone in the house of one Crow, in the said township of Springhill. The Crow family had all been absent during the day, and upon their return in the evening were surprised to find an occupant within, and the doors and windows securely fastened. After reconnoitering the premises the family discovered that it was the manifest intention of the strange intruder to "hold the fort." In this state of the case Mr. Crow proceeded to a neighboring justice of the peace, made complaint, and obtained a warrant, which was placed in the hands of the township constable, who with the aid of the local *posse comitatus* hastily summoned, entered the beleaguered dwelling, arrested the intruder, took him to Uniontown, and lodged him in the county jail, in and around which he remained from that time until the date of his death, which occurred on the 26th day of January, 1883. Soon after his incarceration one John Updergraff was committed to the jail for disorderly conduct on the streets, and after the keys had been turned, "Billy" fell upon the new prisoner, and killed him outright. He was indicted and tried for murder, but acquitted on the plea of insanity, and remanded to jail. Henceforth, and to the time hereafter mentioned, he was heavily ironed and chained fast to the jail floor. William Snyder was elected sheriff in 1847, and a few months after his induction to the office, his wife, who was a good and discerning woman, observed some redeeming qualities in the nature of the chained lunatic, and concluded that it would be wise and safe, as well as humane, to remove his fetters. Accordingly with the aid of her son James, who was a sort of general deputy about the jail and office, she released "Billy" from the chains which had so long bound and chafed him, and permitted him to walk about his dingy cell, untramelled. Gradually he gained the confidence of the sheriff's family and after a season was permitted to enter the official mansion, and move about at pleasure. He showed an inclination to care for the sheriff's horses, and was permitted to feed and clean them, exhibiting much skill in this line. About this time, James Snyder having occasion to visit Monroe, told "Billy" that he might go with him if he chose. Pleased with the opportunity, "Billy" placed saddles and bridles on two horses, mounted one himself, and Snyder the other, and off they sped to Monroe. It was an agreeable trip to "Billy"; the first time in many years, that he had enjoyed the privilege of seeing the country and snuffing the pure air of liberty. After this, he rode out frequently with the deputy to various parts of the county; but his

15ᵃ

mind was never fully restored.   He was incoherent, and given to unintelligible mutterings.   As time wore on, the people of the town became familiar with "Crazy Billy," and as before stated everybody knew him.   He carried letters, and performed errands for the county officers, for many years, and up to the date of his last illness, and his fidelity was proverbial.   Nothing could divert him from the faithful execution of any little mission he undertook.   In addition to his constant mutterings before alluded to, he was a habitual scribbler. He entered any of the offices in the court house at pleasure, and invariably sat down and began to scribble.   He wrote a fairly good hand, but there was no intelligence in his writing, or rather no connected thought.   One of his favorite lines was this: "I am a bold boy in his prime."   He would write this as often as a dozen times a day.   Another of his favorite screeds was this:

> " He drew his sword and pistol,
> And made them for to rattle,
> And the lady held the horse,
> While the soldier fought the battle."

The garb in which "Billy" from day to day appeared, was of the shabby order, and he paid little heed as a rule to personal cleanliness.   His ablutions were periodical, but when he did indulge in them, they were thorough.   He had a habit of rubbing his head with both hands, and would sit engaged in this exercise as long as an hour at a time, with great energy.   He never would submit to an interview.   He talked much, but always on the run.   If approached by anyone with a purpose of conversing with him, he invariably walked off muttering in loud tones as he moved away.   He wore a full beard, which in his latter years was quite gray.   He had a small foot and hand, and many marks of intellectuality.   After his death his body lay in state in the court house at Uniontown, and was viewed by thousands.   He was buried in Oak Grove Cemetery, near Uniontown, with the rites of the Episcopal Church, under direction of the late lamented Rev. R. S. Smith.   A section of one of the stone columns of the old Uniontown court house is made to serve as a monument over his grave.   Maj. Jesse B. Gardner of Uniontown, who attended "Billy" in his last illness, gives the following pathetic narration of his closing hours.   Until the last ebb, he continued to utter the sonorous and unintelligible mutterings so familiar to those who knew him, but in the final throe, he turned his eyes upon his attendant and exclaimed: "Oh, Gardner, if I could only see my mother!"   This was not a lucid interval, in the ordinary meaning of that phrase, but an expiring thought. a final flash of affection, a wonderful testimonial to the sweetest of all names, and a most forcible and striking illustration of the ineffaceable impression made by a mother's care and love, and all the more, since at no time before, during his long sojourn at Uniontown, was he ever known to have mentioned his mother, or his father.   A poor, unfortunate lunatic, separated for more than a half century from the parental roof, a stranger in a strange land, tossed by the billows of a hard fate, and lying down to die, light flashes upon his long distempered mind, and his last and only thought is "MOTHER."

The year 1823 developed one of the most extraordinary examples of grand larceny that ever occurred on the road, and excited the people all along the line from Baltimore to the farthest point west. During the early spring of the year mentioned a merchant whose name was Abraham Boring, doing business in an Ohio town, took passage in a coach of one of the regular stage lines for Baltimore to purchase a stock of fresh goods. At Tomlinson's tavern, west of Cumberland, John Keagy and David Crider, merchants, of Salisbury, Somerset county, Pennsylvania, took seats in the same coach that was conveying Boring, destined also for Baltimore, on a like mission. It required considerable time to reach Baltimore, and passengers in a stage coach became acquainted, one with another. The three merchants not only became personally acquainted with each other, during their long stage ride, but formed strong friendly relations. Reaching Baltimore they stopped together at the same hotel and talked over their business, the quality and quantity of goods required by each, forming the leading topic of their conversation. They went out among the wholesale stores of the city and bought the goods they desired, the stock purchased by Mr. Boring being much larger, finer and more varied than the stock bought by the Somerset county merchants. Upon completing his purchases, Mr. Boring's first thought was to have his goods safely shipped upon the best terms obtainable. Messrs. Keagy and Crider kindly tendered their services to aid him in engaging a trusty wagoner to haul his goods to Ohio, and introduced one Edward Tissue as the right man for that purpose. Tissue was engaged, but one wagon bed would not hold all the goods, and Tissue brought in and introduced another wagoner by the name of Edward Mitchell, who was engaged to haul the remnant that could not be handled by Tissue. Mr. Boring having arranged for the transportation of his goods, said good-bye to his friends Keagy and Crider, and left for his home in Ohio. His goods not arriving when due, he supposed some accident had caused a delay, and that they would be forthcoming as soon as practicable. But days and weeks passed and Mr. Boring began to feel uneasy about the long delay, and wrote the consignors in Baltimore for an explanation. They replied that the goods had been carefully loaded in the wagons of Tissue and Mitchell, according to the agreement, and they knew nothing of their destiny beyond that. Boring then took to the road to find his goods. He went first to Baltimore and learned that Tissue and Mitchell had left the city with the goods in their wagons, and proceeded westward. He traced them as far as Hagerstown, and at that point lost his clue. He proceeded to Cumberland without tidings of his lost goods. From Cumberland he went on, making inquiry at every tavern and toll gate, until he reached Somerfield, but heard nothing of Tissue or his companion,

Mitchell. He put up for the night at a tavern in Somerfield, and while at supper discovered an important clue. The waiting maid at the table wore a tortoise shell comb, resembling very much those in a package he had bought in Baltimore. In polite and delicate terms he inquired of the girl where she obtained so handsome a comb. She replied, "In a store at Salisbury." In an instant Mr. Boring recalled his fellow merchants and recent fellow travelers, Messrs. Keagy and Crider, of Salisbury, but concluding that they had purchased the same quality of combs in Baltimore, went to bed, with a purpose of continuing his researches along the National Road. During the night he changed his purpose, and in the morning returned to Tomlinson's tavern, and thence directly to Salisbury. Reaching Salisbury he entered a store, and to his amazement saw upon the counters and shelves various articles, which he recognized as belonging to his stock. Investigation disclosed a remarkable example of criminal conduct. Keagy, Crider, Tissue and Mitchell entered into a conspiracy to steal Boring's goods. The acquaintance formed in the stage coach constituted the initial point of the scheme, and Keagy and Crider found ready confederates in Tissue and Mitchell. There was of course to be a division of the spoils, but in what proportion never was made public. The wagoners to avoid identification changed the color of their wagon beds, and upon reaching Hagerstown diverged from the National Road and took the country by-ways. The goods were placed at first in a large barn in the vicinity of Salisbury, and thence carried in small lots to the store of Keagy & Co. A portion of the goods consisting of fine china ware, thought to be too expensive for the Salisbury trade, was broken up and buried under ground. There was a third owner of the Salisbury store by the name of Markley, who did not accompany his partners on their tour to raise stock. Boring, after thoroughly satisfying himself that he had found his goods, proceeded to Somerset and swore out a warrant against the parties accused. The warrant was placed for execution in the hands of —— Philson, the sheriff of Somerset county. Keagy was first arrested and promptly gave bail for trial, but goaded by the weight of his offense, soon thereafter committed suicide. Tissue fled the jurisdiction and was never apprehended. Crider also fled and located in some of the wilds of that early day in the State of Ohio, where he married and raised a family, and, it is said, has living descendants to this day. Markley essayed to flee, but made a failure of it. Giving out the impression that he had followed in the wake of Tissue and Crider, he concealed himself in the woods not far from Salisbury, and was supplied with food by a devoted wife. One Sloan, however, happened to fall upon his hiding place and he was arrested. Markley owed Sloan a sum of money and proposed to settle if Sloan would release him from custody. To this Sloan assented. Markley had no ready money, but owned property and proffered his note, which Sloan agreed to accept. But no means were at hand to prepare a note. After canvassing the situation for a while a pen was made from a stick of wood, ink obtained from stump water, and Sloan producing a scrap of paper, a note was prepared and duly signed by Markley for the sum he owed Sloan, and the money subsequently paid by Markley's wife. Sloan promised Markley that he would not make known his hiding place, but it leaked out and he was arrested by the sheriff. He requested permission of the sheriff to go to his house to change his clothes, which was granted him, and taking advantage of the sheriff's indulgence, fled to parts unknown. His wife rejoined him in after years at some point in the West.

Mention was hereinbefore made of the tragical death of Atwell Holland, killed by a fugitive slave on the 4th of July, 1845, at an old tavern in the mountain. In this connection it is proper to state, that fugitive slaves were frequently captured on the National Road, and returned to their masters. Capt. Thomas Endsley, an old tavern keeper, mentioned elsewhere, once had a terrible conflict with three powerful fugitive slaves, at his barn near Somerfield. Without assistance and against most determined resistance, he succeeded in capturing two of them and returning them to their owner or master. The third escaped and became a free man. Capt. Endsley was himself a slave owner as before stated. He owned and used slaves when he lived at Frostburg, and also during his incumbency as landlord at the old Tomlinson tavern, and brought eight with him when he located at Somerfield in 1824. Like all other old slave owners, he thought there was no wrong in owning slaves, and considered it a conscientious duty to aid in capturing and returning fugitives. His sons, however, probably from witnessing the struggles of the slaves to gain their freedom against the efforts of their father, all grew up to be abolitionists, and abide in the anti-slavery faith to this day.

One of the most untiring and devoted friends of escaping slaves, was William Willey of Somerfield. He was a shoemaker without means, yet it is said that he secreted, fed and otherwise aided more fugitive slaves than any other man on the National Road. He is known to have harbored as many as eight and ten in a single night, in his lowly tenement. He was a native of Baltimore, and reared a Democrat. Those of his friends who survive him regard him as a philanthropist, worthy of a granite monument. The wife of William E. Beall, the well known manager of the Uniontown steel mill, a most excellent lady, is a daughter of William Willey, the old friend of the escaping slaves.

In the year 1829 the postoffice at Somerfield was in the brick house, on the south side of the street, known as the Irvin house. John Blocher was postmaster. The old line of coaches, carrying the mail, stopped at the Endsley House. It was customary for the driver after reaching the tavern to carry the way mail pouch on his shoulders to the postoffice. One evening Charley Kemp drove the mail coach in from the west, and upon going to the office with the mail, found the door locked, and was unable, after repeated efforts, to gain admittance. Going around to a window, he looked through the glass into the office, and was horrified by seeing Blocher, the postmaster, lying on the floor, weltering in blood, and forcing his way into the room discovered that his throat was cut. Dr. Frey was summoned, and applied agencies first to arrest the flow of blood, and then sewed up the gash, and to the surprise of all, the man recovered and lived for many years thereafter.

In 1834 John Waters, a cattle drover of Ohio, fell sick at Frazer's tavern, in Somerfield, and languished for many weeks. His mind becoming affected by reason of his severe bodily suffering, he rose from his bed one evening when alone, opened his pocketbook and tore into small fragments a number of good bank notes of the aggregate value of $800. He then deliberately cut his throat. When discovered he was lying on his back on the floor, and small pieces of bank notes were seen floating in blood all around his body. Dr. Frey was summoned on this occasion also, and under his treatment the much dejected old drover was restored, and afterward took many droves of cattle over the road to Baltimore. The fragments of notes were gathered up, carefully cleaned, dried and fitted together with mucilage, so that the loss of money was inconsiderable.

Some time during the year 1840 or '41 a rather tall and cadaverous looking individual, presenting the appearance of a man on a protracted spree, was observed coming down the hill into Somerfield from the east, walking and leading a beautiful bay horse, equipped with a handsome saddle and bridle. The quaint looking and quaint moving stranger halted to converse with a cluster of boys, who were sitting on the pavement in front of Endsley's tavern, near the stone bridge at the Big Crossings. He told the boys so many amusing stories, that they reckoned him to be the clown of a coming circus. That man was Tom Marshall, one of the brightest of Kentucky's many bright sons, a brilliant lawyer, orator and statesman, who carried off the palm in every intellectual combat he ever engaged in save one, and that was when he locked horns with Henry Clay. The horse led by Marshall was a favorite animal which he kept and used in Washington, while attending the sittings of Congress. He frequently passed over the road in the manner described, and often tarried several days and nights in Uniontown. Many of the surviving pike boys remember Marshall with distinctness.

CHAPTER XLVI.

There is no doubt that Dr. John F. Braddee was the most notorious individual that ever lived in Uniontown. The exact date of his advent to that place seems to be unascertainable, but it was more than fifty years ago. The culmination of his remarkable career occurred in 1841. Of his early life but little is accurately known. It is certain that he came to Uniontown from Virginia. Tradition has it that he was born in Kentucky. The story goes that when quite a youth he engaged himself as a stable boy, in the service of a gentleman who dealt in horses in the town of Paris, State of Kentucky. His employer was accustomed to drive horses to the eastern market for sale, and on one of these occasions young Braddee was taken along as an assistant. The horses were driven over what was called the "North Western Pike of Virginia." At some point on this old road Braddee fell sick and was left behind. After his recovery he made his way to Uniontown, stopping for a while in, or about Morgantown. Notwithstanding his robust appearance, which will be remembered by his old acquaintances, it is said that when a boy he was delicate and inclined to consumption. This is the story, whether true or not is immaterial in view of his subsequent history. When he reached Uniontown, he was not known to be the owner of a single dollar, that he might call his own. Without education or professional training, he announced himself a physician, and commenced the practice of medicine. His success was remarkable. He had a commanding personal appearance, a good address, and by these means alone impressed himself upon the confidence of the common mind. He gathered around himself a large circle of friends and admirers, some of doubtful, but not a few of unquestioned reputation. His fame as a doctor extended far and wide, patients flocked to consult him from all points. Many came hundreds of miles. Fifty horses have been seen hitched around his office at one time.

He possessed and cultivated a fondness for fast horses, probably the result of his early education in the stable at Paris, Kentucky. He always kept a number of race horses in training for the turf, and often matched them against others on the race course. In this line his success was varying, sometimes he won and as often lost, but losses did not diminish his love for the race course. The accumulations received from his large practice of medicine, and his winnings on the race course did not satisfy his greed for gain, and he conceived and carried into execution an extraordinary scheme for increasing his gains. It was nothing less than a carefully organized plan to rob the United States mail. His success as a physician had enabled him to acquire property, and he had not been living in Uniontown long until he possessed himself of one of the most handsome and valuable properties in the place, viz: the property known as the "Old National House," on Morgantown street. He bought this property from Hon. Thomas Irwin, who afterwards sat as one of his Judges in the famous trial to be hereafter mentioned. When Braddee bought this property, it contained only a single building, the three story brick on the southern side of the lot. He added the wing to the north, and here he established his headquarters, carrying on his business, professional and unprofessional, with a high hand. His office was convenient, in fact immediately adjoining Stockton's stage yard and coach factory. Into this stage yard, coaches were driven every day. Stockton had the contract for carrying the mails. The old pike was in full blast then, and as many as thirty coaches were driven along it both ways every day. Among the coaches carrying the great and lesser mails, one William Corman was a driver, and Braddee cultivated his acquaintance and secured his confidence. He assured him that money could be made easily by rifling the mail bags, and promised Corman that if he would hand him the bags, he would "go through them" and divide profits with him. Corman consented. It was of course soon discovered that the mails were tampered with, and United States detectives were set upon the tracks of the offenders. They were not long in ascertaining the guilty parties. Corman was arrested and told the whole story. Braddee had other accomplices, viz: P. Mills Strayer, and Dr. Wm. Purnell. Strayer was a saddler, who carried on a shop in Uniontown, and died only a few years ago. Purnell was a sort of body servant of Braddee, and for many years after Braddee's death peddled Braddee's medicine through Fayette and adjoining counties. Braddee was arrested on information made by Wm. Corman, and his arrest caused more excitement than any event that ever transpired in Uniontown.

THE INFORMATION.

Pennsylvania, Fayette County, ss:

George Plitt, agent of the P. O. Department, being duly sworn, says that the United States mail from Wheeling, Virginia, to New York, traveling on the National Road, has been stolen, to-wit: The mails made up at Wheeling on the 13th, 19th, 23d and 29th of November, 1840, and on the 5th, 12th and 18th of December, 1840, and that he has reason to suspect and does suspect and believe that Wm. Corman, who on those days drove the mail stage containing said mail from Washington to Uniontown, Pennsylvania, is guilty, with others of stealing said mails.

GEO. PLITT, *Agt. P.O. Dept.*

Sworn and subscribed this 6th day of January, A. D. 1841, before me.

N. EWING,
Prest. Judge 14th Judicial District, Pennsylvania.

Same day warrant issued, directed to the Sheriff of Washington county, and to all other Sheriffs and Constables within the Fourteenth Judicial District.

George Plitt, agent of the P. O. Department, being duly sworn, says that the United States Mails from Wheeling, Virginia, to New York, traveling on the National Road, has been stolen, to-wit: The mails made up at Wheeling on the 13th, 19th, 23d and 29th of November, 1840, and on the 5th, 12th, and 18th of December, 1840, and that he has reason to suspect, and does suspect and believe that John F. Braddee, William Purnell, and Peter Mills Strayer, with others, are guilty of stealing the mails.

GEO. PLITT, *Agt. P.O. Dept.*

Sworn and subscribed this 7th day of January, A. D. 1841, before

N. EWING,
Prest. Judge 14th Judicial District, Pennsylvania.

Same day warrant issued to George Meason, Esq., Sheriff of Fayette county, and to all constables.

The United States of America vs. John F. Braddee, William Purnell, et al.

William Corman, being duly sworn, says that more than one year ago John F. Braddee repeatedly urged him to let him, the said Braddee, have some of the mail bags from the mail coach, and that he would divide the money taken from them with said Corman. Said Braddee said he had frequently known such things done, and that lots of money had thus been made, and it had never been detected. While said Corman was driving the mail coach between Smithfield and Uniontown last winter, the said Braddee sent Peter Mills Strayer frequently in a sleigh after him to get a mail bag containing a mail—that at length he, said Strayer, took one from the coach, which was then on runners, while he, the said Corman, was watering at Snyder's, east of the Laurel Hill. That Braddee afterwards told him that there was nothing in it.

That he knows of no other mail being taken until within about two months past, when he, the said Corman, was driving between

Uniontown and Washington, and when at the instance and after repeated and urgent requests of said Braddee he commenced leaving a mail pouch or bag in the stage coach, when the coaches were changed at Uniontown, and continued to do so at intervals of (say) a week, ten days or two weeks, until within a week or ten days before Christmas. That the said mail bags were taken from the coach by said Braddee or some one under his direction. That Braddee after the taking of said mails would sometimes say there was nothing in them, and again that others had but little money in them. One he said had but fifteen dollars. The last but one gotten, as before stated, he said had a large amount of money in it, but he was going to keep it secretly—bury it until the fuss was over. That said Braddee said he had a secret place out of doors where he could hide the mail bags so that they could not be found. That said Braddee from time to time gave him three dollars or five dollars as he asked for it, and once ten dollars; and loaned him forty dollars when his (Corman's) wife was going away. That William Purnell several times after a mail bag had been taken, would take him, said Corman, aside and whisper to him that the bag had nothing in it. That on the day before yesterday he was several times at said Braddee's house and Braddee wished him to leave a mail bag in the coach for him when he, said Corman, should return from Washington last night. That said Braddee very often wished him to leave a mail bag when he did not. That he, Braddee, requested him to leave the large mail bag in the coach for him, but he never did do it.

WILLIAM CORMAN.

Sworn and subscribed this 8th day of January, A. D. 1841, before me   N. EWING,

Pres. Judge of the 14th *Jud. Dist., Pa.*

Dr. Howard Kennedy also made a preliminary affidavit, which is given in a previous chapter.

WARRANT OF ARREST.

The United States of America to George Meason, Esq., High Sheriff of Fayette County, Pa., and to all Constables of said County:

WHEREAS, John F. Braddee, William Purnell and Peter Mills Strayer have been charged before me, the President Judge of the Fourteenth Judicial District in the said State, on the oath of George Plitt, an agent of the Post Office Department, with stealing the United States mails from Wheeling to New York, these are therefore to command you, and each of you, to take the said John F. Braddee, William Purnell and Peter Mills Strayer, and bring them before me, or some other Magistrate having jurisdiction, to be dealt with according to law.

Witness the hand and seal of the said N. Ewing, President Judge as aforesaid, at Uniontown, the 7th day of January, A. D. 1841.

N. EWING, [SEAL.]
Pres. Judge of the 14th Jud. Dist., Pa.

Pennsylvania, Fayette County, ss:

The examination of Dr. John F. Braddee, of the borough of Uniontown, Fayette county, Pa., taken before me, N. Ewing, President Judge of the Fourteenth Judicial District of Pennsylvania, the 8th day of January, A. D. 1841.

The said John F. Braddee being brought before me by virtue of a warrant issued by me, on suspicion of stealing the United States Mails from Wheeling, Va., to New York, made up at Wheeling on the 13th, 19th, 23d and 29th days of November, 1840; and on the 5th, 12th and 18th days of December, 1840, says: I know nothing about the alleged stealing of the mails.

his
JOHN F. × BRADDEE,
mark.

Taken and subscribed before me,

N. EWING,
January 8, 1841.   *Pres. Judge 14th Jud. Dist. of Pa.*

Pennsylvania, Fayette County, ss:

The examination of Peter Mills Strayer, of the borough of Uniontown, Fayette county, Pa., taken before me, N. Ewing, President Judge of the Fourteenth Judicial District of Pennsylvania, on the 8th day of January, A. D. 1841.

The said Peter Mills Strayer being brought before me by virtue of a warrant issued by me, on suspicion of stealing the United States Mails from Wheeling, Va., to New York, made up at Wheeling on the 13th, 19th, 23d and 29th days of November, and on the 5th, 12th, and 18th days of December, 1840, says: I know nothing about the mail bags or the stealing of the mails.

P. M. STRAYER.

Taken and subscribed before me,

N. EWING,
January 8, 1841.   *Pres. Judge 14th Dist. of Pa.*

The United States of America, Fayette County, Pennsylvania, ss:

The United States of America vs. John F. Braddee, January 8, 1841, ordered that John F. Braddee enter into security himself in fifty thousand dollars, and two sufficient sureties in $25,000 each. Prisoner remanded until Monday, the 11th instant, at 10 o'clock A. M., to afford time to procure bail.

The same vs. Peter Mills Strayer, January 8th, 1841, ordered that Peter Mills Strayer enter into security himself in $15,000, and two sufficient sureties in $7,500 each. Prisoner remanded until Monday, the 11th instant, at 10 o'clock, to afford time to procure bail.

The same vs. William Purnell. January 8th, 1841. Ordered that William Purnell enter into security himself in $10,000, and two sufficient sureties in $5,000 each. Prisoner remanded as above, etc.

January 11, 1841. Monday, 10 o'clock, A. M. Prisoners ordered before the Judge. Prisoners say they are not provided with bail and ask further time, until say three o'clock P. M. Three o'clock, P. M., no bail being offered the defendants are committed to the custody of the Marshal of the Western District of Pennsylvania.

N. EWING,

Pres. Judge, 14th Jud. Dist., Pa.

MITTIMUS.

The United States of America, Fayette County, Pennsylvania, ss:

The United States of America to the Marshal of the Western District of Pennsylvania, Greeting: WHEREAS, John F. Braddee, of the borough of Uniontown, in the County aforesaid, hath been brought before the Hon. Nathaniel Ewing, President Judge of the Fourteenth Judicial District of Pennsylvania, by virtue of the warrant of the Hon. Nathaniel Ewing, President Judge as aforesaid, charged upon the solemn oath of George Plitt, agent of the General Post Office department, with stealing the United States mails made up at Wheeling, Virginia, for New York, on the 13th, 19th, 23d and 29th days of November, 1840—and on the 5th, 12th and 18th days of December, 1840.

These are therefore to command you the said Marshall to receive the said John F. Braddee, and keep him in safe custody until he be delivered by due course of law. Hereof fail not.

Witness the Hon. Nathaniel Ewing, President Judge as aforesaid, at Uniontown, the eleventh day of January, Anno Domini 1841.

N. EWING,

Pres. Judge of the 14th Jud. Dist., Pa.

The United States of America vs. John F. Braddee, William Purnell, Peter Mills Strayer and William Corman, charged on oath of several robberies of the U. S. Mail.

George Meason tent in $1,000; William Crawford tent in $1,000; William Freeman tent in $1,000; James McCune tent in $1,000.

On this condition, that the said George Meason, William Crawford, William Freeman and James McCune shall be and appear at the next Circuit Court of the United States, to be held for the Western District of Pennsylvania on the third Monday of May next, and give testimony in —— of the said United States against the said John F.

Braddee, William Purnell, Peter Mills Strayer and William Corman, and not depart the court without leave, otherwise the recognizance to be in full force and virtue.

GEO. MEASON, [SEAL.]
WM. CRAWFORD, [SEAL.]
JAS. McCUNE, [SEAL.]
WM. FREEMAN. [SEAL.]

Taken and acknowledged this 13th day of January, A. D. 1841.
Coram,
T. IRWIN,
Dist. Judge of the U. S., Western Dist. of Pa.

U. S. COMMITMENT.

United States of America, Western District of Pennsylvania, ss:

The United States of America to the Marshal of the Western District of Pennsylvania and his deputies, to any constable of the County of Allegheny, and to the jailer of said County of Allegheny, Greeting:

WHEREAS, John F. Braddee, William Purnell and Peter Mills Strayer are now brought before me, the Hon. Thomas Irwin, Esquire, Judge of the District Court of the United States for the Western District of Pennsylvania, charged on the oath of George Plitt, William Corman and others, with stealing the United States mail made up at Wheeling on the 13th, 19th, 23d and 29th days of November, A.D.1840, and on the 5th, 12th and 18th days of December, 1840. These are therefore to command you, the said marshal, constable or jailer, or either of you, to convey the said John F. Braddee, William Purnell and Peter Mills Strayer to the said jailer of Allegheny county, and you, the said jailer, are hereby commanded to receive and keep safely the said John F. Braddee, William Purnell and Peter Mills Strayer in your jail until they thence be discharged by due course of law. For so doing this shall be your warrant.

In testimony whereof the said Hon. Thomas Irwin, Esq., has hereunto set his hand and seal, this 13th day of January, A. D. 1841.

(Signed) TH. IRWIN, [SEAL.]
District Judge, U. S.

PITTSBURG, PENNA., 25th of Jan'y, 1841.

Howard Kennedy, special agent of the Post Office Department, in addition to the testimony given by him before His Honor Judge Ewing, in the case of the United States against Braddee, Purnell, Strayer and Corman, relative to the probable loss of money, drafts, &c., in the stolen mails, further deposes, that since that time he has received reports from various persons and places in the West of letters mailed at dates which would have by due course of mail been in the bags stolen, containing bank notes, scrip, certificates, drafts and checks, amounting to one hundred and two thousand dollars and upwards; that every mail brings him additional reports of losses, and that he believes the amounts reported will not constitute more than one-half of what has been lost in the mails between the 16th of Nov., and the 18th of Dec., 1840, on the route from Wheeling to New York.

HOWARD KENNEDY,
Special Agent P. O. Dep't.

Sworn and subscribed before me the 25th January, 1841.

T. IRWIN,
District Judge.

PETITIONS FOR HABEUS CORPUS.

To the Hon. Thomas Irwin, Judge of the United States Court of the Western District of Pennsylvania:

The petition of William Purnell respectfully represents that your petitioner is now confined in the jail of Allegheny county, in obedience to a warrant of commitment, a true copy of which is prefixed to this petition. Your petitioner humbly prays your Honor to award a *habeas corpus*, that he may be bailed by sufficient sureties, according to the first article and ninth section of the Constitution of the United States, January 29, 1819.

WILLIAM PURNELL.

To the Hon. Thomas Irwin, Judge of the Court of the United States for the Western District of Pennsylvania:

The petition of Doctor John F. Braddee respectfully represents that your petitioner is now confined in the jail of Allegheny county, in obedience to a warrant of commitment, a true copy of which is prefixed to this petition.

Your petitioner humbly prays your Honor to award a *habeas corpus*, that he may be bailed by sufficient sureties, according to the first article and ninth section of the Constitution of the United States.

The United States *vs.* John F. Braddee.

his
JOHN F. × BRADDEE.
mark.

Petition for *habeas corpus* granted, and issued January 28, 1841.

The same *vs.* Wm. Purnell, *alias* William Purnell, January 29, 1841.

United States vs. Braddee.

Let a *habeas corpus* issue in this case according to the prayer of the petitioner, returnable forthwith.

THOMAS IRWIN,
District Judge.

E. J. ROBERTS, Esq., *Clerk.*

January 26, 1841.

United States vs. Purnell.

Let a *habeas corpus* issue in this case according to the prayer of the petitioner, returnable forthwith.

THOMAS IRWIN,
District Judge, Western District of Pennsylvania.

E. J. ROBERTS, Esq., *Cl'k D. Court.*

THE WRIT AND JAILER'S RETURN.

Western District of Pennsylvania, ss:

The President of the United States to the Marshal of said District, and the jailer of Allegheny county, greeting:

We command you the body of John F. Braddee in your custody, under safe and secure conduct before the Hon. Thomas Irwin, Judge of our District Court, at his chambers in the city of Pittsburgh, together with the day and cause of his said caption and detention, forthwith then and there to be subject to whatsoever our said Judge shall consider in that behalf, and have you then there this writ.

Witness the Hon. Thomas Irwin, Judge of the United States for said District, at Pittsburg, the twenty-eighth day of January, A. D. eighteen hundred and forty-one.

E. J. ROBERTS, *Clerk.*

The body of the above named John F. Braddee I have brought before your Honor, together with day and cause of his being detained, in obedience to the writ.

So answers Jas. McCune, jailer of Allegheny county.
To the Hon. Thomas Irwin.

BOND AND BONDSMEN.

The U. S. vs. John F. Braddee. Application to be admitted to bail, Jan. 28, 1841.

The following named persons being sworn, depose, That they are worth severally as follows: Hugh Graham, $20,000; Benjamin Brownfield, $18,000; Isaac Hague, $5,000; Henry Smith, $5,000; R. Laughlin, $4,000; Emanuel Brown, $3,500; B. Brown, $3,000; D. S. Diamond, $1,000; Thomas Moxley, $2,000; Michael Franks, $2,000; Abraham White, $800; Jacob Humbert, $200; Peter Humbert, $1,000; Andrew McClelland, $3,000. *Coram,*

T. IRWIN.

These amounts were taken from the property lists in the Commissioners Office of Fayette county, Pa. Abraham Brown, $3,400; Benjamin Brown, $4,050; Emanuel Brown, $2,925; Benjamin Brownfield, $6,869; Michael Franks, $1,400; Henry Smith, $2,272; Andrew McClelland, $1,170; Peter Humbert, $1,200; Isaac Hague, $3,170; Isaac Brown, $3,552; *Hugh Graham, 3,868; Samuel Hatfield, $4,500; Thomas Moxley, $2,000; *David Chipps, $200. Names marked with a star, are already security for Hugh Keys, Canal Commissioner, with Wm. Searight, for $50,000, and also on the bond of Thompson McKean, late Road Commissioner, for a large amount.

POINTS RAISED BEFORE THE COMMITTING MAGISTRATE:

Quere.—Can bail be given on any other species of property than real estate?

Quere.—Are not these persons indemnified? If so, how? Would it be policy to recognize them as witnesses on the part of the United States?

Quere.—The order is that two sureties in $25,000 each should be furnished—will any other members be taken?

The United States vs. John F. Braddee.

In the Circuit and District Courts of the United States, for the Western District of Pennsylvania, charged with the larceny of the U. S. mail or mails and stealing therefrom. Hugh Graham, Benjamin Brownfield, Isaac Hague, Henry Smith, Robert Laughlin, Emanuel Brown, Daniel Diamond, Thomas Moxley, Michael Franks, Abraham White, Jacob Humbert, Peter Humbert, Andrew McClelland, Lewis Williams, James McLean, David Chipps, James Douglass, John Hague, Abraham Brown, Daniel Franks, John McClelland and William Hague acknowledge themselves to be held and firmly bound unto the United States in the sum of sixty thousand dollars each, lawful money of the United States, to be levied of your goods and chattels, lands and tenements, upon condition that the said John F. Braddee be and appear at a session of the Circuit Court of the United States to be held at the city of Pittsburg the third Monday in May next, to answer the said charges, and such other matters as shall then and there be preferred against him, and that he shall not depart the court without leave. Taken and acknowledged. *Coram,*

T. IRWIN,

January 28, 1841.   *District Judge.*

THE INDICTMENT.

In the Circuit Court of the United States of America, holden in and for the Western District of Pennsylvania, at May sessions, in the year of our Lord one thousand eight hundred and forty-one. Western District of Pennsylvania, to-wit:

The grand inquest of the United States of America, inquiring for the Western District of Pennsylvania, upon their oaths and affirmations respectively do present and say: That John F. Braddee, late of said Western District of Pennsylvania, a practitioner of medicine, did on the twenty-fifth day of January, in the year eighteen hundred and forty, at Uniontown, in the said Western District of Pennsylvania, procure, advise and assist Peter Mills Strayer to steal, take and carry away the mail of the United States of America, then in pro-gress of transmission from the postoffice in Washington City, in the District of Columbia, to the postoffice at Wheeling, in the Western District of Virginia, contrary to the form of the act of Congress of the United States, in such case made and provided, and against the peace, government and dignity of the United States.

C. DARRAGH,
U. S. Attorney for the Western District of Pennsylvania.

True bill—JAMES RIDDLE, Foreman.

May 24th, 1841.—The Grand Jury came into court and presented a bill of indictment against Wm. Purnell for stealing a letter from the mail and other offenses. Same day John F. Braddee by his bail, Hugh Graham, is surrendered into Court and Hugh Graham dis-charged from his recognizance. Same day, on the motion of Mr. Austin, and affidavit of John M. Austin, filed, habeas corpus ad satis-faciendum, issued to the jailor and Sheriff of Fayette county for the body of William Collins. United States vs. John F. Braddee, No. 3 of May Term, 1841. Stealing from the United States mails. And now, to-wit: May 25th, 1841, a jury being called came, to-wit: George Fortune, William Plummer, Samuel Cooper, William Raymond, Ed-ward A. Reynolds, Arnold Eichbaum, James Stewart, John Clemens, Joseph Alexander, Thomas F. Mitchell, Thomas S. Cunningham and Samuel A. Roberts, twelve good and lawful men, duly sworn, sum-moned and balloted for, and sworn and affirmed, do say on their oaths and affirmations that the defendant is guilty on the first, second and fourth counts in the indictment, and not guilty on the third count. Verdict given on the 4th day of June, 1841. The jury was polled at the instance of defendant's counsel.

EXCEPTIONS.

The Court referred to the trial of Robinson, which had taken place at the present term, and in which some of the jurors now em-panneled had rendered a verdict of guilty. It was not pretended that this trial had the remotest connection with the mail robbery at Uniontown, or that the case of Robinson involved any principle of evidence, or consideration as to the credibility of witnesses, analogous to the case under consideration; yet the Court asked the jury to re-flect how it would look, out of doors, after the conviction of a poor friendless boy like Robinson, to acquit such a prisoner as was then on trial; that it might countenance the reproach which had been cast upon the law of permitting big fish to escape while little ones were caught, and that the Court would be deeply mortified at such an appearance. These remarks, which could afford no possible grounds for salutary reflection, were calculated to make the jury

16

forget their oaths; to lead them away from a conscientious and fearless examination of the testimony to calculations upon the probable opinions of others, founded not upon oath or upon a full hearing of the testimony. This, too, in a case where it had been made to appear that the most infamous attempts were resorted to for the purpose of inflaming the public mind by falsehoods through the press. The jury to reflect that if they took a course unpopular at the moment, the whole odium must rest upon them, and that their characters, motives and conduct would be placed in striking contrast with the more popular tone of the Court.

2. That the Court whilst forbearing altogether to notice, or noticing very slightly, the considerations which took all weight from the testimony of Corman and Strayer (witnesses for the prosecution), told the jury it would be a farce to pay any attention to the testimony of Collins and Owens, witnesses for the accused, although the latter stood infinitely fairer before the jury, and had no such powerful inducements as Corman and Strayer to give false testimony.

3. The offense, if any, established against the prisoner, was that of taking the mail with the consent of the person having charge thereof. Yet the Court declined to give the prisoner the benefit of this discrimination.

4. The charge of the Court that the testimony of Turk, as to the non-arrival of the mail at New York, derived from the register, was sufficient, without the production of the register or any copy thereof, or extract therefrom.

United States *vs.* Braddee. Reasons in arrest of judgment.

1. The indictment did not pursue the language of the Act of Congress, but mingles together words which in the act are intended to describe different offences. The accused is consequently not apprised of the clause under which he is indicted, and the especial character of the offence which he must prepare himself to meet. These crimes being statutory, must turn altogether on the language of the Act of Congress. Suppose the same count had charged the accused with robbing, stealing and taking?

The indictment does not allege that the mail stolen or taken contained any valuable thing.

Overruled.

THE SENTENCE.

United States vs. John F. Braddee. May sessions, 1841. Sentence on the first count of the indictment: That you, John F. Braddee, be imprisoned in the Western Penitentiary of Pennsylvania, at hard labor, for and during the term of ten years, and in all respects be subject to the same discipline and treatment as convicts sentenced by the Courts of the State; and that you pay the costs of this prosecution, and stand committed until this sentence be complied with. And while so confined therein you shall be exclusively under the constraint of the officers having charge of said Penitentiary.

DOCKET ENTRIES.

May 27th, 1841.—Test. for United States: J. H. Phillips, J. H. Dieus. Henry H. Beeson, Frederick Byrer, John Keffer, Samuel McLean, Peter Mills Strayer. Amos Jolliff, Samuel Costello, William Wagner. May 28th—Test. for Defendant: John Warner, Thomas Moxley. Adam George, John Hendricks, Uriah Hoke, Aaron Wyatt, James McLean, James Smith, Jacob F. Brant, Robert Carr, Thomas Rowland. Abraham White, Isaac Hague, Jacob Eckel, Decatur Wolfe. May 29th—Test. for Defendant: John Haney, William Collins, Francis Wilkinson. Jesse King, H. Mitchell, David Chipps, Wm. D. Swearingen. Henry Hally, Margaret Collins, William Purnell, John Imbre, John Campbell. John M. Crane, Alfred Core, Seth Holl, John Woodward, Henry Smith, Matthias C. Baker, James Marinder, Madison Mooney, James Owens. May 31st—Test. for Defendant: Jesse Jones, Wm. Hall, T. Shaw, William Ebert, Gideon John, Alexander I. Fowler. John F. Sangston, Benjamin Brownfield. June 1st—Test. for United States: Brown Snyder, George Meason, Robert L. Barry, John Keffer, Alfred McClelland, Ellis Baily, Isaac Nixon, William Nixon, Samuel Nixon, Geo. Rider, J. T. Williams, Jas. McGayen, Wm. Reddick.

June 1. Court took a recess for half an hour. Mr. Black (Col. S. W.), on behalf of the United States, addressed the Court and jury. Mr. William Austin, for defence, addressed the Court and jury. Mr. Darragh, district attorney, addressed the Court and jury. June 2. Mr. Darragh continued and concluded his address. Mr. McCandless, for defense, addressed the Court and jury; Court took a recess for half an hour. Mr. McCandless continued and concluded his address. Mr. Biddle, for the defense, commenced his address to the Court and jury. June 8. Mr. Biddle continued and concluded his address. Mr. Loomis, on behalf of the United States, commenced his address to the Court and jury. The jury, having been charged by Judge Baldwin, retired. Same day rendered a verdict as before mentioned. Mr. McCandless moved the Court in arrest of judgment and for a new trial.

June 5. Affidavits as to the ownership of a portion of the money in the hands of Messrs. Darragh and Kennedy filed. Mr. Finley for Edward H. Brags, moves to take the money out of Court found in the mail stolen, and identified by the affidavits filed. Same gentleman makes the same motion for John J. Young. Both motions referred by the Court to Messrs. Darragh and Kennedy as auditors. Amos Jolliff discharged from his recognizance to attend as a witness. The following report was made to the Court by Messrs. Darragh and Kennedy viz: Pittsburg, June 5, 1841. The undersigned beg leave to report that they have paid out on affidavits to individuals claiming, or their order, the following sums from the money recovered on the premises of John F. Braddee: E. H. Pandell, $250; Timothy Goodman, $1,060; Silas D. Force, $100; James Sproul, $690; H. S. Abbott, $647.10; Sibbett & Jones, $1,127; Haney St. John, $1,455; B. S. Williams, $30; G. G. Moore, $170; A. H. Bangs, $934.90; John S. Young, $190; Chas. S. Bradford, $300; in all $7,154.60. Whole amount recovered, $10,398.60, leaving $3,244 undistributed. Report of auditors confirmed, and claimants who have been paid are directed to give receipts, and the balance unclaimed be deposited in the Bank of Pittsburg to abide the further order of the Court.

United States vs. William Purnell. Wm. Freeman, James McCuen, O. T. Moore, H. H. Turk, A. McClelland and William Crawford each bound in a recognizance of $500 to appear at the next term of the Circuit Court of the United States for the Western District of Pennsylvania, on the 3d Monday of November next, to testify in the above case. J. M. Austin moves the Court to direct the Marshal to pay the witnesses subpœnaed on the part of the defendant in the case of the United States vs. John F. Braddee. Court refused, and ordered that the expenses of compulsory process be paid to the officers by the United States.

United States vs. William Purnell. Defendant tent in $4,000 on condition that he be and appear at the next term of the Circuit Court of the United States, to be held in the city of Pittsburg, on the first Monday of November, next. James L. Bugh, Benjamin Watson and John Hendricks each tent in $1,000 on condition that defendant be and appear as aforesaid.

June 7. The Court overruled the motion for a new trial in the case of the United States vs. Braddee, and also a motion by John M. Austin, esq., to postpone sentence, and the Court sentenced the defendant as before mentioned.

November 16, 1841. The United States vs. Margaret Collins. Stealing from the United States mails. Witnesses sworn before the grand jury: E. S. Harris, Johnze Dicus, A. McClelland. D. H. Phillips, William Ebert, John P. Sturgis, Henry H. Beeson. Abraham Alexander and Dr. Howard Kennedy.

Same vs. Same. Charged with receiving a $500 Treasury note, stolen from the mail, knowing the same to have been stolen.

November 17. Recognizance of William Purnell and his sureties called and forfeited, and the witnesses in this case discharged from their recognizances. The grand jury came into Court and presented true bills of indictment against Margaret Collins.

November 22. Defendant pleads not guilty. Tried and jury could not agree, and were discharged. Margaret Collins was Braddee's mother-in-law. Purnell and Corman were pardoned by the President before trial.

Thus ended the great Braddee trial; an affair that caused more excitement than any local event that ever interested the people of Uniontown. The actors are all dead. Judges Baldwin and Irwin, who heard the cause, are both dead. All the lawyers who were concerned are dead; some of the witnesses are still living. The bondsmen are all dead. Braddee died in the penitentiary about ten years after his incarceration. Many persons believe that he did not die in the penitentiary, but in some manner escaped therefrom. There can be no doubt, however, that he died in the penitentiary.

THE GERMAN D. HAIR HOUSE.

CHAPTER XLVII.

John Quincy Adams visits Uniontown — He is Welcomed by Dr. Hugh Campbell — The National Road a Monument of a Past Age — A Comparison Between the National Road and the Appian Way.

> " We hear no more of the clanging hoof,
> And the stage coach, rattling by;
> For the steam king rules the traveled world,
> And the old pike's left to die."

The foregoing lines were written by one who mourned the departing glories of the old road. When they were written the steam car had taken the place of the four-horse coach, and the writer was giving vent to his grief over the change. Steam has since encountered a formidable competitor in the shape of electricity, and the time is coming when the steam car will follow in the wake of the old stage coach. Progress is the inspiring watchword of the hour, and while there may be nothing new under the sun, old things are certainly presented in a new light, and old agencies applied to new work.

No sound greets the ear of the pike boy now, like the clink of other days. The glory of the old road has departed, but the memory of its better days fades not away. The old tavern has gone with all the rest. The incidents and anecdotes, accidents and episodes of the road have all passed to the domain of history.

In the month of May, 1837, John Quincy Adams visited Uniontown, on his return from Cincinnati, where he had gone to participate in the inauguration of the observatory on Mount Adams, near that city. Dr. Hugh Campbell was appointed to deliver the address of welcome to Mr. Adams on his arrival at Uniontown. The following opening sentences are quoted from Dr. Campbell's address:

"*Venerable Sir:* I have the honor of being the organ of this community to express for them and myself our hearty welcome of you among us. You see here, sir, an assembly of people of every political faith, come together spontaneously as one man to express their respect and veneration for one who has filled so large and distinguished, and I may add, beneficial space in the history and councils of this nation. We stand here, sir, upon the CUMBERLAND ROAD, which has, to some extent, broken down the great wall of the Appallachian mountains, which served to form so natural a barrier between what might have been two great rival nations. This road constitutes we trust, an indissoluble chain of Union, connecting forever as one.

the East and the West. As a people directly interested in this great national work, we are glad to have the opportunity of expressing our acknowledgments to you in person. It is a part of that great system which has always received your support, known as the American System, the happy influence of which you have recently had the pleasure of witnessing in the rapid and extraordinary development of the resources of the West."

Dr. Campbell proceeded at some length in a well conceived and happily expressed address, and concluded as follows:

"Again, sir, I bid you welcome to the hospitalities of our town, and may the God of all grace prolong your existence, and finally receive you to himself."

It is noteworthy, because out of the ordinary line, that two of the ablest debaters and most popular public speakers of Western Pennsylvania, fifty years ago, were physicians—Dr. F. J. Lemoyne, of Washington, and Dr. Hugh Campbell, of Uniontown, the first named an Abolitionist and the other a Whig. Those who have heard them on the stump aver that they never heard better speakers. They were both highly educated, masters of logic, forceful in delivery, and in the modern phrase, "clean cut" in all their utterances.

In the latest map of Fayette county, Pennsylvania, there is a sketch of the National Road, written by the late Hon. James Veech, in which that able man said:

"It is a monument of a past age; but like all other monuments, it is interesting, as well as venerable. It carried thousands of population and millions of wealth into the West; and more than any other material structure in the land, served to harmonize and strengthen, if not to save, the Union."

There was a popular belief, in the olden time, that the National Road was a bond of union between the States, and that it served to harmonize and bring together on friendly terms, people of remote sections, and of different pursuits. This will be seen by the quoted remarks of Dr. Campbell and Mr. Veech. The generation of to-day regards the affection of the old pike boy for the old road, as a mere memory, the recollection of the animated scenes of trade and transportation on the old highway. It is something more. The old pike boy sincerely and truly believes that the old pike was a bond of union, that for years it kept the peace between discordant interests, and prolonged the evil day when the outbreak of disunion came.

The Appian Way was a great road, and is invested with much classic and historic interest, but, unlike the National Road, it did not yield its place to greater lines of progress and improvement. The Appian Way was designed to gratify the pomp and vanity of consuls and pro-consuls, kings and princes, emperors and empires. The National Road was designed to meet the wants of a free and progressive people, and to aid in building up and strengthening a great and growing republic. The Appian Way had more vitality than the government that built it. It outlived its country. The National Road

DR. HUGH CAMPBELL.

served its purpose grandly, was a complete success, the pride and glory of its day and generation, and when it lost its place as a national thoroughfare, the government that made it was all the stronger because it had been made. The average width of the Appian Way was from eighteen to twenty feet, so as to admit of two carriages passing each other, and the expense of constructing the first section of it was so great that it exhausted the public treasury of Rome. The National Road was sixty feet wide, and eight carriages could pass each other within its borders, while the cost of its construction, although a very large sum of money, made so light a draught upon the resources of the public treasury of the United States, in comparison with subsequent appropriations for other objects, as to be scarcely worthy of observation. The Appian Way derived its name from Appius, who was consul of Rome at the time of the undertaking. Its initial southern terminus was Capua, distant from Rome one hundred and twenty-five miles, very nearly the same as the distance from Cumberland to Wheeling. It was subsequently constructed as far as Beneventum, and ultimately to Brundisium, a seaport town of the Adriatic, distant from Rome three hundred and seventy-eight miles. We are informed by Anthon, an ancient classic author of high renown, that the city of Beneventum derived great importance from its position on the Appian Way, and the same can be truthfully said of the towns and cities which were so fortunate as to be located on the National Road.

Paul the apostle traveled over a portion of the Appian Way on his journey from Jerusalem to Rome to carry up his appeal from Agrippa to Cæsar. He intersected the Appian Way at Puteoli, where he remained seven days, and his brethren having learned that he had reached that point, came to meet him as far as Appii Forum and the Three Taverns. The Appii Forum was a station, and the Three Taverns a house for the entertainment of strangers and travelers on the Appian Way. The latter may have been three distinct houses moulded into one, as is sometimes done, or a cluster of taverns consisting of three. That they were taverns, or a tavern, is unquestionable. There was an old tavern on the Mountain division of the National Road, in Fayette county, Pennsylvania, called the Three Cabins. The cabins were put up for boarding and lodging workmen engaged in the construction of the road, and when the work was finished, united and made one. This grotesque old tavern enjoyed a large patronage, and was a source of no little profit to its old-fashioned proprietor.

Horace, as before intimated, was an occasional traveler on the Appian Way, not infrequently accompanied by Virgil, and apparently with no other object than the mere pleasure afforded by the jaunt. These illustrious authors of classic verse were, it is said, given to convivial habits, and we have the word of Horace himself that the wine on the Appian Way was "thick." From some other things said by Horace, it is very evident that the taverns of the Appian Way were inferior to those of the National Road. As an instance, he says that "the bustling landlord of the inn at Beneventum almost burned himself in roasting some lean thrushes." Lean thrushes never entered the well stored larders of the old taverns of the National Road. Fatness was the leading feature of flesh and fowl and bird of every kind that passed inspection of the old-time landlord of our National highway, and fatness distinguished all the surroundings of his overflowing hostelry. Nor was it the habit of our old tavern keepers to do the cooking and roasting of their establishments. All that pertained to the dominion of the landlady, who, as a rule, was tidy and robust, and felt a just pride in her calling. Horace also complained that at an inn at Canusium, on the Appian Way, he was served with "gritty bread." Shades of John N. Dagg, Joseph Hallam, Daniel Brown, Charles Miller, James Workman, Alfred McClelland, Joshua Marsh and Boss Rush, defend us forever against the thought of gritty bread! Horace, in further deprecation of some things on the Appian Way, mentions a little town where "water is sold, though the worst in the world." Generosity was a leading trait of the old tavern keepers of the National Road. There was an inexhaustible supply of water along its line, the best and purest in the world, and no man ever heard of a cup of it being sold for a price. One of the most attractive features of the National Road was the big water-trough that stood by the side of every tavern, filled with fresh, sparkling water, and absolutely free to all comers and goers.

THE BIG WATER-TROUGH ON LAUREL HILL.

APPENDIX.

---

*A Digest of the Laws of Pennsylvania, relating to the Cumberland Road
— Unexpended Balances in Indiana — Accounts of Two Old Com-
missioners — Rates of Toll — Letters of Albert Gallatin, Ebenezer
Finley and Thomas A. Wiley — Curiosities of the old Postal Service.*

1807. Act of April 9th gives the State's consent to the making of
the road within its limits, provided the route be changed to
pass through Uniontown and Washington; also gives the
United States authorities full powei to enter upon lands, dig,
cut and carry away materials, etc., for the purpose of completing and *forever* keeping in repair said road. Pamphlet Laws,
page 185.

1828. February 7th. Joint resolution authorizes the Government of
the United States to erect toll gates, enforce the collection of
tolls, and to do and perform every other act and thing which
may be deemed necessary to insure the PERMANENT repair and
preservation of the road. Andrew Shultz, Governor, Nerr
Middleswarth, Speaker of the House of Representatives, Daniel
Sturgeon, Speaker of the Senate. Pamphlet laws, page 500.

1831. Act of April 11th. Preamble: "Whereas, that part of the
Cumberland Road lying within the State of Pennsylvania is
in many parts in bad condition for want of repairs, and as
doubts have been entertained whether the United States have
authority to erect toll gates on said road and collect toll, and
as a large proportion of the people of this commonwealth are
interested in said road, ITS CONSTANT CONTINUANCE AND PRES-
ERVATION, therefore, etc." The act then goes on and authorizes the erection of at least six gates, designates classes and
persons exempt from toll, provides for the erection of directors
(boards ordering teams, etc., to pass to the right), establishes
rates of tolls, regulates the manner of collecting the same, etc.
Pamphlet Laws, page 419. For a judicial construction of this
act, see case of Hopkins vs. Stockton, 2 Watts and Sargeant,
page 163.

1835. Act of April 1st requires supervisors of highways to make paved valleys or stone culverts where other roads intersect the Cumberland Road and this act also signifies the State's acceptance of the road from the General Government. Pamphlet Laws, page 102.

1836. Act of June 13th provides for payment of half toll by persons carrying the United States mail, and fixes penalties for attempts to defraud the State of toll. Pamphlet Laws, page 534. This act declared inoperative by the Supreme Court of the United States, in so far as it levies toll on mail coaches.

1837. Act of April 4th exempts persons hauling coal for home consumption from payment of tolls. Pamphlet Laws, page 353.

1839. Act of February 5th in form of a joint resolution requires Commissioners to give bond in the sum of $6,000. Pamphlet Laws, page 637. Changed by subsequent acts.

1839. Act of June 17th, in form of a joint resolution, fixes the compensation of Commissioners at $3 per diem, not to exceed one hundred and fifty days in any one year. Pamphlet Laws, page 679. Changed by subsequent acts.

1840. Act of March 24th authorizes the appointment of one Commissioner by the Governor for a term of three years, at a compensation of $3.00 per diem, requiring him to give bond in the sum of $10,000, to keep an account of receipts and expenditures, and publish the same; and further provides for auditors to adjust accounts. Pamphlet Laws, page 207. Partially repealed by subsequent acts.

1843. Act of April 5th authorizes Commissioners to stop mail coaches to enforce payment of tolls. Pamphlet Laws, page 164. This act held to be void by the Supreme Court of the United States, and supplied by act of April 14th, 1845, *postea.*

1845. Act of April 14th (Omnibus Bill).

"Preamble: Whereas, it has lately been decided by the Supreme Court of the United States, that the acts of assembly of this Commonwealth, relating to the collection of tolls on that part of the Cumberland Road which is within this State, passed June 13th, 1836, and April 5th, 1843, do not authorize the collection of any amount of tolls whatever for the passage upon said road of any stage, coach, or other vehicle carrying passengers with their baggage and goods, if such stage, coach, or other vehicle, is at the same time carrying any of the mails or property of the United States; and whereas, the said court sanctions the power of Pennsylvania to provide for the repairs of said road by a general assessment of tolls upon persons traveling thereon, which it is deemed just and right should be paid; and whereas, also, it is found to be impracticable to keep said road in good repair and out of debt by the tolls collectable under the existing laws of this Commonwealth, as interpreted by said Court, therefore," &c. This act then goes on and in section 12 imposes a toll of not less than two nor more than fifteen cents, as shall be fixed and determined by the Commissioner, upon every person riding or traveling in any vehicle carrying the United States mails, for every fourteen miles over which such person shall have been a passenger or traveler, and in proportion for shorter distances, provided that no toll shall be demanded from any guard to the mails, agent of the postoffice, bearer of dispatches for the General or State Government, nor any naval or military officer of the United States or this State, traveling in the discharge of official duty. Section 13 provides the manner of collecting tolls under this act. Section 14 imposes a penalty of fifty dollars on any driver who neglects to report at every gate the number of passengers in his carriage or coach. Section 15 provides that in case of refusal of passengers to pay or neglect of drivers to report, collectors shall charge in a book all unpaid tolls and sue for the same. Section 16 provides that in every case where a collector may be unable from omission or neglect of drivers or passengers to ascertain the number of passengers liable to toll under this act, he may charge and recover for so many as the carriage shall be capable of carrying. Section 17 provides a penalty of twenty dollars for every fraudulent attempt to evade the payment of toll imposed by this act. Pamphlet Laws, pages 430–1. This act is still in force, though mail coaches (rather hacks) have been carrying passengers and freights for many years without paying toll.

1847. Act of March 16th authorizes the Governor to appoint a Commissioner on each side of the Monongahela river, at a salary of $350 each. Pamphlet Laws, page 477. Subsequently repealed.

1848. Act of April 8th provides for the appointment of trustees by the courts of Somerset, Fayette and Washington counties (one in each), said trustees to appoint one or more Commissioners. Pamphlet Laws, page 523. Repealed.

1850. Act of May 3d authorizes the Commissioner and the Court of Quarter Sessions to determine what travel and transportation shall be in part or in whole exempt from toll; also authorizes the imposition of toll upon persons using the road who do not pass through the gates thereon, and prescribes the manner of collecting the same; also authorizes the Commissioner to change the location of gates, and to sell and convey toll houses and grounds, and to purchase sites. Pamphlet Laws, page 682. This act remains in force.

1856. Act of April 22, authorizes the Courts of Fayette and Washington counties to appoint superintendents. Pamphlet Laws, page 523. Prior to the date of this act, the officer in charge of the road was invariably called Commissioner. This act repealed as to that portion of the road east of the Monongahela by Act of May 1, 1861. *Postea.*

1861. Act of May 1, authorizes the Governor to appoint one person as Superintendent for so much of the road as lies within the counties of Fayette and Somerset, and repeals part of the act of April 22, 1856, *supra.* Pamphlet Laws, page 678.

1864. Act of April 13th, requires Superintendents to appropriate fifty per cent. of the tolls to the payment of old debts. Pamphlet Laws, page 408. Repealed.

1865. Act of March 21, repeals so much of the act of April 13th, 1864, *supra,* as requires Superintendents to apply fifty per cent. of tolls to the payment of old debts, and provides that *bona fide* holders of certificates of indebtedness for repairs shall be allowed credit for tolls on their certificates. Pamphlet Laws, page 474.

1865. Act of November 27th, provides for the adjudication and payment of certain claims against the road. Appendix to Pamphlet Laws of 1866, page 1,226.

1867. Act of January 7th, repeals outright *in toto* the act of April 13th, 1864, *supra.* Pamphlet Laws, page 1,543.

1868. Act of March 20th, authorizes and *requires* the Superintendent to repair the road, and keep it in repair, where it passes through any town or borough forming a street thereof in the county of Fayette. Pamphlet Laws, page 444. In force.

1877. Act of April 4th, authorizes the Governor to appoint a Commissioner for that portion of the road lying between the Monongahela river and the line of the State of West Virginia for a term of three years from the termination of the term of incumbent, at a salary of $3.00 per diem, not to exceed $300 per annum, to account under oath to the auditors of Washington county. Pamphlet Laws, page 53.

1893. Act of June 2d, appropriates $1,500 to repair the great stone bridge at the Big Crossings. Pamphlet Laws, page 213.

The following communications and statements show the unexpended balances in 1834 of appropriations made by Congress in preceding years, for constructing the road through the State of Indiana:

WASHINGTON, Jan. 20th, 1835.

Sir : — I have the honor to transmit herewith a report from the Chief Engineer respecting the unexpended balance of the appropriation for the Cumberland Road in Indiana, in answer to the resolution of the House of Representatives, of the 17th instant.

Very respectfully, your most obedient servant,

MAHLON DICKERSON,

Acting Secretary of War.

To Hon. John Bell,

Speaker of the House of Representatives.

ENGINEER DEPARTMENT, Jan. 19th, 1835.

Hon. Lewis Cass, Secretary of War:

SIR:— In obedience to the resolution of the House of Representatives of the 17th instant, I have the honor to hand you the enclosed statement, explaining the difference in the amount of unexpended appropriations on account of the National Road, in the State of Indiana, and furnishing the information called for therein. I beg leave to remark that it is often necessary to close the annual statement of the fiscal operations of the Engineer Department before the returns, &c., from all the work are received. The Department, therefore, can only act on the information before it. This was the case in the present instance, as well as some others included in the same statement.

I have the honor to be, sir, your most obedient servant,

C. GRATIOT, Chief Engineer.

In the tabular statement of the fiscal operations, under the Engineer Department for the year ending the 30th of September, 1834, the unexpended balance of former appropriations is thus stated, relating to the Cumberland Road in Indiana:

Amount undrawn from the Treasury, 30th of September $160,882 00
Amount in the hands of agents, 30th of September 17,631 09

Total...$178,513 09

Which amount was ascertained from the statement of
balances from the Treasury, on the 30th of Sept....$160,882 00

And an acknowledged balance in the hands of
Captain Ogden, on 30th of September....$1,925 79

And from the accounts of Mr. Milroy,
which had been rendered only to
the first quarter of 1834, inclusive, which showed a balance in
his hands, after deducting......$7,218 38

Paid over to Capt.Ogden, credited in his account
current for the 3d quarter of 1834, of....$15,705 30
————— $17,631 09

$178,513 09

Since preparing the annual statement and its transmission to the
War Department, Mr. Milroy has rendered accounts for the 2d
quarter, and part of the 3d quarter of 1834, by which he shows
a balance due him of...... ....$ 1,147 89

So that, had Mr. Milroy's accounts been received to the time of preparing the statement, the amount in the hands of agents would
have been, instead of $17,631 09, only.......................   777 90

Which added to the amount in the Treasury, on the 1st of Oct., 1834. .$160,882 00

Would make available for the service of the 4th quarter of 1834, and
the year 1835... ......$161,659 90

The balance in the Treasury on the 1st of October, 1834, was......$160,882 00

Since which there has been drawn and remitted to the Superinten-
dent, as follows:
October 21, 1834, to Captain Ogden.....................$ 30,000 00
November 25, 1834, to Captain Ogden.................. 17,520 00
January 10, 1835, to Captain Ogden................... 30,000 00
                                                                 $ 77,320 00

Remaining in the Treasury on the 19th of January, 1835.........$ 83,562 00

The following accounts of two of the old Commissioners are interesting as showing the amount of tolls received and disbursements
made for repairs and maintenance at the dates covered, and disclosing the once familiar names of many who had contracts and were
otherwise employed on the road:

ACCOUNT OF WILLIAM HOPKINS,

Commissioner of the Cumberland Road in Pennsylvania, from Nov. 10th, 1840, to Nov.
10th, 1841.

EASTERN DIVISION, EMBRACED IN FAYETTE AND SOMERSET COUNTIES, VIZ:

DR.

To cash received from the National Road Stage Co........				$2,378	12
" " " " Holt & Maltby, supposed..........				113	94
" " " at Gate No. 1, Wm. Condon, collector.. .				1,758	87
" " " " Gate No. 2, Hiram Seaton, "				1,948	24
" " " " Gate No. 3, Wm. D. Beggs, "				769	27
" " " " Gate No. 3, Jas. Reynold, "				1,125	29
" " " a fine collected by Wm. Bradley.........				5	00
" " " " " " John Tunsell				5	00

Total amount received from Nov. 10, 1840, to Nov. 10,
1841..————$ 8,103 73

BY DISBURSEMENTS, VIZ.   CR.

Cash paid Thompson McKean, late Superintendent......$ 50 00
    "   " Henry Woolery in full for work..............   15 62½
    "   " Thompson McKean, late Superintendent.......   40 00

Amount carried forward...........................$ 105 62½

Amount brought forward				$ 105	62½
Cash paid Jackson Brown in full for work				20	75
"	"	George Hensell	ditto	8	22
"	"	Jesse Sachett	ditto	90	00
"	"	John Smalley, hauling stone		34	20
"	"	Peter Leonard, quarry leave.		8	62½
"	"	Elijah Crabb, work		197	95
"	"	Samuel Dean		15	00
"	"	George Colley, quarry leave		100	00
"	"	J. & W. W. Woolery, work		242	40
"	"	Hugh Wilson,	"	2	50
"	"	William Jeffries,	"	83	37
"	"	Isaac Brownfield,	"	59	85
"	"	Thos. McKean,	"	300	00
"	"	John Brownfield,	"	41	25
"	"	John Risler,	"	3	90
"	"	John Dean,	"	106	88
"	"	James Spears,	"	23	25
"	"	Isaac Nixon,	"	125	22
"	"	Elias Gilmore,	"	168	20
"	"	Ephraim Conway,	"	20	00
"	"	A. McDowell,	"	94	63½
"	"	McClean & Emberson,	"	28	92
"	"	C. Rush,	"	4	89
"	"	John Deford, quarry leave		9	04
"	"	Rich'd Beeson, costs, Com. vs. Stockton.		11	83
"	"	S. D. Skeen, in full for work		4	60
"	"	Thomas Prentice	"	6	00
"	"	James Amos,	"	135	31
"	"	Jno. Hatzman,	"	52	84
"	"	William Reynolds,	"	982	66
"	"	Michael S. Miller,	"	38	37½
"	"	James Watkins,	"	2	20
"	"	Jos. M. Sterling,	"	60	00
"	"	Samuel Rush,	"	881	89
"	"	Hiram Hanse,	"	8	00
"	"	Thomas Brown,	"	324	60
"	"	Upton Shaw,	"	314	37
"	"	John Bennington,	"	130	00
"	"	William C. Stevens,	"	5	18¾
"	"	Hugh Graham, work $300 00			
"	"	" " toll house...........200 00		500	00
"	"	James Snyder, on account for work		235	41½
"	"	same in full		28	06
"	"	Charles Kemp, jr.,	"	32	00
"	"	I. & R. Hill,	"	39	64
"	"	Wm. H. Graham,	"	395	67½
"	"	George Colley,	"	80	80
"	"	James Marlow,	"	651	70
"	"	John Bradfield,	"	1,508	64
"	"	John M. Claybaugh,	"	107	63
"	"	Henry G. Brown,	"	24	69
"	"	Joseph Dillon,	"	49	64
"	"	Charles Rush,	"	23	85
"	"	Sam'l McReynolds,	"	29	33
"	"	M. H. Jones,	"	23	32
"	"	Hiram Hayney,	"	50	00
"	"	Morris Mauler	"	69	47½
"	"	Huston Todd, hauling stone		20	00

———————$ 8,722 41

The foregoing items of expenditures were contracts made by Thompson McKean, Esq., late Commissioner, and paid on his certificate.

Cash paid Adam Speer, for work on road.................$		5 00
" " William D. Beggs, do		1 50
" " same do		1 00
" " same salary for keeping Gate No. 3.		83 30
" " James Reynolds, work on road..............		1 50
" " E. Crable, do		2 00
" " Rush & McCollough, do		25 00
" " E. H. Showalter, on account of work on road...		100 00
" " N. Bradley, " " " ...		2 50
" " William Milligan, " " " ...		14 00
" " A. L. Pentland, Esq., costs, Com. v. Stockton...		5 00
" " Wilson McCandless, Esq., Prof. services.......		20 00
" " same " "		30 00
" " R. P. Flenniken, Esq., " "		56 62½
" " John Irons, for advertising...................		4 00
" " Upton Shaw, work on road...................		30 62½
" " Samuel McReynolds, work on road...........		1 25
" " Samuel Lazure, " "		25
" " Robert McDowell...........................		20 00
" " John Bradfield............................		67 50
" " William Reynolds..........................		273 00
" " John L. Dawson, Esq........................		33 62½
" " Nicholas Bradley		58 75
" " William Condon, Gate No. 1, salary....... ...		200 00
" " George Farney, for work on road.............		2 62½
" " John Nelson, " " "		1 50
" " Jas. Reynolds, Gate No. 3, salary....		116 66
" " Hiram Seaton, Gate No. 2, salary.............		200 00
" " McCollough & Rush, for work on road.........		169 55¾
" " Robert S. Brown, " "		169 90½
" " Anthony Yarnell, " "		150 00
" " Sam'l Dean, " "		50 00
" " Henry Showalter, " "		137 50
" " Jackson Brown, " "		65 00
" " John H. Deford, Prof. services................		20 00
" " John Risler, for stone.......................		6 40

Total amount of expenditures on Eastern division.... ————$10,847 98¼

WESTERN DIVISION, LYING IN WASHINGTON COUNTY.

To cash received from Good Intent Stage Co..............$4,246 25		
" " " Moore & Henderson..............		512 16
" " " Wm. R. Cope.................		70 00
" at Gate No. 4, Stephen Phelps, col...............		1,694 23
" " " No. 5, Wm. Hill.........		1,773 36
" " " No. 6, David Guinea.....................		1,569 44
" " " No. 5, in Oct., 1840, under R. Quail.......		150 41
" " " No. 6. Sept. and Oct., 1840, R Quail......		304 67
" a fine collected by John Freeman, Esq...........		5 00

Total amount received............................. ————$10,325 52

Cash paid Egan & Dickey, in full for work on road........	$1,387	00
" " John McDonough " " "	249	22½
" " John Dickey, " " "	50	62½
" " Henry Murry, " " "	889	04
" " same, alleged error in settlement........	150	00
" " Morris Pursell, in full for work on road........	215	87
" " Bradley & Morgan, " " "	234	27
" " Daniel Ward, " " "	746	56
" " Brown & Valentine, " " "	287	00
" " David Guinea, Gate No. 6, salary........	133	18
" " Wm. Hill, Gate No. 5........	66	72
	———$ 4 409 49	

The above items of expenditure were on contracts made by R. Quail, late Commissioner, and paid on his certificate.

Cash paid T. H. Baird, Esq., Prof. services........$	5	00
" " I. P. Morgan, digging well........	32	50
" " Joel Lamborn, building chimney........	11	00
" " William Craven, smith work........	15	80
" " J. T. Rogen, powder........	5	50
" " Amos Griffith, pump........	40	50
" " A. J. Harry, stove pipe........	2	96
" " Robert Bradley, in full work at well........	60	12½
" " Griffith Taylor, wheelbarrow........	1	75
" " John McMath, in full work on road........	8	59
" " John Bausman, printing........	4	00
" " Grayson & Kaine, "	10	25
" " H. Winten, in full for work on road........	27	00
" " Samuel Adams, " "	4	50
" " James P. Morgan, " "	35	31
" " J. Worrell, on account........	7	30
" " same, in full........	2	75
" " J. McGuire, on account........	57	70
" " Jacob Shaffer, stove pipe........	1	37
" " Robert Sprowl, on account work on road........	253	00
" " Thomas Egan, in full........	253	68
" " Henry Murray, stone........	36	86
" " Jacob Stillwagon, on acct. stone........	227	00
" " Anthony Rentz, " "	59	84
" " David Andrews, work........	128	00
" " Joseph Miller, in full, stone........	62	50
" " John Huston, work........	42	00
" " Joseph T. Rogers, powder........	5	50
" " Isaac Leet, Prof. services........	10	00
" " William Watkins, acct. stone........	15	00
" " Stephen Phelps, Gate No. 4, salary........	200	00
" " Robert Bradley, work in full...... .....$122 96		
" " same on account........ 81 16	204	12
" " William Hill, Gate No. 5, salary........	200	00
" " David Guinea, Gate No. 6, "	200	00
" " on acct. book for Superintendent........	3	00
" " counterfeit money received........	11	00
" " Superintendent, for his services, per account filed, 309 days at $3.00 per day........	927	00
" " Auditors, for settling and stating this account, viz:		
H. Langley........$2 00		
J. K. Wilson........ 5 00		
S. Cunningham........ 5 00	12	00
Total expenditures on Western division........———$7,594 09½		

RECAPITULATION.   Dᴿ.

To amount received on the Eastern Division........ ..$ 8,103 73
To amount received on the Western Division.......... 10,325 52
                                            ————$18,429 25

                                                  Cᴿ.

By cash paid out on the Eastern Division, per statement.$10,847 98¼
By cash paid on the Western Division, per statement... 7,594 09½
                                            ————$18,442 07¾

Balance due Wm. Hopkins, Esq., Superintendent, on the
   10th Nov., 1841 ....$ 12 82¾

The undersigned, auditors appointed by the Court of Common Pleas for the county of Washington, Pennsylvania, on the 9th day of November, 1841, to audit, settle and adjust the account of William Hopkins, Esq., Commissioner of the Cumberland Road, having carefully examined the accounts submitted to them by said Commissioner (a full statement of which is herewith presented), and having compared the vouchers with said account, do find that the said William Hopkins, Commissioner as aforesaid, has expended up to the 10th day of November, 1841, the sum of twelve dollars and eighty-two ¾ cents more than came into his hands, and that said sum of twelve dollars and eighty-two ¾ cents was due to him on said day.

In testimony whereof, we have hereto set our hands and seals the 22d day of January, A. D. 1842.

                    SAMUEL CUNNINGHAM, (ꜱᴇᴀʟ)
                    JOHN K. WILSON,   (ꜱᴇᴀʟ) *Auditors.*
                    HENRY LANGLY,   (ꜱᴇᴀʟ)

Wᴀꜱʜɪɴɢᴛᴏɴ Cᴏᴜɴᴛʏ, ꜱꜱ.

   Tʜᴇ Cᴏᴍᴍᴏɴᴡᴇᴀʟᴛʜ ᴏꜰ Pᴇɴɴꜱʏʟᴠᴀɴɪᴀ.

I, John Grayson, prothonotary of the Court of Common Pleas for said county, certify that at a Court of Common Pleas for the county aforesaid, held on the 9th day of November, Anno Domini 1841, Samuel Cunningham, John K. Wilson and Henry Langly were appointed by said Court auditors to settle and adjust the account of William Hopkins, Esq., Commissioner of the Cumberland Road, as appears of record in our said Court.

In testimony whereof, I have hereunto set my hand and affixed the seal of said Court, the 22d day of January, 1842.

   [ꜱᴇᴀʟ]   JOHN GRAYSON, *Prothy.*

ACCOUNT OF WILLIAM SEARIGHT,

Commissioner of the Cumberland Road in Pennsylvania, from the 1st of May, 1843, *to the* 31st *of December,* 1844, *inclusive.*

TO TOLLS RECEIVED ON THE EASTERN DIVISION, VIZ: Dr.

To tolls received from	Thos. Grier, Gate No. 1	.........$ 4,466	24		
" " " "	Robert McDowell, Gate No. 2	 4,102	70		
" " " "	James Reynolds, Gate No. 3	 4,410	43		
" " " "	National Road Stage Co	 3,200	00		
" " " "	Express Co	 254	00		
Total amount received on Eastern Division		....		————$16,433	37

TO TOLLS RECEIVED ON THE WESTERN DIVIISION, VIZ:

From David Mitchell, Gate No 4	....$ 3,509	32		
" Wm. Hill, " No. 5	 3,843	87		
" Wm. McCleary, " No. 6	 4,105	81		
" Good Intent Stage Co	 8,447	30		
Cash received from John S. Brady, on account of Quail's securities	 769	44		
			————$20,675	74

Total receipts...$37,109 11

Cr.

By cash paid	Thomas Grier, collector at Gate No. 1.....$	333	33
" "	Robt. McDowell, " " " No. 2.....	333	33
" "	Jas. Reynolds, " " " No. 3.....	333	33
" "	Dan'l Kaine, for certifying auditors	1	00
" "	D. Kaine, Wm. P. Wells and Joseph Gadd..	12	00
" "	William Jeffries	65	62
" "	Geo. Craft, costs	6	60
" "	Thos. and Robert Brown	330	63
" "	Wm. Hager	3	00
" "	Elias Gilmore	2,737	40
" "	George Palmer	55	25
" "	William C. Stevens	16	80
" "	Peter Kerney	1	50
" "	James Dougan	42	77
" "	Thomas Brownfield	1,922	98
" "	Robert S. Henderson	150	00
" "	John Malone	30	62
" "	Sam'l Shipley, admr. of S. Rush	216	03
" "	Andrew Bryson	3	00
" "	John McCalpin	7	50
" "	Thomas McGrath	485	94
" "	Samuel Harrah	4	87
" "	John Bradfield	1,748	82

Amount carried forward.........................$ 8,842 32

Amount brought forward			8,842	32
By cash paid Robert McDowell		$	1,041	80
"	"	Calvin Perry	44	25
"	"	Wilson Fee	79	93
"	"	Thomas D. Miller	403	66
"	"	James Dolan	92	25
"	"	Upton Shaw	65	75
"	"	Elijah Crable	36	00
"	"	Samuel Shipley	833	38
"	"	Matthew McNeil	107	44
"	"	Fall & Herbertson	24	53
"	"	James White	8	80
"	"	Jackson Brown		50
"	"	J. L. Wylie & Co.	1	44
"	"	Byers & Gregg	35	00
"	"	William Reynolds	698	87
"	"	James Marlow	65	15
"	"	Rudolph Brinkman	82	12
"	"	William Spaw	99	90
"	"	Sebastian Rush	92	75
"	"	John McDowell	809	14
"	"	Edward G. Roddy	49	84
"	"	Isaac McLaughlin	5	25
"	"	George W. Cass	70	00
"	"	John Irons, printing	21	50
"	"	Samuel McDonald, printing	10	00
"	"	J. & G. S. Gideon	24	00
"	"	James Veech, professional services	100	00
"	"	R. P. Flenniken " "	100	00
"	"	Edward Kerven	140	73
"	"	Thomas Hougan	30	00
"	"	Thomas Dougan	51	75
"	"	John Powell	37	75
"	"	George Parmertor	71	75
"	"	Daniel Cannon	329	75
"	"	Hugh Graham	233	95
"	"	Morris Whalen	118	28
"	"	Nicholas Bradley	91	78
"	"	Perry White	116	06
"	"	Simon Deal	96	39
"	"	William McClean	73	23
"	"	James Collins	27	37
"	"	James McCartney	82	08
"	"	Anthony Yarnell	192	65
"	"	William Conard	1	25
"	"	Thomas McCoy	33	00
"	"	James Reynolds	9	47
"	"	John M. Claybaugh	20	43
"	"	Robert McDowell	300	44
"	"	Gadd & Henderson	2,531	50
"	"	Francis L. Wilkinson	12	29
"	"	Kerney & Redfern	44	62
"	"	Matthias Fry	442	67
Depreciated money on hand			10	00
Balance due Commissioner on former settlement			1,580	00
Salary of Commissioner, from May 1st, 1843, to 31st of December, 1844, being 513 days at $3.00 per day			1,539	00
Whole amount expended on Eastern Division		————$22,066	53

BY THE FOLLOWING SUMS EXPENDED ON THE WESTERN DIVISION.

By cash paid David Mitchell, collector Gate No. 4.........$ 333 33
      "   "   William Hill,   "   "   No. 5. .....   333 33
      "   "   Wm. McCleary,   "   "   No. 6........   333 33
      "   "   E. L. Blaine, for use of Patrick Egan........   34 96
      "   "   J. S. Brady, on account of Wm. Paull.......   41 84
      "   "   William McCleary......................   7 00
      "   "   James Denison......................... 213 90
      "   "   Henry Masterson 307 87
      "   "   Hiram Freeman......... .... 1,402 37
      "   "   Charles Kern............................. 136 72
      "   "   Thomas Egan............................ 263 32
      "   "   John McCollough........................ 956 58
      "   "   Robert Sprowl. 2,995 38
      "   "   Adam Fishburn..........................   1 50
      "   "   John Robinson........................... 303 07
      "   "   Joseph Lawson.......................... 1,962 50
      "   "   Patrick Egan............................ 203 00
      "   "   John Bradlley, admr. of R. Bradley......... 221 25
      "   "   Thomas Hagerty.........................   87 95
      "   "   John Huston.............................   20 25
      "   "   George Irvin......... .... 162 07
      "   "   William Hill.............................   2 81
      "   "   William Paull........................... 161 00
      "   "   Samuel Rodgers.........................   3 00
      "   "   Michael Monahan.......................   55 00
      "   "   Thomas Finley..........................   36 25
      "   "   John Curry... ....   6 00
      "   "   Michael Dougan....... ....   9 00
      "   "   McCollough & Gilmore 980 22
      "   "   Charles Murphy.........................   70 00
      "   "   Charles Stillwagon,......................   75 00
      "   "   Jacob Stillwagon........................ 305 21
      "   "   Jacob Daugherty....................... 229 00
      "   "   Anthony Rentz.......................... 534 25
      "   "   Baldwin Miller..........................   3 75
      "   "   William Pepper..........................   13 41
      "   "   Henry Murry 170 66
      "   "   James Thompson......... .... 291 17
      "   "   James Hurley........................... 280 63
      "   "   J. J. Armstrong.........................   58 12
      "   "   B. Forester.............................   25 00
      "   "   John Mitchell...........................   62 71
      "   "   Mark M. Passmore......................   33 75
      "   "   Grayson & Kaine, printing 17 00
      "   "   John Bausman   " 15 00
      "   "   Richard Biddle..........................   60 00
      "   "   Michael Price...........................   21 00
      "   "   William Scott...........................   15 00
      "   "   William Hopkins.........................   52 50
      "   "   E. L. Blaine, costs.......................   11 01
      "   "   Thomas Sprout..........................   14 94
      "   "   John Wheeler...........................   62 87
      "   "   Robert Patrick..........................   45 95
      "   "   Cornelius Daly..........................   37 85
      "   "   James McIntyre......................... 226 50
      "   "   William Hastings........................ 125 62
                                                          ————————
    Amount carried forward.. ....$14,432 70

Amount brought forward............................$14,432 70
By cash paid Jacob Dixon..............................   6 10
  " " Michael Bail 16 00
  " " Keyran Tolbert..........................   55 52
  " " David Butts..............................   2 00
  " " James Redman........................ 160 00
  " " John Gadd............................... 1,556 53
  " " Thomas Hagan......................   34 50
  " " James Gainer......................... 185 56
  " " John Whitmire........................ 150 00
  " " Peter Kerney.........................   51 50
Depreciated money on hand. 5 00
 Whole amount expended on Western Division.......————$16,655 41

 Whole amount expended on Eastern Division....... 22,066 53

 Whole amount expended on both divisions $38,721 94

Balance due Commissioner, December 31, 1844.......... $ 1,612 83

FAYETTE COUNTY, ss.

 We, the undersigned, auditors appointed by the Court of Common Pleas of Fayette county for that purpose, having examined the accounts and vouchers relating to the receipts and expenditures of Wm. Searight, Esq., Superintendent of the Cumberland Road, from the 1st day of May, 1843, to the 31st of December, 1844, inclusive, have found the foregoing statement of the same to be correct and true.   H. CAMPBELL,
           JOHN HUSTON,
           RICHARD BEESON,
                Auditors.

 NOTE.—Gate No. 1 was located at the east end of Petersburg, Gate No. 2 was near Mt. Washington, Gate No. 3 was near Searights, Gate No. 4 was near Beallsville, Gate No. 5 was near Washington, and Gate No. 6 near West Alexander.

RATES OF TOLL.

 The following were the rates of toll fixed by the act of April 11th, 1831, which were subsequently, however, changed: For every score of sheep or hogs, six cents; for every score of cattle, twelve cents; for every led or driven horse, three cents; for every horse and rider, four cents; for every sleigh or sled, for each horse or pair of oxen drawing the same, three cents; for every dearborn, sulky, chair or chaise, with one horse, six cents; for every chariot, coach, coachee, stage, wagon, phaeton, chaise, with two horses and four wheels, twelve cents; for either of the carriages last mentioned with four horses, eighteen cents; for every other carriage of pleasure, under whatever name it may go, the like sum, according to the number of wheels and horses drawing the same; for every cart or wagon whose wheels shall exceed two and one-half inches in breadth, and not exceeding four inches, four cents; for every horse or pair of oxen drawing the same, and every other cart or wagon, whose wheels shall exceed four inches, and not exceeding five inches in breadth, three cents; for every horse or pair of oxen drawing the same, and for every other cart or wagon whose wheels shall exceed six inches, and not more than eight inches, two cents; for every horse or pair of oxen drawing the same, all other carts or wagons whose wheels shall exceed eight inches in breadth, shall pass the gates free of tolls, and no tolls shall be collected from any person or persons passing or repassing from one part of his farm to another, or to or from a mill, or to or from any place of public worship, funeral, militia training, elections, or from any student or child going to or from any school or seminary of learning, or from persons and witnesses going to and returning from courts, or from any wagon or carriage laden with the property of the United States, or any canon or military stores belonging to the United States, or to any State. The reader will note that the exemptions provided for by this act are changed by force of the act of May 3, 1850, which authorized the commissioner and the court of quarter sessions to determine who and what shall be exempt from the payment of toll. A large wide board, having the appearance of a mock window, was firmly fixed in the walls of every toll house, displaying in plain letters the rates above given, so that the wayfarer might not err therein.

MR. GALLATIN DEFINES HIS ATTITUDE AS TO THE LOCATION OF THE ROAD, AND GIVES INSTRUCTIONS TO DAVID SHRIVER, SUPERINTENDENT.

When the road was authorized to be constructed by Congress, Mr. Gallatin was Secretary of the Treasury, and a citizen of Fayette county, Pennsylvania. His home was "Friendship Hill," in Springhill township, near New Geneva, about fifteen miles south of Uniontown, afterward the home of Hon. John L. Dawson. It was intimated in various quarters that Mr. Gallatin was desirous of having the road located through or near his place, and that he used his official influence to further his desire in this regard. The following letter, however, to his old friend David Acheson, of Washington, Pennsylvania, shows that the intimations mentioned were without foundation:

NEW YORK, September 1, 1808.

DAVID ACHESON, ESQ., Washington, Pa.

Dear Sir: On receipt of your letter respecting the Western Road, I immediately transmitted it to the President at Monticello. I was under the impression that he had previously directed the Commissioners to examine both routes and to report to him. It seems, however, that it had not then been yet done. But on the 6th ultimo he wrote to them to make an examination of the best route through Washington to Wheeling, and also to Short Creek, or any other point on the river offering a more advantageous route towards Chillicothe and Cincinnati, and to report to him the material facts with their opinion for consideration.

That it is the sincere wish of the President to obtain all the necessary information in order that the road should pursue the route which will be of the greatest public utility no doubt can exist. So far as relates to myself, after having, with much difficulty, obtained the creation of a fund for opening a great western road, and the act pointing out its general direction, it is sufficiently evident from the spot on the Monongahela which the road strikes, that if there was any subsequent interference on my part it was not of a selfish nature. But the fact is that in the execution of the law I thought myself an improper person, from the situation of my property, to take the direction which would naturally have been placed in my hands, and requested the President to undertake the general superintendence himself. Accept the assurance of friendly remembrance, and of my sincere wishes for your welfare and happiness.

Your obedt servant,
ALBERT GALLATIN.

TREASURY DEPARTMENT, March 9th, 1813.

Sir: You will herewith receive the plot of the road as laid by the Commissioners from the 21st mile to Uniontown.

I approve of having a stone bridge across Little Youghiogheny, and the measures necessary to secure masons should be adopted, but the site cannot be fixed until you have examined whether any alterations in the course be practicable. In that respect I beg leave to refer you to my former letters. As soon as your examination of the ground has taken place, and the alterations you may have found practicable shall have been received and approved, public notice may be given inviting proposals to contract for completing the road as far as Big Yioughiogheny river; an additional appropriation of $140,000 having been made by Congress. You will therefore perceive that in every point of view your examination of the ground is the first object to attend to.

I have the honor to be, respectfully, sir,

Your obt. servant,
ALBERT GALLATIN.

D. Shriver, jr., Cumberland, Md.

TREASURY DEPARTMENT, April 17th, 1813.

Sir: Your letter of the 3d inst. has been duly received. The principal object in finally fixing the course of the road is its permanency and durability without the necessity of perpetual and expensive repairs. To select, therefore, the best ground which that mountainous country will afford, avoiding, as far as practicable, cutting along the side of steep and long hills, always exposed to be washed away, appears to be one of first importance. The other considerations, subordinate to the selection of the best ground, but to be also attended to, are, the expense of making the road, the shortness of the distance and the accommodation (by intersecting lateral roads) of important settlements not on the line of the road.

As an erroneous location would be an irreparable evil, it is better that the contracts for the ensuing twenty miles should be delayed, than to make them before you have had time to take a complete view of the ground. Examine it well before you decide and make your first report. This is more important because it is probable that I will be absent when that report is made, and that it will be decisive, as the acting secretary, to whom the subject will be new and the localities unknown, cannot have time to investigate it critically, and will probably adopt it on your responsibility. If a decisive advantage should arise from an alteration in the last sections already contracted for, and the contractors assent to it, you may, in your report, propose such an alteration. You are authorized for the purpose of facilitating your review of the road, without neglecting the duties of general superintendence, to employ John S. Shriver, or some other able assistant, with a reasonable compensation. You have not stated what this should be, but it is presumed that you will not, in that respect, exceed what is necessary for obtaining the services of a well qualified person. You are authorized to draw for a further sum of twenty thousand dollars; whenever this is nearly exhausted you will apply for a new credit.

With respect to details, they are left at your discretion. You are sensible of the great confidence placed in your abilities and integrity, and I am sure you will not disappoint our expectations.

With perfect consideration and sincere wishes for your welfare, I have the honor to be, sir,

Your obedient servant,

ALBERT GALLATIN.

TREASURY DEPARTMENT, April 20th, 1813.

Sir: You are authorized to employ a surveyor to view the most proper road from Brownsville to Washington in Pennsylvania, and thence to examine the routes to Charlestown, Steubenville, mouth of Short Creek and Wheeling, and report a correct statement of distance and ground on each. If the county road as now established from Brownsville to Washington is not objectionable, it would be eligible to prefer it to any other which might be substituted. The surveyor thus employed will meet with every facility by applying to the gentlemen at Washington who have this alteration in the western road much at heart.

I am respectfully, sir, your obedient servant,

ALBERT GALLATIN.

D. Shriver, Jr., Cumberland, Md.

Treasury Department, April 23rd, 1811.

Sir: Mr. Cochran has signed his contract and bonds for the third and fourth sections of the road at the price agreed on, that is to say, at the rate of twenty-two dollars and fifty cents per rod for the third section, and of sixteen dollars and fifty cents per rod for the fourth section.

I now enclose the contracts and bonds for the first and second sections; that for the first in the name of Henry McKinley, and at the rate of twenty-one dollars and twenty-five cents per rod. The proposal of Mr. Reade was at the rate of thirteen dollars for a road covered with a stratum of stones twelve inches thick, all the stones to pass through a three-inch ring. He did not stay here or return here to complete the business and was not present when the road was altered to a stratum of stones fifteen inches thick. The same additional price, viz: one dollar and a half per rod, is allowed him for that alteration which was by agreement given to all the other contractors, making fourteen dollars and a half as set down in the contract, instead of thirteen. The contracts and bonds are in every respect (the names of sections and difference of price only excepted) verbatim the same as both those signed by Mr. Cochran, and they were as you will perceive all executed by me, and signed by the President. After they shall have been signed by the contractors respectively, they will each keep a copy of their own contracts, and you will return the other copy, together with the bond (both being signed by the contractors respectively) to this office.

If either of the contractors should for any reason whatever refuse to sign the contract, you will return the same to this office, notify the person thus refusing that he is not considered as a contractor, forbid his doing any work, and immediately advertise in Cumberland that you will receive proposals for making the section of the road thus not contracted for. You will afterward transmit the proposals which may accordingly be made.

I also enclose a copy of the contracts for your own use in order that you may in every case be able to secure the additions agreed on.

I have the honor to be with consideration, sir,

Your obedient servant,

ALBERT GALLATIN.

The dates were the only blanks left in the contracts and bonds and must be filled at the time of signing, by the contractors.

A. G.

Mr. David Shriver, Jr., Cumberland, Md.

TREASURY DEPARTMENT, April 30th, 1811.

Sir: Your letter of the 22d inst. has been received. The President has confirmed the alteration in the first section of the road. It will be proper to have a short endorsement to that effect entered on the contract with Mr. McKinley, and signed by him and yourself.

You are authorized to contract for the bridges and mason work on the terms mentioned in your letter, with the exception of the bridges across Clinton's Fork of Braddock's Run, which may perhaps be avoided by the alteration which you contemplate, and which, if necessary, we may, perhaps, considering other expenses, be obliged to contract of cheaper materials. It is left to your discretion to contract for the other mason work as above stated, either with Mr. Kinkead or with the road contractors.

If you shall find it necessary to employ a temporary assistant, you are authorized to do it, provided he shall be employed and paid only when actually necessary. I should think that one dollar and twenty-five, or at most, fifty cents, a day, would in that part of the country be ample compensation.

Respecting side walls no decisive opinion can be given until you shall have matured your ideas on the subject, and formed some estimate of the extent to which they must be adopted and of the expense.

I have the honor to be respectfully, sir,

Your obedient servant,

ALBERT GALLATIN.

MR. DAVID SHRIVER, JR.,

Superintendent of the Cumberland Road, Cumberland, Md.

LETTER FROM EBENEZER FINLEY.

RELEASE, September 1, 1891.

HON. T. B. SEARIGHT,

My much respected friend: In our conversation the other day, I spoke from memory entirely, as I had no statistics from which to quote. Your father bought the stone tavern house at Searights from Joseph Frost. It was unfinished when your father bought it. I knew Joseph Frost, but have no recollection of the family he came from. Your father was a single man, when he bought the house, but married shortly after.

In relation to Mr. Stewart's and Mr. Benton's colloquy about the National Road, Mr. Stewart said that "hay stacks and corn shocks would walk over it." Mr. Benton replied that "he could not conceive how hay stacks and corn shocks could walk over this bowling green road." "Ah!" rejoined Mr. Stewart, "I do not expect to see them walk in the shape of stacks and shocks, but in the shape of fat cattle, hogs, horses and mules from the Western and Southern States." This was in a discussion in Congress, over an appropriation bill for repairing the road. Another conversation with you at some time, would be very much enjoyed by your unworthy scribbler.

P. S. Now, Colonel, since writing the above, many things have come crowding on my memory, and I will mention some of the principal hotels with which I was more or less acquainted. I frequently traveled over the National Road in my younger days. I went often to Cumberland and occasionally to Baltimore. I will begin at Big Crossings (Somerfield). Coming this way, Thomas Brown kept a tavern on the hillside. Next Daniel Collier, then Inks, and next Widow Tantlinger (Boss Rush's place). Next James Sampey at Mt. Washington, then several stopping places before reaching the Stewart stone house, a hotel that was not largely patronized by travelers on the road. Next the Chalk Hill house and then Jimmy Snyder's. Next the first house to the left as you come to Monroe, built by Mr. Deford. Then several other hotels before you come to Uniontown. In Uniontown, the Walker House (now Feather's) was well patronized. Then James Seaton's and Thomas Brownfield's wagon stands. Next the Cuthbert Wiggins wagon stand (later Moxley's), and next the Searight house. Over the hill, next was a house kept by Samuel Woolverton and Hugh Thompson. Then the Robert Johnson (later Hatfield) stone house. Next old Peter Colley, father of Abel, Solomon and John Colley. Then the Bowman house, kept by John Gribble, and next the Brubaker house. Then the first house to the left as you go into Brownsville, kept by Darra Auld, and next the Workman House. But I presume you have all these. Respectfully,

EB. FINLEY.

LETTER FROM THOMAS A. WILEY, A NATIVE OF UNIONTOWN, WHO RODE THE PONY EXPRESS.

BALTIMORE AND OHIO R. R. Co.,
GEN. TICKET AGENT'S OFFICE,
BALTIMORE, July 16, 1892.

T. B. SEARIGHT, ESQ.— *Dear Sir:*—I have been receiving from some one the *Jeffersonian Democrat*, a paper published in my old favorite Uniontown, and have read with great pleasure your publication of things that transpired along the National Road. I knew a great many of the old wagoners, stage drivers and tavern keepers you mention. When I was working for the stage company the Baltimore and Ohio railroad was only completed to Frederic, Maryland, and I used to travel the old pike very often. I hope to be able to come once more to Uniontown before I go hence, where nearly all the rest have gone, and would delight in a long talk with you about old times on the road. In looking over the paper you sent me I scarcely see any names that I used to know in Uniontown. When last in Uniontown I met William Wilson, Ewing Brownfield and Greenberry Crossland, and did not get a chance to see my old friend and shopmate, Philip Bogardus. He and I worked for the Stockton stage company. The shops were on Morgantown street. I understand that since I was out my old friend, Bogardus, has passed away. I recollect the lady he married was a Miss Lincoln, and I also recollect his boy, Winfield Scott. I have been with the Baltimore and Ohio company since October 10th, 1852, and am still in its service. Again thanking you for the paper you sent me, I close, in the hope that God will bless you and spare your life and mine, that we may meet in old time-honored Uniontown, and talk over the glories of the old pike.

Yours most respectfully,

THOMAS A. WILEY.

PROPOSALS FOR CARRYING THE MAILS.

WASHINGTON CITY, September 26, 1831.

We will agree to convey the mail on route No. 1,031, from Philadelphia to Pittsburg, daily in four-horse post coaches, agreeable to advertisement, for the yearly compensation of seven thousand dollars.

Or we will make the following improvements: To convey two daily mails from Philadelphia to Pittsburg: First mail to leave Philadelphia at two o'clock A. M. and arrive at Pittsburg in two days and five hours, so as to arrive in Pittsburg at seven o'clock A. M., and extend the route to Wheeling so as to arrive, including route 1,170, at Wheeling the third day by nine o'clock P. M., from the first of April to first of December, and, from first of December to first of April, to Pittsburg in three and Wheeling in four days; and return from Wheeling by Washington, Pittsburg, and Chambersburg, to Philadelphia within the same time; changing the mail as follows: at Lancaster, Harrisburg, Chambersburg, Bedford, Somerset, Mount Pleasant, and at any other office that is or may be established on the route. The second mail to leave Philadelphia at seven A. M., or immediately after the arrival of the New York mail, and reach Pittsburg in three days and five hours, so as to arrive in Pittsburg by noon, changing the mail at all way offices.

We will agree to carry the mail on route No. 1,198, from Bedford to Washington, Pa., via White House, Somerset, Donegal, Mount Pleasant, McKean's, Old Stand, Robbstown, Gambles, and Parkinson's Ferry, to Washington, Pa., as advertised, for the yearly compensation of twenty-nine hundred dollars.

We do agree to carry the mail on route No. 1,230, from Bedford, Pa., to Cumberland, Md., three times a week in coaches, from the first of April to the first of October, and once a week on horseback from the first of October to the first of April, so as to connect with the Winchester mail at Cumberland, and the Great Eastern and Western mail at Bedford, which is much wanted during the summer season, for the yearly compensation of thirteen hundred dollars.

JAMES REESIDE,
SAMUEL R. SLAYMAKER,
J. TOMLINSON.

To the Hon. WM. T. BARRY,
Postmaster General.

CONTRACT.

This contract, made the fifteenth day of October, in the year one thousand eight hundred and thirty-one, between James Reeside, of Philadelphia, Samuel R. Slaymaker, of Lancaster, and Jesse Tomlinson, of Philadelphia, contractors for carrying the mail of the United States, of one part, and the Postmaster General of the United States of the other part, witnesseth, that said parties have mutually covenanted as follows, viz.: The said contractors covenant with the Postmaster General:

To carry the mails from Pittsburg to Harriottsville, Cannonsburg, Washington, Claysville, West Alexander, and Triadelphia, Va., to Wheeling and back, daily, in four-horse post coaches, the first mail to be changed at each county town through which it passes; the second mail at every office on the route; and to furnish armed guards for the whole, when required by the department, at the rate of six thousand seven hundred and fifty dollars for every quarter of a year, during the continuance of this contract; to be paid in drafts on postmasters on the route above mentioned, or in money, at the option of the Postmaster General, in the months of May, August, November, and February.

That the mails shall be duly delivered at, and taken from each postoffice now established, or that may be established on any post route embraced in this contract, under a penalty of ten dollars for each offence; and a like penalty shall be incurred for each ten minutes' delay in the delivery of the mail after the time fixed for its delivery at any postoffice specified in the schedule hereto annexed; and it is also agreed that the Postmaster General may alter the times of arrival and departure fixed by said schedule, and alter the route (he making an adequate compensation for any extra expense which may be occasioned thereby); and the Postmaster General reserves the right of annulling this contract, in case the contractors do not promptly adopt the alteration required.

If the delay of the arrival of said mail continue until the hour for the departure of any connecting mail, whereby the mails destined for such connecting mails shall miss a trip, it shall be considered a whole trip lost, and a forfeiture of one hundred dollars shall be incurred; and a failure to take the mail, or to make the proper exchange of mails at connecting points, shall be considered a whole trip lost;

and for any delay or failure equal to a trip lost, the Postmaster General shall have full power to annul this contract.

That the said contractors shall be answerable for the persons to whom they shall commit the care and transportation of the mail, and accountable for any damage which may be sustained through their unfaithfulness or want of care.

That seven minutes after the delivery of the mail at any post-office on the aforesaid route named on the annexed schedule, shall be allowed the postmaster for opening the same, and making up another mail to be forwarded.

The contractors agree to discharge any driver or carrier of said mail whenever required to do so by the Postmaster General.

That when the said mail goes by stage, such stage shall be suitable for the comfortable accommodation of at least seven travelers; and the mail shall invariably be carried in a secure dry boot, under the driver's feet, or in the box which constitutes the driver's seat, under a penalty of fifty dollars for each omission; and when it is carried on horseback, or in a vehicle other than a stage, it shall be covered securely with an oil cloth or bear skin, against rain or snow, under a penalty of twenty dollars for each time the mail is wet, without such covering.

Provided always, That this contract shall be null and void in case the contractors or any person that may become interested in this contract, directly or indirectly, shall become a postmaster or an assistant postmaster. No member of Congress shall be admitted to any share or part of this contract or agreement, or to any benefit to arise thereupon; and this contract shall, in all its parts, be subject to its terms and requisitions of an act of Congress, passed on the 21st day of April, in the year of our Lord one thousand eight hundred and eight, entitled, "An act concerning public contracts."

And it is mutually covenanted and agreed by the said parties that this contract shall commence on the first day of January next, and continue in force until the thirty-first day of December, inclusively, which will be in the year one thousand eight hundred and thirty-five.

In witness whereof, They have hereunto interchangeably set their hands and seals the day and year first above written.

(Signed.) JAMES REESIDE. (Seal.)
SAM'L R. SLAYMAKER. (Seal.)
JESSE TOMLINSON. (Seal.)

Signed, sealed and delivered in the presence of

ROB'T D. CARSON.
JACOB SHEARER.

BOND.

Know all men by these presents, That James Reeside, as principal, and Richard Morris and David Dorrance, as sureties, are held and firmly bound unto the Postmaster General of the United States of America, in the just and full sum of two thousand nine hundred dollars, value received, to be paid unto the Postmaster General or his successors in office, or to his or their assigns; to which payment, well and truly to be made, we bind ourselves, our heirs, executors, and administrators, jointly and severally, firmly by these presents. Sealed with our seals, dated the seventeeth day of December, in the year of our Lord one thousand eight hundred and thirty-one.

The condition of this obligation is such that whereas the above bounden James Reeside, by a certain contract bearing date the fifteenth day of October, in the year of our Lord one thousand eight hundred and thirty-one, covenanted with the said Postmaster General to carry the mail of the United States from Bedford to Washington (Pennsylvania), as per contract annexed, commencing the first day of January, one thousand eight hundred and thirty-two, and ending the thirty-first day of December, which will be in the year one thousand eight hundred and thirty-five.

Now, if the said James Reeside shall well and truly perform the covenants in the said indenture expressed on his part to be performed, and shall account for all penalties, and shall promptly repay all balances that may at any time be found due from him, then this bond is to be void; otherwise to remain in full force.

(Signed.) JAMES REESIDE, (Seal.)
RICHARD MORRIS, (Seal.)
DAVID DORRANCE, (Seal.)

Signed, sealed and delivered in the presence of
(Signed.) R. C. WHITESIDE.

A true copy from the original on file in the General Postoffice.
MW. ST. CLAIR CLARKE, Secretary.

CLAIM FOR EXTRA ALLOWANCE.

WASHINGTON CITY, December 28, 1831.

Sir: For the four years which I have been your contractor for transporting the great Eastern mail from New York to Philadelphia, it has happened almost every week, and several times in a week, that arrivals from foreign countries have brought thousands of ship letters to the office of New York just before the time for my departure, and the importance of their being forwarded without delay to the Southern cities has required my detention from one to two hours beyond the ordinary time for me to leave New York. This detention I have been required to gain in speed, and that increased speed has required me always to keep on that route two extra teams of horses, at an extra expense of not less than one thousand dollars per year for each team. During the first year your predecessor made me an extra allowance for this expense, but during the last three years I have received nothing for it. I now submit the subject to you, in the expectation that you will allow the claim; it is certainly but just that I should be relieved, at least in part, of this burden, for the last three years it has subjected me to an expense of not less than six thousand dollars, which I hope you will direct to be paid to me, at least in part, if you do not think me entitled to the whole. I have also, within the same time, transported to New York all the large mail bags which are made in Philadelphia and sent to New York, not with mails, but to be used in New York, and to be sent from New York to other places. These within three years will amount to about five hundred pounds a week, as will appear from accounts of the manufacturers in your office. Wherever I could procure transportation for those bags in wagons, I have uniformly paid $2.50 per hundred pounds for carrying them, rather than overload my coaches in which we carry the great mail. For this service, I hope you will not consider my claim unreasonable, if I charge ten dollars per week for three years. All of which is submitted to your sense of justice for decision.

Very respectfully, your obedient servant,

JAMES REESIDE.

Hon. Wm. T. Barry.

Endorsement — Allowed. Allow $4,500. The residue of the claim is reserved for future consideration. Allow the remaining $1,500.

COULDN'T AFFORD TO CARRY NEWSPAPERS.

Washington, July 12, 1832.

Sir: When we entered into contract with you to run two daily mails between Philadelphia and Pittsburg, one with unexampled rapidity, and the other in three and one-half days, we had no idea whatever of carrying the newspaper mail in our most rapid line, nor do we suppose it was ever contemplated by the department. It was our intention and we so expressed it in all our conversation with you, and with the superintendent of mail contracts, to carry the principal letter mail only in the most rapid line, not believing it practicable to carry the heavy load of newspapers sent to the West with sufficient rapidity to reach Pittsburg in the shortest time specified. Indeed, if we could have supposed that it would ever become necessary to carry the newspapers with that rapidity, we should not have undertaken it for less that fifteen thousand dollars a year beyond what we now receive; but experience soon taught us that great complaints were made against the department and ourselves when the newspapers were not received as soon as the letters, and that these complaints were not confined to Pittsburg, but extended all over the West. To satisfy the public, and sustain the credit of both the department and ourselves as its servant, we made the experiment of trying to carry the newspapers with our most rapid line. We have partially succeeded, but with very great loss. For three days in the week we are

compelled to exclude all passengers, to the loss of not less than one
hundred dollars a day. We are willing to perform our contract to
the full extent of its meaning, but we must relinquish carrying the
newspaper mails by our most rapid line, unless we can in part be re-
munerated for it. If, however, the Postmaster General is willing to
silence the public clamor, which is so great when we carry them in
our slow line, we will carry all the newspaper mails, together with
the letter mail, in our most rapid line to Pittsburg and Wheeling, in
the shortest time specified in our contract, and so arrange the connection of the Baltimore mail at Chambersburg with our swift line,
as to carry the newspapers as well as letter mail, from Baltimore to
Pittsburg in two days, for the additional allowance of ten thousand
dollars per year, from the first of April last. The increased expense
to us will not be less than fifteen thousand dollars a year, and for our
own credit and for the credit of the department, we will make one-
third of the sacrifice and perform the service for ten thousand dollars
a year. We would gladly do it for a less sum if we could afford it,
but we cannot, and at that rate our sacrifice will be as much as we
can bear. It would be much more gratifying to us if the public
would be satisfied without it, but they will not, and our own feelings
will not suffer us to perform a service in which we cannot give satisfaction to the public.

Very respectfully, your obedient servants,

JAS. REESIDE,
SAM'L R. SLAYMAKER.

To the Hon. W. T. Barry,
Postmaster General.

A true copy from the original on file in the General Postoffice.

(The above letter is marked "Granted.")

MW. ST. CLAIR CLARKE, Secretary.

MR. REESIDE DEFIES ALL COMPETITORS.

Philadelphia, January 25, 1833.

Dear Sir: Your favor dated the 22d inst. has just come to hand,
which I have examined with much care, but must confess myself at a
loss to come to the exact meaning it is extended to convey.

That there is at present, and has been for some time back, an express carried on horseback between this city and New York, is a fact
which is well known, and which is publicly acknowledged by the
newspapers in New York. That it is impossible to carry the whole
of the great Eastern mail through in coaches or otherwise with the
same speed as a small package can be carried through on horseback
is a fact that requires no comment.

Not having pointed out this matter clearly in your letter whether
it was the wish of the department that a certain portion of mails

should be sent by express to New York at an earlier hour than it now does.

Should it be the latter, I would at once assure the department of the impossibility of having it carried through in as short a time as it is now carried by express on horseback.

In either case the department may rest assured of my willingness and determination to use every exertion in order to meet the views and wishes of the department. Should you desire it to be sent by express, I have no hesitation in saying that I can have it sent through in a shorter time than it can be done by any other individual in the country. This will be handed to you by Mr. Ewing, whom I have sent on with directions to ascertain from you personally your views of this matter, and who will give you all the information respecting the express that has been sent from this place to New York alluded to in your letter.

With respect, your obedient servant,   JAMES REESIDE.

N. B. I will say to a certainty I will go from this city to New York in six hours, or faster than any other one can do it.

JAMES REESIDE.

To Hon. O. B. Brown,
      Superintendent of Mail Contracts,
            Washington, D. C.

TEAMS READY FOR THE NATIONAL ROAD.

TRENTON, February 25, 1833.

Dear Sir: You will perceive by the enclosed that I have attended to your directions as far as practicable. It is their own exposition of the matter, and such as they gave me.

I neglected to mention to you in my letter of yesterday that the cause of the private express beating that of the Government alluded to in Mr. Mumford's letter, was owing to but one cause.

Their express came through from Washington.

The Government express from Philadelphia, after the arrival of the steamship, giving the newspaper express the start of six hours in advance of that of the Government. The lateness of the succeeding arrivals originated from the cause mentioned in the enclosed letter. No mail having arrived from the South, they supposed, from the lateness of the arrival of the express the following night, that there would not be any more.

This was caused by the late arrival of the steamboat, and no preparation was made on the road for taking it on. This is their excuse; whether it will pass current is for you to determine. I have just received a letter from Mr. Washington on the subject. He attaches the blame to Thompson's bad horse, &c.

I think we shall be able to get the mail through in time to connect with the boat, should the roads not get worse than they now are.

The mail arrived in Philadelphia this morning at 6 o'clock. I have good reasons for believing that it will continue, unless a change should take place in the roads.

The mail has left Jersey City the last few days at a few minutes past three o'clock P. M., and will continue to leave at that hour unless you direct otherwise: that is three o'clock.

The teams intended for the National Road are here to-night, and start to-morrow for the West; they are twelve in number, Jersey stock. Yours respectfully.

D. EWING.

Colonel James Reeside.

P. S. No opposition express for the last four days. Your express horses are in good order, with but two exceptions. D. E.

COPY OF AN ACCOUNT AGAINST COL. JAMES REESIDE.

Col. James Reeside,   To Hutchinson & Weart,   Dr.
1833.

January 31.—To one horse on express		$ 5 00
February 1. " two horses "		10 00
" 2. " two horses "		10 00
" 3. " two horses "		10 00
" 3. " horses and gig, Eastward, making arrangements for regular express		5 00
March 7.—To two horses on express		5 00
" 7. " running express one month and four days, from February 4 to this date, inclusive, between Trenton and New Brunswick		1,885 71
		$1,970 71

The above is a true copy from our books, so far as relates to expresses, and has been paid to us by Col. Reeside.

HUTCHINSON & WEART.

BEDFORD, PA., GETS A DAILY MAIL.

February 14, 1833.

Sir: The citizens of Bedford, Pennsylvania, desire that a daily mail be run between Bedford and Hollidaysburg. The latter being a place of great importance, being at the junction of the Pennsylvania Canal and Railroad, and an intercouse of communication very great between the two points, I will agree to perform the service for a pro rata allowance, and put the arrangement into effect in ten days.

Very respectfully, etc.,

JAMES REESIDE.

Hon. W. T. Barry, Postmaster General.

No. 1215, Pennsylvania. James Reeside proposes to run daily for pro rata; Postmaster General says within "granted;" James Reeside written to 25th February, 1833.

BODKIN, James 180 Wash 179
BOGARDUS, Philip 164 377
William 180
BOGGS, Lydia S 295
BOICE, Robert 214
BOLTON, Gideon 162
BOND, 319
BONEBRAKER, David 178
BONNER, Amariah 181
BONUM, ---- 181 Magnum 181
BORING, Abraham 335 Jesse 179
Mr 336
BOSLEY, William 139
BOSTICK, Charley 172
BOTKINS, G W 317
BOUVIER, Mr 116
BOWER, Charles 140
BOWERS, Joe 156
BOWIE, Lucien B 211 212
BOWLBY, Mrs Amos S 131
BOWMAN, 255
BOYCE, Abram 180 John W 179
Robert 141
BOYD, George 285 Joseph 186
Josh 157 Joshua 169 179 181
Samuel 139 140 Thomas 179
181 William 179 231
BOYER, Dan 156 Daniel 180 181
BOYLE, 133
BRACKEN, Solomon 263
BRADDEE, 242 340 342 350 Dr
165 John F 163 188 241 339
341 342 344-352
BRADDOCK, 133 208 Gen 16 122
229
BRADFIELD, Frank 123 140 John
123 129 140 199 217 218 277
296 320 363 364 367
BRADFORD, Chas S 351
BRADLEY, 319 326 365 Daniel
117 221 320 James 139 173
180 John 117 320 N 364 Nicho-
las 221 320 364 368 R 369
Robert 365 Thomas 180 Wm
362
BRADLLEY, John 369
BRADSHAW, William 300 303
BRADY, J S 369 John S 367
BRAGS, Edward H 351
BRANT, Jacob F 351
BRASHEAR, Bazil 257 Prof 257

BREAKBILL, Jacob 140 Samuel
140
BREAKIRON, Jaccob 124
BRENNARD, David 180 George
180 Jesse 180
BRENTLINGER, John 140
BREWER, Samuel 140 141
BRICELAND, James 278 281
BRIGGS, Alter 300 Ross 302
BRINKMAN, Rudolph 368
BRITTON, James 263
BROOKS, Jacob 305 Joseph 140
William 141
BROSIUS, Jacob 200
BROTHERTON, John 292
BROWER, Charles 166 David 180
William 180
BROWN, 222 365 Abraham 347
348 Abram 135 331 B 347
Barney 210 Bazil 286 287 301
Benjamin 347 Billy 279 Daniel
151 190 258 279 282 356
Elisha 208 Emanuel 347 348
Hannah 135 Henry 125 Henry G
363 Isaac 347 Jackson 320 363
364 368 Jimmy 279 John 180
Josiah 139 Levi 125 Mrs
Jimmy 279 O B 383 Old Billy
278 Robert 320 367 Robert S
364 Samuel 125 Squire 139
Thomas 125 221 257 258 320
363 376 Thos 367 Turner 125
Wilkes 255 William 125
William J 278
BROWNFIELD, Ben 221 247
Benjamin 347 348 351 Benja-
min Jr 117 Ewing 133 377
Isaac 363 John 363 Nathaniel
240 331 Natty 113 230 297
Rachel 312 Thomas 177 216
222 225 240 251 312 320 367
376 William 326
BROWNING, Isaac 135 136 140
200 James 140
BROWNLEE, Elisha 139 James
131 136 139 Widow 286
BROWNS, 125
BROWNSON, Rev Dr 315
BRUBAKER, 256 319 Billy 329
Daniel 255
BRUCE, Andrew 276

CLAY (continued)
Henry 183 186 210 222 245 257
276 286 294 14 130 131 149
152 153 159 166 167 177 183
186 210 222 245 257 276 286
338 Mr 15 16 150 167 Senator
15 William 153
CLAYBAUGH, George W 205
James W 248 John M 363 368
Michael 166
CLEAVENGER, Samuel 116
CLEAVER, Amos 264 Morris 264
CLEMENT, E W 115 233 246 321
Samuel M 225 Wilse 113 136
195 251 296
CLEMENTS, John 349
CLUGGAGE, Robert 264
CLUM, George 141
COCHRAN, James 319 Michael
139 Mordecai 319 Mr 374
Thomas 139
COFFMAN, John 140
COLFLESH, Jerry 241
COLLEY, Abel 131 135 246 250
251 253 263 376 George 253
363 Hannah 135 John 376 Levi
250 Nancy 250 Peter 246 247
250 253 263 301 376 Solomon
253 376 W Searight 250
COLLIER, Daniel 131 222 241
376 John 131 180 222 Thomas
140
COLLINS, 350 Elisha 201 James
368 John 236 Margaret 351 352
Thomas 236 Tom 229 William
349 351
COLQUIT, Capt 311
COLUMBUS, 166
COLVIN, William 247
COLWELL, John 275
CONARD, William 368
CONDON, William 364 Wm 362
CONKLING, Stephen 287
CONN, William 191
CONNELLY, James 216
CONNER, Cyrus L 258 Sandy 191
CONNOR, David 140-142 Neil 140
Sandy 181 212
CONROD, Jacob 206 208
CONWAY, Ephraim 363 John 221
CONWELL, Stokely 247

COOK, John 139 265 301 Solomon
290 Thomas 139
COOPER, 296 297 Samuel 349
William 139
COPE, Wm R 364
COPLAN, William F 52 54 94
247 316
CORBIN, James 181
CORE, Alfred 351 Jesse 267 Otho
W 141
CORMAN, 342 350 352 William
163 181 340-342 344 345 Wm
340 341
CORTS, Benjamin 141
CORWIN, 150 Gov 201 Thomas
124 149 Tom 149
COSGROVE, Robert 131
COSTELLO, Samuel 351
COTRELLS, 202
COUDY, James 190
COULSON, John 284
COWDERY, William F 191
COX, Jacob 141 Jeremiah 307
John 141 Marshall 317 Samuel
S 302 Thomas 180 William
141 240 246 325
CRABB, Elijah 363
CRABLE, E 364 Elijah 368
CRACRAFT, Zadoc 165 242
CRAFT, Geo 367 George 253 317
Jackey 254 John C 251 Joseph
141
CRAIG, Andrew 218 Armor 153
CRAMPTON, John 141 194
Joseph 141 197
CRANE, Allen 226 John M 351
CRANFORD, Wash 302
CRAVEN, 191 William 365
CRAWFORD, Galloway 181
Garret 180 Jonathan 248 Josias
32 Tom 302 West 178 180
William 179 344 352 Wm 345
CRAYTON, 300
CRAZY, BILLY 332 334
CREIGH, Dr 288
CRESAP, Michael 214-216
CRIDER, David 335 Mr 336
CRISFIELD, William 165
CRITTENDEN, 16
CROCKETT, Davy 16 180
CROFT, Thomas 308

CRONCH, Jacob 168
CROSS, Lem 169 Lemuel 191 207 208
CROSSLAND, Caleb 180
CROUSE, Jake 302 Sam 302
CROW, 333 George 180 Mr 333
CRUGER, Daniel 294 295 Lydia S 295
CRUMRINE, 266 286 288 290 Solomon 317
CULP, Daniel 236
CUMMINS, John 261
CUNNINGHAM, S 365 Samuel 366 Thomas S 349
CURRY, John 369
CURTIN, Gov 328
CURTIS, John 138 140 141
CUSIC, 299
DAGG, John N 190 278 279 356
DAGUE, 268
DALLAS, 270
DALY, Cornelius 369
DANFORTH, Charles 190
DANIEL, Justics 19
DANIELS, George W 318
DANNELS, Bernard 139
DARBY, Samuel 180
DARLINGTON, Griffith 139 William 139 229 246
DARR, William 139
DARRAGH, C 349 Mr 351
DARSIE, Allen 318 Allen Jr 318
DAUGHERTY, Jacob 369
DAVIDSON, Thomas R 211
DAVIS, Allen 141 James 141 Joshua 301 Matthew 179
DAWSON, Daniel 180 E B 145 211 212 George 148 186 311 319 John 219 237 247 John L 257 364 371 William 208 261 267
DEAL, Simon 368
DEAN, 66 Daniel 180 Edward 225 Henry Clay 222 James 69 180 John 363 Levi 210 Mrs 195 Sam'l 364 Samuel 363 Thomas 225 Widow 195
DEARTH, George 139 Larkin S 247 Randolph 251
DEDRICK, Abram 156 179

DEETS, John 120 122 145 Michael 120 140
DEFORD, John 232 363 John H 364 Mr 376
DEHAVEN, William 210
DEHOFF, James 193
DEHOOF, James 195
DELAFIELD, Capt 60 97 311 R 69 71 72 75-78 97 98 Rich'd 65 73 78 83 84 97 Richard 67 99
DEMMING, Montgomery 169
DEMMINGS, Amos Frisbie 169
DEMON, Benjamin 265
DENISON, James 369
DENNIS, Robert 181 Samuel 214
DENNISON, James 139 179 232 264 287 296 320 Samuel 281 William 140
DENNY, Isaac 156 180 222
DERLIN, James 179
DETUCK, Michael 141
DEVAN, A Brice 206 Abraham 180 James 180 Robert 180
DEVIL, BILL 128
DIAMOND, D S 347 Daniel 348
DICKERSON, Mahlon 361
DICKEY, 365 John 320 365 William 178 William F 276
DICUS, J H 351 Johnze 352
DILLON, B F 141 Joseph 363 Wm 228
DILLY, Joseph 162 182
DIXON, 113 Frank 301 Jacob 370 Jamees 229 William 140
DOAK, James 140 Joseph 138 140 271 317 Robert 140 Samuel 290
DODD, Charles 275 John 274 275
DOHERTY, 319
DOLAN, James 368
DONALDSON, Maj 165 Richard 278 281 William A 165
DONEHO, Edward 318
DONEHOE, Justice 277
DONLEY, Samuel 275
DORRANCE, David 379 380
DORSIE, Allen 194 James B 261
DOUGAN, James 367 Michael 369 Thomas 368
DOUGHERTY, Jacob 289 320 John W 248 Michael 289

FERGUSON, John 276 William 301
FERRELL, Andrew 180 Joseph 300
FERREN, John 137 139
FINCH, Edward 140
FINK, John 141 179 Ross 141
FINLEY, Eb 376 Ebenezer 250 Mr 351 Thomas 369
FINNEGAN, James 181
FISHBURN, Adam 369
FISHER, 159 George 158 Henry 232 John 276 William 180
FISK, James 180 Leander 179
FLACK, John 111 112 Thomas 139 140
FLAGLE, Isaac 180
FLAXEY, 157
FLECK, John 140
FLEMING, Elizabeth 276 John 281 Robert Q 130
FLENNIKEN, Andrew 220 R P 313 364 368 Robert P 19
FLETCHER, 203 Philip 202
FLOWERS, Samuel 138 269
FORCE, Silas D 351
FORD, John 180 William 140
FORESTER, B 369
FORSYTH, John 88
FORSYTHE, 113 James H 297 Leonard 297
FORTUNE, George 349
FOSNOCK, Henry 197 Jacob 197 Susan 197
FOSTER, Henry 132 James 180 John 179 180 191 228 251 John D 293 Mary 293
FOUCH, Isaiah 139 Jerry 139 John 180
FOWLER, Alex 165 Alexander I 351 Peter 139 Rob 194 Robert 196 197 William 140 179
FOX, One 276
FRANCIS, James 311 Maj 312
FRANKENBERRY, Milton K 153
FRANKS, Conrad 113 Daniel 348 Jesse 113 Michael 347 348
FRANTZ, Richard 180 Tom 156
FRASHER, Alexander 317 Fielding 254 Henry 139 John 141

FRASHER (continued)
L H 254 Peter 138 139 251 254 255
FRAZEE, Isaac 156 181 Richard 180 Samuel 218
FRAZER, Samuel 226
FREEMAN, Elias 139 Hiram 320 369 John 364 Joseph 141 William 344 Wm 345 352
FREIGER, George 180
FREY, Dr 338 Kim 241 Russell 241
FRICK, H Clay 126
FRIEND, George 255
FRISBIE, Amos 169
FROCK, Mr 238
FROST, 205 James 248 Joseph 142 375 Meshach 90 Mesheck 55 Westley 166 230 257 William 207
FRY, Lewis 248 M 233 Matthias 114 216 232 248 320 368
FULLER, Henry 209 Isaiah 180 Jane 228 John 247 Smith 128 171 228
FULTON, Henry 281
FUNK, John 197
GADD, 368 John 320 370 Joseph 367
GADDE, John 254
GADDIS, Perry 128 William 164
GAINER, James 370
GAITHER, Wm S 228
GALLATIN, 51 Albert 42 43 372–375 Mr 14 371
GALT, 288
GALWIX, John 125 136 140 197 Widow 197
GAMS, William 239
GANS, William 258
GARDENER, Mr 308
GARDNER, James 136 Jesse B 132 242 334 Maj 248
GARFIELD, 112
GARRARD, George 259
GARRETT, 278 James 278 William 256 257 263
GARVER, Joe 196
GATE, BOB 229
GAVIN, Edward 132

GEARS, 127
GENEWINE, Charles 142
GEORGE, Adam 351 Billy 200
   William 140
GETZENDANNER, 195
GIBSON, Daniel P 127 John 267
GIDDINGS, John 180
GIDEON, G S 368 J 368
GIESEY, 66 Mr 60 61 Valentine
   320
GILBERT, 307 323 Harry 233 238
   Joseph W 306
GILES, Mr 46
GILFILLAN, John 191 Silver 290
   291
GILLESPIE, 261 Neil 259
GILLIS, Samuel 209
GILMORE, 128 169 369 Capt 128
   David 247 Elias 127 320 321
   363 367 James 137 Judge 185
   Mrs Judge 189
GLEAVES, Isaac 299 300 302 303
GOLDEN, Stephen 136
GOOD, Jacob 276
GOODING, John 290 Mrs 293 294
   320
GOODINGS, Widow 295
GOODMAN, Timothy 351
GOODRIDGE, Rock 181
GOODWIN, Benjamin 139
GORDON, David 146 155-157 J A
   286 James 150 Marion 141
   William F 290
GORE, Thomas 125 126
GORMLEY, 319
GOSLIN, 193
GOW, John L 282
GRACE, George 139 John 113
   Thomas 181 Thompson 156
GRAHAM, Hugh 320 347-349 363
   368 John 296 Thomas B 245
   William H 320 Wm H 363
GRANGER, 154 Theodore 190
GRATIOT, Brig Gen 299 311 C 60
   62 63 67 69 71 76-78 87-90 93
   95-99 361 Charles 65 73 76 78
   84 96 97 Chas 60
GRAY, James 181 John 246-248
   Joseph 248 Richard 140 Wil-
   liam 139
GRAYSON, 365 369 John 366

GREEN, Gretna 291
GREENFIELD, William 265 Wm
   265
GREENLAND, David 141
GREER, Alex 140
GREGG, 236-238 368 James 237
   Nancy 237
GREGORY, James 140
GRIBBLE, John 136 178 254 376
   Lewis 178
GRIER, Thomas 367 Thos 367
GRIFFIN, Dumb Ike 329 Isaac
   329 William 222 320
GRIFFITH, Amos 365 Charles
   116 Emanuel 135 140 James
   179 John 178 Joseph 301
GRIM, George 179 William 179
   180
GRIMES, Darius 131 250 251
   Elijah 301
GROVE, Harvey 139
GRUMMON, Ichabod 301
GUINEA, David 364 365
GUMP, George W 204
GUTTERY, Charles 137 174 251
   264 John 139 146 173 174
   Samuel 140
HACKNEY, Hiram 138 139
HADDEN, Armstrong 166 Brown
   216 231
HAGAN, J Squire 323 John 228
   Nancy 323 Peter 195 Robert
   228 Squire 218 323 331
   Thomas 370
HAGEN, John 319
HAGER, Peter 140 203 Thomas
   180 Wm 367
HAGERTY, Thomas 369
HAGUE, Isaac 347 348 351 John
   348 William 348
HAIR, German D 228 233 320
   John 168
HALDEMAN, 188 Abe 188 Abram
   166 Mrs 210 Pete 188 Widow
   210
HALDERMAN, Abe 156 Peter 157
HALL, Abram 139 Alby 140
   Edward 180 James 141 Robert
   138 286 William 123 124 138
   182 215 318 Wm 351
HALLAM, Charles 290

HALLAM (continued)
George 111 139 Joseph 274 275
356 Lewis 139
HALLY, Henry 351
HALSTED, Samuel 156
HAMILTON, Harvey 140 Samuel
202 Susan R 189 W T 177
HAMMERS, Harry 179 Jack 179
Nelse 179 William 179
HAMMOND, Geo T 276 George T
281 Maj 150
HAMPSON, John 267
HANEY, Alfred 179 John 351
HANKINS, James 133 William
132
HANSE, Hiram 363
HARBAUGH, Jacob 237 238
HARDIN, Jesse 139 180 258 John
139 320 William 320
HARR, David 130 Emanuel 196
HARRAH, Samuel 367
HARRIS, E S 352 J G 280 John
180 Richard 181 Samuel 139
HARRISON, 16 165 167 Benjamin
134 Gen 134 165 166 President
308 William Henry 134
HARRY, A J 365
HART, Jacob 141 William 179
239
HARTER, Philip 307
HARTMAN, William 258
HARTZELL, Capt 311 David 317
Otho 139 277
HARVEY, John 134 211 212
HASS, Charles D 290
HASTINGS, Doc 140 John 140
Thomas 132 269 270 William
140 320 369
HATCHET, FACE 157
HATFIELD, 118 251 Judge 251
252 254 Samuel 139 347 Wil-
liam 172 247 251-253 320
HATZMAN, Jno 363
HAUTE, Terre 123
HAWES, Peter 140 199
HAYES, 179 C 279 281 282 S B
279 281 282
HAYMAKER, Lee 211 Thomas
166
HAYNEY, Hiram 363

HAYS, Edward 162 John 275 S B
239 241 Thomas 300
HAZARD, Daniel 248
HEAD, Walter 179
HEBNER, Andrew 140
HECK, Andrew 179 James 180
Jerome 139 Peter 150
HECKROTE, 225
HEINSELMAN, John 178
HENDERSON, 364 368 George 180
Joseph 146 178 268 277 Robert
139 Robert S 320 367 Stewart
139 Thomas 180
HENDRICKS, John 351 352
HENDRICKSON, Joseph 216
HENDRIX, James W 317 John
179
HENSEL, Washington 226
HENSELL, George 363
HENSHAW, James 139
HERBERTSON, 368
HERR, Abram 140 Christian 136
David 140 Fred 140
HERRICK, Henry 180
HERSING, Capt 301
HEZLOP, John McClure 256
HIBBS, Caleb 139
HICKMAN, Bill 329 Peter 317
William 180
HICKS, Gov 124 Robert 124
HIGH, John 156 157
HIGHT, Henry 302
HIGINBOTHAM, W F 259
HILEMAN, Abram 140 Joseph 140
HILL, Alex J 312 David 114 139
Dr 114 I 363 R 363 Robert 305
306 Stephen 52 54 94 150 186
266 267 316 317 Thomas 267
William 271 365 369 Wm 364
365 367
HINTON, Otho 303
HITCHIN, Barney 140
HOBLITZELL, Dennis 201 211
212 Jacob 147 Sarah E 213
HODGENS, Isaac 112
HOGE, John 236
HOGG, George E 256 Mr 257
William 129
HOGSETT, Mr 227 228 Robert 136
137 139 227 251 321

HOKE, Uriah 351
HOLL, Seth 351
HOLLAND, 224 Atwell 223 337 J
	W 271
HOLLY, Frank 191
HOLMES, Hiram 251 257
HOLSTED, Samuel 181
HOLSWORTH, Caldwell 141
HOLT, 293 362
HOLTON, Evans 180
HOOK, 133 P U 133 Peter Uriah
	239
HOOVER, Christian 140 Christo-
	pher 300 David 140 Jacob A
	137 William 140
HOPKINS, 357 Col 315 316 321
	John 112 Speaker 315 Thomas
	H 261 Thomas Hamen 261
	William 256 312 314 316 317
	362 366 369 Wm 366
HOPWOOD, Rice G 182 211
HORN, Martin 139
HORRELL, John 180
HOUCK, Mart 302
HOUGAN, Thomas 368
HOUSER, Simeon 170 171 237
HOUSTON, Sam 16
HOWARD, John 203
HOWELL, Alfred 189 Amos 237
	Charles 156 Charley 176 177
	183 Flinger 242 Seth 242
HOYE, John 55 88 90 93
HUBBARD, Judge 280
HUDDLESON, Jesse 208 Jonathan
	203 318
HUEY, John 281
HUFF, George 140
HUFFMAN, Vin 178
HUGHES, Joseph 173 Samuel 270
HUHN, John 146 161 180
HUMBERT, Jacob 347 348
	Michael 140 Peter 347 348
HUMES, 167
HUMPHREYS, Robert 290
HUNSUCKER, Suboy Bill 331
	William 331
HUNTER, Benjamin 141 Mrs 216
	Robert 211 216 246
HURD, Seth T 287
HURLEY, James 369
HURST, Isaac 133

HURTON, Eberon 139
HUSTED, Moses 139
HUSTON, John 261 365 369 370
	Joseph 276 Mrs 276 William B
	276
HUTCHINSON, 149 384 Clark 139
	Mr 189 Wyatt 301
HUTTON, Nathan 147
IMBRE, John 351
IMHOFF, William 218
INGLE, Mr 73
INKS, George 225
IRONS, John 281 290 364 368
IRVIN, James 140 142 John 219
	221
IRVINE, James 234
IRWIN, George 369 Judge 241 352
	Martin 141 T 189 345-348
	Thomas 241 345-347 William
	179
JACK, Dandy 180
JACKSON, 16 161 247 271 Andrew
	193 186 276 278 Gen 16 45 166
	176 239 256 272 312 Oliver 180
	President 183 Robert 179
	Samuel 141
JACO, Samuel 156 177 181
JAMES, David 181
JEFFERSON, 13 51 Mr 45 46 238
	President 238 TH 27 Th 28 38
JEFFREYS, Joseph B 263
JEFFRIES, Abraham 307 Dar-
	lington 139 Mifflin 139 Wil-
	liam 363 367
JEHUS, 302
JENK, Joseph 180
JENNING, Henry 241
JENNINGS, Moses 217 218
JEROME, Sam 157 180
JOHN, Gideon 351
JOHNSON, 264 Alexander 247 Col
	187 David 156 180 181 208 212
	213 318 David D 331 Elias 180
	Issac 331 James 141 John 141
	180 277 Joshua 140 163 207
	Miss 251 Mr 283 Nimrod 309
	Old Sandy 180 Richard M 187
	Robert 251 376 Thomas 180
	206 Tom 142 William 131
	William F 170 170 Richard M
	134

MARTIN (continued)
James 139 Jonathan 271
MASON, Barnes 199 Morgan 258
MASSEY, Martin 147
MASTERSON, Henry 320 369
MATTHERS, James 290 296
MATTHEWS, Jesse 180 Joseph
180 William 180
MATTINGLY, George 204
MAULER, James 117 Morris 116
148 221 223 224 228 363
MAXON, Elijah 132
MAXY, Virgil 187
MAY, John 275
MAYES, Charles 290 Joseph F
291
MCALEER, Charles 140
MCALPIN, John 367
MCBRIDE, 142 143 Westly 140
MCCAFFFREY, 299
MCCALL, William 290
MCCAMANT, James 277
MCCAMBRIDGE, Francis 211
MCCANDLESS, Mr 351 Wilson
364
MCCANN, 319
MCCARTNEY, 117 224 James
140 368 Mr 225 Nicholas 117
223 225 320
MCCAULEY, James 163 181
MCCLEAN, 363 Col 235 Ephraim
231 245 Justices 19 Mrs 245
William 368
MCCLEARY, Ewing 239 William
179 289 369 Wm 367 369
MCCLELLAND, A 352 Alfred 213
240 351 356 Andrew 347 348
John 348 Jospeh P 153 Mrs
201 211 212 Sarah E 241
Thomas 180 Widow 286 William 240
MCCLINTOCK, William 140
MCCLOUD, Edward 301
MCCLOY, Mary 323
MCCLUNEY, John 274
MCCLUNG, James 180
MCCLUNY, John 277
MCCLURE, John 139 141 Robert
236
MCCLUSKEY, John 291

MCCOLLOUGH, 117 364 369 Jim
223 John 179 224 369 John W
223 320 Nick 223 224
MCCONOUGHY, David 274
MCCORMICK, Alfred 248 Caleb
215 George 275 Noble 137 215
229 Provance 247
MCCORTNEY, 296 John 295
MCCOY, Thomas 368
MCCRACKIN, John 161
MCCREARY, James 296
MCCUEN, James 352 Mr 301
MCCUNE, James 344 Jas 345 347
MCCURDY, 212 258 John 139 208
Samuel 208
MCCUTCHEON, William 290
MCDONALD, Andrew 283 Lewis
301 Parker 139 255 Samuel 330
368 Thomas 141 William 141
211 301
MCDONOUGH, John 320 365
MCDOWELL, A 363 Alex 320
Bob Gate 321 John 317 368
John W 270 320 Robert 229
317 320 364 367 368 Robert S
128 321 Robt 367
MCFARLAND, Mrs 275
MCGAYEN, Jas 351
MCGIDIGEN, James 180 William
180
MCGIFFIN, Norton 266 Thomas
266 319 320
MCGINNIS, Edward 180 Thomas
180
MCGRATH, Thomas 320 367
MCGREGOR, Alex 140 Archy 180
MCGRUDER, Elias 141 Emanuel
140 George 140 Henry 141
Levi 202 Widow 195
MCGUIRE, J 365
MCHAHON, Erin 299
MCHUGH, William A 238
MCILHENEY, Robert 179
MCILHENY, Robert 179
MCILLREE, James 179
MCILLVAINE, John 302
MCILREE, James 179 John 138
179 287
MCINTYRE, James 320 369
MCKAIG, 143

RANKIN, 133
RANKLIN, John 139 283 Widow
283
RAPP, Jacob 181
RATLIFF, Joseph C 305
RAYMOND, Henry J 175 William
349
READE, Mr 374
REAMER, Fred 166
RECKNOR, John 207 Mrs 207
Widow 211
REDBURN, James T 241
REDDICK, Charles 139 John 139
Wm 351
REDFERN, 368
REDMAN, James 370
REED, Mr 288
REESIDE, 187 Col 384 Commo-
dore 162 Edward 185 James
148 156 169 176 182 183 185
187 378-381 383 384 Janet
Alexander 185 Jas 382 John E
156 161 216 Mr 163 186
REINHART, John 140
RENGER, Henry 140
RENSHAW, 242 Samuel 139
RENTZ, Anthony 320 365 369
RETTIG, Charles 190 271 277
RETTIGG, John 275
REYNOLDS, David 179 Edward A
349 James 169 179 213 364
367 368 Jas 362 364 367 Jim
157 John 138 258 William 138
141 213 216 257 258 320 363
364 368
RHODES, James 117 177 Moses
299 Mrs 292 Widow 130 292
RICE, Dan 286 287 296
RICHARDS, George 120 254 Jacob
221 John 218
RICHARDSON, Dicky 139
RICHER, Moses 139
RICHMIRE, Charles 180 George
180
RIDDLE, James 349
RIDDLEMOSER, Samuel 195
RIDER, Arthur 30 Geo 351
RIGDON, Henry J 247
RIGGLE, Zeph 139 264 267
Zephania 263

RILEY, James 129 180 John 132
259
RINE, Macon W 240
RINEHART, John 139
RINGLAND, George 267 272 278
Thomas 267
RISLER, 242 John 116 216 225
229 248 320 363 364 Mr 216
Mrs 248
RISLY, John 190
RITCHIE, Marion 142
RITTER, John 146 150 Johnny
150
ROACH, William 177
ROBBIN, George 180
ROBBINS, George 180
ROBERTS, Benjamin 252 253 Col
253 E J 346 347 Samuel A 349
William 178 William B 165
253
ROBINSON, 156 349 Arthur 139
Billy 267 John 181 320 369
Thomas 203 William 139 146
156 176 267
RODDY, Edward G 368 William
216 317
RODGERS, Samuel 369
ROE, Nicholas 293
ROGEN, J T 365
ROGERS, 289 Abram 166 Hugh
166 John 263 Joseph T 263 365
Mr 263 Robert 263 Samuel 141
ROLF, Herman 142
RONEY, 292
ROOT, Sylvester 302
ROSE, Levi 191
ROSS, Moses A 216
ROTROFF, 274
ROWALT, Samuel 180
ROWE, James 180
ROWLAND, Jonathan 236
Thomas 351
RUBY, Mrs 237
RUFF, Joseph 180
RUSH, 364 Boss 128 167 168 228
230 246 356 376 Boss Jr 226 C
363 Charles 224-226 320 363
Charles H 241 318 Charley 122
224 225 Henry Clay 114 206
224 226 231 246 248 320

RUSH (continued)
James 166 John 128 181 226
228 229 Marker 225 Mr 224 S
367 Samuel 225 320 363 Sebas-
tian 117 226 317 318 368
Widow 224
RUSSELL, Abraham 148
RUTH, John 179 180
RUTLEDGE, John 139 Rafe 141
RYAN, Ira 140
RYAN, John 140
S, Mr 47 48 50
SACHETT, Jesse 363
SAINT, William 178
SAINTCLAIR, Arthur 299
SAINTJOHN, Haney 351
SALTER, Mrs 238 Samuel 236
William 236
SAMPBELL, Isaac 166 Simon 166
SAMPEY, Henry 320 James 179
180 223 227 228 376
SAMPLE, John 272
SANDS, Widow 233
SANGSTON, John A 116 John F
351
SANTA, ANNA 166 238
SARGEANT, 357 James 275-277
286
SARGENT, James 290
SAYERS, Pierson 237
SCARBOROUGH, Samuel 129
William 129
SCHAFFER, George 141
SCHARTS, 175
SCHAVERNS, James 179
SCHENCK, John 180
SCHOOLFIELD, Samuel 309
SCHROYER, Harvey 257 Widow
258
SCHUCK, Henry 180
SCOTT, 16 279 285 John 276 298
William 146 154 190 369
Winfield 186 377
SCROGGINS, John 140
SEABURN, Elliot 281 Elliott 146
SEAMAN, John 179 180
SEAMANS, Thomas 137
SEARIGHT, 131 253 321 329
Ewing 248 312 318 James 257
281 Mr 120 Rachel 312 T B
142 376

SEARIGHT (continued)
William 18 137 203 247 248
258 270 281 282 312-314 317
Wm 348 370
SEATON, 241 242 C S 228
Charles H 241 Hiram 228 241
362 364 James 241 376 James
C 241 John 241 Mrs 241
SEIBERT, John 141
SHADBURN, Dick 202 Richard
202
SHAFER, James 233
SHAFFER, 168 Andrew 148 179
George 139 Isaac 141 Jacob
365 James 139 141 John 148
179 218 William 167
SHANE, John 200
SHAW, John 301 Joseph 142
Robert 128 133 229 T 351
Tavern Keeper Billy 248 Upton
363 364 368 Wagoner Billy 18
137 248 William 210 222 229
230 248
SHAWN, Grafton 141
SHEARER, Jacob 379
SHEARL, Doug 142
SHEERES, John 140
SHEETS, Bazil 139 327 Perry 180
Sarah 326 William 142 211 325
326
SHELBY, 16
SHELDEN, Bony 302
SHEPHERD, Lydia 294 Lydia S
295 Moses 294 295 320
SHEVERNER, Andrew 141
SHIPLEY, 117 179 Fred 140
Frederic 204 Milford 230 Sam'l
367 Samuel 230 233 320 368
William 230
SHIRES, Peter 139
SHIRLS, 279
SHOAF, Samuel 140
SHOBWORTH, Caldwell 141
SHOCK, Jacob 181
SHORT, John 135
SHOUSE, William 140
SHOW, Daniel 217 Henry 320
SHOWALTER, Ben 152 E H 364
Henry 320 364
SHRIVER, 113 148 D Jr 372 374
Daniel 180

SHRIVER (continued)
David 166 245 270 S319 371
David Jr 374 375 John S 373
Thomas 149 175
SHUCK, George 178 Jacob 168
SHULTZ, Adam 209 Andrew 357
Perry 209 212
SHULTZE, Gov 314
SHUTE, Philip 260 261
SIBBETT, 351
SIBLEY, David 151 152 Sam 16
Samuel 152
SIDEBOTTOM, Samuel 139
SIDES, Jacob 148 207 327 Julia
323 P R 218 323 Pate 156 157
188 191 Pete 188 Peyton R 156
SIMMS, 150 186 Richard 296
SINSABAUGH, Hiram 301 Mr 301
SKEEN, S D 363
SKELLY, Joseph 140
SKILES, A 233 Archibald 132 233
Isaac 120 Peter 136
SKINNER, John 216
SLACK, John 236 244 245
SLAMS, Widow 301
SLATER, Mr 301
SLAVE, Peter Butler 325 Phebe
Butler 325
SLAYMAKER, Sam'l R 379 382
Samuel R 378
SLICER, John 209 210 Miss 163
Mr 178 Nathaniel 210 Samuel
177 William 210
SLIFE, Philip 140
SLIFER, 197
SLIFERS, 203
SLIPE, Philip 139
SLOAN, 300 336 337 Daniel D 306
John 140
SMALLEY, John 363
SMASHER, John 132
SMITH, 274 Aquila 146 Bate 180
302 303 Bill 302 Eli 140 142
George W 317 Gilbert 303
Hank 178 Henry 141 180 347
348 351 James 131 139 299
301 351 Jim 302 Jo 302 John
139 140 John A 140 141 Lewis
204 Louis 140 Marion 248 329
Nat 146 302 303 Nathan 148
Neri 134 Quil 302

SMITH (continued)
Quill 148 303 R S 334 Robert
284 Sam 302 Samuel 300 303
Samuel Jr 303 William L 224
SMOUSE, Daniel 210 George 209
211
SNELL, John 178
SNIDER, Anthony 199 John 111
122 135 140 199 201 204 206
321
SNOWDEN, John 312
SNYDER, 242 Brown 351 James
230 320 333 363 Jimmy 114
376 John 141 178 179 231
Lewis M 320 Philip 141 Simon
37 Stephen W 216 231 Thomas
143 William 229 333
SOPHER, Jack 125 139 179
Joseph 119 125 139 179
Nimrod 125 139 179 William
125 179
SPALDING, 283
SPARKER, John 178
SPAW, William 368
SPEARS, James 363
SPEELMAN, Jonas 140 141
SPEER, Adam 364
SPEERS, Adam 320 Alexander
221 300 James 320 Stewart 165
SPERRY, David G 241
SPIGOT, Dirty 199
SPIKER, Philip 206
SPRINGER, 139 180 233 241 242
Abner 130 Calvin 139 180 233
241 242 Dennis 247 Levi 139
247 William 242
SPROUL, James 351
SPROUT, Thomas 369
SPROWL, Robert 140 365 369
STACY, Joseph C 241
STANFORD, William 333
STARR, Charles W 306 Ebenezer
165 George 165 Mathiot 165
Matthews 165 Thomas 132
STCLAIR, Gen 166
STEDLER, Martin 180
STEELE, 148 William F 149
STEENROD, Daniel 15 295 320
Lewis 15 177 295
STEEP, John 180
STEINER, Archibald 209 210

404

STEINER (continued)
Solomon 209
STELLE, Mr 189 Widow 296
William H 166 189 296
STENTZ, John 139 Philip D 139
237
STENZ, Philip D 241
STERLING, Jos M 363
STEVENS, Dr 159 William C 320
363 367
STEVENSON, T K 280
STEWART, Andrew 14 15 46 177
219 229 242 245 247 256 319
James 349 Leroy 166 Mr 50
375 Thomas 166 William 180
STICKLE, Henry 141
STILLWAGON, Charles 320 369
Jacob 320 365 369
STINSON, David 177
STOCKTON, 186 187 212 357 364
Daniel Moore 184 Elias Boudi-
not 185 Elizabeth C 184 Ellen
184 Henrietta Maria 185 Katha-
rine 184 185 L W 59 166 178
183 189 191 242 Lucius W 18
148 Lucius Witham 183 184
Margaret 184 Miss 185 Mr 18
19 147 148 152 158 161 164
165 177 185 190 324 325 Philip
183 Rebecca 184 Richard 183
Richard C 184 185 William
185
STOCKWELL, Elisha 180
STODDARD, 212 James 186 208
211
STOKES, 186 187 Richard 148
STONE, Aaron 239 Bishop 185
William 134 William A 222
STORY, Matthew 258 259
STOTLER, John 162
STOY, Dr 257
STRADER, Barney 178
STRAUSER, John 141
STRAWN, Jerry 139 William 295
STRAYER, 350 P M 343 P Mills
340 Peter Mills 188 341 343–
345 349 351
STREAN, Robert 275
STREETS, Thomas 203
STRICKLE, Henry 140
STRICKLER, Jacob 139

STRONG, Ira 139 John 136 Joseph
140
STROTHER, Westley 115
STUCK, Isaac 134
STURGEON, Daniel 15 237 313
David 177 357
STURGIS, John P 128 352
SULLIVAN, William 139
SUMNY, Isaac 275
SUNEFRANK, Jacob 301
SURRATT, James F 281 Samuel
281
SUTTON, Harvey 139 Hiram 140
142 206 213 Mr 301
SWAGGART, David 140
SWAN, James 241 John 318
Thomas 241 William 241
SWEARINGEN, Maj 229 Wm D
351
TAGGART, A A 247
TALMADGE, N P 299 303
TAMON, Jacob 141 James 141
TANEY, Chief Justice 19 Mr 99
TANTLINGER, J 218 Widow 226
376
TATE, Oliver 139
TAYLOR, 16 167 Alexander 300
Bry 262 Gen 161 175 176 242
Griffith 365 Henry 267 J 122
James 261–263 John 267
Kizzie 262 263 Noble 300
President 175 Pryn 140 Tim
140
TEDRICK, George 139
TEED, John 173 Mrs 173
TEETERS, Joseph 274 296
Michael 129 136
TELFORD, 66 Thomas 69
TERRY, William 191
THAYER, Dr 162
THEAKSTON, 258
THISTLE, Thomas 208 318
THOMAS, 169 James 90 91 93
John 115 140 Michael 320
Widow 169 William 140
THOMPSON, 112 300 Alexander
156 179 Col 293 Hugh 251 376
J V 144 James 140 320 369
John 111 159 285 Joseph 114
Josias 29 319 Samuel 140 217
218 Superintendent 320

405

WELLS, Joseph 139 Wm P 367
WELSH, John 206 214 Robert 318
    Widow 264
WELTY, Michael 140
WENTLING, Henry 216
WESLEY, Black 136
WEST, Maj 152
WESTLEY, Black 135 200
WESTOVER, Homer 152
WEYMAN, John 141
WHALEN, John 194 Morris 320
    368
WHALEY, James 151 William
    151
WHALON, John 122
WHARTON, Frank 195
WHEELER, John 369
WHETSTONE, Joseph 215
WHETZEL, John 126 Johnny 126
WHISSON, Joseph 139 162 Watt
    179
WHITE, Abraham 347 348 351
    Battelly 240 Battley 111 264
    Benjamin 282 Benny 282 Frank
    180 James 368 John 292
    Joseph 295 Perry 320 368 Seth
    166 William 156 179
WHITESIDE, R C 380
WHITMIRE, John 320 370
WHITNEY, 163 John 162
WHITSETT, Henry 263
WHITTLE, John 141 William 140
    141
WHITTON, Jonathan 141
WHOLLERY, John 320
WIDDLE, George 115
WIGGINS, Cuthbert 116 229 236
    254 326 376 George 179 Harri-
    son 116 165 179 216 246 254
    Isaac 326 327 James H 326
    Joseph 327 Sarah 326
WIGLINGTON, William 142
WILEY, John 180 Thomas A 191
    212 376 377 William 180
WILHELM, George 139
WILKINSON, Francis 351 Francis
    L 368 Frank 166 William 181
WILLARD, Larry 180
WILLEY, William 337
WILLIAMS, B S 351 Capt 311 Col
    286 Eli 28 35 40 J T 351

WILLIAMS (continued)
    Joe 331 John 139 Judge 331
    Lewis 348 Peter 254 William
    W 254 258
WILLIS, Billy 181 William 181
    182
WILLISON, Ashael 135 178
    Hanson 147 149 178 183 185
    Isaac 192
WILLSON, Ashael 140 Hanson
    140 Justice 236
WILSON, Amos 258 Center Billy
    277 Colin 159 Hugh 275 363 J
    K 365 James 180 274 275 John
    267 274 John K 366 Levi 284
    Mr 263
WILSON, William 277 301 377
WINDELL, John 178
WINDOM, William B 308
WINSLOW, Bernard 242
WINTEN, H 365
WINTERMUTE, George 252
WIRT, 149 John A 189
WISE, Henry A 161 Morgan R 161
WISHART, Alexander 184 Capt
    184 Dr 280 Ellen 184 John 184
    Mrs 185 Rebecca 184 185
WITHAM, William 178
WITHROW, John 252
WOLF, 176 285 Alfred 172 Chris-
    tly 285 George 52 Jacob 139
    Martha 172
WOLFE, Decatur 351
WOLSEY, Conrod 199
WOLVERTON, Samuel 251
WOODBURN, John 290
WOODING, Mrs 208 Widow 208
    209
WOODS, Alexander 212 Henry 212
    John 212 213 Thomas 212
WOODWARD, Ellis B 118 John
    351 Reuben 139
WOOLERY, Henry 362 J 363 W
    W 363
WOOLEY, Thomas 191
WOOLLEY, Joseph 152-154
    William 153 154
WOOLVERTON, Samuel 376
WORKMAN, 257 James 256 276
    281 356 William 272
WORRELL, J 365

WORTHINGTON, John 233 321
William 114
WRENCH, John 207 John B 198
John D 209 210
WRIGHT, Edward 293 John 136
208 211 Joseph 242 Robert 181
WYATT, Aaron 124 148 177 179
214 218 221 239 256 351
James 239 Kate 239 Mrs Aaron
239 William 241 256
WYLIE, J L 368
WYNING, George W 208
YARDLEY, Gus 137 John 137
William 137

YARNELL, Anthony 320 364 368
Mordecai 296
YEAST, Adam 139 212 224 Peter
142 208 209 214 William 140
YORTY, Henry 268 Mrs 268
YOUMAN, 131 Israel 131 Samuel
130 181 267
YOUNG, Ezra 140 141 Isaac 139
141 Israel 141 John J 351 John
S 351 Thornton 259
ZANE, George 141 John 179
ZETTLE, Peter 196
ZIMMERMAN, Frederic 180